Women before the Bar

Women

before the Bar

GENDER, LAW, AND SOCIETY IN CONNECTICUT,

1639–1789

Cornelia Hughes Dayton

PUBLISHED FOR THE

INSTITUTE OF EARLY AMERICAN HISTORY AND CULTURE,

WILLIAMSBURG, VIRGINIA,

BY THE UNIVERSITY OF NORTH CAROLINA PRESS,

CHAPEL HILL AND LONDON

The Institute of Early American History and Culture
is sponsored jointly by the College of William and Mary and
the Colonial Williamsburg Foundation

Library of Congress Cataloging-in-Publication Data
Dayton, Cornelia Hughes.
Women before the bar : gender, law, and society in Connecticut,
1639–1789 / by Cornelia Hughes Dayton.
p.   cm.
Includes bibliographical references and index.
ISBN 0-8078-2244-2 (cloth : alk. paper).
— ISBN 0-8078-4561-2 (pbk. : alk. paper)
1. Women — Legal status, laws, etc. — Connecticut — History.
2. Courts — Connecticut — History.   3. Connecticut — History — Colonial
period, ca. 1600–1775.   I. Title
KFC3691.W6D39   1995
340'.082 — dc20   95-20116
CIP

This volume received indirect support from an unrestricted book publication grant awarded
to the Institute by the L. J. Skaggs and Mary C. Skaggs Foundation of Oakland, California.

99   98   97   96   95   5   4   3   2   1

TO MY PARENTS,

William Berrian Dayton & Ruth Eades MacLaren Dayton,

with all my love

Acknowledgments

From its beginnings, this project was blessed by many supporters. Stanley N. Katz is surely the wisest and most humane mentor a young scholar could have. He pointed me in the direction of colonial court records in manuscript, knowing them to be the mother lode that they are, and I have been happy in the archives ever since. John M. Murrin contributed untold gifts as First Reader: amazing bibliographic memory and depth of knowledge about early American primary sources, a mischievous sense of humor, and an uncannily powerful skill at summarizing my own work back to me. I am deeply grateful also to other scholars who befriended the project and offered intellectual advice, close readings, and stimulating conversations at critical points along the way: Marylynn Salmon, Mary Maples Dunn, Linda K. Kerber, Allan Kulikoff, Laurel Thatcher Ulrich, Bruce H. Mann, the late Stephen Botein, Norma Basch, Carol F. Karlsen, Carole Shammas, David Thomas Konig, Mary Beth Norton, William Nelson, John Phillip Reid, David D. Hall, Patricia J. Tracy, Joanna Bowen Gillespie, Alison Duncan Hirsch, and Paul Clemens.

In order to write this book I nearly made a home at the Connecticut State Library in Hartford, planting myself there for months at a time. The expertise, patience, and good humor of numerous present and former staff members contributed enormously to my progress. I wish to thank especially Dr. Mark H. Jones (State Archivist), Theodore Wohlsen (History and Genealogy Unit Head), Ann Barry, David Corrigan, Eunice DiBella, Marguerite Giguerre-Davis, Denise Jernigan, Kevin Johnson, Kristin O. Johnson, Beverly Naylor, Sandra Perlman, Carolyn M. Picciano, Richard C. Roberts, and Elroy Velasquez. I am also grateful to the staffs of the American Antiquarian Society, the Connecticut Historical Society, Firestone Library at Princeton University, the Huntington Library, the Massachusetts Historical Society, and the Sterling Memorial and Beinecke Libraries at Yale University for help in consulting their collections.

As a dissertation, this project was supported by grants from Princeton University, the Woodrow Wilson Foundation (for research in Women's Studies), the Mark DeWolfe Howe Fund (Harvard Law School), the Charlotte W. Newcombe Foundation, and the Samuel I. Goleib Fellowship at New York University School of Law. The revisions for publication were made possible by the generous provisions of a postdoctoral fellowship at the Institute of Early American History and Culture (one year of which was sponsored by the National Endowment for the Humanities), a University of California–Irvine Faculty Career Development award, and University of California sabbatical leave. Serendipitously, my research for other projects on fellowships at the American Antiquarian Society and the Massachusetts Historical Society added small treasures that enhanced this study. I was fortunate in being able to try out early versions of chapters in several collegial settings where commentators and audience pushed me to refine my thinking: the Berkshire Conferences on the History of Women, the Clark Library, the Association for the Study of Connecticut History, the Philadelphia Center for Early American Studies, the American Society for Legal History, the Legal History Colloquium at New York University School of Law, and the Institute of Early American History and Culture colloquium series. At Princeton, the opportunity to publish a different form of portions of Chapter 4 in *Critical Matrix: Princeton Working Papers in Women's Studies* provided early, valuable exposure to the rigors of rewriting and responding to astute editors.

Perhaps the sweetest moment in the completion of a book is the chance to put into print one's thanks to friends who aided and abetted the project but who were often not in a position to choose their involvement. During my years in Princeton, Hartford, and New York, and in many cases beyond, Ann Barry and Dennis Landes, Victoria Bernal and Tekle Woldemikael, Richard Bernstein, Caroline Danchak, Daniel Ernst, Mary Harper and Al Cavallo, Alison Duncan Hirsch, John Jefferson Looney, Amy Ragsdale, Linda Rodgers, Frederick Tibbetts, Paige Tolbert and Jim Mulholland, and members of the E. Bright Wilson family were welcoming hosts, listened with grace and wit to tales drawn from the old court records, and offered perspective and succor in a myriad of ways. The Institute of Early American History and Culture provides a wonderful way station and training ground for early Americanists; my sojourn there was especially enriched by the friendship and support of Thad W. Tate, Cynthia, Ed, and Eleanor Ayres, Alan Taylor, Michael Meranze, and Fredrika Teute and Clyde Haulman. Fredrika, now my editor, Ron Hoffman, current Director of the Institute, and Gil Kelly, expert copy-editor, shepherded the book to completion with wisdom, superb skill, and marvelous forbearance for my faults. In California, I could not have been favored by stauncher friends than Robert Moeller and Lynn and Nora Mally, Ellen Broidy and Joan Ariel, Sharon Salinger, Marjorie Beale, Anne Walthall, Patricia O'Brien, Jonathan Dewald, James Given, and Terri Snyder. My colleagues at the Early Americanists seminar at the

Huntington Library, the Teaching Workshop in U.S. Women's History, and, most of all, the History Department at University of California–Irvine (including a host of enthusiastic graduate students) have immeasurably bolstered my confidence and sense of mission. In the final throes of writing and checking footnotes, Sharon Block and Ann Little liberally gave me tips and help based on their exciting, fresh research. Finally, I wish to pay tribute to the extraordinary generosity of several whose faith sustained my spirit: D. Fairchild Ruggles, Marjorie Tichenor, James Shilts Boster, and Katie Sky.

This book is dedicated to my parents as an emblem of the depth of their commitment to a daughter's education and as a tribute to what they together have bequeathed to me — the gift of love.

Contents

Illustrations and Tables

Abbreviations of Works Cited

CHS   Connecticut Historical Society, Hartford

CSL   State Archives, Connecticut State Library, Hartford

FANH,   Donald Lines Jacobus, comp. *Families of Ancient New Haven.*
Jacobus   3 vols. 1922–1932; rpt., Baltimore, 1981

NHCC   New Haven County Court, Record Books and Files, R. G. 3, Connecticut State Library, Hartford

NHCR, I   Charles J. Hoadly, ed. *Records of the Colony and Plantation of New Haven, from 1638 to 1649.* Hartford, 1857

NHCR, II   Charles J. Hoadly, ed. *Records of the Colony or Jurisdiction of New Haven, from May, 1653, to the Union.* Hartford, 1858

NHSC Files   New Haven County Superior Court Files, R. G. 3, Connecticut State Library, Hartford

NHTR   Franklin Bowditch Dexter and Zara Jones Powers, eds. *New Haven Town Records.* 3 vols. Ancient Town Records. New Haven, 1917–1962

PR   J. Hammond Trumbull and Charles J. Hoadly, eds. *The Public Records of the Colony of Connecticut, 1636–1776.* 15 vols. Hartford, 1850–1890

PRS   Charles J. Hoadly et al., comps. *The Public Records of the State of Connecticut, [1776–1803].* 11 vols. Hartford, 1894–1967

Recs. Ct.   Norbert B. Lacy, ed. "Records of the Court of Assistants of
of Assts.,   Connecticut, 1665–1701." 2 vols. Master's thesis, Yale Uni-
Lacy   versity, 1937
transcript

SCR   Superior Court, Record Books, R. G. 3, Connecticut State Library, Hartford

WMQ   *William and Mary Quarterly,* 3d Ser.

Women before the Bar

Introduction

More than half a century separated the first and last courtroom appearances of Rebecca Baldwin of Milford, Connecticut. In 1719, when she was seventeen, Rebecca came before the bar in the New Haven courthouse to confess to the crime of fornication; her father, a prosperous wheelwright, paid her fine of forty-three shillings. The man whom Rebecca named as the father of her infant was a newly married local physician, from whom the court extracted a pledge of child support. Despite the embarrassment of bearing a child out of wedlock, Rebecca avoided forfeiting the respectable status of the family she was born into. At age 24, she married her first cousin Phineas Baldwin; they soon became full church members and had three children, all of whom survived to marry well. In her thirties Rebecca inherited two small tracts of land and one hundred pounds from her father and in her sixties a generous testamentary property settlement when her husband died. In 1775 and 1778—well before her death at age 89—Rebecca again crossed the threshold of the courthouse, now as a widow and the sole surviving executor of her husband's estate.[1]

Rebecca Baldwin's adult life was thus bracketed by two quintessential encounters with the law among those experienced by the hundreds of New England women in each county jurisdiction who found their way into court. Although many women never made the trip to the courthouse, the presence of women in court was not unusual. In the early part of the colonial period, spectators on court days would have found it routine that one-third of those waiting to plead or to give testimony were women. Taking shame upon oneself for the illicit act of fornication, as young Rebecca Baldwin did, and suing to collect a debt, as Rebecca did as a widow, were the most common guises in which Connecticut women appeared before the judges of the county courts, the forums to which the bulk of civil and criminal cases were funneled. In addition, scores of

1. Rex v. Rebecca Baldwin (Nov. 1719, Apr. 1720), NHCC, III, 107, 138, VIII, 177, 351, and NHCC Files, drawer 6; Milford Deeds, VIII, 471, IX, 97, CSL; New Haven District Probate Court, VI, 234–235, X, 182–183, 185–186, CSL. Rebecca also came into court jointly with her husband in 1759 when she was serving as executor of a deceased woman, possibly her mother, and suing for a debt due the estate (NHCC, V, 224).

women came into county court to sue over slanderous words or inheritance disputes. In Connecticut, the Superior Court, which rode circuit holding sessions in each county seat, heard a smattering of felony and capital cases inherently involving women — rape, adultery, infanticide — amid a much larger stream of divorce petitions, most of which were brought by deserted wives.

This study takes as its central subjects the many women who entered early Connecticut courtrooms: women suing and being sued over debt and slander, women petitioning for divorce, women prosecuted for sexual transgressions, women advancing rape charges. To ask what the everyday practice of the law courts meant for women is to ask how both women *and* men used available legal procedures to advance their own interests and in what ways they were treated by magistrates and the panoply of community members who, as grand jurors, jurors, and witnesses, made the legal system function. Drawing on colonywide criminal cases and the extensive court records of one jurisdiction, New Haven, in its incarnation as a separate colony until 1665 and afterward as a Connecticut county, this work traces how the gendered patterns of civil, criminal, and divorce litigation changed over 150 years.[2]

Although it follows a design uniquely its own, this investigation builds on three types of scholarly works: analyses of litigation patterns in a single jurisdiction over time, in-depth community studies of towns and their inhabitants, and inquiries into specific aspects of women's relationship to the law.[3] When I began this project, excellent work was emerging

2. One obstacle in working on New Haven is that no modern community studies of the area or any of its towns have been undertaken. Such work could illuminate leadership patterns, deviant families, and wealth stratification in sharper detail than my own scrutiny of public records has allowed. Tax records survive for only a few years for the town of New Haven and for a fuller run for Guilford. For social history analysis of the latter, see John Waters, "Patrimony, Succession, and Social Stability: Guilford, Connecticut in the Eighteenth Century," *Perspectives in American History*, X (1976), 129–160.

3. Among the relatively few quantitative and social history approaches to litigation or prosecution patterns in United States courts, see Lawrence M. Friedman and Robert V. Percival, *The Roots of Justice: Crime and Punishment in Alameda County, California, 1870–1910* (Chapel Hill, N.C., 1981); Robert A. Silverman, *Law and Urban Growth: Civil Litigation in the Boston Trial Courts, 1880–1900* (Princeton, N.J., 1981); Michael Stephen Hindus, *Prison and Plantation: Crime, Justice, and Authority in Massachusetts and South Carolina, 1767–1878* (Chapel Hill, N.C., 1980). Examples of community studies of early New England towns for which all extant records were read and family reconstructions completed are John Demos, *A Little Commonwealth:*

on women's legal position as it was defined by colonial statutes, early modern English treatises, and late-eighteenth-century appellate case law, but gender as an important analytical category was missing from new studies on the actual workings of early American courts.[4] Setting out to remedy the deficit, I chose to eschew sampling, a traditional social science technique that can yield a useful portrait of a legal system but that fails to capture all the courtroom encounters that individuals like Rebecca Baldwin might have had over their lifetime. In order to paint an accurate and telling portrait of the early American courts' treatment of subordinate groups such as women, African-Americans, and Indians, the best strategy, I believe, is a systematic profiling of everything occurring in court in a given jurisdiction.

The extensive, nearly complete records surviving for colonial Connecticut and New Haven make this study possible. For the seventeenth

---

Family Life in Plymouth Colony (New York, 1970); Philip J. Greven, Jr., *Four Generations: Population, Land, and Family in Colonial Andover, Massachusetts* (Ithaca, N.Y., 1970); Kenneth Lockridge, *A New England Town, the First Hundred Years: Dedham, Massachusetts, 1636–1736* (New York, 1970); and Stephen Innes, *Labor in a New Land: Economy and Society in Seventeenth-Century Springfield* (Princeton, N.J., 1983). Studies of gender and early American law have tended to focus on either the civil or criminal realms or on one area of women's contact with courts. Sample titles include N. E. H. Hull, *Female Felons: Women and Serious Crime in Colonial Massachusetts* (Urbana, Ill., 1987); G. S. Rowe, "Women's Crime and Criminal Administration in Pennsylvania, 1763–1790," *Pennsylvania Magazine of History and Biography,* CIX (1985), 335–368; Barbara S. Lindemann, " 'To Ravish and Carnally Know': Rape in Eighteenth-Century Massachusetts," *Signs: Journal of Women in Culture and Society,* X (1984–1985), 63–82; Nancy F. Cott, "Divorce and the Changing Status of Women in Eighteenth-Century Massachusetts," *WMQ,* XXXIII (1976), 586–614; Joan R. Gundersen and Gwen Victor Gampel, "Married Women's Legal Status in Eighteenth-Century New York and Virginia," *WMQ,* XXXIX (1982), 114–134; and Linda E. Speth, "More than Her 'Thirds': Wives and Widows in Colonial Virginia," *Women and History,* no. 4 (1982), 5–41.

4. Marylynn Salmon, *Women and the Law of Property in Early America* (Chapel Hill, N.C., 1986); Linda K. Kerber, *Women of the Republic: Intellect and Ideology in Revolutionary America* (Chapel Hill, N.C., 1980), chap. 5. Otherwise illuminating legal histories that pay little attention to gender include William E. Nelson, *Americanization of the Common Law: The Impact of Legal Change on Massachusetts Society, 1760–1830* (Cambridge, Mass., 1975), and *Dispute and Conflict Resolution in Plymouth County, Massachusetts, 1725–1825* (Chapel Hill, N.C., 1981); David Thomas Konig, *Law and Society in Puritan Massachusetts: Essex County, 1629–1692* (Chapel Hill, N.C., 1979); Bruce H. Mann, *Neighbors and Strangers: Law and Community in Early Connecticut* (Chapel Hill, N.C., 1987).

and eighteenth centuries, court records provide an extraordinary window into behaviors, self-fashionings, and idiomatic uses of language that would otherwise go unrecorded. In a period when few adults left letters or diaries, women and men speak through court records more openly than through almost any other set of documents. Slander writs quote speech fragments verbatim, depositions offer a person's deliberate construction of events, and local magistrates' records transcribe criminals' examinations in a question-and-answer format.[5] Thus we can hear women talking and being talked to, we can see the extent to which they were recognized or ignored in the courtroom, in a more tangible way than is possible for other public settings, such as the tavern, the street, and the meetinghouse.

Besides their usefulness in capturing random, individual voices and in documenting the literal and symbolic work of an important public institution, court records disclose the agency of laypersons. In the seventeenth and eighteenth centuries the legal system could function only with the cooperation of ordinary men and women. New Englanders with legal standing could choose, after all, whether to submit their disputes to the magistrates and courts or resort instead to other forms of mediation, such as the parish or neighborhood arbitration.[6] Indeed, because civil litigation occupied the bulk of the courts' business, local inhabitants by their decisions on whom to sue and how to plead gave shape to the rhythms of court sessions and breathed life into, spelled atrophy for, or prompted modification of legal forms and actions. Similarly, in the realm of criminal justice, without the modern-day apparatus of police, prosecutors, and investigators, the colonial court's effectiveness in keeping the peace depended on the public's willingness to bring complaints and testimony to it.

As members of the lay population, women could contribute to the dynamics of legal business as litigants, witnesses, and criminal defendants. Indeed, they did so with unparalleled frequency in the earliest decades of settlement, when simplified legal rules and a ban on lawyers gave all residents direct access to the legal system. But women stood

---

5. These and many other types of legal documents (including divorce petitions) continued to be handwritten throughout the 1700s, thus combining formulaic with idiosyncratic phrasing. The one major exception was the printed writs used in nearly all debt suits beginning in the second quarter of the 18th century.

6. On parish- and court-sponsored arbitration in New England, see Nelson, *Dispute and Conflict Resolution in Plymouth;* and Mann, *Neighbors and Strangers,* chap. 4.

outside the loose group of brokers who coalesced in the early eighteenth century, a group I call the legal fraternity. Wider than the clusters of judges, justices of the peace, and professional attorneys serving each county, the legal fraternity should be seen as encompassing the many propertied heads of household who rotated on and off duty as trial jurors and grand jurors. Since the men chosen as jurors were typically in their thirties or forties with average landholdings and dense kinship networks in Connecticut, the system ensured that legal decisions were influenced by men of middling ranks, not just the wealthiest, most prominent figures in the county or those few trained in the law.[7] Thus, after 1700, women's cases were filtered through several layers of men dispensing legal advice and decrees. For New Haven women encountering the law in the eighteenth century, this arrangement represented a different sort of paternalism from that exemplified by the unmediated power of seventeenth-century magistrates. As in affairs of church governance, women operated informally, behind the scenes, to shape legal outcomes, but with the expansion of the legal fraternity through the century their activities became more and more invisible to the public record.[8]

Alongside any brief for the value of early modern court records must come recognition of their recalcitrance. Writs in certain civil actions, notably debt, assault, and trespass, usually fail to record the actual nature of the underlying transaction or conflict. Moreover, no matter how voluminous the depositions surviving in a particular case, as historians we can capture only a small fraction of the information that came before the bench and jury. There were no stenographers in colonial Connecticut courtrooms to transcribe oral testimony, lawyers' arguments, and defendants' exact words. The gestures of the various participants, the gasps and sighs and catcalls of the audience, and in general the dramaturgy of early New England courtrooms — these are almost always lost to us.[9]

7. No study exists profiling age and property holdings of trial and grand jurors, but presumably they were drawn from the pool of minor officeholders described by Edward M. Cook, Jr., *The Fathers of the Towns: Leadership and Community Structure in Eighteenth-Century New England* (Baltimore, 1976), 32. On the church affiliation of Massachusetts jurors, see Nelson, *Dispute and Conflict Resolution in Plymouth*, 24–26.

8. Laurel Thatcher Ulrich, " 'Daughters of Liberty': Religious Women in Revolutionary New England," in Ronald Hoffman and Peter J. Albert, eds., *Women in the Age of the American Revolution* (Charlottesville, Va., 1989), 211–243.

9. Since no written record was made of the oral testimony given in court, the only testimony that survives comes from those witnesses who were exempted from coming in person to court. By statute, one was allowed to send a written deposition if one

Much of what the judges said from the bench went unrecorded, including instructions to juries in criminal trials. The practice of issuing judicial opinions to explain rulings and verdicts began, spottily, only in the 1780s. Few eighteenth-century Connecticut judges and lawyers wrote diaries or left papers containing legal briefs and correspondence.[10] Lay men and women, introspective over spiritual matters but not yet inspired to self-revelatory consciousness by Romanticism or modernist impulses, would never have conceived the value of recording in detail what motivated them to attend court, what they observed in the courtroom, or why they might have altered their testimony from one hearing to the next.

Thus our interpretations of what happened in court are inevitably dependent on records full of omissions and silences and on testimonies refracted through faulty memories and calculation. Supplemental information from nonlegal sources can shed light on such issues as who was in court by age or social status and what sorts of disputes failed to come before the bar, but it rarely supplies direct evidence on the attitudes and motivations of courtroom actors. Court records, of course, can be a springboard to investigations of all sorts of topics — from witchcraft beliefs and courtship rituals to credit networks. Yet principally the record books and file papers speak to what issues came before the courts and how laypeople and officials negotiated the terrain marked as law. Thus, the present study keeps a steady focus on the courtroom itself. In its pursuit of the story of New Englanders' use of and reception by the courts over time, it is institutional history. In its close attention to the gender, age, and social standing of litigants, it relies heavily on social history methods. Above all, it is meant to contribute to our understand-

---

lived more than 20 miles from the court or could claim illness, pregnancy, or a nursing child.

A. G. Roeber analyzes early Virginia court proceedings in terms of their panoply and dramaturgy in "Authority, Law, and Custom: The Rituals of Court Day in Tidewater Virginia, 1720–1750," *WMQ*, XXXVII (1980), 29–52.

10. The 1784 statute creating the Supreme Court of Errors stipulated that the justices' rulings be written (Charles J. Hoadley et al., comps., *Public Records of the State of Connecticut, 1776–1803* [Hartford, 1894–1967], V, 323–324). Ephraim Kirby compiled the first printed court reports for the state (*Reports of Cases Adjudged in the Superior Court of the State of Connecticut, from the Year 1785, to January 1789; with Some Determinations in the Supreme Court of Errors* [Hartford, 1939 (orig. publ. 1789)]).

A notable exception to not leaving legal papers is John T. Farrell, ed., *The Superior Court Diary of William Samuel Johnson, 1772–1773* ... (Washington, D.C., 1942).

ing of change in early American legal culture and in gender relations and gender ideology.

After sketching the broad outlines of change in law and society in early New Haven and Connecticut, the study is arranged according to major legal actions that brought women into court. Five topical categories—debt, divorce, illicit consensual sex, rape, and slander—were chosen because of the sheer quantity of cases or the utility of the legal record for illuminating important aspects of women's relationship to the courts over time. For example, women were party to more than a thousand debt suits in New Haven County alone in the seventeenth and eighteenth centuries. A comparison of women's and men's litigated debt significantly expands our grasp of an understudied aspect of colonial development—the gendered dimensions of commercialization and rural economic growth.[11] In contrast, cases involving rape were few, yet file papers permit us to reconstruct women's and men's conflicting stories and to compare community responses to charges against acquaintances and outsiders, whites and blacks. Considering major aspects of civil, criminal, and divorce law together highlights important currents of legal and social change that can remain obscured when legal actions are studied in isolation.

I make no claim, however, that the study covers every aspect of women's experience before the courts in early New England. Readers will not find extended discussions of several issues. Witchcraft is omitted because the number of cases in New Haven was small and because two fine, in-depth studies of early New England witch-hunting exist that cover Connecticut, including one that makes gender central to its analysis. Furthermore, singular criminal cases in which women played a central role, like a rare 1740s Connecticut abortion prosecution of a doctor and his alleged accomplices, did not fit easily into a study that was geared to examine change in legal actions over time. Finally, legal scholars may argue for the importance of studying women's roles in land and inheri-

---

11. The outstanding sleuthing of Laurel Thatcher Ulrich in recreating the "female economy" of late-18th-century Hallowell, Maine, lays the crucial groundwork for studies of rural women (*A Midwife's Tale: The Life of Martha Ballard, Based on Her Diary, 1785–1812* [New York, 1990], esp. chap. 2). For an examination of one aspect of women's involvement in urban markets, see Patricia A. Cleary, " 'She Merchants' of Colonial America: Women and Commerce on the Eve of the Revolution" (Ph.D. diss., Northwestern University, 1989).

tance disputes, but I found it difficult to tease conclusions about gender out of the records for trespass, ejectment, trover, or inheritance suits, since most involved joint heirs—siblings suing together.[12] To my mind, the differential pattern of men's and women's participation in debt litigation was the most important area of private law to address: debt, after all, was the major engine of change in the colonial legal system.

As each chapter of this work illustrates, the courtrooms of the seventeenth-century New Haven and Connecticut colonies had a very different character from those of the late eighteenth century. I argue that the most critical period of change for women's relation to the public space of the courtroom came in the decades surrounding the end of the seventeenth century. By then a collective commitment to upholding a God-fearing society through the courts had been abandoned, and Puritan resistance to the technicalities of English common law practice had faded. From the 1690s to the 1720s rules were implemented that shifted New Haven courtrooms from the utopian reform platform of the Puritan founders to a selective embrace of English formalism. Toward the end of that transition, an enormous expansion in indebtedness reshaped civil litigation. As a result of these transformations in law and society, by the end of the colonial period women's presence in court declined dramatically.

In essence, women's courtroom participation throws into sharp relief the realignment of court and community. The seventeenth-century courts had been occupied by the sorts of community activities to which women were integral: maintaining harmonious neighborly relations, ensuring equitable local trading, and monitoring sexual and moral conduct. After the turn of the century, the courts increasingly became adjuncts and facilitators of vast credit networks that provided farmers and

12. Carol F. Karlsen, *The Devil in the Shape of a Woman: Witchcraft in Colonial New England* (New York, 1987); John Putnam Demos, *Entertaining Satan: Witchcraft and the Culture of Early New England* (New York, 1982); Cornelia Hughes Dayton, "Taking the Trade: Abortion and Gender Relations in an Eighteenth-Century New England Village," *WMQ*, XLVIII (1991), 19–49.

Because so few women turned up as defendants, accomplices, or victims in murder, burglary, counterfeiting, or other felony prosecutions, such cases are omitted from this study.

For brief discussions of the gender of parties to 18th-century land litigation, see Cornelia Hughes Dayton, "Women before the Bar: Gender, Law, and Society in Connecticut, 1710–1790" (Ph.D. diss., Princeton University, 1986), 40–42, 59–60, 66, 68–69.

tradesmen with the capital to expand their farms and enterprises. The constituency served by the courts narrowed to propertied men active in the expanding economy; at the same time the volume of court business was growing exponentially. Women's economic and social activities did not change markedly at the beginning of the eighteenth century, but in a schematic sense what was happening in court reveals a new set of divergences in men's and women's spheres taking hold gradually throughout the century. These divergences—in women's and men's relations to commercialization, to the public theater of the courtroom, and to religious attitudes toward sin and human culpability—were silent foreshadowings of the more explicit nineteenth-century ideology that reserved the public realms of commerce, law, and politics to men and gave white women moral dominion over privatized families.

If New Haven's evolving courtroom scenes illumine the restructuring of public and private space, putting law at the center of the story of gender and social change in early New England also enables us to perceive important shifts in a system of power relations that is often viewed as static: patriarchy, or the legal and cultural rules by which men held authority over women in the household and polity. It is my contention that the seventeenth-century Puritan courtroom occupies an anomalous position in the long histories of Anglo-American law and of patriarchy. The New England Puritans struck out on idiosyncratic legal paths, the twisted strands of which included some policies harshly intolerant of unsubmissive women and others remarkably unforgiving of men's ungodly behavior.

On the one hand, the familiar characterization of Puritan justice as repressive of women is borne out in many respects. Puritan legal regimes across New England unquestioningly cast women as witches and condoned a prosecutorial double standard for accused men and women such that twenty-eight women and only seven men were hanged for the crime of witchcraft. In the 1630s and 1640s, New England's leaders used showcase trials against Anne Hutchinson and other female dissenters to silence women as political beings and religious leaders.[13] Finally, the

---

13. Karlsen, *Devil in the Shape of a Woman*, 48–49. Karlsen deftly shows how disproportionately more men than women had their cases dismissed at each stage of the criminal process (47–52). On female dissenters, see Lyle Koehler, "The Case of the American Jezebels: Anne Hutchinson and Female Agitation during the Years of Antinomian Turmoil, 1636–1640," *WMQ*, XXXI (1974), 55–78; Jane Neill Kamensky, "Governing the Tongue: Speech and Society in Early New England" (Ph.D. diss., Yale University, 1993), chap. 3.

Puritan compulsion to punish a wide range of moral lapses with whippings meant that women were frequently haled before the bar to confess their sins publicly and to submit to the lash.

On the other hand, Puritan jurisprudence, by encouraging lay pleading and by insisting on godly rules, created unusual opportunities for women's voices to be heard in court. The prohibition against lawyers, the simplification of procedural rules, and the magistrates' confidence that God would help them discern the truth behind a dispute or criminal charge meant that women's testimony was invited and encouraged in ways that clashed with English legal traditions. Not only was women's access to courts eased, but the Puritans' emphasis on each individual's obedience to God's strictures led them to insist on punishing men's abuse of authority and sinful behavior. In cases of sexual assault, wife-abuse, and premarital sex, seventeenth-century magistrates gave credence to women's charges and meted out swift, severe sentences to men. Indeed, New Haven Colony came close to establishing a single standard for men and women in the areas of sexual and moral conduct. In sum, policies that were intended to create the most God-fearing society possible operated to reduce the near-absolute power that English men by law wielded over their wives, to undercut men's sense of sexual entitlement to women's bodies, and to relieve women in some situations from their extreme dependency on men. Thus, when Puritanism ceased to be the organizing force in New England society and courtrooms, there were losses for women as well as gains.

Along with new work on the Chesapeake, this study urges that we examine the early and middle decades of the eighteenth century as a period that saw the return to a more traditional type of patriarchy in Britain's New World colonies. Quite different material and ideological conditions explain why some traditional supports of patriarchy were loosened in seventeenth-century colonies as distinct as Virginia and Connecticut and why women in various regions encountered a tightening of patriarchal authority in the eighteenth century.[14] In this study I

14. Terri Lynne Snyder, " 'Rich Widows Are the Best Commodity This Country Affords': Gender Relations and the Rehabilitation of Patriarchy in Virginia, 1660–1700" (Ph.D. diss., University of Iowa, 1992); Kathleen Mary Brown, "Gender and the Genesis of a Race and Class System in Virginia, 1630–1750" (Ph.D. diss., University of Wisconsin, 1990); Carole Shammas, "Anglo-American Household Government in Comparative Perspective," *WMQ*, LII (1995), 104–150.

attempt to account only for women's experience in New Haven as suggestive of the cultural shifts characterizing colonies that began as intensely Puritan settlements. Here, judges, lawmakers, and other men of influence and wealth launched no coordinated, self-conscious campaign to roll back the slight openings and advances women had enjoyed under seventeenth-century legal approaches. Rather, their implicit endorsement of rules and practices that would reinforce male authority was integrally bound up in their promulgation of two pervasive cultural trends: anglicization and embourgeoisement.

Anglicization, the importation of English ways by colonists newly and self-consciously eager to bind themselves to the cultural sophistication of the empire's urban centers, has gained much attention in recent years. In the realm of law, the process can be discerned in early-eighteenth-century New England not only in the licensing of professional attorneys but also in the stricter attention paid to common law procedures and rules of evidence. These shifts internal to the legal system raised barriers to women's easy use of the courts and introduced skeptical attitudes toward the reliability of women's charges of male abuse. Beyond the law, newspapers and almanacs show that by midcentury New England culture also became more English (and more European) in its new toleration of misogynist, antimatrimonial, and bawdy themes. Having been invoked by historians to illuminate such diverse areas as professionalization, political culture, consumer tastes, and national integration, anglicization needs also to be recognized as the bearer of ideas about woman's nature that had been largely suppressed in seventeenth-century New England.[15]

15. John M. Murrin, "Anglicizing an American Colony: The Transformation of Provincial Massachusetts" (Ph.D. diss., Yale University, 1966); Murrin, "The Legal Transformation: The Bench and Bar of Eighteenth-Century Massachusetts," in Stanley N. Katz and Murrin, eds., *Colonial America: Essays in Politics and Social Development*, 3d ed. (New York, 1983), 540–572; Cornelia Hughes Dayton, "Satire and Sensationalism: The Emergence of Misogyny in Mid-Eighteenth-Century New England Newspapers and Almanacs," paper presented to the New England Seminar in American History, Worcester, Mass., Nov. 15, 1991. One of the few historians to discuss misogyny in the 18th-century North American context, Kenneth A. Lockridge offers close readings of the commonplace books that two elite Virginians kept as young men (*On the Sources of Patriarchal Rage: The Commonplace Books of William Byrd and Thomas Jefferson and the Gendering of Power in the Eighteenth Century* [New York, 1992]).

On the links between consumer taste and national integration, see T. H. Breen,

Although there has been much hesitation over applying the language of class to early America before wage dependency was extensive, a social stratum and a set of practices later identified as middle-class were emerging in the eighteenth century. The various processes that one scholar calls the "refinement of America" reflect not just the formation of a distinct American gentry but also the fact that many colonials were taking on genteel habits that the post-Independence, republican context would remake into bourgeois habits.[16] The signs of interest in acquiring the badges of cultivation appeared as early as the 1690s. Expanded trade and sources of credit, denser kinship networks, and ideological shifts released New Englanders from insular preoccupations with family and community survival. Wealthy and ambitious families became caught up in elaborating their material world by adding rooms to their dwelling houses, dividing household space into public and private areas, and acquiring luxury goods. Along with those trends came a new ethic of privacy among the emergent bourgeoisie. The social, religious, and political values of the men who breathed life into the legal system no longer called upon them to insist that their dependents or peers submit moral transgressions — slander, premarital sex, drunkenness — to the regulation of the community embodied in the county court. In the area of regulating premarital sexual relations, for example, Connecticut officials moved toward a narrowly selective approach targeting poor, marginal women and sheltering the middling classes from public scrutiny, humiliation, and penalty. These changes in the types of transgressors and transgressions subject to legal action point to a general reformulation of status and identity, a reformulation that authorized propertied male family heads to distance themselves from general reformulation of status and identity, a reformulation that authorized propertied male family heads to distance themselves from some of the key communal values espoused by Puritan founders. What was at work was a simulta-

---

"An Empire of Goods: The Anglicization of Colonial America, 1690–1776," *Journal of British Studies,* XXV (1986), 467–499.

16. Richard L. Bushman, *The Refinement of America: Persons, Houses, Cities* (New York, 1992). Bushman argues for a complex blending of gentility and class identity in the 18th century while locating the spread of genteel tastes to the middle-class in the 19th century (xii–xviii, 182–186). For a perceptive comment on gender and the emergence of a class structure in the 18th century, see Carroll Smith-Rosenberg, "Dis-Covering the Subject of the 'Great Constitutional Discussion,' 1786–1789," *Journal of American History,* LXXIX (1992–1993), 859n.

neous intensification of class definitions and a "restructuring of morality as a category of private or individual rather than communal life."[17]

Studying gendered patterns of litigation and criminal prosecution over 150 years of New Haven's and Connecticut's shared early history allows us to glimpse not only forces that dramatically changed the face of court business but also divergences in women's and men's lives that led to a redefinition of the public space of the courtroom as a male arena. Crucial to this process were both material conditions, as in women's increasingly attenuated link to their menfolks' economic dealings, and cultural fashions, notably perceptions of appropriate behavior for respectable women. Moreover, that women's voices were largely emptied out of the theater of the courtroom by the era of the new Republic was not a maneuver engineered by elites. Laypersons, through their strategies in civil suits, their pleas in criminal cases, and the wording of their writs and petitions, were critical participants in the renegotiations played out in the courts over how reputation was measured, how culpability for sexual transgressions was calculated, how male power within marriage would be buttressed, and how much women could manage property and have access to credit networks.

Men's and women's actions together, then, over the eighteenth century reshaped the county court from an inclusive forum representative of community to a rationalized institution serving the interests of commercially active men. The refashioning of the court into a public space designed solely to shape and nurture the civic identity of bourgeois men powerfully illustrates that fraternity in its deliberately gendered sense would determine access to the new nation's political and public spheres.[18] The refusal of the statesmen, jurists, and political pamphleteers of the Revolutionary and nation-building era to see women as anything but dependent, apolitical beings emerges clearly in their writings.[19] It is through the narrative trail left in court records predating the Constitu-

17. Joan B. Landes, *Women and the Public Sphere in the Age of the French Revolution* (Ithaca, N.Y., 1988), 61. For an argument on privatization similar to mine, see Helena M. Wall, *Fierce Communion: Family and Community in Early America* (Cambridge, Mass., 1990).

18. Landes, *Women in the Age of Revolution*, 12; Carole Pateman, *The Sexual Contract* (Stanford, Calif., 1988).

19. L. H. Butterfield et al., eds., *The Book of Abigail and John: Selected Letters of the Adams Family, 1762–1784* (Cambridge, Mass., 1975), 120–123; Linda K. Kerber, "The Paradox of Women's Citizenship in the Early Republic: The Case of *Martin vs.*

tion that we can discern that writing women out of the original American political contract had a structural history and experiential base many decades in the making.

Massachusetts, 1805," *American Historical Review,* XCVII (1992), 349–378; Kerber, *Women of the Republic,* chap. 1.

1

From Godly Rules to

Lawyerly Habits

SCENES FROM THE NEW HAVEN COURTROOM

Mary Kirby, a former servant and new bride, suing with her husband to collect unpaid wages — Elizabeth Gaskell, a widow and shopkeeper, bringing her account book into court to prove unpaid debts — Bethia Hawes, confessing to fornication after being reminded of the "allseeing God, who can write her sin in her forehead" — Elizabeth Bissell, unable to make a rape charge stick against a neighborhood youth whom she had flirted with — Hannah Sanford, an unmarried, part-time nurse and helper, suing to protect her reputation from defamatory, lampooning tales: Each of these women, sometime between the first meeting of English courts in 1639 and the close of the eighteenth century, made the journey to the "fair" green of New Haven to attend court.[1] They walked;

---

1. Joseph and Mary Kirby v. John Plum (Apr. 1708), NHCC, II, 305; Elizabeth Gaskell v. Caleb Ray (Nov. 1720), III, 120–125; Gaskell v. Thomas Wilshire (Nov. 1721), III, 133–139; Hannah Sanford v. Jedediah Andrews (Jan. 1747/8), NHCC

or, if they lived in an outlying town, they rode horseback, sometimes doubling up with a spouse, or perhaps hitched up a team and cart to bring along family members, witnesses, and supporters.

The last few steps leading to the building where the court was appointed to meet could be daunting. During the years in which New Haven was a separate colony, pretrial examinations were held in Governor Theophilus Eaton's mansion house. There, amid furnishings fit for nobility, many defendants must have quaked before a man whose learning and vaunted saintlike probity they could not hope to aspire to. For trials, the town and colony courts convened in the meetinghouse, the largest interior space in the county. Later in the seventeenth century, court sessions often took place in taverns, predominantly male social spaces and thus unfamiliar territory to most women.[2] After 1718, the makeshift efforts to create court spaces out of rooms in taverns and private houses were no longer needed. Men and women attending court would mount the steps of a two-story edifice that was built on the green as a combined courthouse and town hall. Once inside, one confronted a proper English courtroom fitted with the permanent architectural features that symbolized the power of the king to dispense justice through his officers. A raised bench, wainscoted and doubtless embellished with carving by the best local craftsmen, a clerk's and lawyer's table below it, jury boxes to the left and right: these framed what was the focal point of the secular sanctuary—the space before the bar. A woman petitioning for divorce or suing to collect a debt came forward from the crowd to

---

Files, dr. 19, NHSC Files (1749), dr. 327, and Connecticut Archives, Private Controversies, 1st Ser., IV, 121, 133–143, CSL.

2. Gail Sussman Marcus, " 'Due Execution of the Generall Rules of Righteousnesse': Criminal Procedures in New Haven Town and Colony, 1638–1658," in David D. Hall et al., eds., *Saints and Revolutionaries: Essays on Early American History* (New York, 1984), 115, 123–124. Cotton Mather said of Eaton, "He was the Terror of Evil Doers" (*Magnalia Christi Americana, Books I and II*, ed. Kenneth B. Murdock [Cambridge, Mass., 1977], 257).

One piece of evidence for the early-18th-century Hartford County Court suggests that the bar in the decades before formal courtrooms existed was a table at which the judges sat. Note the two terms used to describe the barrier between judges and litigant in the case against Bevil Waters. Waters was convicted of contempt of court for his response to losing a civil suit: "As he departed from the Barr" (or "Table" in one version), he said "to the Court . . . God blesse you" over his left shoulder (*Recs. Ct. of Assts.*, Lacy transcipt, II, 483–484; Conn. Archives, Crimes and Misdemeanors, 1st Ser., I, 389–392.

occupy this space alone; but if she had been charged with a crime, she stood before the bar guarded by the arresting constables.[3]

The degree of drama in the court scene, whether it was staged in a wealthy magistrate's house, in a barroom, or in a specially designed space, varied according to an individual litigant's temperament, her status, and the nature of her case. Varying over time were both the townscape that those attending court looked out on as they left a session and the rural landscape they passed through on their way home. In the 1640s, when the white population of New Haven Colony numbered two thousand at most, men and women from outlying farms and settlements entered the small, isolated town through the gate of a stout palisade (see Plate 1). On day trips necessitated by a court case, the earliest Europeans in the area must have been haunted by the implications of their sparse presence in the forested "wilderness," by the seemingly enormous distance to the next English village, and by the fear of raids from roving enemy Indians or competitive Dutchmen from the outposts of New Netherlands to the west. Court sessions in those early decades and until the end of the seventeenth century typically lasted a single day.[4]

By the 1780s, sessions stretched over three or four weeks, and county residents venturing toward court journeyed through a countryside that

3. This description is based on the earliest known existing plan for a New England courtroom: a drawing of the 1718 Salem, Mass., court chamber made in 1763 to indicate minor alterations. Martha J. McNamara discovered the drawing at the James Duncan Phillips Library, Peabody and Essex Museum, in Salem. For discussions of the 1763 Salem plan, the extent of other evidence on colonial New England court interiors, and the dearth of pictorial representations of courtrooms, see McNamara, "Disciplining Justice: Massachusetts Courthouses and the Legal Profession, 1750–1850" (Ph.D. diss., Boston University, 1995), 30–34, 40–47, 68–70, 198. I am deeply grateful to McNamara for making her work available to me. No plans for the interior of New Haven's 1719 wooden or 1764 brick courthouses survive, but it is highly likely that their interior designs were similar to the Salem plan.

4. Rollin G. Osterweis, *Three Centuries of New Haven, 1638–1938* (New Haven, 1953), 12; Floyd Shumway and Richard Hegel, eds., *New Haven: An Illustrated History* (Woodland Hills, Calif., 1981), 13. For the Reverend John Davenport's emphasis on wilderness in the first sermon ever delivered in New Haven, see John Warner Barber, *Connecticut Historical Collections, . . . Relating to History and Antiquities of Every Town . . .* (New Haven, 1838), 135. Neal W. Allen, Jr., offers an evocative, detailed reconstruction of a single-day session in the early 18th century for the court of general sessions of the peace in York Co., Mass. ("Law and Authority to the Eastward: Maine Courts, Magistrates, and Lawyers, 1690–1730," in Daniel R. Coquillette, ed., *Law in Colonial Massachusetts, 1630–1800* [Colonial Society of Massachusetts, *Publications*, LXII (Boston, 1984)], 290–311).

PLATE 1. Early New Haven. *An artist's imaginative sketch, with palisade sur-rounding town. From Charles Hervey Townshend,* A Pictorial History of Raynham and Its Vicinity *(New Haven, 1900)*

bore many marks of English "improvement." In many stretches all the arable land had yielded to clearing and fences. Surveying the distance, the eye looked out on a "medley of fine green plains," "rockey and woody hills, caped over . . . with bushes," and "very fertile valleys" in which "corn, buckwheat, flax, and hemp grow perfectly." Foreign visitors who were well acquainted with cities such as Edinburgh, London, and Rome found New Haven reminiscent of an English trading town or provincial seat. It was "pritty," especially since it was "inclosed" "upon all sides (excepting the south which faces the Sound) . . . with ranges of little hills as old Jerusalem was." The houses were "all built in the English fashion," they noted approvingly, and the "harbor [was] full of vessels." But the streets ("unsurfaced and sandy") were not as impressive as the "well compacted" lanes or "very stately and high" brick buildings of New York, Philadelphia, and Boston. With just a fraction of the population of Philadelphia, the largest North American city, New Haven after 1770 could boast, not of metropolitan distinctions like competing couturier shops and coffeehouses, but rather of more modest attainments: a bustling port, a skyline punctuated by six steeples, a sixteen-acre central green lined with half-grown elms (see Plate 2), and a social season climaxed by the pageantry of a college commencement.[5]

5. Carl Bridenbaugh, ed., *Gentleman's Progress: The Itinerarium of Dr. Alexander Ham-*

PLATE 2. Southeast View of New Haven, 1786. *Woodcut from the masthead of the* New Haven Chronicle, *showing city and harbor. Courtesy of the Connecticut State Library*

Throughout the fifteen decades following Theophilus Eaton's first New Haven court, women's formal legal status remained fixed in the mold of English common law. Single women over the age of majority (eighteen) and widowed women had legal standing before the courts, meaning they could sue and be sued in their own names, convey property, and write wills. However, when a woman married (and at least 95 percent of colonial women did), she was prohibited from alienating property, entering into contracts, bringing lawsuits, or making a will without the consent and, often, the joint action of her husband. As the great explicator of the common law, William Blackstone, put it, "The very being or legal existence of the woman is suspended during the

ilton, 1744 (Pittsburgh, 1992), 165–166; Antonio Pace, ed. and trans., *Luigi Castiglioni's Viaggio: Travels in the United States of North America, 1785–87* (Syracuse, N.Y., 1983), 249; Thomas Pownall on his 1754 visit, quoted in Osterweis, *Three Centuries of New Haven,* 76; Sargent Bush, Jr., ed., "The Journal of Madam [Sarah Kemble] Knight [1704]," in William L. Andrews, ed., *Journeys in New Worlds: Early American Women's Narratives* (Madison, Wis., 1990), 109. The public house kept by Amy(?) Smith in 1786 was known as "the Coffeehouse," according to a plaintiff in an assault case (Northrop v. Brush and Isaacs, NHCC Files, dr. 77 [writ]). It was also referred to in the *Connecticut Journal* (New Haven), May 1, 1783. According to a 1774 census, the number of people living within the bounds of the town of New Haven was 8,295; by Ezra Stiles's estimate, 2,000 lived in the town center. In contrast, Philadelphia, the largest city in the Atlantic British colonies, housed at least 40,000. Evarts B. Greene and Virginia D. Harrington, *American Population before the Federal Census of 1790* (New York, 1932), 59; and Bruce C. Daniels, *The Connecticut Town: Growth and Development, 1635–1790* (Middletown, Conn., 1979), 160, app. 10.

marriage, or at least is . . . consolidated into that of the husband: under whose wing, protection, and *cover,* she performs every thing; . . . in our law-french . . . her condition . . . is called her *coverture.*"[6]

Besides their silent incorporation of the principles of coverture, colonial legal codes endorsed the premise that male family heads constituted the relevant recipients of rights. Through the guise of a definitively gendered use of the word "man," this assumption made its most overt appearance in the grand statements of civil liberties set forth in the earliest legal codes of both New Haven and Connecticut colonies:

> No man's Life shall be taken away; no man's Honour or good Name shall be stained; no man's Person shall be Arrested . . . [or] Punished; No man shall be deprived of his Wife, or Children . . . : Unless it be by the vertue or equity of some express Law of this Colony warranting the same.[7]

Although all women were denied voting rights and married women had to be accompanied by their husbands in legal proceedings, the early Connecticut legal system claimed to extend procedural due process to women and members of other excluded groups. Reflecting the accretion through the centuries by the English legal system of rights and remedies open to all comers, one Connecticut statute in force throughout the colonial period promised "all persons within this Colony, whether they be Inhabitants or Forreiners," white or black, male or female, "the same Justice . . . without partiality or delay." Assured access to the courts and legislatures as petitioners and litigants, women did not find it incongruous with their subordinate social and political status to claim the right to be heard or to be given their due. In a 1726 inheritance dispute that wound its way up to the General Assembly, these striking claims were made for Elizabeth Durand by her husband: she should "have the Law ["which measures out Equal Justice to all men"] as

6. Jackson Turner Main, *Society and Economy in Colonial Connecticut* (Princeton, N.J., 1985), 13–14, 18n; William Blackstone, *Commentaries on the Laws of England,* 1st ed., 4 vols. (1765–1769; rpt., Chicago, 1979), I, 430.

7. This version is that appearing in *Acts and Laws, of His Majesties Colony of Connecticut in New-England* (New London, 1715), 1. Clauses with nearly identical wording are found in New Haven Colony's 1656 Code (*NHCR,* I, 571) and Connecticut Colony's Codes of 1650 (*PR,* I, 509) and 1672 (John D. Cushing, ed., *The Earliest Laws of the New Haven and Connecticut Colonies, 1639–1673* [Wilmington, Del., 1977], 75).

her Sheild," and she should not be "cut of[f as] one of his majesties Subjects from the Priviledges of the magna Charta."[8]

In New Haven as in England, custom dictated that, along with children, "idiots," Indians, blacks, and propertyless white men, white women were debarred from serving as jurors, voters, and officeholders. Yet in certain legal situations, white matrons and midwives served the court in a quasi-official capacity. In rape, infanticide, and witchcraft cases, judges often named a panel of such women to search the body of the woman involved. Requisite to a fornication prosecution or paternity suit against a man was the midwife's testimony about whom the mother had named while in the throes of childbirth as the father of her infant.[9] As long as such cases occupied a significant portion of the courts' business, the sight of women on court days — mingling with the audience, testifying on oath, familiarizing themselves with court procedures — was ensured.

For all the fixity of women's formal legal status as adults who lost their legal being upon marriage and as inhabitants who had access to the courts but no voice in legal governance, the forces that changed the landscape of New Haven between 1639 and 1790 profoundly affected women's experiences before the bar. In that period, the New Haven region witnessed the eclipse of a distinctively Puritan legal regime, it prospered from a long-awaited economic boom, and it shared in far-reaching social and cultural changes that touched all of New England. To begin to understand the complex interplay between New Haven's unstatic legal culture, the social forces outside its courtroom walls, and gender relations in the white community, we need to begin with The-

8. "An Act for Administring Equal Justice," in *Acts and Laws* (1715), 64 (similar wording appeared in the New Haven Colony's magistrate's oath [*NHCR*, II, 616] and the 1672 Connecticut Code [Cushing, ed., *Earliest Laws of New Haven and Connecticut*, 111]); Remonstrance of John Durand (Oct. 18, 1726), Administrators of Abigail Bryan v. John Durand, Conn. Archives, Private Controversies, 2d Ser., V, 23.

9. An early use in New Haven of a matrons' jury occurred in the October 1662 prosecution of John Frost for "defiling" Mercy Payne (Records of the Colony of New Haven, original MS, Ib, 331, CSL). For examples of cases outside New Haven, see Lyle Koehler, *A Search for Power: The "Weaker Sex" in Seventeenth-Century New England* (Urbana, Ill., 1980), 117, 131 n. 42. On the midwife's testimony in late-18th-century Maine, see Laurel Thatcher Ulrich, *A Midwife's Tale: The Life of Martha Ballard, Based on Her Diary, 1785–1812* (New York, 1990), 149–152.

ophilus Eaton and the company that staked its hopes on the colony along the Quinnipiac.

The origin of the English settlement in New Haven can be traced to St. Stephen's, the Coleman Street parish in London that was home in the 1620s to the two men most responsible for the colony's founding, Theophilus Eaton and John Davenport. Eaton, a minister's son, had risen to become a London "Merchant of great Credit and Fashion," notwithstanding his strong Puritan beliefs. While making his fortune in the Baltic trade, Eaton had served as deputy governor of the East-Land Company, lived for several years in Denmark, and been entrusted with carrying out trade negotiations with the Danish king. Davenport, a childhood friend and schoolmate of Eaton, became vicar of St. Stephen's in 1624. The ward was known as the residence of many prosperous merchants and "as a veritable Puritan stronghold." Davenport proved to be a popular preacher, garnering the support and sympathy of many of his parishioners as he investigated the opportunities for emigrating to the New World in the late 1620s and as he moved increasingly toward nonconformity with Anglican orthodoxy in the early 1630s. Disgusted by the tight discipline and liturgical requirements of Archbishop William Laud, Davenport quietly resigned his post in 1633 and took pastoral positions in Amsterdam and Rotterdam. Returning to England in disguise in 1636, he teamed with Eaton to form a company to plant yet another group of dissenters in the Massachusetts Bay Colony. Investing their whole estates in the plan, Davenport and Eaton persuaded a nucleus of the St. Stephen's parishioners, in addition to other Puritan families, to join the company.[10] The emigrants, among whom were several merchants besides Eaton, were motivated both by the vision of establishing a

---

10. Benjamin Trumbull, *A Complete History of Connecticut, Civil and Ecclesiastical, from the Emigration of Its First Planters* . . . (Hartford, 1797–1818), I, 94; Mather, *Magnalia*, ed. Murdock, 255–256; Charles M. Andrews, *The Fathers of New England: A Chronicle of the Puritan Commonwealths* (New Haven, 1921), 67; Andrews, *The Colonial Period of American History,* II, (New Haven, 1936), 146; Elizabeth Tucker Van Beek, "Piety and Profit: English Puritans and the Shaping of a Godly Marketplace in the New Haven Colony" (Ph.D. diss., University of Virginia, 1993), 78–116, 190–206; Isabel MacBeath Calder, *The New Haven Colony* (1934; rpt., New Haven, 1970), chap. 1; Trumbull, *Complete History of Connecticut,* I, 89. Eaton and Davenport both contributed funds to the Massachusetts Bay Company and attended its London meetings, yet without any intention to join the emigration.

port town that would thrive on commerce with London and by the desire to live in a more godly spiritual community than the Church of England then allowed.

The *Hector,* the vessel chartered by Eaton and Davenport, arrived in Boston in June 1637 with about 250 people aboard. Many of the arrivals had been involved in the initial planning of the Bay Colony and could count on being greeted in Boston by former associates and fellow believers. Fully intending to fix on a coastal site within Massachusetts, Eaton and his partners considered several nominated locations but were disappointed. Late in the summer they began to hear high praise of a region just west of the Connecticut Colony, called Quinnipiac after a river that flowed into the Long Island Sound to form a harbor. Eaton and a small group went to investigate, sailing into the harbor that a later visitor described as "a Circle two miles in Diameter" with an "Entrance formed by two tongues of Land," sandy banks on the west and wooded shores on the east. The scouting party pronounced the site acceptable and left a few men to build huts and winter over while Eaton returned to Boston to prepare for a spring departure and to solicit settlers among the original *Hector* company and others in the Bay Colony. Davenport and Eaton and their adherents did not depart out of any disagreement on points of theology or governance from the Puritan leaders of Massachusetts Bay. Rather, by starting a separate colony, they could not only distance themselves from the dissension then wracking the Bay Colony but also try their own hands at designing "a civil and religious constitution as near as possible to scriptural precept and example." That they brazenly set out on their own without a charter or any legitimacy in the eyes of the crown and Parliament was a mark of both their desire for independence and their spiritual zeal.[11]

Eaton's company disembarked on the shore of the Quinnipiac harbor on April 24, 1638. The next day, being the Sabbath, they broke off from digging the cellars that would house them in the early months, to hear John Davenport preach. The settlers' plans found favor with local native

---

11. Osterweis, *Three Centuries of New Haven,* 22; Capt. Patrick Ferguson to Sir Henry Clements, May 27, 1779, quoted in Lloyd A. Brown, *Loyalist Operations at New Haven* (Meriden, Conn., 1938), [4]. On the decision to depart, see Trumbull, *Complete History of Connecticut,* I, 91; Calder, *New Haven Colony,* chap. 2; Albert E. Van Dusen, *Connecticut* (New York, 1961), 49–50. Another factor was the rumor that Massachusetts might lose its charter and, thus, its Puritan features (Andrews, *Colonial Period,* II, 151).

American sachems who, in 1638 and over the next few years, agreed to sell them substantial parcels of land along the coast and inland up the river. During that first summer, the town site on the northwestern side of the harbor was given its grid: a surveyor laid out nine large squares. Town plots were distributed according to status and wealth, frame houses began to go up, and the outer perimeter was palisaded.[12]

The following summer, in June, the male settlers gathered to sign the Fundamental Agreement, articles that laid out the civil government for the jurisdiction, which then consisted only of the palisaded town. The agreement emphasized that the franchise would be limited, as it was in the Bay Colony, to male church members, those who had made a convincing public relation of their conversion and faith and who were then the only worshipers who took communion on Sacrament Sundays and voted in church affairs. This linkage between civic voting and church membership was one of the defining features of New Haven Colony, one that other towns had to agree to before joining the colony. In August 1639, the church was gathered, and Davenport chosen as its pastor. Two months later, Eaton, "a man well known and approved . . . as fittly quallified for thatt office," was elected as the town's chief magistrate. Davenport, who believed firmly that God's hand guided the election of magistrates, preached from Exodus 18:21: "Provide thou among all the people men of courage, fearing God, men dealing truely, hating covetousnes: and appoint *suche* over them *to be* rulers over thousandes." On the following day, October 26, 1639, Eaton convened a court in the new settlement to hear its first criminal case. Nearly a year later, inhabitants chose the name New Haven for their town, thus dismissing the native American signifier in favor of a thoroughly English image conjuring up the spiritual and economic promise of a harbor (or haven).[13]

12. Calder, *New Haven Colony*, chap. 3; Van Dusen, *Connecticut*, 50; Osterweis, *Three Centuries of New Haven*, 12–14.

13. *NHCR*, I, 12–19, 20–21, 22; Marcus, " 'Due Execution of the Rules of Righteousnesse,' " in Hall et al., eds., *Saints and Revolutionaries*, 102, 123; Osterweis, *Three Centuries of New Haven*, 20. Edmund S. Morgan offers a succinct and lucid account of how the Puritan test for church membership evolved in 17th-century New England (*Visible Saints: The History of a Puritan Idea* [New York, 1963]). The idea that voters were the instruments of God and thus that the elected officeholders were God's chosen persisted in New England through the century (Richard L. Bushman, *From Puritan to Yankee: Character and the Social Order in Connecticut, 1690–1765* [New York, 1967], 9; T. H. Breen, *The Character of the Good Ruler: A Study of Puritan Political Ideas in New England, 1630–1730* [New Haven, 1970]).

It was not until 1643 that New Haven became a colony, with jurisdiction over a sizable, if fragmented, territory and a structure of government to match. By the autumn of that year, the tiny coastal settlements of Guilford, Branford, and Milford (which were adjacent to New Haven), Stamford (further down the coast), and Southold (on Long Island) had agreed to join themselves to New Haven. A General Court, or unicameral legislature, would meet twice a year in New Haven. Presided over by a governor and deputy governor, this assembly was a small gathering, given that the six towns each sent from two to four deputies. Theophilus Eaton, elected the first governor, continued to serve in that post until his death in 1658.

With the coalescence of the colony, what was in practice a bilevel court system was put into place. Town, or "plantation," courts would try small civil and criminal causes. The bench for these local courts consisted of magistrates nominated by the towns but officially named by the assembly and the town's deputies, who were instructed to assist them. A higher court, the Colony Court of Magistrates, sat twice a year or in special session in New Haven. Made up of the magistrates from all the towns, first among whom was Governor Eaton, this court heard "weighty and capitall cases, whether civill or criminall," in addition to appeals from the town courts.[14]

What made the colony's government vulnerable was, not its structure, which resembled that of Massachusetts Bay and Connecticut, but its lack of a charter. Protected because of its Puritan credentials during Oliver Cromwell's accession to power, New Haven after the restoration of Charles II in 1660 proved to be on shakier ground than Connecticut, the neighboring colony founded in 1656 also without a charter. Unable to secure their own charter and threatened with consolidation with the

14. *NHCR*, I, 110–116 (quote on 114); Calder, *New Haven Colony*, 123–125; Marcus, " 'Due Execution of the Rules of Righteousnesse,' " in Hall et al., eds., *Saints and Revolutionaries*, 105, 108–111. The General Court was to act as a final court of appeal only for civil cases, but since the civil caseload was so small, almost all judicial matters were resolved in the Colony Court of Magistrates (108n). In the latter court, a quorum of four was required. Votes in all courts were by the majority. Note that no magistrate sitting alone could adjudicate cases.

Historians agree that New Haven Colony's legal records are fuller than those for any of its early New England counterparts. However, records for the Colony Court of Magistrates and the General Court are missing for the terms between April 1644 and May 1653 (*NHCR*, I, iv). The records of the New Haven town court survive for that period.

very un-Puritan, newly conquered English colony of New York, New Haven's leaders in 1664 would reluctantly accede to their colony's absorption into Connecticut. The implementation of that union in May 1665 brought to an abrupt conclusion a colonization effort that was at its outset, in material resources and singleness of purpose, perhaps one of the most promising in North America.[15]

As all commentators in the seventeenth century and ever since have pointed out, New Haven was distinctive among New England's earliest European settlements for the wealth of its founders. The early settlers brought to the "wilderness" thirty-six thousand pounds, an awesome sum in the context of New World colonization efforts. As "Men of Traffick and Business" in London, ten of the planters had amassed "Considerable estates" of at least one thousand pounds; Eaton himself had assets valued at three thousand pounds in 1643. This unusual combination of capital manifested itself in the ease with which Indian lands were purchased, the prompt construction of a fifty-foot-square meetinghouse with tower and turret, and the "stately and costly houses" that rose in the town center not long after 1638. Residents of modest worth, owning perhaps a two-room house, ninety acres, a few beds, and a single chest, must have looked in awe at Davenport and his compeers whose houses might contain not only many "chambers" with beds decked resplendently in "Tapestry" coverings but public rooms outfitted with "great" chairs, "Turky" carpets, shelves of books, silver plate, and other opulent goods.[16] The middling sort also must have anticipated sharing in some of the employment and profits that were expected to accrue from the commercial ventures instigated by New Haven's leaders. A fur-trading colony on the Delaware, the launching of a "Great Ship" to jump-start direct trade with London merchant houses, and the encouragement of an ironworks were all enterprises entered into enthusiastically by New Haveners in the 1640s and 1650s. All failed miserably. In the wake of

15. Calder, *New Haven Colony,* 207–217; Osterweis, *Three Centuries of New Haven,* 60–64, chap. 9; Andrews, *Colonial Period,* II, 73, 140–141, 192–194; *PR,* I, 441.

16. Andrews, *Colonial Period,* II, 172; William Hubbard, *A General History of New England from the Discovery to MDCLXXX,* 2d ed. (1848; rpt., New York, 1968), 318; *NHCR,* I, 91–93; Van Dusen, *Connecticut,* 53; Shumway and Hegel, eds., *New Haven,* 12–13; Trumbull, *Complete History of Connecticut,* I, 94; Van Beek, "Piety and Profit," 352, 449–459, 472–486. Charles McLean Andrews contends that depictions of these houses as having 13 fireplaces (as in Shumway and Hegel, eds., *New Haven,* 12) are exaggerated (*Colonial Period,* II, 154n).

such discouragements, mercantile and commercial efforts declined, and householders settled for lives structured around farming, with surpluses funneled to Boston or New Amsterdam merchants who monopolized the overseas trade. By 1660, one observer said of New Haven: "The Merchants [are] either dead or come away, the rest gotten to their Farmes. The Towne is not so glorious as once it was."[17]

If New Haven's potential economic glories dimmed all too quickly, Eaton and Davenport might have taken consolation in the success with which they fashioned a legal system that epitomized Puritan principles. The colony along the Quinnipiac, historians have claimed, not only reached for a "purer Puritanism" but achieved "in practice" a more "rigorous working out" of Protestant dissenting notions of secular government than its neighbors, Massachusetts Bay and Connecticut. Learned emigrants brought with them strong opinions about the corrupt nature of the English legal system and the ways in which it cried out for reform. Given the chance to start from scratch, Eaton and his colleagues rejoiced in their ability to ban lawyers, insist on simplified pleadings comprehensible to laypersons, and issue equitable, ad hoc remedies and swift criminal sentences. Yet, despite their posture as literal followers of Mosaic law, many of the premises and much of the structure of their legal system came directly from English experience. In effect, New Haven's founders put in place those features of English institutions and procedures that were consonant with Scripture, with New World conditions, and with their particular vision of an efficacious and godly legal regime.[18]

Two objects were central to the New Haveners' mission of establishing

17. Mather, *Magnalia*, ed. Murdock, 169–170; Shumway and Hegel, eds., *New Haven*, 16–17; Andrews, *Colonial Period*, II, 172–173, 175–176; Thomas Rutherford Trowbridge, Jr., "History of Ancient Maritime Interests of New Haven," New Haven Colony Historical Society, *Papers*, III (1882), 85–112; Osterweis, *Three Centuries of New Haven*, 27–30; Calder, *New Haven Colony*, 160–169; Samuel Maverick, "A Briefe Discription of New England and the Severall Townes Therein, Together with the Present Government Thereof," Massachusetts Historical Society, *Proceedings*, 2d Ser., I (1884–1885), 245.

18. Marcus, " 'Due Execution of the Rules of Righteousnesse,' " in Hall et al., eds., *Saints and Revolutionaries*, 101, 109; Perry Miller, review of *The New Haven Colony*, by Isabel M. Calder, *New England Quarterly*, VIII (1935), 583; G. B. Warden, "Law Reform in England and New England, 1620 to 1660," *WMQ*, XXXV (1978), 668–690; Andrews, *Colonial Period*, II, 156–157; Richard B. Morris, *Studies in the History of American Law: With Special Reference to the Seventeenth and Eighteenth Centuries*, 2d ed. (New York, 1974), 27–39.

a "civill order . . . most p[leas]ing unto God": placing righteous men in office and punishing sin wherever it festered. The first would be achieved, they believed, by restricting voting and officeholding to those pious few who passed the rigorous test for church membership. Such trustworthy voters would have the foresight — and the divine inspiration — to return year after year to the bench magistrates who, while not clerics themselves, would be guided by a thorough knowledge of the Scriptures and would be eager to consult with "Men of God" (that is, local clergymen) "in all hard cases." Magistrates were expected to have the skill and the awe-inspiring presence to accomplish the colony's second goal: allowing no sin to go uncovered. A majestic countenance, uncommon degrees of discretion and gravity, and "Ungainsayable *Authority*" all gave Theophilus Eaton the power, Cotton Mather later rhapsodized, to cajole just about any miscreant, even the most obstinate, into truth telling and repentance. Puritans were convinced that God's favor could be courted *only* if magistrates and residents did their utmost to uncover and punish all sin. Bearing witness to an omniscient God thus meant extracting full confessions from criminals and meting out severe, public punishments to transgressors "without partiality."[19]

Justice could be dispensed impartially, Theophilus Eaton was convinced, without the English system of petit trial juries and grand juries. Indeed, in historical accounts, the great hallmark of New Haven Colony's peculiar legal regime has been its strong antijury stance. Without direct documentation why New Haven and no other early New England jurisdiction dispensed with juries, we can safely surmise that Eaton's rationale was twofold. Like Puritan law reformers in England, he could claim that juries lacked any scriptural basis. Moreover, given the tiny number of male voters from whom jurors could be called, finding enough disinterested men could prove impossible. The colony in effect made the town deputies (elected legislators) who sat alongside the magistrates at town courts fulfill the function of jurors.[20]

19. *NHCR*, I, 11; John Cotton [John Davenport], *A Discourse about Civil Government in a New Plantation Whose Design Is Religion* (Cambridge, Mass., 1663), 15; Mather, *Magnalia*, ed. Murdock, 257; *NHCR*, II, 616.

20. John M. Murrin, "Magistrates, Sinners, and a Precarious Liberty: Trial by Jury in Seventeenth-Century New England," in Hall et al., eds., *Saints and Revolutionaries*, 170, 182; Marcus, " 'Due Execution of the Rules of Righteousnesse,' " ibid., 109– 111; Calder, *New Haven Colony*, 125–126; Warden, "Law Reform in England and New England," *WMQ*, XXXV (1978), 677.

Seemingly just as peculiar as abolishing juries was the magistrates' extreme reluctance to admit testimony on oath. Flying in the face of English practice, New Haven judges allowed very few defendants or witnesses to take oaths. Since swearing an oath was an "Extraordinary act of Religion," most fallible humans if required to swear would fall into the pit of perjury. Magistrates who condoned any degree of lying, the logic went, would bring down God's wrath on the colony. Thus in the great majority of legal cases, the judges relied on unsworn testimony, permitting witnesses to swear on rare occasions, and only after they had been grilled and were thought to be telling the truth.[21]

New Haven Colony's legal system lived up to the ideals of Puritan jurisprudence to a remarkable extent. This feat was partly due to the stability of its leadership. Theophilus Eaton presided over practically every pretrial examination and court session convened in New Haven until his death in January 1658.[22] Davenport, the other lodestar for many who ended up making the trip from St. Stephen's to the Quinnipiac, exerted great influence on the community and its governance until 1667, when he left Connecticut behind to become minister of the First Church of Boston.

Surveying developments in the 1640s and 1650s, Eaton and Davenport could count many signs of success. First, most New Haveners took their leaders' advice to settle disputes over debt and property by informal conciliation or neighborhood arbitration: examples of formal civil litigation rarely appear in the record books. Second, the founders' emphasis on pursuing sin and maintaining watchfulness "produced a phenomenally law-abiding society," with little violent crime or sexual misconduct. Inhabitants apparently accepted the broad powers of the magistrates to ferret out sin: very few suspected criminals had to be jailed before trial, and witnesses "faithfully appeared" when asked to give testimony. Third, justice was indeed swift. Almost all criminal cases concluded within a month of their commencement.[23] Fourth, New Haven

---

21. Marcus, " 'Due Execution of the Rules of Righteousnesse,' " in Hall et al., eds., *Saints and Revolutionaries,* 112; Murrin, "Magistrates, Sinners, and a Precarious Liberty," ibid., 175.

22. Marcus, " 'Due Execution of the Rules of Righteousnesse,' " ibid., 123.

23. Ibid., 104–105, 108, 136; Murrin, "Magistrates, Sinners, and a Precarious Liberty," ibid., 173, 176. A further example of New Haven's selective rejection of English legal approaches was reflected in the blurring of criminal and civil actions. Rather than follow common law forms and sort their court sessions into common

magistrates adhered to Deuteronomy's evidentiary rule in criminal cases: in the event that the suspect refused to confess, the bench could convict only with two witnesses to the crime. For "secret" crimes where eyewitnessing was unlikely, Eaton and his fellow judges followed the Bay Colony's interpretation that "one clear witness" backed up by strong circumstanial evidence would suffice. Eaton's conscience could be clear: despite his reluctance to see defendants go unpunished whom he personally believed guilty, there were occasions on which the colony courts dismissed men and women accused of theft, bestiality, and witchcraft for lack of evidence. Finally, Eaton's reputation and his powers as an interrogator convinced the great majority of criminal defendants that it would be for their "spiritual good" to break down and reveal the full extent of their complicity. After many denials, John Frost, having been told by the bench "that his countenance argued guilt," finally conceded that he knew "he must owne . . . [the charge] one day if it was true, if not now." That 85 percent of criminal defendants confessed before conviction (and typically they did so more readily than John Frost) demonstrates how distant New Haven colony's legal culture was from modern, adversarial modes of prosecuting.[24]

The fashioning of a distinctly Puritan legal regime in New Haven had significant consequences for women. Although the Puritan scheme for

---

pleas and general sessions, colony magistrates were more interested in arriving at the "truth" behind any misconduct and forging a remedy. See Marcus, " 'Due Execution of the Rules of Righteousnesse,' " ibid., 105n.

24. Deut. 17:16, 19:15; John Winthrop, *The History of New England from 1630 to 1649*, ed. James Savage (Boston, 1853), II, 56–57; Marcus, " 'Due Execution of the Rules of Righteousnesse,' " in Hall et al., eds., *Saints and Revolutionaries*, 111–112, 116–118, and Murrin, "Magistrates, Sinners, and a Precarious Liberty," 175–176; *NHTR*, I, 249–251, 252–253; *NHCR*, I, 454–455, 471, II, 263–268, 289–291. In cases of witchcraft, Marcus points out that New Haven magistrates would not convict on supernatural evidence alone (116).

"Spiritual good": Cotton [Davenport], *Discourse*, 17. John Frost: Records of the Colony of New Haven, original manuscript, Ib, 331, CSL. Confessions: Marcus, " 'Due Execution of the Rules of Righteousnesse,' " in Hall et al., eds., *Saints and Revolutionaries*, 122, 132–133. John Langbein's work reminds us that, while the 17th-century English system was more formal and addicted to legal fictions than New Haven's, it was neither fully adversarial nor committed to granting many procedural rights to the accused ("The Criminal Trial before the Lawyers," *University of Chicago Law Review*, XLV [1978], 263–316, and *Prosecuting Crime in the Renaissance: England, Germany, France* [Cambridge, Mass., 1974]).

legal reform contained no call for improving women's legal status, several of its approaches made the courtroom more hospitable to women than were the king's courts in England. Generally, the relaxation of common law rules helped women and all those not learned in the law to bring complaints to court without fear of making mistakes and without paying fees. More specifically, the magistrates' zeal for pursuing the truth led them to permit wives to testify alongside their husbands when disputes touching the household economy found their way into court.[25] Thus women found fewer barriers to coming to court over civil matters than they would confront in courtrooms hewing rigidly to common law procedures. New Haven Puritans also dispensed with the restrictive policy of English ecclesiastical courts on marital separation and divorce. The 1656 New Haven code cited Matthew 19:9 and 1 Corinthians 7:15 when it permitted divorces on the basis of adultery, male impotence, and confirmed desertion. In making available a full divorce with permission granted to "the innocent party . . . to marry again," the lawmakers gave abandoned wives a chance to extricate themselves from legal limbo, economic uncertainty, and sinful sexual temptation.[26] During the colony's existence, only two residents (both women) took advantage of the law. However, the spirit and letter of New Haven's precocious divorce policy lived on after 1665, offering to Connecticut women a remedy that wives in other colonies could rarely obtain.

In the criminal sphere, colony judges strove to implement a single standard. They were motivated by a strongly held belief that godly behavior should be the measure for *all* inhabitants. Hence sinners, whether women or men, servants or wealthy church members, could expect to be lectured from the bench to follow "the rule" of neighborly kindness, to refrain from "wicked" "uncleanness," or to emulate such familiar biblical figures as "Micaell the Archangell." Indeed, in this age in which nearly all those convicted of serious crimes received whipping, men tended to be punished more severely than women for sexual misconduct. At the same time that colony magistrates eschewed delivering condemnations of vice in markedly gendered language, they explicitly endorsed the premise that women who advanced charges of rape or sexual

25. Richard B. Morris notes that the common law rule incapacitating spouses' testimony was flouted in several 17th-century colonial jurisdictions influenced by Protestant reform ideology (*Studies in the History of American Law,* 197–200).

26. Cushing, ed., *Earliest Laws of New Haven and Connecticut,* 28. Before 1667, the colony of Connecticut granted some divorces ad hoc, but it had no divorce statute.

harassment would not lie. After young Mercy Payne had given "a large relation" of the many times she had attempted to resist John Frost's advances, the magistrates challenged Frost over his denials: "What temptation should shee bee under to bring such a thing out to her owne shame?" Eaton and his judicial colleagues, having arrogated to themselves the power to discern truthfulness in witnesses, used that power to support women who righteously revealed great sins, to wring confessions from male assailants, and to hand out severe punishments as warning to others.[27] Women thus had good reason to believe that their voices would not be ignored and that the men elected to the bench would not reflexively use whatever skeptical views they harbored of woman's nature to shield accused men from exposure and penalty.

Although Scripture- and reform-inspired departures from English legal traditions favored women in important ways, the colony was hardly a haven for equality between men and women. Eaton and Davenport might have respected women's capacity for godliness and acknowledged their essential economic roles in a frontier setting, but they had no interest in subverting the inherited gender system that emphatically subordinated women to men in the family and the polity. The Puritans' rejection of the double standard in fornication cases — and their abhorrence of bawdy and satirical jesting that often targeted women — flowed, not from a conviction that women were oppressed, but from other strong intolerances, including revulsion at seeing any sinner go unpunished and hearing the sanctity of marriage impugned. When it came to adultery or witchcraft, colony magistrates were prepared to believe the worst of women. Choosing a definition of adultery that would remain on the books in Connecticut for two centuries, New Haven Colony lawmakers followed the narrow Old Testament concept that adultery was an act committed with a married woman. Thus married men who had affairs with single women were exempted from adultery's penalties. New Haven's magistrates were not more immune than their counterparts in Massachusetts Bay from the implicit belief that women were more prone than men to the most damning sin of all — renouncing God in order to serve Satan. Indeed, concerns that wives would turn rebellious and over-

27. *NHCR*, I, 77, 247, 471, 476. Frost: Records of the Colony of New Haven, orig. ms., Ib, 331. Note that New Haven Colony judges, while sympathetic to the trauma that assaulted women experienced, still meted out whippings or harsh reprimands to women who hid their rape stories or who could be interpreted as having encouraged a dalliance.

throw male household governance or disrupt paternal bloodlines through illicit sex crop up repeatedly in witchcraft, adultery, and heresy proceedings against women in early New England. New Haven never experienced an outbreak of witchcraft accusations, but the colony's most prominent leaders had staked out clear positions condemning dissident women. Davenport, while in Boston in 1637, had supported the proceedings against Anne Hutchinson. And Eaton complied with the 1644 excommunication of his wife, Anne Yale Eaton, for her unorthodox opinions. Through these postures and others, they linked themselves to centuries-old European ideas about the inferiority and necessary submission of the female sex.[28]

Yet what an inquiry into patterns of adjudication in New Haven Colony illustrates is that, historically, patriarchy has not always worn the same face. In the cause of creating an earthly community pleasing to their God, New Haven's founders implemented legal policies that served to blunt the sharpness of patriarchy as it was typically enforced in seventeenth-century England's hierarchical institutions. If Puritan approaches to the law, such as simplifying civil procedure, punishing men and women equally, and receiving women's stories of abuse supportively, had been retained as permanent fixtures of the evolving American legal system, the result would have been a less patriarchal society in the long run. But such a system, preoccupied as it was with criminal behavior and reliant on judges' intimate knowledge of the men and women before the

28. Carol F. Karlsen, *The Devil in the Shape of a Woman: Witchcraft in Colonial New England* (New York, 1987); Calder, *New Haven Colony*, 36; Murrin, "Magistrates, Sinners, and a Precarious Liberty," in Hall et al., eds., *Saints and Revolutionaries*, 172. For the proceedings against Anne Eaton, see Newman Smyth, ed., "Mrs. Eaton's Trial (in 1644): As It Appears upon the Records of the First Church of New Haven," New Haven Colony Historical Society, *Papers*, V (1894), 133–148.
There were four prosecutions and two slander suits over witchcraft in New Haven Colony (John Putnam Demos, *Entertaining Satan: Witchcraft and the Culture of Early New England* [New York, 1982], 401–409). Records survive for prosecutions against Elizabeth Godman and Nicholas and Eleanor Bayley. The Bayleys were banished from the colony, and Godman was strongly reprimanded for suspicion of witchcraft and required to post bond for her good behavior. Most of the documents for these cases are reprinted in David D. Hall, ed., *Witchhunting in Seventeenth-Century New England: A Documentary History, 1638–1692* (Boston, 1991), 61–73, 92–95. A Goody Knapp was executed in 1653 in Fairfield under New Haven's jurisdiction, but the trial record does not survive. Suspicion that Mary Staples was a witch was the subject of a slander suit (*NHCR*, II, 88–89; Hall, ed., *Witchhunting in New England*, 75–86).

bar, would not accommodate the type of litigation generated by a commercializing, transatlantic economy and by rapid population growth.
Although many tenets of Puritan jurisprudence were kept alive in New
Haven's courtrooms for some time after the colony passed out of existence, their ultimate fate was sealed when New England underwent a
major cultural shift at the end of the seventeenth century. In response to
tightening oversight by the crown and a series of crises in the 1680s and
1690s, lawmakers and judges in Massachusetts and Connecticut began
to align courtroom practice more closely with that of the parent country.
The single-minded pursuit of godly communities that had been Theophilus Eaton's dream was no longer the organizing principle of New
England society. As New England's legal culture became more and more
English as the eighteenth century progressed, New Haven Colony's distinctive regime began to look like an aberration, a blip on the screen, in
the long evolution of the common law.

The experience of New Haven men and women before the bar in the
four decades following union with Connecticut was not as novel as one
might expect. Court sessions remained small, intimate affairs where business was wrapped up by the end of the day. Given the option of jury trials,
some civil litigants chose to place their disputes before the twelve-man
panels, but others continued in the old way and requested the bench to
rule on their cases. Among those charged with criminal misdemeanors,
the general habit of confessing persisted until the 1690s, and thus juries
were rarely needed. In felony cases, grand juries were often but not
invariably convened to hear the evidence and return an indictment.
Indicted defendants frequently pleaded not guilty and desired to be
tried "by God and the country" (that is, by a petit trial jury). The process
became more streamlined by the end of the century. In the late 1690s
Daniel Clark, a respected justice of the peace and militia captain, was
appointed case by case as king's attorney for the colony, assuring that
one man knowledgeable in criminal procedure brought serious cases to
trial in an organized fashion.[29]

---

29. Murrin, "Magistrates, Sinners, and a Precarious Liberty," in Hall et al., eds.,
Saints and Revolutionaries, 181–182; NHCC, I; Rex v. Nicholas Sension (May 1677),
Recs. Ct. of Assts., Lacy transcript, I, 67–68. A grand jury was instructed to return an
indictment marked either "Ignoramus," meaning they found insufficient evidence
to try the suspect, or "Billa Vera" (a true bill), indicating they found enough evi-

Besides the introduction of juries, the union with Connecticut meant that New Haven became a county. In 1666 the General Assembly of the newly enlarged Connecticut Colony divided the colony into four counties and stipulated that each have a county court. New Haven County was to stretch "from the east bounds of Guilford unto the west bounds of Millford," and from Long Island Sound north to the boundary line of Hartford County. In 1666 it contained only four towns, New Haven, Branford, Guilford, and Milford, but, by 1675, two new towns had been carved out of the old: Wallingford (1671) and Derby (1675). By 1728, when two more towns, Durham in the northeastern corner and Waterbury in the northwestern corner, were added, the structure of the county became clear. It consisted of two tiers of towns laid out east to west, one being landlocked (Derby, Waterbury, Wallingford, and Durham), and the other skirting the Sound (Milford, New Haven, Branford, and Guilford) (see Map 1).[30] Colonial almanacs show that most of the county's town centers were ten to twelve miles by road from their neighboring counterparts. Thus the New Haven courthouse was about a ten-mile ride for most denizens of adjacent towns (Wallingford, Branford,

---

dence for the case to proceed to trial. Record keeping was still not exacting in the late 17th century; the Court of Assistants clerk failed to note the pleas of many indicted persons. For examples of cases that proceeded without a formal indictment and by a verdict from the bench, see *Recs. Ct. of Assts.,* Lacy transcript, I: Rex v. Samuel Lauson (May 1670), 21–22; Rex v. John Orton and Hannah North (May 1683), 121; Rex v. Abraham, "a negro" (May 1698), 279.

Although no legislative record remains of Daniel Clark's appointment as "Attorney for his Majesty and this Corporation," the Court of Assistants records name him as presenting the capital cases against some defendants starting in October 1694 (*Recs. Ct. of Assts.,* Lacy transcript, I, 214–215, 262–263, 290–291). For a similar ad hoc approach in Connecticut Colony in 1664, see John T. Farrell, ed., *The Superior Court Diary of William Samuel Johnson, 1772–1773* . . . (Washington, D.C., 1942), xxxix. Persons who attempted to act as attorneys for criminal defendants were to be fined 10s. (*PR,* II, 59). Besides the indictment process, criminal cases could come before the higher court by a private person's complaint, by presentment by the county court grand jurors, or by the direct request of the bench. In 1704, the colony switched to appointing a prosecuting attorney for each county (*PR,* IV, 460).

30. *PR,* II, 34–35. At various times in the 1700s, noncontiguous towns were temporarily annexed to New Haven County before they had found a permanent berth in Litchfield County (created in 1752). Legal cases from New Milford, Sharon, and Salisbury appeared sporadically in the New Haven County Court from 1706 to 1752. In the 1780s, new towns such as Cheshire and Woodbridge were split off from Wallingford and New Haven.

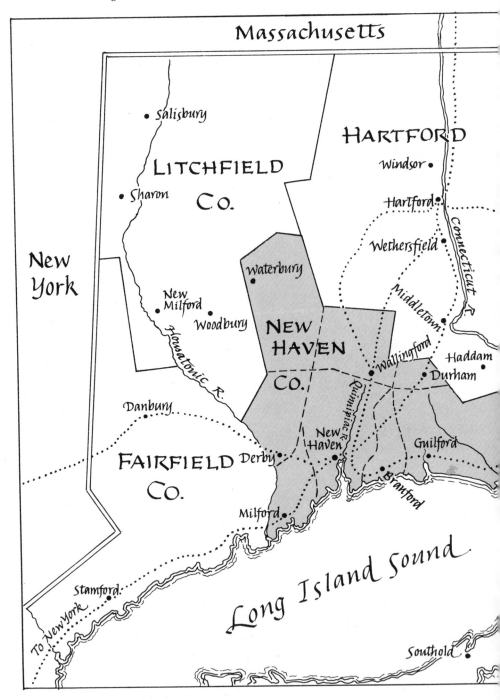

Massachusetts

New York

HARTFORD

Windsor •

Hartford •

Wethersfield •

Connecticut R.

LITCHFIELD
CO.

• Salisbury

• Sharon

Waterbury •

New
Milford •

Woodbury •

NEW
HAVEN
CO.

Middletown •

Wallingford •

Haddam •

Durham •

Housatonic R.

Quinnipiac R.

New
Haven •

Guilford •

Danbury •

FAIRFIELD
CO.

Derby •

Branford

Milford •

Stamford •

To New York

Long Island Sound

Southold •

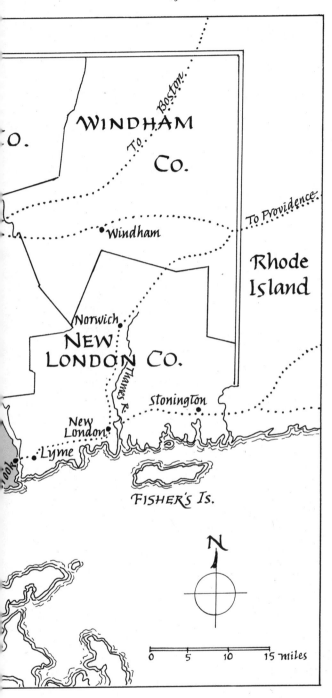

MAP 1.
Connecticut in
the 1700s.
*Drawn by
Richard Stinely*

Milford), but a trip of fifteen to thirty for those in the farther corners of the county.

From 1666 on into the nineteenth century, New Haven County and other Connecticut residents would be served by four levels of courts. In each town, one or more justices of the peace were authorized to hold pretrial hearings in criminal cases and rule on petty misdemeanors and civil suits.[31] Justices also attested to depositions taken down locally and sent on to higher courts, and they were often asked by townspeople for legal advice. Thus this site for the transaction of legal business, literally the cramped quarters of a justice's parlor, was undoubtedly the one most familiar to ordinary men and women. At the next level was the workhorse of the system, the county court. With original jurisdiction over civil litigation and noncapital crimes, these courts in any era after their 1666 creation handled the lion's share of the colony's legal business. The county court exercised limited equity jurisdiction and supervised administrative duties such as laying out roads, overseeing the poor, licensing tavernkeepers and attorneys, and, before 1716, handling probate matters. Grand jurors drawn from the various towns constituted an important element of the criminal justice system; these minor officeholders were required to report to the county court annually "the breaches of any laws . . . or any other misdemeanors they shal know of." Convening in magistrates' houses or well-known taverns near the New Haven green, the county court met twice yearly for regular sessions and usually more often for adjourned and special sessions.[32]

31. Initially, in a holdover from the pre-1666 period, a single justice (called a commissioner until 1698) was authorized to sit with town selectmen in deciding cases "to the value of forty shillings" (*PR*, II, 34, 108). For the justices' commissions and powers in 1698 and after, see ibid., IV, 235–236, 259–260, 357–358, VI, 22, 559–560; Bruce H. Mann, *Neighbors and Strangers: Law and Community in Early Connecticut* (Chapel Hill, N.C., 1987), 7. In 1698, 8 justices served for New Haven County; the number grew to 34 in 1750 and 45 in 1773. Note that all assistants could serve as single magistrates in their home counties. Except for a brief experiment in 1702, justices of the peace and county court justices were appointed by the Assembly, not elected (Farrell, ed., *Superior Court Diary of William Samuel Johnson*, xv).

32. *PR*, II, 61, 98–99. By the 1667 law, grand jurymen were summoned once a year by the county court clerk and approved as qualified to serve by the bench; the jury was to contain at least one man from each incorporated town. In 1712, the system changed: every town at its annual election meeting was to choose "two or more sober, discreet persons . . . to serve as Grand Jurors for the ensuing year" (ibid., V, 324). These men submitted in person lists of presentments to the county court and throughout the year brought written presentments informing on those sus-

Beyond the county court, Connecticut residents might come into contact with two higher courts. In the 1666–1710 period, the appellate court for the colony was called the Court of Assistants. With its bench made up of a quorum of the assistants, the court met in Hartford until 1701, but thereafter it rotated its sessions between Hartford and New Haven, newly declared the colony's co-capital.[33] The court exercised jurisdiction over all criminal cases punishable by "life, limb, or banishment," all actions brought by appeal from the county and probate courts, certain equity matters, and, in the wake of a 1667 statute allowing divorce on certain grounds, all divorce petitions. In 1711, the Superior Court, with a bench consisting of a chief justice and four men with judicial experience (most of whom were assistants also), replaced the Court of Assistants. What was new was that this court rode circuit, convening in each county seat twice a year.[34]

Finally, until the adoption of the 1818 constitution, the General Court was recognized as Connecticut's supreme judicial body. Initially, the General Court was a unicameral legislature, consisting of two deputies from each town, and the governor, deputy governor, and twelve

---

pected of fornication, drunkenness, and so forth to local justices of the peace. For a thorough account of the evolving use of grand jurors, see Farrell, ed., *Superior Court Diary of William Samuel Johnson*, xl–xlii.

From 1666 to 1698, at least one assistant and two commissioners constituted the county court bench (*PR*, II, 35). From 1698 on, the bench consisted of a presiding judge and three or more justices of the quorum — all appointed by the General Assembly from among the most prominent justices of the peace in the county (Mann, *Neighbors and Strangers*, 90–91; *PR*, IV, 220, 235–236).

33. Assistants were chosen by the members of the General Court until an act of 1708 established colonywide elections by the freemen for the offices of governor, deputy governor, and assistant.

34. *PR*, II, 28–29, 38–39, 328, V, 238–241. The Superior Court retained the jurisdiction of the court it replaced. Colonial Connecticut has earned the label the "land of steady habits" partly because assistants, Superior Court, and county court judges typically served more than 10 years and were drawn from the colony's chief towns and all the counties (Edward M. Cook, Jr., *The Fathers of the Towns: Leadership and Community Structure in Eighteenth-Century New England* [Baltimore, 1976], 154–156). For a summary of criminal trial procedures before the Superior Court, see Farrell, ed., *Superior Court Diary of William Samuel Johnson*, xxxix–xlv. In 1784 the Supreme Court of Errors, defined as a court of "Dernier resort of all Matters brought by way of Error or Complaint from the Judgment or Decree of the Superior Court in Matters of Law or Equity," was created (*PRS*, V, 323–324). It consisted of the lieutenant governor and the council.

assistants, whom the members of the General Court elected each May. After a 1698 overhaul of the legislative and judicial system, the court was divided into two houses, with the assistants forming an upper house. It exercised no original jurisdiction except over some equity matters. Until 1697, the legislature took appeals from the Court of Assistants; thereafter it accepted petitions for relief from losing litigants in the lower courts who believed themselves wronged and "without further remedy." The affirmative votes of both houses were needed to grant a petition.[35]

Within this fairly simple judicial structure, the county court would have been the site that seventeenth-century New Haven women anticipated visiting for the one legal adventure that typically punctuated a woman's life: the probating of her husband's estate. Women had to prepare themselves for this for two reasons. First, husbands tended to predecease their wives in early New England, because they married women a few years younger than themselves and because mortality in childbirth was not as high in the healthy New England climate as it was on the other side of the Atlantic. Second, husbands as testators typically named their wives as executors, and probate judges followed suit in their appointment of administrators.

Appointing the widow to settle the estate and pay the debts was not seen in the seventeenth century as granting her a dangerous degree of independence. Rather, the responsibility was both a natural outgrowth of her partnership in the household economy during her husband's lifetime and a logical complement to her role in widowhood as guardian of the couple's minor children. As long as a widow respected the superior wisdom of her husband and obeyed his will, her assumption of male duties was perceived, not as a threat to male governance, but as a mark of loyalty to spouse and family. Being administrator or executor made her an agent of her husband, the temporary treasurer and accountant for the household, the keeper of the family document box. It did *not* give her control over the most valuable resource in early American society: land. Whether she was administrator or not, a widow came into her

35. Cushing, ed., *Earliest Laws of New Haven and Connecticut,* 91; *PR,* III, 267. For the rules governing the submission to the Assembly of "Petitions in Controversial Matters," see *Acts and Laws* (1715), 94, 208; and Mann, *Neighbors and Strangers,* 132–134. In 1770, the procedures were revised (*PR,* XIII, 301, XIV, 361). The petitions and their accompanying papers have been preserved, indexed, and microfilmed as Connecticut Archives, Private Controversies, 1st and 2d Ser. In theory, appeals to the Privy Council were possible, but only nine Connecticut parties thus appealed before 1783 (Mann, *Neighbors and Strangers,* 8n).

"thirds," or dower, at her spouse's death. That meant, first, that if her husband died intestate (without a will), she owned outright one-third of his personal estate — his livestock, furnishings, linens, pots and pans, and tools, all items that she would need to keep her household running.[36] Second, she was granted the *use only* of one-third of her husband's real estate, his land and buildings. In effect she was both a trustee *of* the land and maintained *by* it until it could pass on to her husband's heirs (who were usually her children) upon her death.[37] So great was the reluctance of colonial lawmakers to jeopardize the transmission of landed property to heirs that, if a widow-adminstrator needed to sell part of the land for her family's survival, she was required to get the legislature's approval through a private bill.

That recently bereaved widows rarely declined the post of administrator suggests that they considered managing probate affairs part of their duty as a capable consort. Since probating an estate entailed a multitude of steps stretching over months and often years, female administrators grew familiar with the ritual of handing over a succession of documents — perhaps first a will, then guardian bonds, inventories, receipts, accounts of debts, and distributions — to the judge and receiving further instructions from him. Most women got a chance to watch their mothers, aunts, or sisters go through the process before their turn came. Few families hired a lawyer to help with the settling of an estate, and, although some women must have called on the assistance of a son or brother or male neighbor, no female administrator escaped responsibility for marshaling and understanding the documents that attested to the proper ordering of the family property.[38]

36. Laurel Thatcher Ulrich, *Good Wives: Image and Reality in the Lives of Women in Northern New England, 1650–1750* (New York, 1982), 7–8. By writing a will, a husband could leave his wife more than her thirds. Some men did leave their wives land outright, but the vast majority of widows inherited the traditional thirds. Creditors had a claim on the personal property if the "Just debts" owed by the deceased man had not been paid before the property was divided among the widow and the heirs (Toby L. Ditz, *Property and Kinship: Inheritance in Early Connecticut, 1750–1820* [Princeton, N.J., 1986], 126, 130–131).

37. Connecticut Code of 1672, in Cushing, ed., *Earliest Laws of New Haven and Connecticut*, 95, 104, 110. The grant of the use of real estate to a widow is called a life estate. By will, husbands could give their wives land outright, but very few did so (Ditz, *Property and Kinship*, 129–130, 133–134).

38. Here and in successive sentences, the term "administrator" encompasses executors also. Following 1716 legislation, probate matters came under the jurisdiction of an appointed probate judge, who convened probate court sessions in his own

There was a good chance that a female administrator who came into county court over probate affairs would either observe another woman engaged in civil litigation or be a party to a suit herself. In the first five decades of the New Haven County Court's existence, one-sixth of civil suits involved a woman as plaintiff or defendant, and 40 percent of the women litigating did so in the role of an estate administrator. Although court business and town meetings were spheres that boys and not girls were brought up to be conversant in, women who found it necessary to initiate or answer a suit might not have found the process particularly daunting. Civil litigation was a much more visible part of the court case-load than it had been in New Haven Colony, and it was more formal, meaning that the plaintiff had to specify the action correctly and give the adverse party sufficient notice through the serving of a writ. But even if the county court began to bear some resemblance to an English inferior court of common pleas, Puritan ideas about law shaped civil disputation in the post-1666 Connecticut courts: litigants did not resort to lawyers; judges kept rules of pleading simple; writs containing technical mistakes were overlooked or amended without penalty.

Furthermore, New Haven–area residents in this period used litigation to air grievances and repair neighborly relations that had been badly rent by discord. Thus civil suits in the late seventeenth century often revolved around the details of the daily rounds of visiting and exchanges that constituted the rural economy. Witnesses were called to testify, for example, concerning who had made an entry in an account book and when. All of this was quite within the ken of yeomen's wives and daughters, who were essential accessories to, and often central participants in, neighborhood transactions. In essence, litigating in the seventeenth century was more about preserving social bonds and community than promoting the self. Moreover, the men on the bench made certain to maintain an atmosphere and set of rules that nurtured communal modes of disputing.[39]

In other areas of court business, too, Puritan legal approaches that eschewed hostility toward women lived on. Some of the justices ap-

---

house (*PR*, V, 564–566). For a discussion of the decreasing role of wives as administrators in 18th-century New Haven County, see below, in Chapter 2. An excellent study of probate procedures is found in Ditz, *Property and Kinship*, chap. 8.

39. This interpretation owes a great deal to the research and insights of Mann, *Neighbors and Strangers*, and David Thomas Konig, *Law and Society in Puritan Massachusetts: Essex County, 1629–1692* (Chapel Hill, N.C., 1979).

pointed to the county court in the years immediately following union had served as magistrates on the New Haven town and colony courts. They continued to expect that women and men suspected of fornication would be presented, pressured to confess, and punished together; the grand jurors in charge of presentments and the defendants called before the bar complied. On the subject of divorce, Connecticut defiantly adhered to a liberal policy that took its inspiration from Martin Luther's teachings and was in clear conflict with English law. Moreover, when handing out divorce decrees before 1710, the Court of Assistants was willing to ignore various English legal principles when it deemed moral issues paramount. Adhering to the spirit of ad hoc, equitable adjudicating that was prevalent in seventeenth-century New England courts, the assistants went out of their way to award child custody and generous property settlements to mothers if the guilty, divorced father had conducted himself irresponsibly and immorally. In England, even when separations were granted to women, fathers retained rights to children and to two-thirds of the marital property.

Although the bias of seventeenth-century judicial authorities toward communal and equitable remedies meant that women's voices and needs were not ignored in the courts, the grand structure of rules for property transmission established in this period militated against women. A revision of the law book completed in 1672 stipulated that a widow was no longer guaranteed one-third of her husband's personal property; although few husbands failed to give their wives the traditional thirds, they now had the legal right to devise their household goods by will to whomever they chose. Furthermore, a woman's dower in her husband's land would rest only in what he was possessed of at his death. Although the first clause echoed a shift in policy embraced by English courts and other colonies by the end of the century, the second was a departure from the traditional common law, and a negative one for women. Probably Connecticut authorities understood their action as a means to simplify conveyancing procedures and as a mark of trust in husbands' and wives' capacities to agree on property management without interference by the state. Nonetheless, the effect of the restrictive dower policy was, first, to leave Connecticut women potentially with fewer resources at widowhood than they would have controlled in neighboring colonies and, second, to open the possibility that disgruntled husbands would convey all their land away before death, thus leaving their widows with nothing. Two further inheritance laws underscore the reluctance of early Connecticut authorities to concede to wives any control over property. Until 1723 a woman who brought inherited land into her marriage had absolutely no say in how her husband disposed of it. Similarly, official policy prohibited separate estates (instruments authorizing the wife or a third party to manage her inherited property during her coverture) while it permitted jointures (premarital agreements stipulating the property the wife would receive upon widowhood).[40]

These policies made Connecticut the colony most restrictive of a woman's claims to marital property. However, in practice, they might have made little difference. Most early American wives readily waived their dower rights in small pieces of land that their husbands sold during marriage, expecting to share along with other family members in the gains from the sale. In Connecticut, as in other colonies, most couples worked out in advance arrangements for the woman's adequate subsistence after her husband's death. If her children were grown, typically she was authorized to inhabit part of the homestead (for example, the "western chambers") and have access to the well, the orchards, and the gardens; meanwhile, her sons were to provide her with an annual complement of firewood and other provisions. Nevertheless, that lawmakers were willing to sacrifice the well-being of widows and further diminish women's already limited leverage over landed property illustrates that their aversion to the idea of independent female control over family property ran deep.[41]

For New Haveners, the most dramatic shift in the atmosphere of their courtrooms occurred, not with the demise of New Haven Colony, but

40. Cushing, ed., *Earliest Laws of New Haven and Connecticut*, 95; Marylynn Salmon, *Women and the Law of Property in Early America* (Chapel Hill, N.C., 1986), 6, 122–123, 148–149, 160–161; Ditz, *Property and Kinship*, 125–126. Restricting a widow's dower in real estate to that held by a husband at death was a policy copied only by Pennsylvania. In October 1723, the Assembly noted the rising value of real estate and passed a requirement that all married women consent by their hand and seal to any sale of their inherited land (*PR*, VI, 425).

41. Alexander Keyssar, "Widowhood in Eighteenth-Century Massachusetts: A Problem in the History of the Family," *Perspectives in American History*, VIII (1974), 103–104, 106–110; Salmon, *Women and the Law of Property*, 9; Karlsen, *Devil in the Shape of a Woman*, esp. chap. 3; Ditz, *Property and Kinship*, 127–130, 132–134. The English aversion to placing property in women's hands emerges in sharp relief when compared to the lack of similar anxieties in the New World Hispanic jurisdictions (Patricia Seed, "American Law, Hispanic Traces: Some Contemporary Entanglements of Community Property," *WMQ*, LII [1995], 157–162).

with the gradual institution of new procedural rules beginning in the 1690s and with the flood of debt litigation that clogged county court dockets from the 1720s on. These two trends shattered forever both the ease with which ordinary folk had transformed themselves into litigants on court day and the brevity and immediacy of the encounter between the people and the judges. An expanding economy and stricter attention to often mystifying English legal procedure would lead the county court slowly but inexorably down the road to complexity, professionalism, and rationalization. The court in 1790 — housed in an elegant brick statehouse that in its Georgian symmetries and elaborate workmanship made an opposite architectural statement to the plain style of the long-defunct 1639 meetinghouse — was an institution that Theophilus Eaton would not have recognized.

The political crises in New England at the end of the seventeenth century appear to have been the factor that convinced judges and lawmakers across the region to strip their courtrooms of many of the vestiges of informal Puritan jurisprudence. New Englanders were thoroughly shaken when the Bay Colony's charter was revoked in 1684 and a new governing structure, the Dominion of New England, was imposed, with the hated Sir Edmund Andros as its "president." Through obstinacy and sleight of hand, Connecticut managed never to surrender its charter. The high moment of drama came on October 31, 1687, when Andros arrived in Hartford with sixty soldiers and spent the day in the General Court debating with the governor and delegates over the charter's fate. Tradition has it that in the evening hours, when the charter was laid out on the table between the contending parties, someone extinguished the candles. In the darkness and confusion, the hallowed document was spirited away to a hiding place in a hollow oak tree. In the short term, this was no obstacle to Andros's taking control of Connecticut, suspending its system of representation and its courts, and annexing it to the Dominion. In the long run, however, the light-fingered Connecticut deputies triumphed: the Andros regime ended in 1688 with the Glorious Revolution, the constitutional settlement that put William and Mary on the throne. In May 1689, Connecticut's leaders reassumed the reins of government, put the charter system back into motion, and convened county courts again. Some months later the crown ruled that Connecticut's charter had never been suspended and that the colonists could proceed under its aegis.[42]

42. Trumbull, *Complete History of Connecticut*, II, 386–399. James II had begun quo

In the wake of this major governmental disruption, formal English rules relating to writs, pleading, evidence, and courtroom etiquette began to infiltrate courts at all levels across New England. Massachusetts courts retained some of the changes instituted when Andros insisted that outward forms and procedures resemble English practice. Connecticut's first step, taken immediately after the Dominion's close, was to force litigants to make a more particular distinction between forms of land actions. Its second step was an overhaul of the court system in 1698.[43] Over the next few decades, lawmakers and judges implemented stricter legal rules in piecemeal fashion under the influence of several factors. Apprehension that Connecticut's charter was vulnerable was confirmed in 1704 when the royal governors of Massachusetts and New York launched a campaign to challenge their neighbor's existence. An agent for the colony appeared in Parliament and successfully headed off this effort, but the concern for the future stability of the polity lingered. Connecticut's authorities might have felt that, by enforcing "orderly pleading" and some of the niceties of common law form, their judicial system would stand up to criticism and attacks that could precipitate the loss of the charter.[44] But the new rules stemmed, too, from the esteem in

---

warranto proceedings against Connecticut, questioning its charter, in July 1685 (ibid., 386–387).

43. Mann, *Neighbors and Strangers,* 88–89; Konig, *Law and Society in Puritan Massachusetts,* 160–165; *PR,* III, 267–268. It was at this point too, 10 years after the Andros regime, that Connecticut shifted to "regular English nomenclature" for justices of the peace and justices, discarding the Puritan vocabulary of "commissioners" and "magistrates" (Farrell, ed., *Superior Court Diary of William Samuel Johnson,* xiv). However, at this juncture, Connecticut, unlike Massachusetts, failed to adopt the English model of separate courts of general sessions and common pleas at the county level. Yet, misleadingly, throughout the 1700s Connecticut statutes and other public documents referred to county courts as the courts of common pleas.

44. Trumbull, *Complete History of Connecticut,* II, 429–443; *PR,* IV, 4, 68. Two Connecticut laws were disallowed in 1705 and 1728, one against "Hereticks" and one setting forth procedures for settling intestate estates (*PR,* III, 546; Elmer Beecher Russell, *The Review of American Colonial Legislation by the King in Council* [1915; rpt., New York, 1976], 102–106).

One serious episode of criticism occurred in 1733, when Francis Fane, king's counsel and standing counsel to the Board of Trade, examined Connecticut's statutes and reported several incompatibilities with English law (including the divorce policy), but the Privy Council never acted (Fane, *Reports on the Laws of Connecticut,* ed. Charles M. Andrews [New Haven, 1915]).

which a new breed of political men held the formality of English law. The two rivals who shaped the course of Connecticut politics in the 1690s, James Fitch and Fitz-John Winthrop, both admired "procedural propriety" and legal tactics that allowed lawyers to make a game of courtroom strategy. The pleas that came into vogue involved technical objections to the writ or how it was served; they were "dilatory" in that they forced a delay or an appeal to a higher court before the legal issue could be joined. Because of changes in pleading and changes in the most frequent type of debt being sued over, litigants had less and less of a chance to raise issues related to neighborly conflict in the course of a lawsuit.[45]

The wording of the new guidelines suggests that the seventeenth-century courtroom might have been a chaotic and extremely informal place, where adversaries talked at the same time and audience members shouted out their opinions. The Assembly in 1704 directed the courts "to oblige all parties concerned to speake one after another in their turnes." Judges were to direct the choreography of the players — litigants, lawyers, witnesses, jurors, audience — so that "there may not be clamours and noise to pervert justice." Even earlier, the New Haven County Court had promulgated rules for courtroom etiquette: all parties were to "direct theire Speech to the Moderator" (the presiding judge) and not "presume to Interrupt without Leave." Beyond establishing decorum, the magistrates moved to eliminate "disorderly pleading." This meant tutoring litigants not just on when to speak up but also on what days they must enter various pleas and on how the technicalities of demurring, pleading in bar, amending a plea, reviewing, and appealing worked. The New Haven County bench issued such rules for its sessions in 1694, 1713, and 1730, and the General Assembly enacted directives for its own deliberation and for all Connecticut courts in 1698, 1704, 1709, 1711, and 1720.[46]

In the midst of this campaign to tighten discipline in the courtroom, the General Assembly decided to regulate professional lawyers. Commencing in 1708, all attorneys would have to be officially admitted to the bar in a Connecticut court before they could plead cases. In seventeenth-century courtrooms the only attorneys present had been attorneys-in-

45. Mann, *Neighbors and Strangers,* 90–91, 93.
46. *PR,* IV, 266, 468, V, 106, 233–234, VI, 186, 495–496; NHCC, I, 229, III, 3–5, 325–326.

fact, persons designated through the document of a power of attorney to appear in the stead of a litigant. This had been a common practice only among mariners and merchants whose occupations took them away for lengthy periods. After 1700 some New Haven County litigants began to bring an attorney-at-law along with them on court day. These lawyers were professionals because they were paid a fee for offering their expertise and pleading the case before the bar. Yet none of the early Connecticut lawyers had any formal legal training. They taught themselves the common law by reading English manuals and treatises. The earliest lawyers in New Haven County argued cases to supplement their earnings as farmers, traders, and artisans. In skill, they ranged from Jeremiah Osborne, who had long served as justice of the peace, to cordwainer Joseph Tuttle, who managed to lose most of his clients' cases.[47]

For a time after 1708, the two types of attorneys appeared in county courts in similar numbers, and many litigants continued to represent themselves. Accustomed to courtrooms where the intricate motions and fictions of English common law pleading were suspended, many plaintiffs and defendants, the court records reveal, manifested confusion and made mistakes. One rare surviving written note shows an attorney-at-law, Thomas Fitch, giving advice to an attorney-in-fact, Mary Miles, the wife of mariner Samuel Miles: "Mistress Miles you must get the writ sined served and prepared for Court and I hope to be at Court. [Crossed out:] get Capt Whiting to Look over and Correct any Mistakes that may be observed in Relating the Story." The note hints at the apprehension many people felt about shepherding their own cases through an in-

---

47. On licensing, *PR*, V, 48. The licensing process involved pledging on oath that "you shall . . . [perform] to the best of your learning and discretion" and "delay no man for lucre or malice." For subsequent regulation of attorneys and their fees, see VII, 279–280, 358.

On early lawyers: Mann, *Neighbors and Strangers*, 93–98, 100. Not until the 1750s did a handful of New England lawyers manage to attract enough business to practice full-time. For a sketch of William Samuel Johnson, who was most probably the colony's first full-time practitioner, see Farrell, ed., *Supreme Court Diary of William Samuel Johnson*, xlv–liv. For a portrait of what it meant to enter law practice through an apprenticeship in the 1750s, see Richard D. Brown, *Knowledge Is Power: The Diffusion of Information in Early America, 1700–1865* (New York, 1989), chap. 4.

Even though they hired lawyers, litigants were required to appear in court in person unless they appointed a substitute through a power of attorney or unless they were confessing or defaulting under specific circumstances.

creasingly complicated writ system and rules of pleading "best understood by lawyers."[48]

Changes spiraled up from below, too. The lawyers who were most masterful at exploiting technical, dilatory pleading to gain advantage for their clients forced not only their adversaries but also any onlookers contemplating future litigation to learn the new strategies or hire attorneys. By the 1730s, nearly all civil litigants had given up trying to plead their own cases. Indeed, almost every contested suit was argued by two pairs of lawyers, one representing each side. Thus, in the middle and late decades of the century, "litigation became sparring matches controlled by technical rules in which lawyers were the actors, the nominal litigants were mute spectators," and the communal mode of disputing that allowed ordinary folk to air a broad range of grievances no longer was an option.[49]

If litigating meant hiring attorneys and confronting the possibility of a drawn-out process, many Connecticut residents might have been scared off by the prospect of the costs involved. Plaintiffs were required at the outset to pay a number of fees in cash: in 1712 standard fees included sixpence to the constable for every summons, one shilling to the county court clerk to enter the action, eightpence for a written copy of the judgment. The costs could mount up if the plaintiff called many witnesses (two shillings eightpence for each warrant), opted for a jury trial (twelve shillings), or appealed a disappointing result to the higher court (twelve shillings). Attorneys' fees were set in 1731 at ten shillings in county court cases and twenty shillings in the Superior Court. Throughout the 1700s, the average final bill of costs assessed on the losing party in New Haven County Court hovered between one and two pounds.[50] Many households evidently had this amount in specie or bills at hand — perhaps as a stash earmarked for potential litigation. Since the heavy

---

48. Mann, *Neighbors and Strangers*, 92–93, 165; Samuel Miles v. Joseph Smith, Jr. (Apr., Nov. 1734), NHCC Files, dr. 10 (writ). Fitch's wife was the plaintiff's first cousin.

49. Mann, *Neighbors and Strangers*, 95–100, 165.

50. "An Act for Regulating of Fees," *PR*, IV, 312–314. For changes in the schedules, see VI, 18, 207, 566, VII, 391–392, 524–527. The law stipulated that attorney's fees be included in the losing party's bill of costs (VII, 280). In range, some bills came in as low as six or nine pence while others, particularly after a review, climbed to nine pounds or higher. In the first half of the century, the final bill was often split between a payment in cash and in "pay" (or provisions).

odds were for the plaintiff in debt cases, the onus was on the defendant to calculate whether risking the likely prospect of paying costs or settling out of court was preferable. Many poor laborers and householders must have maneuvered as far as was possible to avoid being sued and thus saddled with what could be a two-pound bill on top of the outstanding debt. Certainly, very few of the many New Haven–area widows with meager resources ever appeared in debt litigation. But while the issue of costs might have operated as a barrier for the lowest rung of taxpayers, the Connecticut General Assembly seems to have established court fees at levels that permitted middling property owners relatively easy access to the courts.[51]

For potential litigants in the early eighteenth century, a further complication was added to the burdens of mastering legal procedures and anticipating costs. By the 1710s regular county court sessions stretched from Tuesday to Saturday, and litigants were required to be familiar with the sequence of activities presided over by the bench each day.[52] On the first day, judicial attendance was taken. The judges called out the cases on the docket, and plaintiffs stepped forward to pay various court and clerk's fees in advance. On the next day, the judges ran through the civil

51. With pre-1770 tax records surviving for only a part of one New Haven County town (Guilford), correlating litigants appearing in court with quintiles of taxpayers is not feasible for New Haven. Studying mid- to late-18th-century Kent, Conn., Charles S. Grant found few small property owners participating in debt litigation (*Democracy in the Connecticut Frontier Town of Kent* [New York, 1972], 70–73).

52. The following account of court days and the structure of courts draws on my own research in the New Haven County and Connecticut court records; various Connecticut statutes governing civil procedure (see *Acts and Laws* [1715], 2–4, 117–118, 143, 150, 188; *PR*, VI, 106); Bruce Hartling Mann, "Parishes, Law, and Community in Connecticut, 1700–1760" (Ph.D. diss., Yale University, 1977), 19–25; and Farrell, ed., *Superior Court Diary of William Samuel Johnson*, xiii–xix.

To get a civil suit on the court docket, a plaintiff first had to draw up a writ (or purchase a printed writ and fill in the blanks), taking care to state accurately the names of the parties, their residences, and the nature of the action to ensure that the suit would not be abated over technicalities and dismissed at the plaintiff's expense. Once drawn up, the writ was taken to a local justice (who received a fee for his signature and formal issuing. A sheriff or constable (also for a fee) then served it on the defendant by reading it aloud to the defendant or affixing it to his or her "last place of abode." If the writ was properly served and returned more than five days before the meeting of the next county court, then the action would be entered on the court docket. For more on this process, see Farrell, ed., *Superior Court Diary of William Samuel Johnson*, xix–xxi.

suits again, and both plaintiffs and defendants came forward and offered pleas. Three types of cases were resolved at this juncture — nonsuits, defaults, and confessions. Nonsuits were the rarest; here, the plaintiff failed to appear, and the defendant could move to collect costs. A second category of uncontested civil case involved the default, or nonappearance, of the defendant. Confronted with this behavior in the early decades of the eighteenth century, the county court issued an attachment against the defendant's property or person to force him or her into court at the next session. Later, when defaults became common, the justices entered judgment for the plaintiff immediately. At any time thereafter, the party with a judgment could request a writ of execution to collect the sum due. A third outcome saw the defendant's confessing judgment in court and arranging to pay the amount sued for and the costs incurred by the plaintiff.

It was not until the third day of the typical early-eighteenth-century county court session that the proceedings ceased to be a routine matter of recording motions and became potentially the stuff of courtroom dramas. Now contested cases, in which both parties had appeared to plead and "join issue," were heard. The witnesses summoned at the behest of each of the contending parties presented their evidence and were cross-examined by the "adverse party." If a deponent was ill or lived more than twenty miles from the court, he or she was permitted to send a sworn, written statement through a justice of the peace.[53] If the parties chose to submit the issue and evidence to a petit jury, the jurors consulted (often without leaving the room) and returned a verdict on a slip of paper. If the judges believed the jury had misconstrued the evidence or the matter of law, they could twice require the jurors to reconsider the matter, but they could not overrule a jury after its third consideration. The losing party had the right either to "review" the case for a trial de novo at the next county court or to appeal the case to the Superior Court, where it was tried de novo. Throughout the 1700s, a majority of contested cases were appealed.

In addition to the scene of witnesses testifying and jurors deliberating in civil suits, audiences attending the final days of a county court session would see the trial of any criminal defendants brought before the bar

53. No stenographers recorded oral testimony given in county court or Superior Court sessions. The only testimony that comes down to us is depositions sent by ailing or distant witnesses or, in criminal cases, justices' records of the preliminary examinations of witnesses.

that term. If the defendant confessed, the bench could quickly pass on to the next case. If the accused pleaded not guilty, however, the crown — in the guise of either the king's attorney for the county or the local grand jurors who might have originally complained against the defendant — would present its evidence, and the defendant could summon witnesses in his or her own defense. Prosecutors were not always diligent in lining up witnesses; in many criminal cases, "proclamation was made," and no one appeared to object against the defendant, who was then dismissed on paying costs. If a defendant found guilty by bench or jury could not pay the charges of the prosecution, the court was authorized to bind the convicted criminal "in service to any inhabitant in this colony" willing to pay the charges in exchange for the "delinquent's" labor.[54]

Prolonged and rationally segmented court sessions, the increasing visibility of attorneys-at-law looking for clients, and judges who welcomed legal practice in the English model: all of these had become fixed features of court days by the 1720s.[55] But more than political exigency and changing legal fashion spurred the shift away from informal approaches to disputing. At the end of Queen Anne's War in 1713, Connecticut began to experience dramatic, sustained population growth and expanding economic activity. Although the colony's total fleet of oceangoing vessels was still small, coastal traders worked assiduously to increase the volume of foodstuffs and livestock exported to the West Indies. With the population doubling every thirty years, more land was cleared to go under tillage, and more surpluses arrived at the marketplaces. The paper money first issued by the colony in 1709 to fund wartime expeditions was followed by more emissions, which served to slake the thirst of farmers and tradesmen for currency with which to increase production and pay debts. The ubiquitous small-scale expansion and entrepreneurial activities were funded almost entirely by credit extended by merchants and wealthy elites through promissory notes. Suits to collect on these notes became the most common legal action

54. *PR*, VI, 560. See the various acts relating to criminal procedure in *Acts and Laws* (1715), esp. 26–27, 59. A criminal defendant (in a noncapital case) might also avoid trial by demonstrating that the official complaint against him or her had been entered more than one year after the offense was allegedly committed.

55. Richard B. Morris argued that tightening imperial discipline, the growth of a propertied class, and the emergence of an American bar led to stricter attention to common law rules in all colonies (*Studies in the History of American Law*, 41–45, 59–60, 62–67).

before the county courts, and debt litigation grew at a rate far exceeding population growth.[56] All of the components of the transition from a Puritan to a more English legal culture—the more orderly courtroom, the presence of professional lawyers, and the predictability of procedural rules—suited a populace increasingly caught up in commercial activity.

New Haven was hardly exempt from the changes at work across Connecticut. When it was named the colony's co-capital in 1701, the town along the Quinnipiac was still a sleepy county seat, and the population of the county had risen to only about five thousand persons. New Haven's harbor was home to a handful of rather paltry vessels, public buildings to grace the central square were almost nonexistent beyond the wooden meetinghouse, and the population of about five hundred in the center of town did not make for a scene of urban bustle. By 1719 the town had more of a prosperous air: not only had a combined courthouse and townhouse been erected, but the first Yale College building had gone up, a long, narrow, three-story clapboard structure. Because of increases in coastal trading and exporting to the West Indies, more warehouses lined the water's edge, and more single-masted sloops were moored in the harbor. A new wagon line was authorized to operate monthly between New Haven and Hartford. New Haven had snapped out of the economic stagnation that had set in during the seventeenth century; signs multiplied suggesting that, as an entrepôt of trade, the site might finally fulfill the hopes of its Puritan founders.[57]

The town witnessed its greatest spurt of economic growth in the thirty years preceding the Revolution. Under the aegis of a new group of merchants such as Benedict Arnold and Roger Sherman, "the amount of tonnage in the harbor increased [by] . . . fortyfold." One historian estimates that one-fourth of male townsmen "worked at occupations directly connected with the sea and shipping." Mercantile trade and new sources of credit encouraged farmers in the countryside to raise "im-

56. Bruce C. Daniels, "Economic Development in Colonial and Revolutionary Connecticut: An Overview," *WMQ*, XXXVII (1980), 432–433; Trumbull, *Complete History of Connecticut*, II, 383; Mann, *Neighbors and Strangers*, 13–14, 31–32; Richard L. Bushman, *From Puritan to Yankee: Character and the Social Order in Connecticut, 1690–1765* (New York, 1967), 107–136.

57. Trowbridge, "Ancient Maritime Interests of New Haven," New Haven Colony Historical Society, *Papers*, III (1882), 109, 111–112; Shumway and Hegel, eds., *New Haven*, 16; Osterweis, *Three Centuries of New Haven*, 74, 98–101.

PLATE 3.
Plan of New Haven, 1748. *Detail from* A Plan of the Town of New Haven, with All the Buildings in 1748. *Engraving by T. Kensett from a copy made by William Lyon of James Wadsworth's original drawing. Courtesy of Yale University*

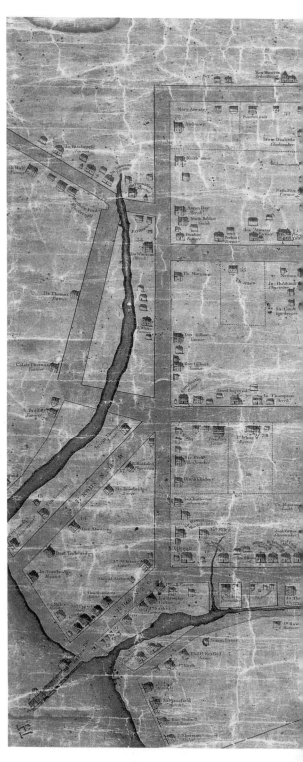

mense quantities of flax" for export. In 1756, officials at Whitehall decided that a customhouse was needed in New Haven. By 1770, thirty seaworthy vessels departed from the county's principal port on regular overseas voyages. New Haven the town had been transformed into a prosperous commercial port, but without a deep harbor and an inland waterway it would always play second fiddle in trade to Boston and New York.[58]

Outside the county seat, the impact of expanding commerce was more visible in coastal than inland communities. Throughout the eighteenth century, the towns in the upper, landlocked tier—Derby, Waterbury, Wallingford, and Durham—retained the characteristics of what Bruce Daniels calls "country towns." Their town centers offered the limited range of services of a few retail shops, a couple of artisans and mills, and probably several taverns. Only a few merchants and professional men resided here, and the distribution of wealth among householders was not large. Most families engaged exclusively in farming, raising crops for family and local consumption and for sale at the markets held on the southern border of New Haven's central square.[59]

In contrast, by midcentury, the county's three smaller coastal towns— Milford, Branford, and Guilford—had developed into secondary economic centers. Each housed several full-scale merchants who carried on extensive coastal trading and also direct trade with the West Indies. Pressure on the land in these fertile towns encouraged farmers to specialize in livestock, dairy farming, and sheep raising. While the subsistence-plus economy of colonial Connecticut had always meant that members of farm families crafted tools, engaged in weaving, and sold homespun woolens, especially in the winter months, the commercial development of the region prompted farmers increasingly to engage in trading on the side. The expanding economy also lured more artisans to the coastal town centers, although most plied their craft part-time, simultaneously running small farms.[60]

---

58. Osterweis, *Three Centuries of New Haven*, 101–105; Trowbridge, "Ancient Maritime Interests of New Haven," New Haven Colony Historical Society, *Papers*, III (1882), 112–114. Although the sex ratio for the county was dead even in 1774, it had reached 1.09 in the town of New Haven (Robert V. Wells, *The Population of the British Colonies in America before 1776* [Princeton, N.J., 1975], 93). For discussions of New Haven in the context of other Connecticut entrepôts, see Mann, *Neighbors and Strangers*, 47–49; and Main, *Society and Economy in Colonial Connecticut*, 132–133.

59. Daniels, *Connecticut Town*, 156–157; Mann, *Neighbors and Strangers*, 51–52.

60. Mann, *Neighbors and Strangers*, 32; Daniels, *Connecticut Town*, 151–155; Dan-

Settlement patterns became much denser in the New Haven region over the course of the eighteenth century. Even as late as 1744 a visitor found the area's towns "sparse and thin sowed." But by 1785 a traveling London merchant setting out from New Haven's green could exclaim: "I don't think any part of England is thicker settled. . . . There are houses about the whole way from Newhaven" north to Hartford. At the beginning of the century, when the county population stood at about 5,000, town sizes ranged from newly settled Durham with only fifteen families to New Haven, always the largest, with perhaps 1,500 persons living within its bounds. Between 1710 and 1760, the county population grew in step with the colony's at a rate of 28 percent each decade. By the first colonywide census, taken in 1756, Durham, still the smallest town, had some 800 residents, and New Haven was home to 5,000. Wallingford was the next largest, with 3,700 inhabitants, and the population for the remaining five towns ranged from 2,300 down to 1,000. Town centers were much smaller, of course, since at least two-thirds of any town's residents lived on outlying farms or in parish villages. For example, a map of the center of Guilford in the 1770s shows about 50 buildings, thus indicating a cluster of 350 residents, only 12 percent of the town's overall population. On the eve of Independence, the county population had just surpassed the size of New York City's 25,000 inhabitants, and its seat, New Haven, might finally be called urban, at least in the colonial context. Ezra Stiles's count of 328 dwelling houses in the town center in 1775 indicates a population of about 2,000 within the grid of nine squares. By 1784, the year in which New Haven was incorporated as a city, residents could boast of an urban economy that supported 56 shops and a cluster of public buildings that included the brick state- and court-house as well as three churches each capable of holding more than 800 congregants.[61]

---

iels, "Economic Development in Colonial and Revolutionary Connecticut," *WMQ*, XXXVII (1980), 433, 439–442. Daniels reports that in the 1770s "the average farmer possessed ten cattle, sixteen sheep, six pigs, two horses, and a team of oxen" (433). For a slightly different typology in which to fit New Haven towns, see Main, *Society and Economy in Colonial Connecticut*, 133–135.

61. Bridenbaugh, ed., *Gentleman's Progress: The Itinerarium of Dr. Alexander Hamilton, 1744*, 165; Louis B. Wright and Marion Tinling, eds., *Quebec to Carolina in 1785–1786: Being the Travel Diary and Observations of Robert Hunter, Jr., a Young Merchant of London* (San Marino, Calif., 1943), 149.

The population figures for the early 18th century are backward projections from the 1756 census. Daniels calculates that population densities for the county grew

The growing economy did not change the rhythm of New Haven County women's lives as much as it distanced them from the changing world of men's dealings and the litigation those dealings engendered. From 1639 on, the dictates of maintaining farming households gave women broad responsibilities. Without attracting criticism for transgressing gender roles, women took on hard physical tasks around the house and yard, rode through the woods alone to visit ailing relatives, and negotiated to hire young girls to help with household work. Although most of the transactions and reckonings that women participated in were part of the female economy, custom and necessity often dictated that a woman act as her husband's partner, agent, or (if he were absent a long time) competent surrogate.[62] In the seventeenth century the economic activities of both women and men were circumscribed within the local sphere. As the economy expanded and credit through transferable notes of hand became increasingly available, male householders found themselves frequently transacting business and involved in credit relationships with men outside their own town and their established social network. Although women's neighborhood trading remained critical to the household economy in this period, women who were single or widowed rarely participated in the new credit relations. Women's presence in what I call the "litigated economy" — the transactions that wound up in court — declined in 1720 from close to 20 percent to a plateau of 10 percent. In the early 1770s when judges were processing as many as two hundred debt suits at a session, women appeared as plaintiffs or defendants in only 5 percent of civil suits.

---

from 10 to 40 persons per square mile between 1710 and 1774 (see *Connecticut Town*, 50–63). For Durham, see Greene and Harrington, *American Population*, 57; and William Chauncey Fowler, *History of Durham, Connecticut, from the First Grant of Land in 1662 to 1866* (Hartford, 1866), 21. The censuses of 1756 and 1774 are found in Greene and Harrington, *American Population*, 58–59. See also Wells, *Population of the British Colonies in America*, 88–90. The totals for New Haven County were 18,181 in 1756 (including 226 blacks, found living in four of the eight towns), and 26,819 in 1774 (including 925 blacks, or 3.6%).

For Guilford, see Daniels, *Connecticut Town*, 152. Greene and Harrington calculate seven persons per house (*American Population*, xxiii). On Stiles, see Edmund S. Morgan, *The Gentle Puritan: A Life of Ezra Stiles, 1727–1795* (New Haven, 1962), 311. On a chart of cities just before Independence, New Haven ranks as the sixth largest (Carl Bridenbaugh, *Cities in Revolt: Urban Life in America, 1743–1776* [New York, 1955], 216–217). For the 1780s, see Franklin Bowditch Dexter, "New Haven in 1784," New Haven Colony Historical Society, *Papers*, IV (1888), 119–120.

62. Ulrich, *Good Wives*, 8, chaps. 1–2; and *A Midwife's Tale*, chap. 2.

Like many householders with limited resources, widows who did engage in borrowing and lending on a small scale might have been discouraged from using the courts to collect debts after the introduction of formalized procedures. Certainly, women were less apt to have the attributes that allowed some laymen to master the new legal procedures — extensive courtroom experience, reading and writing skills, access to law books. Moreover, many widows simply could not afford the costs of hiring an attorney and paying a series of fees up front. Another disincentive stemmed from the changing gender mix present on court days. The resort to lawyers by litigants in contested cases meant that, typically, four men were added to the scene of plaintiff and defendant poised before the bench and jury. Among witnessses waiting in the audience to be called, women were fewer after 1740 because the taking of evidence from midwives and matrons for fornication cases was removed to justice of the peace courts. The diminished presence of women conveyed the message that the legal arena was properly a ground of contest between men. Visually at least, women who entered the field were oddities.

In rejecting the anti-English elements of their founding heritage, the eighteenth-century legal fraternity fundamentally changed the ways in which women were received in court not just in debt ligitation but also when marital trouble and crimes involving women's bodies were at issue. New attitudes about the reliability of evidence affected profoundly the outcome of fornication and rape trials and, to a lesser extent, divorce petitions. Given the turn-of-the-century climate of uncertainty over the fate of New England's charters, Connecticut men training themselves in the law and reading English treatises would have been especially alert to pronounced discrepancies between their colony's procedures and the home country's. The issue of adequate evidence in criminal trials was particularly sensitive in early-eighteenth-century New England amid the recriminations that followed the Salem witchcraft trials. In 1691 the court of oyer and terminer in Salem had allowed nineteen people to be convicted and hanged largely on spectral evidence — evidence that did not meet a strict application of the two-witness rule.[63] Watching judges like Samuel Sewall acknowledge after the fact that they had sent innocent women and men to their deaths jarred jurists all over New England

63. For examples of both colonial departures from English law and 18th-century introductions of common law rules, see Morris, *Studies in the History of American Law*, 45, 59–60, 197–198. On the Salem witchcraft trials, see Perry Miller, *The New England Mind: From Colony to Province* (Boston, 1953), chap. 13.

into scrutinizing their instructions to juries and their own deliberations in criminal trials.

One glaring difference between English and New Haven practice at the outset of the eighteenth century occurred in the most frequently prosecuted crime — fornication. Whereas English law authorized collecting child support from a man on the basis of the single mother's "constant accusation" (her swearing to the identity of her infant's father both in childbirth and on oath in court), Connecticut law permitted the woman's word to lead not only to a child support order but also to a criminal conviction, meaning a whipping or a fine. After 1700, this tradition came under attack from two directions. First, young men prosecuted for fornication hired lawyers, pleaded not guilty, and requested jury trials. Their arguments emphasized the unfairness (and un-Englishness) of basing a conviction on presumptive evidence from an interested party, with no direct or corroborating third-party witness to the act of fornication itself. A class-based rhetoric unheard of in New Haven's seventeenth-century courts appeared, borrowed from the English poor law tradition that linked "lewd," resourceless women with out-of-wedlock births. Lawyers urged jurors to reject a procedure by which "the safety of mens names and Estates doe depend" upon "the accusation of a Naughty Woman."[64] Jurors heard this new line of thinking on the adequacy of evidence in fornication cases from a second source: the bench. Several times in the 1710s and 1720s the county court justices sent the jurors back to consider a man's case until they returned with a not guilty verdict. By 1740, the Puritan system of prosecuting and punishing men alongside women for fornication had collapsed. Lawyers, judges, and sexually active young men had brought off a coup: men would be exempted from confessing to philandering while women, still presented for the crime and convicted by both their confessions and their pregnancies, would continue to appear in public as repentant sinners until the end of the century.

Skepticism over woman's word became a central feature of rape prosecutions in the eighteenth century, especially when the alleged assailant was a settled, white resident of the colony and not an outsider by race or ethnicity. Once again, defense lawyers, judges, and jurors heeded the warnings of widely read English treatise writers to beware "easy" accusations that could be made, not just by "lewd" women, but by all women.

---

64. Matters of Law pleaded in behalfe of Matthew Woodruff, John Rew v. Woodruff (Oct. 1686 General Assembly), Conn. Archives, Crimes and Misdemeanors, 1st Ser., I, 159.

The most famous dictum of the period was Sir Matthew Hale's: "It must be remembered that [rape] is an accusation easily to be made and hard to be proved, and harder to be defended by the party accused, tho never so innocent." Given the rigorous scrutiny applied to the circumstantial evidence that existed to support a woman's charge, trial juries often voted to acquit, grand juries found bills of indictment ignoramus, and women were discouraged from pressing charges against fellow townsmen. Thus many of the hallmarks of modern-day rape trials made their first appearance in New England courts in the eighteenth century.[65] Part of the reluctance to convict in rape cases reflected broad trends in eighteenth-century England and the colonies. Juries increasingly looked for reasons to find the evidence insufficient to send a defendant to the gallows. In the case of infanticide, which attracted heightened prosecutorial interest at midcentury, women's lives were spared because of jurors' qualms. On the other hand, the devaluing of women's word in cases of sexual assault reinforced the message of fornication cases: male sexual license and assertions of entitlement to women's bodies would generally be condoned, but women's sexual behavior would continue to be regulated.

Although Connecticut's divorce policy by and large favored women with its offer of a full divorce if a husband's adultery or three-year desertion was proved, the Superior Court's shift away from the ad hoc approaches of the seventeenth century did militate against women in certain situations. For the first time, the judges granted divorces to men who discovered upon marriage that their wives were pregnant by another man. Such decrees underscored the urgency of making paternal bloodlines certain, and they echoed the theme emerging in the areas of fornication and rape that cast women as deceitful. The eighteenth-century bench also refused any longer, in cases where guilty husbands had been exceptionally irresponsible or immoral, to endow divorcing women with child custody or most of the marital property. With this reversal, the judges in effect announced that the eighteenth century would be an era when male property rights and men's absolute common law rights to their children would be kept inviolate. Finally, the judges altered their approach to cases in which the wife had "deserted" by moving to a

65. Sir Matthew Hale, *Historia Placitorum Coronae: The History of the Pleas of the Crown* (London, 1736), I, 635; Barbara S. Lindemann, "'To Ravish and Carnally Know': Rape in Eighteenth-Century Massachusetts," *Signs: Journal of Women in Culture and Society,* X (1984–1985), 63–82.

nearby house or town to protest her husband's cruelty. In the seventeenth century, magistrates had counseled mediation and reconciliation in such estrangement cases and had refused to acquiesce in the peremptory demands of husbands to be rid of uppity wives. In the wake of the Merriman divorce suit, a highly contentious case that stretched over much of the 1710s, the judges sided with husbands' arguments that wives who left the marital household and obstinately challenged their spouse's governance should be labeled "rebellious" and pronounced the guilty party.[66] Few women could afford the high social and emotional costs and the economic deprivation that walking out, and thus severing ties with children and community, entailed. Women who were physically beaten by their husbands had little recourse in the eighteenth century: Connecticut judges and lawmakers held the line against approving cruelty-based divorce petitions, and the criminal complaint process against an abusive husband was largely ineffectual and thus rarely invoked. In sum, Connecticut's late-colonial divorce policy, despite its generous terms, moved in the direction of reinforcing male authority in the household at the same time that it paralleled the handling of rape in its disavowal of male violence.

As the county court grew away from its origins as an intimate public space congenial to lay pleading and communal modes of disputing, its evolution mirrored the gendering of the increasingly distinct public and private spheres that came to characterize mid- and late-eighteenth-century New England society. With respect to women's presence in court, this complex process was perhaps best epitomized by the growing tendency of men and probate judges to appoint as estate administrators sons, lawyers, or male kin, not wives. Women themselves might often have asked not to serve. This backing off from expecting a widow to act as her husband's agent and trustee reflected an important shift in the ideology of gender as it was practiced among elite and prosperous families. Bathsheba of Proverbs 31 had been the biblical, female archetype most suited to material conditions and Puritan culture in the earliest generations of white settlers. Bathsheba, the virtuous wife and skilled household manager whose price was "far above rubies," combined the qualities of prudence, frugality, and quiet piety with generosity to the poor, wisdom and kindness in speaking, and acquiescence to her hus-

66. The divorce case of Hannah and John Merriman is discussed in Chapter 3, below.

band's ultimate will.[67] With the advent of a less Puritan climate in the eighteenth century, the Bathsheba model did not lose its power or relevance for shaping expectations of womanly behavior. Most New Englanders, after all, continued to earn their livelihood from farming and interpret their world through the prism of familiar Old Testament stories. But cultural and economic forces prompted the discourse of the elite about women to expand and shift in significant ways. Helped along by Cotton Mather's observation in 1691 that women made up three-quarters of the full members of his church, a tradition grew up in New England of emphasizing women's special capacity for piety and the Christian virtues. On appropriate occasions, men were praised as pious too, of course, but reflected in the plaudits for "daughters of Zion" was a nagging recognition that men were increasingly opting to center their lives around secular pursuits.[68]

By the mid-eighteenth century the material lives of some New England women, particularly those living in large port towns like New Haven, had shifted in important respects off the axes that undergirded the Bathsheba archetype. Gradually a commensurate ideology of womanhood emerged. As more male household heads became involved in commercial transactions and specialized, often nonagricultural work, the complementarity of economic tasks of husband and wife became attenuated. As manufactured goods such as chairs, looking glasses, forks, linens, and teacups became increasingly available to prosperous New Englanders, wives and daughters began to devote more of their time and energies to elaborate housewifery skills, to social rituals such as tea drinking, and to the purchase of fashionable apparel and other goods sym-

67. Ulrich, *Good Wives*, pt. 1. One of the best articulations of this ideal is Thomas Clap's private memoir of his first wife, who died in 1736 (Edwin Stanley Welles, ed., "Memoirs of a College President: Womanhood in Early America," *Journal of American History*, II [1908], 473–478).

68. Mather is quoted in Richard D. Shiels, "The Feminization of American Congregationalism, 1730–1835," *American Quarterly*, XXXIII (1981), 46. For further examples of high female church memberships and the ensuing clerical attention to women, see Barbara E. Lacey, "Gender, Piety, and Secularization in Connecticut Religion, 1720–1775," *Journal of Social History*, XXIV (1990–1991), esp. 802–803, 805–808; Ulrich, *Good Wives*, 215–216; Mary Maples Dunn, "Saints and Sisters: Congregational and Quaker Women in the Early Colonial Period," *American Quarterly*, XXX (1978), 590–595; Lonna M. Malmsheimer, "Daughters of Zion: New England Roots of American Feminism," *New England Quarterly*, L (1977), 484–504.

bolizing refinement. For middle- and upper-class women, the new emphasis on gentility was often accompanied by a withdrawal from hard
physical labor and a disengagement from detailed knowledge of her
husband's business affairs.[69]

As the material worlds, childhood training, and gender role expectations of elite and professional families grew increasingly distant from
those of modest farm families, young New Haven women reaching adult-
hood became overtly aware of class gradations. Sarah Welles, coming of
age in the early 1770s, practiced the refined arts of penmanship and
letter writing by scratching out epistles, "Little bit[s] of paper," to her
friend Rebecca Woolsey late at night, "all alone, papa asleep by the fire."
"Sometimes I fancy mySelf Some great Lady rideing in my Coach," Sarah
mused, "and Some times I am a poor Country farmers wife mounted on
my old 'pye bawld mare' carrying fowl and eggs to market to buy my old
man A holland Shirt but when I come to think in earnest about these
affairs if I know my Self I shall Choose the midle way between these two
'for that which make's our lives delightfull' / 'is A genteel Sufficiency
and love.' "[70] Of course, Sarah's contrasting images of archetypal aristo-
cratic and poor women might have come as much from reading English
novels and poetry as from her observations of New Haven society. Strikingly, her self-consciously literary prose encapsulates many of the distinctive aspects of middle-class formation in British America: the emphasis
on choice rather than birth, the seeming rejection of aristocracy for a
middle way that nevertheless was rooted in gentility, and the implicit
recognition that genteel women would not be directly involved in the
market as deputy husbands.

With the narrowing of elite women's economic roles came a redefinition of their moral attributes. By the late eighteenth century, the ideal
woman was seen to function as a civilizing, softening, and Christian
influence on her sons and husband, who increasingly spent their days in
the secular, masculine worlds of commerce, law, and politics. Finally,
under the influence of British evangelical thought, woman's sexual
power and interest were downplayed. Instead, it was assumed that her

69. Ulrich, *Good Wives*, chap. 4, esp. 69–71; Carole Shammas, "The Domestic
Environment in Early Modern England and America," *Journal of Social History*, XIV
(1980–1981), 3–24.

70. S. Welles to R. Woolsey, Nov. 8, 1771, Hillhouse Family Papers, box 1, folder 2,
Yale University Library, Manuscripts and Archives.

natural proclivity for delicacy and chastity could be harnessed as a purifying force that would tame the excessive sexual desires of men.[71]

In the courtrooms of the mid-eighteenth century the new model of woman as virtuous ornament worked both to exclude most women and to expose the deficiencies of women who could not hope to aspire to gentility and leisured motherhood—women working for wages, non-white women, women without a fixed residence. Whereas the resources of the early-seventeenth-century court system had been marshaled to call all sinners to account—men and women, rich and poor—the men who ran the legal system increasingly toward the end of the colonial period sheltered middle-class women from court appearances and singled out poorer women for reprimand and regulation. A sudden rise in infanticide prosecutions in the 1750s and the steady barrage of newspaper reports on the subject reflected the anxiety of the elite about the rising numbers of poor, unmarried women who traveled from town to town looking for work.[72] Young women of marginal economic circumstances who bore children repeatedly with little hope of marrying were the major target of midcentury fornication prosecutions in New Haven county, but grand jurors increasingly ignored the childbearing of single women whose fathers were respectable yeomen and officeholders. Well-connected families often chose to protect themselves from the scandal of a paternity suit by hiring a lawyer to settle the matter out of court. In this legal world in which magistrates were *not* cut out of the same cloth as Theophilus Eaton—being neither all-seeing nor interested in extracting public confessions from high-status sinners as well as low—laboring men and women and the poor found themselves ill served by the courts. The

71. The literature on the emergence of a domestic, privatized role for middle-class women is extensive. See Janet Wilson James, "Changing Ideas about Women in the United States, 1776–1825" (Ph.D. diss., Radcliffe College, 1954), 34–64; Linda Kerber, "The Republican Mother: Women and the Enlightenment—An American Perspective," *American Quarterly*, XXVIII (1976), 187–205; Mary Beth Norton, "The Evolution of White Women's Experience in Early America," *American Historical Review*, LXXXIX (1984), 593–619; Ulrich, *Good Wives*, 103–105; Nancy F. Cott, *The Bonds of Womanhood: Woman's Sphere in New England, 1780–1825* (New Haven, 1977); and Cott, "Passionlessness: An Interpretation of Victorian Sexual Ideology, 1790–1850," *Signs*, IV (1978–1979), 219–236.

72. Douglas Lamar Jones, "Poverty and Vagabondage: The Process of Survival in Eighteenth-Century Massachusetts," *New England Historical and Genealogical Register*, CXXXIII (1979), 246–250.

barriers to initiating or even defending oneself in a civil suit were too high. The county court had become a forum almost exclusively about property, and it operated in symbiosis with the network of men active in trade and the extension of credit.

––––––––

If we were to follow the legal history of any New England community from the 1630s to the ratification of the Constitution, we would witness the courtroom scene responding, as New Haven's courts did, to the major social forces that marked the eighteenth century off from the seventeenth. But in New Haven the operation of those forces — secularization, commercialization, rapid population growth, increasing class consciousness, professionalization, and the anglicization of culture — had a special meaning. Along the Quinnipiac, as with other New World settlements founded on utopian principles, sustained growth along with regional and national integration stripped the polity of its uniqueness. By 1790, New Haveners had few grounds for claiming that their city and county were materially or ideologically exceptional.

Theophilus Eaton's New Haven Colony, Perry Miller declared in 1935, provides "the ideal laboratory in which to study the germ of Puritanism." For students of gender relations, the gradual evanescence of New Haven's distinctive legal regime affords an equally promising line of inquiry. Although no bastion of gender equality, the colony's legal culture worked counter to the tendencies of English law that rendered women invisible, silent, and morally more culpable than men. Because of that exceptional beginning, the story of New Haven's transition from frontier outpost to cosmopolitan province can be told, more dramatically perhaps than for other regions, as a case study of how patriarchal authority reconstituted itself in British North America after the turn of the eighteenth century.[73]

When New Haven's magistrates reversed themselves and began to

73. Miller, review of Calder, *New England Quarterly,* VIII (1935), 583. Under quite different ideological and material conditions, colonial Virginia is now thought to have undergone a similar transition (Terri Lynne Snyder, " 'Rich Widows Are the Best Commodity This Country Affords': Gender Relations and the Rehabilitation of Patriarchy in Virginia, 1660–1700" [Ph.D. diss., University of Iowa, 1992]; Kathleen Mary Brown, "Gender and the Genesis of a Race and Class System in Virginia, 1630–1750" [Ph.D. diss., University of Wisconsin, 1990]); Carole Shammas, "Anglo-American Household Government in Comparative Perspective," *WMQ,* LII (1995), 104–144.

treat women's charges of rape, wife-abuse, and fornication with a great deal of skepticism; when judges and Assembly delegates erected a wall against women's pleading for divorce on cruelty grounds; when women were entrusted less often with the duties of estate administration: at all of these junctures Connecticut men implicitly signaled that they wished to curb the power of women in the courtroom to challenge and disrupt white men's authority and entitlement. Uncomfortable with the ad hoc, moralistic, seventeenth-century adjudicating style that had allowed women more voice and more leverage over the outcome of conflict, the men who shaped the law—legislators, judges, jurors, lawyers, testators—collectively manifested an impulse to reassert legal rules and approaches that buttressed male authority and male property rights. As increasingly proud, if independent, members of the empire, the embrace by the New England elites of English legal approaches, including those that silenced women, made sense. Not anticipating that they would be goaded into leaving the empire by the duo of an unresponsive, corrupted Parliament and an unhearing, unfeeling, arbitrary monarch, New Haveners imported English cloth and books, told English jokes, and drank tea with as much avidity as other colonials.[74] In the decades leading up to 1776 and after, very few harbored regrets about abandoning the old New England ways: ways that had sketched paths not taken in gender relations.

Women's revolt against the paths taken—against the eighteenth century's entrenchment of patriarchal authority—would find its source in the domestic and religious sphere created by and for middle-class women as their exclusion from public life became manifest. Empowered by the ideology that ascribed virtue and refinement to women, female reformers would gain enough bittersweet experience as activists by the 1840s to know that their chief target should be the law. Mocking the fraternal male order that had deceptively declared "all men are created equal," the women at Seneca Falls in 1848 mimicked the Declaration of Independence with their own Declaration of Sentiments, turning the phrases of the 1776 document inside out to demand not only the right

74. The classic statement on anglicization in New England is John M. Murrin, "Anglicizing an American Colony: The Transformation of Provincial Massachusetts" (Ph.D. diss., Yale University, 1966). T. H. Breen argues that consumer choices and buying patterns bound disparate colonists and helped create a national consciousness in the mid-18th century (" 'Baubles of Britain': The American and Consumer Revolutions of the Eighteenth Century," *Past and Present*, no.119 [May 1988], 73–104).

to manage their own property and to speak for themselves in public and in court but also effective laws to curb men's cruelty and tyranny in marriage and to undercut the double standard.[75]

Although Elizabeth Cady Stanton and Lucretia Mott would not have thought of themselves as operating within a Puritan framework, many of their demands had once been met for women before the bar in courts that cleaved to Puritan jurisprudence. Theophilus Eaton would, of course, have shuddered at being linked even conceptually with his religious archenemies, the Quakers, whose explicit teachings on the equality of men and women inspired so many of the nineteenth-century women reformers. He would also have found alien the existence of a self-conscious, collective, woman-centered reform movement, a development that was precluded by social and cultural conditions in the seventeenth and eighteenth centuries. While in the late twentieth century we celebrate and feel kinship with the earliest humanitarian and feminist reformers, what the following chapters aim to illustrate is that, historically, renegotiations of patriarchy have often taken place without fanfare, without deliberate mobilization, almost imperceptibly to contemporaries.

75. For the tale of a post-Revolutionary legal ruling that rejected innovation in the concept of women's political membership, see Linda K. Kerber, "The Paradox of Women's Citizenship in the Early Republic: The Case of *Martin vs. Massachusetts, 1805,*" *American Historical Review,* XCVII (1992), 349–378. On middle-class women's domesticity and piety as sources for female activism, see Kerber, *Women of the Republic: Intellect and Ideology in Revolutionary America* (Chapel Hill, N.C., 1980), chaps. 7–9; and Cott, *The Bonds of Womanhood.* For the text of the 1848 Declaration of Sentiments and Resolutions, see Miriam Schneir, ed., *Feminism: The Essential Historical Writings* (New York, 1972), 76–82. On the sources of the 19th-century women's rights movement, see Ellen Carol Dubois, *Feminism and Suffrage: The Emergence of an Independent Woman's Movement in America, 1848–1869* (Ithaca, N.Y., 1978), chap. 1; Keith E. Melder, *Beginnings of Sisterhood: The American Woman's Rights Movement, 1800–1850* (New York, 1977); Margaret Hope Bacon, *Mothers of Feminism: The Story of Quaker Women in America* (San Francisco, 1986).

2

Toward Marginality

WOMEN AND THE LITIGATED ECONOMY

Shortly after her husband died, Elizabeth Peakin sued a fellow New Haven resident, John Thompson, Jr., for wages and expenses her spouse had incurred as "master workeman" supervising a crew of men to complete a job contracted by Thompson for his ship. The year was 1658, and, in the lawyer-free legal environment established by Puritan leaders, Widow Peakin argued her own case before the bench. She presented as evidence, first, her husband's account book, where, as she declared, the demanded sum "appeare[d] clearly due"; second, a written agreement signed by the two men; and, third, testimony that her husband had been at the job each day "early and late." The magistrates ruled that the widow should collect the just debt, but they admonished her for being "very quick in prosecuting, seeing the money were due but yesterday." Peakin rejoined that she had ignored the customary period of forbearance, "not knowing but before another Court" Thompson "might be gone abroad to sea, and she hath need of her due." Widow Peakin's precipitous lawsuit was probably intended to broach a grievance larger than the debt: Thompson had gone about town accusing Goodman Peakin and another skilled artisan of overcharging, thus shattering the ethic of trust and reciprocity that bound together the small cluster of

New Haven men involved in maritime trades. Unable to bring a slander suit on her dead husband's behalf, Elizabeth translated her knowledge of his local business dealings into an effective forum for defending the family's honor and good name.[1]

Widow Peakin's case illustrates key aspects of the intersection between legal culture, gender roles, and the rural New England economy in the first half of the colonial period. As a public space, the courtroom with its small caseloads and simplified rules of pleading afforded ordinary men and women satisfying chances to air long-standing neighborhood disputes. Before 1666, loose evidentiary rules allowing hearsay and the introduction of a wide range of issues frequently prompted men to ask their wives to testify in civil suits. These women, like Elizabeth Peakin, demonstrated a detailed grasp of their families' local economic entanglements. Few households in the seventeenth century had reason to look for credit, exchanges, or materials beyond town lines. John Peakin, New Haven's only rope- and sailmaker, was unusual in this respect, and his long-distance dealings with men in Boston or Salem reveal the limits of his wife's ken. She reported "she hath heard of some debts owing to her husband in the Bay, but knowes not by whom nor how much."[2] But in cases involving local exchanges, many early New England women entered the courtroom to claim their legal and economic rights with a confidence similar to that of Widow Peakin. It was a confidence partly born of status and wealth; John Peakin, a former magistrate and deputy, left his wife in charge of a sizable estate. Poorer women adopted different strategies in response to debt and the prospect of litigation.

The area of law that touched the most people in early New England was, not crime, but civil litigation, especially suits for debt. Most householders at some point in their lifetime could expect to be threatened by a creditor with a lawsuit, see a cow led away in attachment for an unpaid debt, or be forced themselves to sue a debtor whom they feared was

1. Widow Peakin's case is found in *NHTR*, I, 333–334. The court made the widow pay half the costs because she had declined Thompson's offers to settle privately out of court or to submit their differences to arbitrators. For Thompson's accusations against Peakin and his proclivity for "unrighteous" and "offensive carriage" "to the Court and others," see Thomas Morris's slander suit, *NHTR*, I, 365–367, 371–375, 385–389.

2. Bruce H. Mann, *Neighbors and Strangers: Law and Community in Early Connecticut* (Chapel Hill, N.C., 1987), 21–27; *NHTR*, I, 343.

about to leave the country.[3] Certainly the topics of who was close to bankruptcy, which struggling families merited a creditor's forbearance, and how litigants and witnesses had behaved at the most recent court were the stuff of daily conversation in the towns and farmsteads of coastal and interior Connecticut. This was primarily men's talk, just as at least eight of ten parties in debt litigation were men. But women — as housewives, widows, and grown daughters — overheard and participated in these conversations that fueled the rural economy. Indeed, women would continue to keep abreast of their menfolk's credit relations as long as Connecticut houses remained small and cramped and as long as the economic sphere relevant to householders' livelihoods remained locally bounded. Moreover, given the interdependence of neighboring households in the early New England economy, housewives' swapping of goods and services among themselves and their occasional side businesses were critical to each family's well-being. In the early decades of settlement, women's work gained ideological support through the clergy's praise of their prudence and skills in the "oeconomical" sphere.[4] While subordinate to male authority in family and state, women nonetheless were perceived as integral to the local economy, and that integration brought far more women into colonial courts than the crimes such as fornication and adultery that the Puritans are so famous for prosecuting.

In the eighteenth century, the New England economy underwent dramatic changes. Whereas the nineteenth century would witness the rise of large-scale manufacturing and permanent wagework, the eighteenth saw a diffusion of credit through the countryside that altered the

3. Mann, *Neighbors and Strangers*, 6. For calculations of the proportion of adult male residents involved in litigation, see below at note 38. Such estimates do not account for men who appeared as witnesses, posted security for litigants, or sat in the audience at court sessions.

4. Samuel Willard, *A Compleat Body of Divinity* . . . (Boston, 1726). The best discussion of New England women's neighborhood trading activities is found in Laurel Thatcher Ulrich's work: " 'A Friendly Neighbor': Social Dimensions of Daily Work in Northern Colonial New England," *Feminist Studies,* VI (1980), 392–405, and "Martha Ballard and Her Girls: Women's Work in Eighteenth-Century Maine," in Stephen Innes, ed., *Work and Labor in Early America* (Chapel Hill, N.C., 1988), 70–105. On the valorization of women's economic roles in the 17th century, see Jeanne Boydston, *Home and Work: Housework, Wages, and the Ideology of Labor in the Early Republic* (New York, 1990), 5–11.

ways in which farmers and traders, neighbors and strangers, and husbands and wives interacted. While daily work and trading patterns for most Connecticut women changed very little over the century, the larger economy was changing around them. As men's routine economic dealings became more commercial and cash-based, women were largely excluded from the realm of greatly expanded credit relations. Levels of indebtedness increased enormously, and so too did the volume of debts litigated at each session of the county court. Confident litigating women like Widow Peakin did not disappear from the courtroom, but their presence became more anomalous, and their relationship to the legal system — a system transmogrified by 1770 into a giant debt-collecting machine — resoundingly marginal.

The "litigated economy" thus reveals that the economic spheres of men and women were diverging in critical ways before the nineteenth century and the separation of home and workplace.[5] If we pursue the subject of gender and credit relations, the 1700s come into sharper focus as a key transitional period between a rural, early modern economy that acknowledged women's household work and facility in local trade and an era that associated middle-class wives exclusively with consumption and motherhood.

———

On a summer day Betty Keeny stood in her husband's house in Derby and declared to assembled neighbors that Eliphalet Beecher "Dares not Come here for he owes us Money . . . and We never Expect to Get [it]." Mistress Keeny spoke as her husband's partner, his helpmeet, his complement, his stand-in when necessary — a self-definition shared by most housewives in seventeenth- and eighteenth-century New England. Although their daily arenas of work and trade typically were distinct, husbands and wives geared their activities to the same ends: preserving the

5. By litigated economy I mean all economic dealings that became the subject of civil litigation. These made up only a small subset of all transactions, of course, but even with their multifarious biases they provide us with the most accessible serial record reflecting general economic change. I have focused on debt because it made up the vast majority of civil cases and because it reveals creditor-debtor relations fairly transparently. Writs and surviving loose papers for trespass, assault, and land claims, in contrast, often obscure the core dispute between adversaries. For a helpful comparison between litigated debt and the universe of debts created at probate for men in Kent, Conn., 1773–1777, see Charles S. Grant, *Democracy in the Connecticut Frontier Town of Kent* (New York, 1972), chap. 5.

independence and good name of the family and securing enough property, in land and movables, to give each grown child an adequate portion.[6] It was the complementarity of men's and women's work in the household economy that allowed Betty Keeny to think in terms of "our" debts and credits — not simply her assertive temperament.

Court records for the most part obscure the productive contributions of married women — or, as one husband phrased it for the bench, "the Domestick business of . . . house and family" which his wife "most advantageously . . . Discharge[d]."[7] Coverture, the common law principle that submerged the adult identity of a wife into that of her husband, ensured that, when judges strictly enforced English rules, few married women appeared in court as litigants or witnesses. Yet the testimonies supplied to buttress the arguments of contending debtors and creditors offer glimpses of housewives' roles in the local economy. For New Haven County, this strand of evidence is richest for the decades preceding 1720. By the second quarter of the eighteenth century, changing legal and economic forces began pushing credit relations in new directions, directions that would gradually erode the close complementarity that had previously bound husbands and wives.

It is difficult for us to imagine the extent to which economic transactions in the seventeenth and eighteenth centuries were based on oral exchanges and dependent on the parties' memory for their final resolution. Written notations of debts or contracts, if they existed at all, served as aide-mémoire, prompters to the recall of the conversations out of which the bargain was made. This "memory economy" demanded that its participants develop an acute ability to recollect talk from an early age. Male householders whose dealings ended up in court often depended on the power of their wives and daughters to remember the details of oral agreements made months and even years before. If their witnessing was to be reliable, girls' upbringing had to include familiarity with the language and logic of men's bargaining. Amy and Obedience

6. Daniel Vickers, "Competency and Competition: Economic Culture in Early America," *WMQ*, XLVII (1990), 3–12; James A. Henretta, "Families and Farms: *Mentalité* in Pre-Industrial America," *WMQ*, XXXV (1978), 3–32.

Keeny's statement precipitated a slander suit: Eliphalet Beecher v. Ebenezer and Betty Keeny (Aug. 1762), NHSC Files, drawer 330. Both men were traders. Betty Keeny also denounced Beecher as "a Knave and a Cheat," a liar and a bankrupt, among other things.

7. The declaration of John Prinn in his suit against Mary Allen for assaulting Prinn's wife: Prinn v. Allen (Jan. 1739/40), NHCC Files, dr. 10.

Smith met the test: they were able to testify to the details of the workman-ship agreed on when their father hired George Clinton to clapboard his house. And they could report that they had been present later when Smith and Clinton took out their books and "Concluded . . . to mak a Jumping Reckoning as tis Sum time called."[8]

Women both young and old were privy to such negotiations partly because the spatial arrangements of New England houses and home lots were not as yet highly specialized. In short, to be at home was to overhear men's reckonings. Even by the early 1700s when prosperous yeomen typically lived in two-story houses with six to eight rooms, conversations between a visiting creditor and the household head would have taken place in the hall, parlor, or yard—within close range of women's work spaces. In this context, a woman well apprised of her husband's accounts and suspicious of a creditor's trustworthiness might choose to intervene. When Clement Ellsworth and Thomas Johnson met to "make up ac-counts" in the fall of 1725, the process came to an abrupt halt because "Mr. Ellsworth's wife broke out into a passion." As a result of her inter-ference, the issue was only settled fifteen years later, after Ellsworth's death.[9]

The spatial aspects of men's and women's daily work patterns also contributed to women's necessary entanglement with their husbands' dealings. Given that farm holdings were typically dispersed and distant from the homestead, men spent much of their day beyond calling dis-tance from their residence. In contrast, the tasks central to women's domestic work—food preparation and child care—kept women close to home, even though related duties such as tending livestock, picking herbs and berries, and the cooperative tasks accomplished through "vis-iting" with other women extended their orbit beyond the house to the

8. Laurel Thatcher Ulrich, *A Midwife's Tale: The Life of Martha Ballard, Based on Her Diary, 1785–1812* (New York, 1990), 86; Deposition of Obedience and Amy Smith, in Gideon Candee v. Capt. Samuel Smith (Jan. 1743/4), NHCC Files, dr. 14. For other examples of women recounting at length intricate oral agreements, see the Deposition of Alice Rawlings, *NHCR*, II, 394–396, and Deposition of Anna Hopkins, in George Nickols v. John Hopkins (Jan. 1743/4), NHCC Files, dr. 17.

9. Robert Blair St. George, " 'Set Thine House in Order': The Domestication of the Yeomanry in Seventeenth-Century New England," in Jonathan L. Fairbanks and Robert F. Trent, eds., *New England Begins: The Seventeenth Century* (Boston, 1982), II, 165–173; Cornelius Kerstead and William Ellsworth as Executors of Clement Ells-worth v. Thomas Johnson (Jan. 1740/1), NHCC Files, dr. 16.

neighborhood.[10] Thus when creditors and debtors came to call, they often found only the wife and children at home.

In November 1712 Samuel Pond was evidently at home when Abraham Hoadley came by to make the first payment due according to an arbitrated settlement. But a month later, Pond's wife Abigail placed *her* mark on the receipt recording Hoadley's next payment. In 1706, the merchant Louis Liron stopped to offer his wares at the house of Benjamin Barnes. Barnes's wife Sarah explained that she must follow family guidelines for trading on credit. She recalled telling Liron, "I must not trad with him unles he would take hops [in payment at a later date] and he consented," letting her take the goods she had selected. A third case provides an arresting image. In 1658 Goodwife Jeffries was at home when her husband's fishing partner, John Griffen, came by to collect Jeffries's half of a joint debt that was being called in. Griffen must have been traveling without a purse or saddlebag large enough to hold sixteen shillings worth of wampum, because Goodwife Jeffries placed the shells in one of her pewter dishes, pledging Griffen to return the empty vessel to her that day.[11]

The Jeffries's pewter pot and its out-of-the-ordinary journey are apt symbols for one of the roles any early New England woman was often called upon to play: agent or vessel, bearing her husband's messages or implementing his wishes. The fluidity of gender roles in the rural economy had a one-way dimension: adult women were expected to act in their husbands' steads when the need arose, but men are rarely if ever glimpsed in surviving records tackling cooking or housework. Communities assumed that wives of men whose occupations took them away for long periods would carry on the family farm or business. Such women routinely bought and sold livestock, hired help, and kept up the family accounts. When long-distance trade was involved, married women were sometimes careful to underscore their "deputy husband" role. In 1714 a

10. Laurel Thatcher Ulrich, "Housewife and Gadder: Themes of Self-Sufficiency and Community in Eighteenth-Century New England," in Carol Groneman and Mary Beth Norton, eds., *"To Toil the Livelong Day": America's Women at Work, 1780–1980* (Ithaca, N.Y., 1987), 21–34, and *Good Wives: Image and Reality in the Lives of Women in Northern New England, 1650–1750* (New York, 1982), 39.

11. Pond v. Hoadley (1715), NHSC Files, dr. 323; Louis Liron v. Benjamin Barnes (1706), NHCC Files, dr. 2; Sgt. Thomas Jeffries v. Estate of John Griffen (March 1657/8), *NHTR*, I, 335, 344.

mariner's wife appended this note to her detailed directions to a captain sailing for the West Indies with her husband's goods: "My husband being Absent you may Take this for your orders."[12]

A woman's duty to act as agent for her spouse extended beyond his death. Because of at least a two-year age gap on average between husbands and wives at first marriage and similar life expectancies for men and women, perhaps 60 percent of all married women in early New England experienced widowhood. They approached it, not as a period of sudden emancipation and autonomy, but rather as an office of trusteeship and stewardship. Kin, neighbors, and probate judges expected a widow to be diligent in preserving the family estate and carrying out the instructions left by her husband. In an era in which wives rather than lawyers or male relatives were typically appointed estate administrators, a widow was plunged immediately into the world of men's reckonings. Not only did the probate process require her to locate all records documenting her husband's unsettled accounts, but very soon a stream of creditors and debtors arrived to make or demand payments. In fact, a woman's married life was in one sense a preparation for widowhood: spouses knew that most women outlived their husbands and that it was wise policy for women to be kept informed of the state of the household's indebtedness.[13]

12. Ulrich, *Good Wives*, chap. 2; Christopher Clark, *The Roots of Rural Capitalism: Western Massachusetts, 1780–1860* (Ithaca, N.Y., 1990), 26; papers dated February 1714/5 for an action never entered in the county court record book: Richard Hall v. Benjamin Smith, NHCC Files, dr. 1. After Richard died, Hannah continued to run their tavern and appeared in civil litigation 15 times before her death in 1741.

The early New Haven court records reveal married women making deals independently of their husbands, deals that their spouses allowed and were ultimately responsible for in court. See *NHCR*, I, 416–417, II, 121–122, 192–194; *NHTR*, II, 2, 9, 227.

13. For age at marriage and death, see Philip J. Greven, Jr., *Four Generations: Population, Land, and Family in Colonial Andover, Massachusetts* (Ithaca, N.Y., 1970), 33, 35, 109, 118, 120, 193–196, 206–208. For analyses of women's likelihood to become widows, see Alexander Keyssar, "Widowhood in Eighteenth-Century Massachusetts: A Problem in the History of the Family," *Perspectives in American History*, VIII (1974), 83–119; and William F. Ricketson, "To Be Young, Poor, and Alone: The Experience of Widowhood in the Massachusetts Bay Colony, 1675–1676," *New England Quarterly*, LXIV (1991), 115.

An example of gathering accounts for probate is Elizabeth Judson, widowed for the third time, who in 1663 "attested to the fulnes" of the inventory of her late husband's estate "soe far as is clearly knowne at prsent, there being one booke

This functional arrangement, encompassing as it did interdependence between the sexes and broad responsibilities for housewives, by no means undermined the man's position of ultimate authority in the household. He could countermand his consort's orders to her children or servants, he could deny her any voice in decisions affecting family property or credit relations, and he could at any time inform all the neighborhood that he would not honor her debts. But such an authoritarian pose would not only prove counterproductive to the material, let alone the emotional, well-being of the family. It would also fly in the face of the steady stream of advice emanating from Puritan divines on the Christian duty in marriage and on proper household management.[14] Finally, in denying a capable wife the role of partner, a man courted the opprobrium of neighbors and kin. Most husbands probably exercised their punitive powers sparingly, just as most wives accepted it as their duty to obey their husband and follow his lead in setting household policies.

One final circumstance contributing to early Connecticut women's knowledge of their husbands' economic affairs was the noncommercial nature of debt relations in the seventeenth century. Given the scarcity of specie and the absence of a local currency between the 1650s (when wampum disappeared) and 1709 (when Connecticut began issuing paper money), residents paid for goods and services "in kind" — several hours of haying work for a promise to be paid later with a barrel of cider, for example. If these debt obligations were written down at all, it was in householders' account books. Debts created in this way did not bear

---

wanting (as she apprhended) of some accounts" (*NHTR*, II, 33). For a similar case, see *NHCR*, II, 203.

Lisa Wilson Waciega makes a smiliar point about spouses' sharing knowledge of family finances, in "A 'Man of Business': The Widow of Means in Southeastern Pennsylvania, 1750–1850," *WMQ*, XLIV (1987), 51. See also the careful analysis of how women as executors and administrators operated, in Suzanne Lebsock, *The Free Women of Petersburg: Status and Culture in a Southern Town, 1784–1860* (New York, 1984), 36–37, 120–125.

14. For excellent analyses of the balance of power between men and women in colonial households, see Nancy F. Folbre, "Patriarchy in Colonial New England," *Review of Radical Political Economics*, XII (1980), 8–11; and Toby L. Ditz, *Property and Kinship: Inheritance in Early Connecticut, 1750–1820* (Princeton, N.J., 1986), 127–128. Carol F. Karlsen places Puritan writing on marriage in the New England context, in *The Devil in the Shape of a Woman: Witchcraft in Colonial New England* (New York, 1987), 160–171.

interest and did not require payment at any particular time, only when the creditor chose to request it or when two men with many exchanges between them agreed to "reckon" or "balance accounts." Since a yeoman's book rarely traveled outside the confines of the homestead, women were likely to be present when their husbands entered debits and credits at the end of each day. Moreover, the bookkeeping system of most New England farmers was extremely simple. A woman who was not adept at writing but could read and also pen some words and figures might have learned the formula for ledger entries well enough to make an entry if her husband was away when a debtor came to call.[15]

Simply put, the locus of the account book and the informality of local debt relations made men's dealings familiar to women. Book debt persisted throughout the eighteenth century as a common method of recording exchanges and obligations, particularly at the local level.[16] However, after 1720, promissory notes became increasingly prevalent in the Connecticut countryside. Signing a note enmeshed a householder in a very different form of debt from relying on running book accounts. First, each note (sometimes printed, but often handwritten) bound the signatory to pay the principal by a given date. If he was able to make payments only in installments that stretched well beyond the due date, as was often the case, interest was computed and added to the sum due. Second,

15. On book debt, see Mann, *Neighbors and Strangers,* 11–27; and Clark, *Roots of Rural Capitalism,* 32–38, 69–70.

Since historians now agree that signatures do *not* reflect ability to read or even to write in a limited fashion, Kenneth Lockridge's estimate that only 30%–50% of rural New England women were "literate" must be discarded (*Literacy in Colonial New England: An Enquiry into the Social Context of Literacy in the Early Modern West* [New York, 1974], 15, 38–43). Two later studies argue effectively that practically all New Englanders, men and women, could read: David D. Hall, *Worlds of Wonder, Days of Judgment: Popular Religious Belief in Early New England* (New York, 1989); and E. Jennifer Monaghan, "Literacy Instruction and Gender in Colonial New England," *American Quarterly,* XL (1988), 18–41.

My point about a housewife's ability to make entries in the family account book is speculative. The relationship between men's and women's accounting capabilities and preferred forms of bookkeeping calls out for further research.

16. Asked to testify to their activities on a particular day for a paternity suit, one Waterbury couple provided a compelling image of spouses who acted jointly and almost ritually to take care of family obligations to pay taxes and support the church: "We went to Mr C—— and pade him his minister Rate that day and he charged it on his Book in our sight" (Joint deposition of Roger and Anne Pritchard, Mar. 31, 1764, in Dorcas Fulford v. Alling Sage [Apr. 1764], NHCC Files, dr. 32).

notes were assignable to third parties. By the 1740s, not only did the typical propertied householder hold several notes in his document box, but, unless he was very wealthy, he had probably signed a greater number. Some of these had doubtless been reassigned since the original credit transaction, leaving our householder a debtor or creditor to men who lived at some distance, persons with whom he had little knowledge and no other ties. Thus, while male New Englanders continued to be embedded in dense social and economic dealings with their neighbors, the expanding regional economy drew them increasingly into more impersonal, purely financial ties with strangers.[17]

The attributes of promissory notes must have distanced many Connecticut housewives from a confident ken of their husbands' debt obligations. Given their portability, notes were not as tied to the homestead as account books were. They also required more sophisticated skills in writing and numeracy. Some women, of course, learned enough about accounting to aid their spouses as knowledgeable monitors of the full range of the household's credit relations. But the formality of written instruments like notes, the possibility that the wife would not know the other party, the precise wording of the written promise, and the computations of principal and interest that were often required probably hindered many mid- to late-eighteenth-century housewives from attaining much more than a vague sense of the family's overall indebtedness.

––––––––

Our focus now turns to the courtroom. Coverture ensured that married women's trading activities could not be the subject of litigation except when disguised as their husbands' dealings. Thus court records remain silent about a huge proportion of female economic activity. But court dockets *do* capture debts that directly involved three sorts of women — widows, single women who had reached the age of majority (eighteen), and newly married women who had unsettled accounts reaching back before marriage. Since New England county courts were destined by the end of the colonial period to be occupied almost entirely with debt cases, the fate of women's relationship to the legal system rested largely on the complex set of factors that brought female creditors and debtors into court.

17. The best analysis of changing credit relations is found in Mann, *Neighbors and Strangers*, 27–41. As notes became popular, sums due on book accounts were often transferred to obligations due by note.

The Colony period of New Haven's history (1639–1665) marked a unique legal regime in the adjudication of debt no less than in other judicial matters. Between 1638 and the establishment of a county court in 1666, the godly men sitting as judges favored courtroom procedures designed to get at the truth and to coax adversaries to reconcile. In their eyes, most of the procedural rules, legal fictions, and lawyerly traditions that had accreted as part of English common law were not suitable to a biblical commonwealth. These Puritan leaders believed that householders who could not settle their differences privately or before arbitrators should be able to argue their case face to face in court, using everyday language, introducing any material they felt relevant, and calling any witness who could speak to the issues.[18]

One result was that married women could testify for their husbands in civil suits. Male litigants asked their wives to recall for the court critical conversations and actions that had originated the debt or led to an impasse over repayment. On some occasions, women verified the incidents recollected by their spouses; at other times they spoke of sales, purchases, or agreements they had made on their own. Thus in the earliest decades of settlement, women's economic roles were *not* invisible, but rather were acknowledged publicly in the discourse that filled the courtroom and made its way into official records.[19] Because of the informality dictated by Puritan legal tenets, the pre-1666 records convey the realities of economic life for early New England women and men

18. This characterization is based on my reading of the surviving colony and town court records for 1638–1666. I have found no contemporaneous statement for New Haven Colony of procedures to be followed in civil litigation. With their concern for shaping remedies around the just price and the restoration of brotherly behavior, New Haven magistrates showed their preference for "equity in its popular sense." For the application of Puritan law reform in New England, see G. B. Warden, "Law Reform in England and New England, 1620 to 1660," *WMQ*, XXXV (1978), 676–683 (677 for the quoted phrase).

19. Wives also testified in suits across a wider range of economic transactions than debt. For examples, see *NHTR*, I, 29, 157, 162, 262–263, 305; *NHCR*, I, 330, 416–417, II, 276–284, 382, 396. William Blackstone interpreted coverture as barring husband and wife from testifying for or against each other (*Commentaries on the Laws of England* [1765–1769; rpt., Chicago, 1979], I, 431).

In its inclusion and acknowledgment of married women's economic activities, the New Haven Colony legal system was not unlike that of New Netherland, where women (including wives) participated in 26% of the 195 debt cases considered in 1663 (David E. Narrett, *Inheritance and Family Life in Colonial New York City* [Ithaca, N.Y., 1992], 48–49).

much more clearly than records of any later period. For the historian, the informal labeling and handling of disputes make futile any attempt to quantify or categorize civil suits brought before the town and colony courts. Debt suits were inconsistently differentiated from trespass, trover, or case. Magistrates often urged parties to end their unspecified differences privately, or they referred the matter to arbitrators; we cannot know to what extent these unnamed disputes involved formal debts. Moreover, the town court doubled as a probate court, and magistrates approved creditors' claims on decedents' estates without requiring the parties to undertake formal debt litigation.[20]

With the union of the Connecticut and New Haven colonies and the establishment of county courts in 1666, juries were introduced, and justices began to follow common law guidelines more assiduously. However, in this second stage of civil litigation in New Haven, stretching through the 1710s, the rules of pleading were deliberately kept simple, discouraging the emergence of lawyers. Local litigants for the most part continued to plead their own cases. Despite the steady growth of civil suits from 1680 on, the scale of civil business at county court sessions remained manageable. Two sorts of debts predominated: first, book debts and obligations based on oral promises between neighbors or fellow townsmen, and, second, debts arising out of mercantile trade between New Haveners and more distant New Englanders.[21]

The court's efficacy in the 1670–1719 period as an accessible institu-

20. For examples of these judicial habits that acted to discourage or obscure litigated debt, see *NHTR*, I, 30, 51, 58, 125, 183, 417–418. I count 105 clearly identified actions for debt in the surviving records for the colony's Court of Magistrates (1641–1649, 1654–1661) and the particular court of the town of New Haven (1650–1665). Women litigants apppeared in at least 16% of these ($N = 17$); this figure surely undercounts women, since administrators appearing to litigate were often not named.

Action on the case, a common law form that no longer exists, was designed to provide a writ for damage suits over wrongs that were not committed by force or that were otherwise not sustainable under trespass or other actions. See *Black's Law Dictionary*, 5th ed. (St. Paul, Minn., 1979), s.v. "action on the case."

21. On the late-17th-century regime, see Mann, *Neighbors and Strangers*, 84–92. For the earliest decades of county court records, up to about 1710, one can accurately distinguish neither between book debt and other types of debt nor between debt and other civil suits. Between 1670 and 1710, only half of civil actions are identified as debt, but surely many among the 38% of suits called "Case" actually involved debt. By the 1710s actions clearly labeled book debt had climbed to 62% of the debt caseload.

tion that proffered a communal mode of disputing to litigants is demonstrated by the two most common choices that adversaries made when their cases were called up. Before 1710, a notable one-quarter of plaintiffs withdrew their actions, many informing the court that they had settled privately. The very process of suing out a writ before the county court had thus compelled the adversaries to reconcile their differences, without resorting even to formal arbitration. In the bulk of the remaining cases (nearly 60 percent) the defendant opted to contest the suit so that the issues under dispute could be laid before audience, bench, and jury. Since the era's most common form of action (book debt) allowed litigants to raise a wide range of factual issues relating to their dealings, the late-seventeenth-century courtroom enabled people to air accumulated grievances and resume the day-to-day social and material exchanges of neighborly relations afterward.[22]

For the presiding judge and his typical complement of four associates, the civil caseload was not much of a burden. Never before 1710 did the justices hear more than eleven civil suits at a session, and not infrequently in these decades the men on the bench outnumbered the debt and trespass cases on the docket. Most of the time they dispensed with three to five civil suits before calling up a clutch of repentant fornicators and tipplers.[23]

For several of its sessions between 1703 and 1706, the New Haven County Court met at the house of John Miles, a site much like others where the court had convened over the preceding three decades. John Miles was a respected townsman and captain of New Haven's Second Militia Company. One downstairs room in his house near the central square had served as an "Ordinary" since 1692. The justices believed this room to be sufficiently commodious (it was probably no more than fifteen by twenty feet) to accommodate county court sessions.[24] Lacking

22. Between 1670 and 1710, of 442 civil suits, 254 (58%) were contested; 164 were uncontested (13 confessions, 16 defaults, 22 nonsuits [nonappearance of plaintiff], and 113 withdrawals). Only 3 suits in this period were referred to arbitration. For the remaining 21 cases, no resolution is noted in the records.

On 17th-century civil suits as safety valves for residents striving for community harmony, see Mann, *Neighbors and Strangers*, 9, 21–27; and David Thomas Konig, *Law and Society in Puritan Massachusetts, 1629–1692* (Chapel Hill, N.C., 1979), 107–116, 188–191.

23. During the 1666–1719 period the bench dispensed with five or fewer civil cases at two-thirds of all sessions where civil suits were heard.

24. For sources on John Miles, see Jacobus, *FANH*, 1182–1183; *PR*, IV, 25, 33, 42,

an official courthouse, the court had for decades met in the best avail-able rooms of private houses at the center of town.

In late 1704 and 1705 there was something different about the ses-sions at the Miles tavern. They marked perhaps the only time in the county's history when litigants were summoned to a county court held at a house and establishment presided over by a woman. Captain Miles had died on November 7, 1704, leaving his business, household, and the administration of his estate in the hands of his second wife, Mary. Mary managed the tavern until her death in October 1705 at age fifty-one. In the intervening months, six court sittings were called to meet "at the house of Mrs. Mary Miles." And in the March after her husband's death, widow and administratror Miles made the one appearance of her life-time as a county court litigant — in her own parlor.[25]

Mary Miles figures as an unusual emblem of the familiarity that some colonial women had for the goings-on of the courtroom. Women who lived near the central square of the county seat, women who were mem-bers of households where court business was conducted or discussed, women who were entrusted with management of family property for significant stretches of time — these women were part of the extended constituency regularly served by the county court in the early colonial period. Mary's unmarried sister and near neighbor, Hannah Alsop, was another exemplar of such litigation-savvy women. Addressed by the hon-orific title "Mistress," Hannah came into county court three times in four years suing for debts as administrator for both her father and one of her brothers. For these two sisters, going to court meant stepping into a familiar room, accumulating no traveling expenses, and disrupting the constant daily cycle of household tasks only minimally. To women who lived in outlying county towns or who had lesser means, the decision to pursue a debtor in county court was a more burdensome, and a more remote, possibility.[26]

88; NHCC, I, 199 (tavern license). For evidence that the court met at Miles's house, see scattered summonses in NHCC Files, dr. 1.

25. Mary Miles v. Richard Blackleach (Mar. 1704/5), NHCC, II, 178. Mrs. Miles may have been aided in running the tavern by her son Daniel, then in his early 20s. At her death, the house became his, and county courts continued to convene there.

26. For Alsop's three appearances, at least one of which was at the Miles house, see NHCC, II, 27, 139, 162. On the Alsop family, see Jacobus, *FANH,* 39. Hannah wrote a 1701 will naming John Miles her executor, but she lived many years beyond him, dying in 1722 possessed of a warehouse, half a home lot, several small plots of land, and other movables totaling £104 (New Haven Probate District Court Records,

TABLE 1

Female Litigants and the Civil Caseload, 1670–1749,
New Haven County Court

	Total Caseload	Cases Involving Female Litigants
1670–1719		
1670–1679	83	15 (18%)
1680–1689	64	13 (20%)
1690–1699	133	19 (14%)
1700–1709	163	21 (13%)
1710–1719	337	64 (19%)
Overall	780	132 (17%)
1720–1749		
1720–1729	537	54 (10%)
1730–1739	1,100	107 (10%)
1740–1749	2,139	204 (10%)
Overall	3,776	365 (10%)

Source: New Haven County Court Records and Files, 1670–1749.

In the intimate atmosphere of the court session of the late seventeenth and early eighteenth centuries, women appeared as litigants in one of every six civil suits, and in at least one of seven debt cases (see Tables 1 and 2).[27] Among the 97 individual women who made 160 ap-

---

V, 107, 121 [microfilm], CSL).

Geographically, of 16 women initiating 26 civil suits as sole plaintiffs between 1670 and 1710, 10 (or 62%) hailed from New Haven, 3 from Milford, and 1 from Branford. Wallingford and Guilford were each represented by 1 defendant among the 81 appearances by women in this period.

27. Under the rubric of female civil or debt litigants, this analysis includes administrators (whether male or female) appearing on behalf of a deceased woman's estate, since such cases represent debts or contracts entered into by women.

TABLE 2
Female Litigants and the Debt Caseload, 1670–1749,
New Haven County Court

	Total Debt Caseload	Cases Involving Female Litigants
	1670–1719	
1670–1679	38	4 (11%)
1680–1689	27	6 (22%)
1690–1699	56	6 (11%)
1700–1709	98	15 (15%)
1710–1719	237	39 (16%)
Overall	456	70 (15%)
	1720–1749	
1720–1729	424	36 (8%)
1730–1739	920	89 (10%)
1740–1749	1,676	153 (9%)
Overall	3,020	278 (9%)

Source: New Haven County Court Records and Files, 1670–1749.

pearances, Hannah Alsop was unusual: only 2 other single (never-married) women ventured into court for a civil dispute before 1710, and only 5 more did so in the next decade. But in another respect, Mistress Alsop, along with her sister Mary Miles, *was* representative of many of the women in court: it was her job as an administrator that drew her into litigation. Indeed, almost 40 percent of female civil litigants before 1720 entered the court's dockets because of their duty to shepherd the estate of a husband or relative through probate and to settle all debts. Another fifth were widows, suing or being sued over debts or transactions contracted during widowhood. The credit networks of these litigating widows were much more circumscribed than those of the men suing in county court: each woman contended against someone from her own town, whereas male debt litigants were more often pitted against parties from outside the county.[28]

Hundreds of women lived as widows for ten years or longer without ever entering the litigation rolls. While the norm throughout the colonial period for widows of all wealth backgrounds was to manage their economic dealings without becoming entangled in lawsuits, widows who came alone (not in plural parties) into court more than once over debt usually belonged to at least one of three distinct profiles. Such county women had husbands who had left large estates, or they carried on shopkeeping or taverns after a spouse's death, or they had been entrusted as sole administrator of one or more wealthy, commercially active kinsmen.[29] Although these repeaters constituted only a handful of individuals (eight in the 1670–1719 years, eighteen in the next three decades), they accounted for two-thirds of widows' appearances as lone litigants in debt suits throughout the pre-1750 period.

Despite their importance in registering a presence for women in debt litigation, before 1720 repeating widows almost never came into court more than three times.[30] The phenomenon of a widow whose familiarity

28. Of 160 appearances by women between 1670 and 1720, 60 (38%) were by female administrators, and 30 (19%) were by widows *not* suing as administrators. (Appearances encompass every court appearance of a woman or female minor, whether in a suit alone or in a plural party.) My data on the geographical relationship of parties in debt suits cover the 1670–1709 period. Of the 188 debt suits involving male litigants only, 33% were between fellow townsmen, 10% were between residents of different New Haven County towns, and 56% were across county or colony lines (in 5% a geographical relation could not be determined). Twelve personal debt suits involving widows can be identified for these four decades: 10 were intratown, and in 2 the residence of the widow's adversary is unknown.

29. For 6 of 7 New Haven County widows who repeated as sole debt litigants in the 1670–1719 years, inventories for their husbands survive (the 8th was from Hartford): their mean value was £455, and the median was £532. For 16 county widows appearing only once, husbands' inventories survive or can be reliably estimated in 9 cases: these yield a mean of £288 and a median of £230. Again in the 1720–1749 period, widows who appeared more than once had on average far wealthier husbands (median estate = £1,206, mean estate = £3,512, with 11 of 16 known) than widows appearing one time only in debt litigation.

30. Three came in twice, another three participated in 3 suits, one appeared 5 times, and Sibella Bryan Grey (who is profiled below) appeared 15 times. These counts focus on widows' appearances alone in debt litigation, leaving out other occasions when some of these women appeared in land or trespass suits or pursued civil litgation in plural parties.

with litigation stemmed from fifteen appearances over thirteen years was limited to one individual, twice-widowed Sibella Whiting Bryan Grey. The daughter of a Hartford minister, Sibella served as sole administrator of her husband, "Gentleman" Alexander Bryan, whose 1700 estate exceeded £590 and included warehouses, slaves, and a sizable library. Upon Alexander's death, Sibella also took on her husband's role as administrator of the estate of his father, an extremely wealthy Milford merchant.[31] Sibella Bryan was typical of widows appearing in the turn-of-the-century court in that thirteen of her fifteen appearances were as an administrator and only two as a plaintiff or defendant representing her own credit transactions. After this active litigator's death (circa 1715), the growing popularity of promissory notes gave widows greater chances to earn interest as frequent, small lenders. In an unrelated development, more families by midcentury chose to vest administration duties with male kinsmen. The two trends meant that wealthy widows like Sibella Bryan would come into court dramatically less often as agents resolving the debt obligations of deceased men and more as propertied women protecting their own modest interventions in the commercializing economy.

In 1719 the two-story wooden frame of an official courthouse was finally raised on the northeast corner of New Haven's central square. Over the next ten years, women's participation in civil cases declined by 40 percent. This was a permanent falling off from the presence women had sustained over the previous five decades (Table 1). Although the new courthouse in and of itself did not act as an intimidating edifice to members of the "weaker sex," the era in which it served the county witnessed far-reaching transitions in both the litigated economy and court culture, transitions that turned the county courtroom into more and more of a male preserve.

First, ordinary litigants encountered a jarring set of new rules of conduct in the courtroom. By the 1720s, county court justices were vigorously enforcing the rules of "orderly" pleading, a movement that had been under way since the 1690s. The heightened formality enforced by

---

31. Jacobus, *FANH,* 1971; Susan Woodruff Abbott, comp., *Families of Early Milford, Connecticut* (Baltimore, 1979), 124–125; New Haven District Probate Court Records, II, 13, 253 (microfilm). Sibella also appeared twice in court with her second husband, Hugh Grey, as administrator of the two Bryans' estates until Grey's death in 1707. In subsequent years, she entered court for her own debts and for outstanding cases involving the Bryan estates, but not as Grey's administrator. For Sibella's civil cases, see NHCC, II, 72–74, 278, 361, 373–374, 376–377, 388, III, 36.

the judges and the increasing number of licensed lawyers contributed to the quick spread of technical, dilatory pleading tactics. Such strategies were well known in English common law courts but alien to seventeenth-century New England courtrooms and to yeoman litigants who were used to pleading their own cases. Whereas almost all contested suits before 1710 were tried in such a way that litigants could debate the merits of the case, in the 1710s and 1720s a growing majority of defendants chose pleas that objected to the suit on narrow, technical legal grounds. This shift meant that fewer and fewer civil disputes went to juries. And it meant that by the 1730s most litigants paid the standard two-pound fee to ensure they had the expertise of an attorney on their side. The lay, communal approach to settling economic disputes was fast disappearing from Connecticut's courtrooms.[32]

The shift toward orderly pleading and the use of lawyers had a long-lasting impact on the county court's accessibility to the poor. In what can be seen as a process of mutual exclusion, judges constructed rules that discouraged the uninitiated from bringing civil disputes to county court, at the same time as the poorer sort began to develop strategies to avoid being sued. Unfortunately, colonial Connecticut court records do not assign occupational labels to litigants, so we can only hypothesize a diminishing presence in court for those categories of men, whether humble yeomen farmers, laborers, or mariners, who controlled little property, eked out a marginal existence, or simply did not join in the new investment opportunities offered by the growing economy. A 1709 case illustrates how courtroom disputing was beginning to turn an uncongenial face to those who continued to rely on oral trading networks. James Humphrey was forced to withdraw his suit and pay the costs when he admitted to the bench "that he had no account" with the man who owed him three pounds except "what he had in his head."[33]

32. The most common strategy adopted by litigants shifted from directly pleading the general issue (as was done in nearly all contested cases before 1700) to initially demurring or pleading in abatement or in bar. The former allowed a range of factual issues to be raised, and the latter avoided the merits of the dispute and focused on legal technicalities (for example, Was the writ correctly served? Did it name the proper defendant?). Bruce Mann documents this shift for Hartford County and notes that litigants in the transitional 1710–1730 period exhibited confusion at the newly prevalent pleading tactics (*Neighbors and Strangers,* chap. 3, esp. 81–84, 92–93, and tables 15 and 16 at 185–186). The same revolution in pleading occurred in the New Haven County Court, but its records do not lend themselves to quantification on this score.

33. In his survey of debt cases involving residents of the town of Kent in the

Faced with the new necessity of choosing proper pleas or hiring an attorney, many women might have balked at the idea of going to court. By paying debts when demanded of them, women could by their own conscious behavior avoid going to court—at least as debtors. Indeed, until 1720 slightly fewer than half of the women appearing in debt litigation were defendants, but in the decades thereafter only two of ten came into court as debtors.[34] Resistance to the prospect of being hauled into court as a debtor was voiced resoundingly by one Branford widow in 1713. On receiving a summons to answer for a debt owed by her husband before his death, forty-three-year-old Mary Foot marched to the house of her creditor, Nathaniel Johnson, trailing two male witnesses behind her. There she "desired Johnson to reckon with her, and further said to him that if She owed him anything she would pay him every penny and rather than go to Court she would pay him 20 shillings more." Meeting with a refusal, Mary offered this parting shot to her creditor: "She was very sorry . . . he would not reckon, for she had as live [lief] go to prison as to Court."[35]

A second engine pulling litigation away from informal seventeenth-century patterns was Connecticut's expanding economy. After the turn

---

Litchfield County Court for the years 1752 and 1786, Charles S. Grant found few small farmers among either debtors or creditors (*Democracy in Kent,* 70–73). For the 1709 case, see Humphrey v. John Weed, NHCC, II, 335, 343–344, and *Recs. Ct. of Assts.,* Lacy transcript, II, 690–691, 708.

34. Apparently women were not resorting to local justices of the peace more often than to county courts for debt resolution. Surviving justice of peace records from Hartford County (none exists for New Haven County before 1776) indicate that the proportion of women suing and being sued for debt before single magistrates (thus, over sums less than 40s.) in that populous and commercializing region mirrored the presence of women in the 1740s New Haven County Court civil caseload (see Tables 1 and 2). Of 116 suits labeled debt or "plea demanding" recorded by Justice of Peace Joseph Willcockson of Simsbury, 1742–1753, 11, or 9.5%, involved a female litigant (Simsbury Inferior Court, Records, 1742–Nov. 1, 1753 [microfilm], CHS).

Of the 78 parties that comprised or included a female litigant in debt cases 1670–1719, 44, or 56%, were plaintiffs. In the 1720–1749 period, 79% (*N* = 222 of 284) of such parties came into court as plaintiffs. For widows appearing alone over their own debts (as nonadministrators), the imbalance was even more striking: 62% appeared as plaintiffs in the 1670–1719 period, 87% in 1720–1749.

35. Johnson v. Foot (Jan. 1712/3), NHCC, III, 22, and NHCC Files, dr. 2. John Foot had died in early 1713, leaving only 18 acres, a log-and-stone house, and a barn (New Haven Probate District Estate Papers for John Foot [1713], 3943, R.G. 4 [microfilm], CSL).

of the century agricultural output and the volume of coastal trading increased in dramatic spurts, driven partly by population growth and partly by the availability of cash in the form of paper money. This boom motivated householders to look for new sources of credit to finance investments in more land and livestock or in tools to begin a winter business. Merchants and shopkeepers in towns throughout the countryside offered cash advances in exchange for interest-bearing notes. Thus farmers and artisans found themselves in an economy no longer dependent solely on barter and commodity money and in a world of credit no longer characterized chiefly by book debt and oral promises to pay.[36]

The proliferation of notes — and other written instruments such as bonds and bills — fueled an enormous rise in debt litigation across New England, an expansion that far outstripped population growth. In the New Haven County Court, the debt caseload grew each decade between 1710 and 1750 at rates ranging from 80 percent to 120 percent (Table 2). And much of the new litigation concerned notes and bonds: by 1740 suits over written instruments had edged out book debt actions by a ratio of three to one. A widow suing her debtors in the 1730s and 1740s frequently would have sat through long, tedious court sessions at which the bench processed 35–70 civil cases. A depression in agricultural prices in the late 1730s prompted particularly high caseloads from 1740 through 1742, as county residents intensified their pursuit of debts.[37] After 1744 the extra flurry of debt collection died down, and the caseload returned to the level it had reached by the late 1730s — about 140 cases per year, 40 cases per sitting.

The swelled caseload meant that an ever-increasing proportion of county inhabitants participated in economic dealings that wound up in court. Rough calculations indicate that during the 1710s, just fewer than 4 percent of adult male residents of New Haven County appeared in civil litigation annually. For the 1740s, the figure rises to 12.5 percent. If we look at the volume of litigation over a decade (a span that better approxi-

36. Mann, *Neighbors and Strangers*, 30–33; Richard L. Bushman, *From Puritan to Yankee: Character and the Social Order in Connecticut, 1690–1765* (New York, 1970), 107–137; Jackson Turner Main, *Society and Economy in Colonial Connecticut* (Princeton, N.J., 1985), chap. 4.

37. Bruce C. Daniels estimates the decadal population growth for Connecticut in these years was 28% (*The Connecticut Town: Growth and Development, 1635–1790* [Middletown, Conn., 1979], chap. 2, esp. 46). On depression, see Main, *Society and Economy*, 18, 121–123, 380.

mates the chances of coming into court once in a lifetime), men's appearances corresponded to 41 percent of the adult male population in the 1710s and rose to the equivalent of one litigant per adult male resident in the 1740s.[38] Clearly, litigious behavior and familiarity with the courthouse scene punctuated the lives of almost all white men in the county by the mid-eighteenth century.

Something more than lawyerly procedures separated men's midcentury experience of debt litigation from the days when court sessions had met in John Miles's barroom. Suing over notes and bonds was very different from suing over book debt. A debtor could challenge a written obligation only by contending that the piece of paper was not his or her deed. Thus very few suits to collect on notes and bonds were contested. The predictability of getting a judgment made this form of debt obligation particularly attractive to creditors. Indeed, it was this feature of written instruments that turned eighteenth-century debt litigation into a recording device: by midcentury, debtors defaulted or confessed judgment in more than 90 percent of cases, and creditors waited to execute those easily won judgments until they wished to call in the debt.[39]

A search for explanations why women's presence in debt litigation descended to a plateau of 9 percent in the 1720–1750 period must focus on the two groups who had comprised the bulk of female litigants up to that juncture: estate administrators and widows suing over personal transactions. Before 1720, a solid majority—60 percent—of women coming into the New Haven court for debt were present as estate administrators.[40] Thus, any shift in the appointment practices of testators and probate judges away from naming widows would spell a probable decline in the overall presence of women in the courtroom. As for widows whose independent economic dealings might involve them in litigation, their rootedness in local, informal trading and lending networks did not fore-

38. For New Haven County population, I have estimated backward from the 1756 census. Following Robert V. Wells's analysis of the 1774 census, I have assumed that adult males and adult females each made up 22% of the population (*The Population of the British Colonies in America before 1776* [Princeton, N.J., 1975], 88–94). My computations for men do not account for noncounty men appearing or for parties with plural male litigants. The figures assume two male litigants per case. See the method applied in John M. Murrin, review essay, *History and Theory*, XI (1972), 250n.

39. On the process of litigating over notes and for figures on the rise of uncontested cases in Hartford County, see Mann, *Neighbors and Strangers*, 12–27, 181.

40. My discussion and figures treat executors (named by a will) and administrators (appointed by the probate court) as one group.

bode an active presence for them in the proliferating exchanges of notes and bonds across town, county, and colony lines. Unless new opportunities for earning a livelihood and investing were opened to widows, they were fated to be increasingly marginal actors way in the litigated economy.

Historians studying the mid-Atlantic and Chesapeake colonies have found that, after an initial period in which widows almost invariably took charge of their husbands' estates, wealthier male testators at some point in the eighteenth century began to relieve their wives of the burden of administration. They did this either by appointing a son or male relative alongside their wife or by sparing her entirely. It is probable that at about the same time women themselves increasingly declined the job of administration when their husbands failed to leave wills and that probate judges encouraged this trend away from placing the management of family property in women's hands. The complicated work involved in sorting out household accounts, along with a new concern among the genteel to protect women from the cares of commerce, hastened the process.[41]

In the New Haven area, court records indicate that the shift was well

41. For a comparative table based on a range of studies of widows named as executors, see Carole Shammas, Marylynn Salmon, and Michel Dahlin, *Inheritance in America from Colonial Times to the Present* (New Brunswick, N.J., 1987), 59–61. Further analysis can be found in Narrett, *Inheritance and Family Life in Colonial New York City*, 106–113, 204–205; Ditz, *Property and Kinship*, 144–148; Allan Kulikoff, *Tobacco and Slaves: The Development of Southern Cultures in the Chesapeake, 1680–1800* (Chapel Hill, N.C., 1986), 189–193; Lebsock, *Free Women of Petersburg*, 36–40, 120–125; and Deborah Mathias Gough, "A Further Look at Widows in Early Southeastern Pennsylvania," *WMQ*, XLIV (1987), 833–835. Data for 17th-century New England areas are given in Lyle Koehler, *A Search for Power: The "Weaker Sex" in Seventeenth-Century New England* (Urbana, Ill., 1980), 312–314; and Rachelle E. Friedman, "To My Well-Beloved Wife: Testamentary Patterns and Female Authority in Boston, 1650–1725," paper presented at the Annual Meeting of the Organization of American Historians, Anaheim, Calif., Apr. 15–18, 1993. To my knowledge, no study has systematically examined appointment practices in intestate cases for the colonial period.

Mary Beth Norton discusses middle-class women's lack of knowledge of household finances in "Eighteenth-Century American Women in Peace and War: The Case of the Loyalists," *WMQ*, XXXIII (1976), 386–409. Margaret Rose Hunt traces the English pamphlet debate in which Daniel Defoe and others urged that women in trading familes should be trained to cast accounts. Defoe's arguments were heeded less and less during the 1700s. See Hunt, "English Urban Families in Trade, 1660–1800: The Culture of Early Modern Capitalism" (Ph.D. diss., New York University, 1986), chap. 4.

under way by midcentury. It manifested itself in two ways. Until the 1730s, three-quarters of women administrators appearing in debt cases had undertaken the job of administration alone. By the 1740s and 1750s, women appeared more frequently as joint than sole administrators; indeed, only one-third of the women administrators appearing in court for debt were managing estates officially without male help. Second, the number of women administrators collecting their husbands' debts fell in proportion to widows, single women, and married women pursuing their own debts in court. In other words, their participation in debt cases grew at a far more modest rate than the increase for women appearing as *non*administrators.[42] The fact that the presence of female administrators in the overall debt caseload slid from 10 percent in 1670–1729 to 4 percent in the following three decades goes much of the way toward accounting for the diminished proportion of women among civil litigants in the second quarter of the eighteenth century.

If Mary Miles serves as an appropriate representative of women who came into court between 1670 and 1720, then her daughter Hannah offers an equally good example of the next generation of female litigants. Hannah's husband, Richard Hall, died when she was forty-five, and she lived out her remaining sixteen years without remarrying. Following in the footsteps of Hannah's parents, the Halls had converted part of their New Haven house into a tavern in 1713, and Hannah continued the business throughout her widowhood. As her husband's executor, only once did she enter the doors of the county courthouse to collect a debt. Rather, it was her own dealings as a tavernkeeper that gave her the most experience as a county court litigator. Between 1735 and her death in 1741, Widow Hall sued fourteen debtors, securing judgments on seven bonds valued at eighty pounds, three notes worth seventeen pounds, and seventeen pounds more in accounts recorded in her book (see Plates 4 and 5).[43]

42. Between 1710 and 1760, women administrators' presence grew every 20 years by 70%, and the number of women appearing over their personal debts quadrupled. In the category of sole administrator, I have not included women who remarried and appeared in court as administrators or executors accompanied by their new husbands.

43. All of Hall's suits were uncontested. Twice the court allowed an attorney to appear in her stead. Hall's litigation history was rounded out by two suits brought in the January 1745/6 term by her son-in-law executor to collect sums due to her by bond. Sources on Hannah Hall: Jacobus, *FANH*, 717–718, 1182; NHCC, III, 236, 442, 479, 484, 523, IV, 38, 46, 73–75, 78, 89, 271.

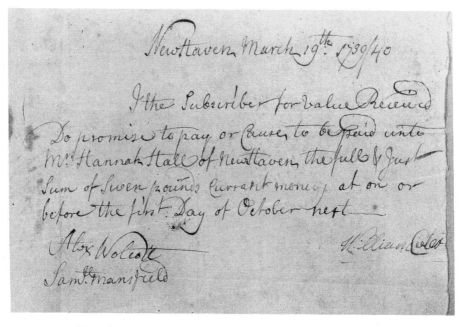

PLATE 4. Promissory Note. *Submitted as evidence in debt suit of Hannah Hall against William Carter, January 1740/1. New Haven County Court, Files, dr. 16, R.G. 3. Courtesy of the Connecticut State Library*

Although her numerous appearances were unusual, Hannah Hall's profile as a litigant—widow, nonadministrator, plaintiff—was shared by 40 percent of the individual women in debt litigation between 1710 and 1750. Only a handful of New Haven County widows ran taverns, and only a few widows kept their own account books. But, like Hall, the widows who entered the litigation rolls did so as net creditors: nearly 90 percent of litigating widows had extended small amounts of credit by note. Thus some widows, whether they were running a family enterprise or augmenting their income through cautious lending, displayed considerable facility with written credit instruments. The number of widows appearing in county court to sue or be sued over their own debts (rather than their husbands') increased about sevenfold between the 1710s and 1750s, just as men's litigiousness did. Thus the court records provide indirect evidence that well-propertied widows in the most expansive decades of New England's preindustrial history played a role similar to that of wealthy widows in commercializing regions of early modern England: they were an important source of both consumer and commercial loans and therefore, it must be acknowledged, played a modest but significant

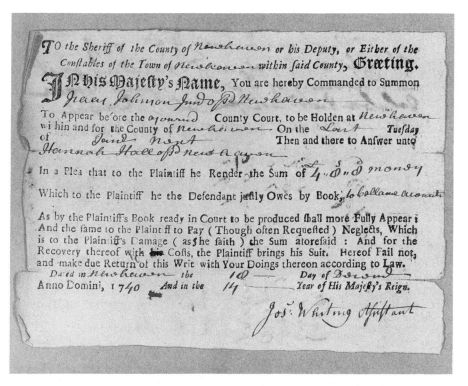

PLATE 5. Writ in Book Debt Suit. *In suit of Hannah Hall against Isaac Johnson, January 1740/1. New Haven County Court, Files, dr. 16, R.G. 3. Courtesy of the Connecticut State Library*

part in the capitalization and commercial development of the countryside.[44]

44. On women's account books: From 1700 (when types of debt were first enumerated in the court records) through 1779, New Haven County Court records document 30 individual femes sole and 12 newly married women suing on their own book accounts. Although no surviving account books belonging to colonial Connecticut women are known to exist (Ulrich, *Good Wives*, 44), these suits are a strong indication that some widows maintained their husband's book and that single women often kept a ledger of their own. For example, in December 1773, auditors awarded £6 12s. to David and Anna Bronson, a sum owed to Anna "while sole and before her intermarriage as by her book appears" (writ, Bronson v. Upson, NHCC Files, dr. 56).

For details on the activities of post-1780 widows as creditors and financial managers and on the real estate market, see Lebsock, *Free Women of Petersburg*, 128–129; and Lisa Wilson, *Life after Death: Widows in Pennsylvania, 1750–1850* (Philadelphia,

The litigated economy indicates that widows' roles as actors and catalysts in the economic expansion were limited in two respects: they did not aggressively seek out loans and thus were rarely if ever overextended; and when they did extend credit themselves, it was to local residents. Almost never appearing as debt defendants, propertied widows apparently were not engaged in extensive borrowing. Evidently they contributed to the expanding economy as local lenders but not as active entrepreneurs or risk-taking investors.[45] The few women who did appear as debtors in court were widowed or divorced women with precarious economic toeholds in their communities, yet they usually appeared only once, not as defendants hounded by a series of worried creditors. Widows' own strategies to avoid being sued, the dependence of many widows on their childrens' support, and, finally, lingering traditions heeding biblical prescriptions for forgiving poor widows' small debts effectively shielded many elderly and resourceless women from county court appearances.[46]

However actively certain independent women participated in the circulation of notes up through 1750, patterns of debt litigation show that

---

1992), esp. chap. 4.

See William Chester Jordan, *Women and Credit in Pre-Industrial and Developing Societies* (Philadelphia, 1993), 67–69, 77, for a succinct and extremely useful synthesis of the scholarly research on women's roles in lending and trade, comparing late-medieval and early modern Europe with modern Africa, Asia, and Latin America.

45. On the rarity of widows' risk-taking investments in preindustrial England, see Jordan, *Women and Credit*, 69. To illuminate the nature and range of widows' economic activities in commercializing areas of colonial British North America, a systematic study is needed of, first, widows' assets at death (especially notes, other credits, and cash) and, second, widows' appearances as creditors in decedents' estates. One limitation of court and probate records, however, is that the nature of the credit transaction—whether it consisted of direct moneylending or delayed payment on a purchase—is typically not noted.

46. Of the 163 appearances made by widows or once-married women alone (including plaintiffs and defendants, administrators and nonadministrators) between 1720 and 1750, only 15 were by women being sued over their own debts. Six of the 15 resided outside the county. Seven of the 9 county women can be identified as having few resources: 4 were recently divorced women without much property, 1 boarded and had been abandoned by her spouse, and 2 others were widows left with small estates.

For illustrations and discussion of widows' dependency, see Keyssar, "Widowhood in Massachusetts," *Perspectives in American History*, VIII (1974), 103–117; and Ditz, *Property and Kinship*, 128–134.

their role was limited in one significant respect. Just as Hannah Hall sued fellow New Haveners at all but one of her court appearances, litigating widows tended to be bound in debt relations with people they must have known well, men and women who lived not more than a few miles away. The contrast between women and men with respect to the "geographic reach of credit relations" emerges most clearly in book debt actions: 93 percent of widows' suits but only 40 percent of men's were with fellow town residents. The gender gap is less dramatic but still significant if we look at book debt actions combined with the more numerous suits over notes and bonds. Widows appeared in three debt cases against fellow townspeople for every two suits in which they engaged with a litigant across town, county, or colony lines. The ratio was reversed for male litigants: not only were they pitted against a distant adversary in three of five cases, but they were 20 percent *less* likely to sue a fellow townsman and 15 percent *more* likely than widows to be contending with someone from another county or colony.[47]

That female creditors and debtors were far less involved in intertown or intercounty debt suits than men suggests that they were not participating as frequently in the increasingly impersonal credit relations that extended beyond town lines. Given their lack of resources, accounting skills, and commercial contacts, this finding should not surprise us. However, widows still played active roles in the world of local credit, a realm that over the second half of the century would come to occupy an ever smaller proportion of both the litigated economy and the economy at large.

What is striking about the 1720–1750 period is that, following a sharp decline, women maintained a remarkably steady presence in civil litigation. While the litigated economy of New Haven County became increasingly marked by the use of notes and by suits that were no longer

47. The quoted phrase is from Mann, *Neighbors and Strangers,* 34. All figures in this paragraph apply to 1710–1749. Of 18 widows appearing in book debt actions as nonadministrators, 15 came up against a fellow town resident (one of these cases involved New Haveners). The geographic distribution of widows' adversarial relationships for all types of debt not involving estate administration ($N = 122$) was as follows: 58% intratown ($N = 72$), 16% intertown within the county ($N = 20$), and 24% across county or colony lines ($N = 30$). The distribution for debt cases involving men only was: 38% intratown, 23% intertown, and 39% intercounty or intercolony. Figures for men are based on all cases filed in 1712, 1715, 1717, 1719, 1722, 1725, 1727, 1729, 1732, 1735, 1742. This sampling method yields 42 cases for the 1710s, 162 for the 1720s, 281 for the 1730s, and 265 for the 1740s.

real disputes, but uncontested legal moves to guarantee payment, women's litigation patterns did not depart radically from men's.[48] Only in the geographic relations between creditors and debtors do we see a persistent divergence between men and women. Despite commercializing trends, New Haven County remained a predominantly rural society in which women's work played a crucial role in household production and in which women were expected to shoulder the tasks of household and property management when their husbands were away or deceased. Indeed, widows' appearances in court as creditors who had extended small loans locally rose at the same dramatic rate that men's appearances did. A continuing decline in the participation of women in debt litigation after 1720 would have signaled a dramatic disengagement by women from the economy. Such a precipitous change would have been neither pragmatic nor even thinkable for the hundreds of farm and artisanal households that forged subsistence with family labor. As scattered extant diaries show, from the mid-seventeenth century to the early nineteenth, the daily and seasonal work of New England farm families followed much the same rhythms.[49] The third quarter of the eighteenth century, however, brought renewed economic growth, regional agricultural specialization, and commercial activity to the New Haven area, along with the continued diffusion of cash and notes passing as currency through the countryside. By the early 1770s, the pressure of trends already under way — newly structured credit relations, intimidating procedural courtroom rules, and an ever-rising, bloated civil caseload — would combine with new cultural forces to slash the presence of women in debt litigation yet again by nearly one-half.

48. Women were almost as likely to sue over debt as men were: debt comprised 76% of civil cases involving female litigants and 80% of the entire civil caseload. Throughout the pre-1750 period, however, women appeared proportionately more frequently in suits over land title and trespass than in any other type of civil action. One-fifth of the 365 land-related cases in the New Haven County Court, 1666–1749, involved female litigants, almost always appearing in plural parties of joint heirs. Hence litigation patterns bear out Toby Ditz's finding that New England daughters routinely inherited small parcels of land (*Property and Kinship*, chap. 4).

49. Compare the diaries of Thomas Minor, Joshua Hempstead, and Matthew Patten: *The Diary of Thomas Minor, Stonington, Connecticut, 1653 to 1684* (New London, 1899); *Diary of Joshua Hempstead of New London, Connecticut . . . from September, 1711, to November, 1758*, New London County Historical Society, Collections, I, (New London, 1901); *The Diary of Matthew Patten of Bedford, N.H.* (Concord, N.H., 1903). See the analysis in Clark, *Roots of Rural Capitalism*, chaps. 2–4.

In 1775 the civil caseload of the New Haven County Court peaked for the colonial period at 865 suits. Between the late 1740s (when the annual caseload settled at a plateau of about 150 cases) and the Revolution, litigation rates had more than quintupled. The docket was so large in the early 1770s that the bench sat at some sessions for as long as four weeks. Two professional attorneys represented litigants in all contested cases. As a public forum the county court had lost all vestiges of its previous embodiment as a local, intimate, dispute-resolving institution. Simply to get their business done, court officials were forced to adopt streamlined, rationalized procedures that must have meant that their endeavor smacked more often of administrative tedium than the exalted obligation to mete out justice. The court record books reveal the most striking hallmark of the new bureaucratic atmosphere of the late-eighteenth-century court: the clerk now separated contested cases from uncontested ones, and the latter category for a single session might occupy forty pages of the record book. We can imagine that the justices spent several days simply listening to the clerk call out these cases (which constituted 80 percent of the civil caseload), record the default of the debtor, and enter judgment for the plaintiff.

The separation of uncontested and contested actions in the 1770s symbolized the divergence of men's and women's spheres within the litigated economy. Women continued to appear in at least 10 percent of all contested suits, two-thirds of which were over land, inheritance, slander, and other nondebt matters. But women participated in fewer than 4 percent of the huge numbers of uncontested actions, 92 percent of which were debt suits. Female litigants were thus represented in only 5 percent of the entire civil caseload — half the level of their participation in the second quarter of the century (see Table 3). And there can be no doubt that their visibility on court days was greatly reduced. At an average sitting, the bench heard 150–200 cases, only 6 or 7 of which might include a woman litigant.[50]

Women had by no means disappeared from the litigated economy by the eve of the Revolution. Indeed, their litigation patterns in the 1770s

50. As in earlier decades, women evidently were not resorting more frequently to justice of the peace courts than to county courts. Of the debt cases that came before Justice of the Peace Thomas Clark of Derby, Conn., March 1778–May 1789, only 4% involved a woman litigant (Justice of the Peace Records of Thomas Clark, CSL).

TABLE 3

Female Litigants and the Debt Caseload, 1770–1773,
New Haven County Court

	No. of Cases (Proportion Involving Women)			
	Contested	Uncontested	Arbitrated	Overall
1770	35 (6%)	313 (3%)	16 (6%)	364 (3%)
1771	32 (16%)	342 (5%)	11 (9%)	385 (6%)
1772	36 (14%)	425 (4%)	22 (4%)	483 (5%)
1773	49 (12%)	683 (3%)[a]	17 (12%)	749 (4%)[a]
Overall	152 (12%)	1,763 (4%)[a]	66 (8%)	1,981 (4%)[a]

[a]The figure and proportion are estimations.

Source: New Haven County Court Records and Files, 1770–1773.

suggest the stability of their economic activities over the century. As in the 1720–1749 period, close to 80 percent of female litigants who came into court in the 1773–1775 years appeared as plaintiffs. Many of these were widows who brought a succession of suits both as administrators and as creditors in their own right. Hannah Gibb and Martha Baker, for example, had not only inherited unusual amounts of property before widowhood but also had married shopkeepers; both came into court over debt only as plaintiffs—Baker did so five times in four years, and Gibb twenty-two times over five years.[51] The high proportion of plaintiffs among women suing alone indicates that most widows continued to

51. For Gibb's court appearances, see NHCC, VII, 499, 529, VIII, 16, 43, 169. For Baker, see VII, 290, 428, 431, VIII, 104. Hannah (Allen) Gibb had received £608 in land and goods from her brother Gideon's 1749 estate settlement, and £250 old tenor according to her father's 1751 will. Her husband, Thomas Gibb, left her two slaves and half his land and movables outright (Fairfield Probate District Estate Papers for Gideon Allen [1748], 7059, [1752], 7060 [microfilm], CSL; Thomas Gibb: New Haven District Probate Court Records, X, 571–572, XI, 156–157, 304 [microfilm]). Before coming into her thirds of shopkeeper husband Samuel's 1767 estate, Martha Baker had inherited land and goods from her father, the Reverend John Davenport of Stamford, and from her first husband, whose 1746 estate was assessed at £5,583 (Stamford District Probate Court Records, I, 10–21, 221 [microfilm], CSL; New Haven Probate District Estate Papers for Thomas Goodsell [1746], 4371 [microfilm]).

actively avoid coming into court as debtors and that wealthy widows engaged in frequent lending, but not borrowing. Finally, when women did appear in uncontested debt suits, their credit relations were predominantly with fellow townspeople and rarely extended outside the county.[52]

Because the civil caseload had grown so much faster than the population, the percentage of the adult female population of New Haven County appearing in court annually in the mid-1770s was actually *higher* than it had been at any time in the early part of the century.[53] That women's presence was drowned out by the enormous increases in men's litigiousness perhaps registered differently in the minds of men and women familiar with the court scene. Likely to be from wealthy families, the women who appeared in debt litigation on the eve of the Revolution could have seen themselves as linked to previous generations of widows who had not hesitated to resort to county court suits when necessary. By the 1770s, dense kin networks in the county meant that well-off women would often have had mothers, mothers-in-law, aunts, sisters, or even grandmothers who could recount their own courtroom experiences as creditors or administrators. Indeed, the implications of the transformation in the court scene might have dawned initially and more tellingly on the men — litigants and lawyers — who routinely attended county court sessions rather than on the substratum of county women from whom frequent female litigants were drawn. The scores of men gathered in and near the courthouse during sessions facilitated male sociability and cast any women's appearance as an anomalous event. That very anomaly

52. The breakdown for the 57 uncontested debt cases involving women (as either plaintiff or defendant), 1773–1775, was 56% intratown ($N = 32$), 28% intertown ($N = 15$), and 18% intercounty ($N = 10$). Comparable figures for the 464 uncontested cases between men in 1774 were 45% intratown, 24% intertown, and 33% intercounty and intercolony. Of course, the New Haven County Court records do not capture county women who sued a debtor in another county. We can assume, however, that these missing female litigators are counterbalanced in roughly equal number by the noncounty women (from Hartford or Fairfield or Boston, for example) who brought debt suits in New Haven County Court.

53. The 91 New Haven County women appearing as litigants in 1774 correspond to 1.5% of the adult female population, which I have calculated as 22% of the county population as counted in the 1774 census ($N = 5,900$ of 26,819). The figures for the average number of county women appearing in court each year in the first half of the century are as follows (based on estimated population): .5% of the adult female population in the 1710s, .3% in the 1720s, .4% in the 1730s, and .7% in the 1740s.

might have led middling and wealthy men, consciously or unconsciously, to shield their wives and daughters as far as possible from legal and financial responsibilities that in the late eighteenth century were becoming marked as masculine.[54]

The commercializing trends that made New Haven a bustling, prosperous port by 1760 did not signal a drastic curtailment in the daily, face-to-face trading activities in which New England women had always engaged. Neighborhood women, whether wives or widows, doubtless continued to engage in largely informal, oral, petty trading of goods and services. The larger regional economy, however, had changed around them. In essence, the burgeoning volume of uncontested debt cases represented the capitalization of the New England economy. Debt litigation had become a recording device for the easy credit available to propertied and professional men, craftsmen, and entrepreneurs eager to expand their landholdings and businesses. Although many New England women continued to play a crucial role in household management and the local economy, the worlds of commerce and credit in which their menfolk partook were increasingly unknown and alien to them.

Several factors must have accounted for the near exclusion of women from this new realm of credit relations. If writing skills and strict accounting procedures were becoming more integral to credit transactions in the colonies, as they were in England, then women, whose writing and ciphering skills in the 1770s remained distinctly inferior to men's, were at a clear disadvantage. Further, few women had the economic resources or the intercolonial contacts that would have facilitated their entry into entrepreneurship, speculation, and interregional credit. And among the small substratum of women who controlled substantial property on their husbands' death, a new ethic of gentility was gradually, if unevenly, gaining ground. The notions of respectability and refinement that steered elite women increasingly into the roles of consumers of luxury goods, mistresses of "the rituals of the table and the garden," and moral educators within the private domain of the nuclear family replaced older images of wives as prudent, frugal, hardworking Bathshebas. In the middle decades of the eighteenth century, the importation of European

54. For an analysis of testators' appointments of wives as executors that breaks down testators by occupational groups and reveals that only among mariners did wives predominate as executors in 18th-century New York City, see Narrett, *Inheritance and Family Life in Colonial New York City*, 106–109, 184–185.

traditions of satire and polite literature became more visible in New England in the guise of stories and poems mocking women's extravagant tastes and spendthrift habits.[55] Thus, in the realms of iconography and ideological discourse, two prominent developments that accompanied commercial expansion were a downplaying of the image of the industrious yeoman farmer's wife and a new criticism of women's indulgent and wasteful consumption patterns.

The representation of women as excessive consumers and the diminished presence of women in debt caseloads were trends that had significant implications for how female citizenship would be defined after 1776. If middle-class women were prone to frivolity and waste and lower-class women to idleness and dangerous sexuality, how could one entrust women with civic responsibility? If women were not visible in two of the most important spheres where a citizen took on identity—the expanding economy and the courtroom—then why should lawmakers and constitution drafters have made a special effort to overcome centuries of Western tradition that disassociated women from politics? Resoundingly, Revolutionary leaders chose not to take the opportunity offered by the break with Britain to relieve women under the law from their dependence on men.[56] As the Puritans had inadvertently shown, only challenging or making exceptions to coverture would reverse the invisibility of women in the public sphere that included the litigated economy. The role that widows played as investors and extenders of local credit in the

55. On writing and accounting skills, see Hunt, "English Urban Families," chaps. 2 and 4; and Patricia Cline Cohen, *A Calculating People: Numeracy in Early America* (Chicago, 1982). On new images of women emphasizing domesticity, see Ulrich, *Good Wives,* chap. 4, esp. 76–77; Boydston, *Home and Work,* 26–29; Norton, "Eighteenth-Century Women in Peace and War," *WMQ,* XXXIII (1976), 386–409; Nancy F. Cott, *The Bonds of Womanhood: "Woman's Sphere" in New England, 1780–1825* (New Haven, 1977).

On changing representations of women, work and consumption, see Boydston, *Home and Work,* 25–27; and Cornelia Hughes Dayton, "Satire and Sensationalism: The Emergence of Misogyny in Mid-Eighteenth-Century New England Newspapers and Almanacs," paper presented to the New England Seminar in American History, Worcester, Mass., Nov. 15, 1991.

56. Marylynn Salmon, *Women and the Law of Property in Early America* (Chapel Hill, N.C., 1986), xv; Linda K. Kerber, " 'History Can Do It No Justice': Women and the Reinterpretation of the American Revolution," in Hoffman and Albert, eds., *Women in the Age of the American Revolution,* 3–42; Kerber, "The Paradox of Women's Citizenship in the Early Republic: The Case of *Martin vs. Massachusetts,* 1805," *American Historical Review,* XCVII (1992), 349–378.

eighteenth-century commercialization of the colonial economy did not lead to changes in legal rules, economic structures, or understandings of political economy that would free women to engage throughout their adult lives in the sorts of economic activities that won public and political recognition. Propertied white male householders liberated themselves from monarchical tyranny, but the ties that bound women to the largely informal, local economy helped to doom their eligibility for full citizenship in the new fraternal republican order.[57]

57. Ironically, wartime and postwar conditions would temporarily increase the proportion of women appearing in civil litigation. For the 1776–1789 years, both the annual volume of civil cases in the New Haven County Court and the proportion of cases involving women litigants fluctuated considerably. Caseloads ranged from 71 suits in 1779 to 593 in 1782, with an average of 307 for the 14 years. In some years, women were parties to 6%–9% of civil suits, and in other years their participation topped 20%. None of this should be surprising, given that the war produced a sharp rise in the number of widows of all ages and the likelihood that they ran family farms and businesses, served as administrators, and failed to remarry far more often than widows in the 1750s and 1760s.

For discussions of women's exclusion from political membership, see Linda K. Kerber, " 'I Have Don . . . much to Carrey on the Warr': Women and the Shaping of Republican Ideology after the American Revolution," in Harriet B. Applewhite and Darline G. Levy, eds., *Women and Politics in the Age of the Democratic Revolution* (Ann Arbor, Mich., 1990), esp. 232–235; and Joan R. Gundersen, "Independence, Citizenship, and the American Revolution," *Signs: Journal of Women in Culture and Society,* XIII (1987–1988), 59–77.

3

Divorce

THE LIMITS OF A PURITAN REMEDY

Mary Larkham could claim none of the grounds for divorce established by early Connecticut law. Her husband Job had neither deserted her nor committed adultery; when they wed, he had not been impotent or guilty of hiding a preexisting marriage. But during six years of marriage and childbearing Mary endured repeated beatings (by horsewhip, halter, and ax), strangling attempts, a mock hanging, and expulsions from the house—all accompanied by Job's vow that he would "be the Death" of her. These actions by a disturbed, sadistic man were not legitimate grounds for divorce, and Mary had little recourse beyond appealing to family members and neighbors for succor and mediation. Although Connecticut had long administered the most generous divorce policy in the British Empire, no woman had been granted a divorce solely on evidence of cruelty by the Superior Court, the body with primary jurisdiction. Spouses whose marital grievance was without remedy under statute law could petition the General Assembly in its capacity as a court of equity. In her petition of May 1753, Mary Larkham detailed the abuses she had suffered from Job and reported that she had been "forced to leave" his house two months earlier "to secure my own life and Prevent him from Murthering me." Larkham's petition occasioned the only decree granting a Connecticut woman a divorce explicitly and solely on cruelty grounds in the century and a half prior to the late 1780s. The legislators' decision did not stem merely from the sympathy generated by Mary's wrenching narrative or her lawyer's arguments. Job Larkham appeared before the assembled deputies and Assistants and "Confest himself . . . Guilty" of the "Barbarous and Inhuman . . . carryage" alleged against him. Thus it took a husband's oral public confirmation of his utter failure to be a proper household head and family protector to convince early Connecticut authorities that a woman's story of cruelty should merit a divorce.[1]

Since wives were discouraged from bringing cruelty-based cases to the Connecticut courts beginning in the 1650s, when divorce petitions were first heard, allegations of wife-abuse emerged in divorce suits in two ways. First, successful women petitioners periodically told the court that they had been pushed into the fire or "Barbarously" beaten by their spouses; this information, however, was largely irrelevant, since these wives had procured clinching evidence of desertion or adultery.[2] The most explicit tales of cruelty might surface when a woman, lacking evidence of adultery or desertion, left an abusive husband and was then cast as the deserter when he sued for divorce. To defend her reputation as a long-suffering but dutiful wife and, more crucially, to protect against losing all claims to marital property and to her children, a woman might contest her spouse's suit by introducing cruelty charges. Seventeenth-century judges, faced with a handful of such cases, were swayed by wifely protests

1. Petition of Mary Larkham (May 1753), Petition passed by the Assembly and Council, Connecticut Archives, Crimes and Misdemeanors, 1st Ser., IV, 361–362; see also *PR*, X, 168–169. Local authorities confirmed the dangerous nature of Job's threats by confining him in jail temporarily in spring 1753, presumably on formal wife-abuse charges. Mary Larkham refers to the confinement in her May 1753 petition. A clause in the divorce bill requiring Job to pay Mary five pounds annual support was eliminated from the final legislative act.

For a pre-1790 Superior Court decree where horrific male violence and, this time, insanity were involved, see n. 74, below. Frances E. Dolan argues that the increasing tendency in late-17th-century English fiction and crime tales to equate murderous husbands with lunatics was a way of avoiding the message "that marriage is arbitrary, tyrannous, and exploitative, or that wives' rebellion might be justified" (*Dangerous Familiars: Representations of Domestic Crime in England, 1550–1700* [Ithaca, N.Y., 1994], 120).

2. Petition of Mary McFarnel (Aug. 1778), Petition of Sarah Brown (Feb. 1738/9), NHSC Files, drawer 716.

to deny divorces to allegedly abusive or difficult husbands. However, after the turn of the century, men who sued over their spouses' desertion amid competing charges of mistreatment usually found their prayers for a divorce answered.

Only in the late 1780s did the Connecticut legislature, the body that presided over out-of-the-ordinary divorce cases, begin to approve petitions based solely on cruelty (see Appendix 2). Responsive to transatlantic intellectual currents decrying intemperance and popularizing sentimentalized images of female virtue and republican motherhood, lawmakers began to make regular exceptions to the state's divorce law for women like Eunice Pardee.[3] Pardee, or more likely her lawyer, crafted a compelling petition chronicling how the threats and weapons brandished by her "almost continually" intoxicated husband had caused her to deem "it absolutely necessary" to flee "for the preservation of her life."[4] The sudden legitimization of cruelty-based petitions by the Connecticut Assembly permitted Tapping Reeve to reassure readers of the earliest American treatise on domestic relations, *The Law of Baron and Femme* (1816): "that if a husband turns his wife out of doors, and so abuses her, that she cannot live with him safely, and she departs from him; that this is not a willful absence on her part, but that it is so on his."[5]

3. Ruth H. Bloch, "The Gendered Meanings of Virtue in Revolutionary America," *Signs: Journal of Women in Culture and Society*, XIII (1987–1988), 37–58; G. J. Barker-Benfield, *The Culture of Sensibility: Sex and Society in Eighteenth-Century Britain* (Chicago, 1992), esp. 224–247. By 1795, the jurist Zephaniah Swift could report that the legislature had "adopted as a general rule, that in all cases of intolerable cruelty, . . . divorces may be granted" (*A System of the Laws of the State of Connecticut* [New York, 1972 (orig. publ. Windham, Conn., 1795–1796)], I, 193).

Starting with Susanna Widger's petition, 21 of 23 women successfully requesting divorces from the Assembly between 1786 and 1800 listed cruelty as primary, if not exclusive, grounds. Two men citing their wives' cruelty also won divorces. Summaries of these cases can be found in *PRS* and the indexes of Conn. Archives, Lotteries and Divorces, 1st and 2d Ser.

Of the 35 divorce petitions submitted by women to the Connecticut Assembly, 1784–1799, 10 mentioned spousal intemperance; 6 were granted.

4. Petition of Eunice Pardee (Oct. 1798), Conn. Archives, Lotteries and Divorces, 2d Ser., I, 133. After Larkham's 1753 divorce, the next two Assembly acts to award divorces to abused wives who fled their husbands granted them to Mary Loomis (Oct. 1790) and Abiah Twitchell (Dec. 1790).

5. Tapping Reeve, *The Law of Baron and Femme, of Parent and Child, Guardian and Ward, Master and Servant . . .* (New Haven, 1816), 207–208. Omitting case citations, Reeve left unspecified what sort of judicial bodies (legislatures or courts) had autho-

Casting an abusive husband as the willful deserter and thus the guilty party in a divorce was not the colonial New England way. Yet New England's early leaders, building on the Protestant concept of marriage as a civil contract, forged divorce policies that were, for the preindustrial era, remarkably generous in extending relief to men and women in troubled or failed marriages. Because Connecticut granted more divorces than any other jurisdiction before 1800, it affords an excellent base for analyzing how religious belief, legal culture, and gender ideology variously legitimized and constrained divorce petitioners and judges' decrees. Indeed, a study of divorce spotlights the shifting tides of patriarchy in early Connecticut. When the colony's policy crystallized in the early eighteenth century, it offered precociously liberal grounds in defiance of English legal custom.[6] However, it continued to breathe life into a power structure within marriage that authorized a man to think of his wife as property, as a package of rights he could lay claim to.

———

If divorce was a limited remedy for women in early New England, the fact that it was available to inhabitants of all classes marked a sharp departure from English practice. In the parent country, all marital matters fell under the jurisdiction of church courts, which could approve only two sorts of breakups: annulments (based on an impediment predating the wedding, such as impotence) and legal separations (divorces from bed and board, or a mensa et thoro), which gave neither party the right to

———

rized divorces that recognized abusive husbands as deserters.

The story of Connecticut's transition from issuing exceptional decrees like Pardee's to adding "intolerable cruelty" to statutory divorce grounds in the 1840s belongs in a history of 19th-century American family law and marital separation policies. See Michael Grossberg, *Governing the Hearth: Law and the Family in Nineteenth-Century America* (Chapel Hill, N.C., 1985), for aspects of family law other than divorce. There exists no modern study offering an overview of changes in divorce law in the United States for the post-1790 period.

6. When Francis Fane, king's counsel and standing counsel to the Board of Trade, submitted a report in 1733 on the compatibility of Connecticut laws with the law of England, his succinct comment on the colony's divorce statute was, "This Act is very different from the Law of England and seems proper to be repealed tho' the making [of] some law about divorces in particular cases may not be unreasonable." Although not a royal colony, Connecticut was bound by imperial policy not to pass laws at variance with English law. See Francis Fane, *Reports on the Laws of Connecticut*, ed. Charles M. Andrews ([New Haven], 1915), 10, 23, 29, 73–74.

remarry. From the 1690s on, Parliament sparingly granted divorces a vinculo (with permission to remarry) to noble or wealthy men who assumed the high costs of pursuing a private bill in order to rid themselves of an adulterous and estranged wife.[7]

The Puritan founders of New England took a very different approach to troubled marriages. Because they viewed marriage as a civil contract rather than a sacrament, marital disputes could properly fall under the aegis of secular courts. Furthermore, the New Englanders followed Martin Luther's reasoning: as with any other contract, the gross misbehavior of one spouse in breaking the terms, notably through neglect or infidelity, should abrogate the contract and free the aggrieved party to remarry. Finally, Puritan divines promoting law reform in seventeenth-century England urged that the sexes be treated equally with respect to grounds for divorce, just as they urged men and women be held equally accountable for sexual transgressions. Consequently, the colonies of New Haven, Connecticut, and Massachusetts Bay each agreed to hear divorce petitions and granted selected petitions as early as the 1630s.[8]

Beyond their argument with Anglican definitions of marriage, early New England lawmakers conceived of divorce as a means to forestall the widespread practice of bigamy that afflicted Britain and colonial jurisdictions where divorce was unavailable. In early modern Britain the poor and nonelite resorted to several mechanisms of self-divorce: most often through desertion and illegal remarriage, although sometimes with community sanction through regional folk customs such as wife sales or returning the wedding ring. English historians conclude that in many of these broken marriages the deserted wife and her children were left

---

7. Lawrence Stone, *Road to Divorce: England, 1530–1987* (New York, 1990), chaps. 6–10; Sybil Wolfram, "Divorce in England, 1700–1857," *Oxford Journal of Legal Studies*, V (1985), 155–186. The third option open to the wealthy, a private deed of separation, did not emanate from a judicial or legislative decree.

8. On Puritans' ideas about divorce, see Chilton Latham Powell, *English Domestic Relations, 1487–1653* . . . (New York, 1917), 69–100; Nancy F. Cott, "Divorce and the Changing Status of Women in Eighteenth-Century Massachusetts," *WMQ*, XXXIII (1976), 589, 600; Linda K. Kerber, *Women of the Republic: Intellect and Ideology in Revolutionary America* (Chapel Hill, N.C., 1980), 159–160. Keith Thomas discusses Puritans' emphasis on equal treatment of the sexes in "The Double Standard," *Journal of the History of Ideas*, XX (1959), 203–204. In barring the guilty party from remarriage, early New Englanders followed the "Reformatio Legum Ecclesiasticarum," canon law reforms proposed by radical Protestants in the mid-16th century (Stone, *Road to Divorce*, 302).

destitute and forced onto the poor rolls or into the workhouse.[9] In the North American colonies, ending an unhappy marriage through mutual agreement or desertion was not infrequent. Abandoned wives, still formally under the disabilities of coverture and thus theoretically unable to engage independently in economic transactions and lawsuits, often coped by joining their parents' or siblings' households. Alternatively, communities appear to have protected abandoned women by sanctioning their self-support through industry or remarriage, under the collective pretense that the husbands were dead. Nonetheless, the property and status of such family units lacking a legitimate male head were inevitably precarious, being continually subject to legal challenge or the husband's surprise return. In their concern to provide women with an escape from such uncertainty, New England authorities demonstrated their anxiety over both the perceived instability of female-headed families and the sexual temptation that might lure abandoned wives into adultery.[10]

In the early decades of settlement, magistrates across New England eschewed a double standard when they considered men's and women's divorce petitions based on desertion or adultery. Consequently, since most broken marriages in this era were caused by a husband's flight, women in seventeenth-century Massachusetts Bay and Connecticut petitioned for divorce three or four times more often than men, nearly two-thirds of them citing desertion and at least 80 percent of them winning

9. Lawrence Stone, *The Family, Sex, and Marriage in England, 1500–1800* (New York, 1977), 38–41; Samuel Pyeatt Menefee, *Wives for Sale: An Ethnographic Study of British Popular Divorce* (New York, 1981), esp. 20–23, 27; Stone, *Road to Divorce,* chap. 6.

10. Stone, *Road to Divorce,* 161; Mary Beth Norton, *Liberty's Daughters: The Revolutionary Experience of American Women, 1750–1800* (Boston, 1980), 47; remarks by Norma Basch, "An Open Discussion on Women's Legal History, 1730–1830," 14th Annual Meeting of the American Society for Legal History, Newark, N.J., Oct. 19, 1984. For local magistrates who overlooked self-divorces and remarriages, see Powell, *English Domestic Relations,* 66–100.

For a discussion of the rationale for divorce in early Massachusetts Bay, see D. Kelly Weisberg, " 'Under Greet Temptations Heer': Women and Divorce in Puritan Massachusetts," *Feminist Studies,* II (1975), 186–189. The concern over how abandoned wives could support themselves persisted into the 18th century. In a 1717 exchange of letters between educated gentlemen over a deserted wife, Samuel Mix reported, "I think the poor woman hath been much pinched and streightened thro the want of a sutable provider" (Mix to Mr. Richard Edwards, Sept. 19, 1717, Conn. Archives, Crimes and Misdemeanors, 1st Ser., III, 295).

the desired separation.[11] The pattern changed, however, in eighteenth-century Massachusetts when county courts no longer granted divorces. The governor and Council now heard divorce pleas, and, since no colony statute on divorce existed, they hewed closely to the canon law guidelines for marital separation that were followed in English ecclesiastical courts. This meant that they discouraged petitions based on desertion and cruelty. Indeed, in the 1692–1786 period only slightly more wives than husbands requested separations; furthermore, husbands enjoyed a higher success rate. Although nearly all of the Massachusetts wives who had cited adultery as primary or secondary grounds before 1700 won divorces, between 1700 and 1774 wives dared to cite adultery only with other grounds, and even then they met with a success rate under 50 percent. Clearly, a double standard with respect to adultery characterized Massachusetts divorce practice from the early 1700s until the Revolutionary era.[12]

Connecticut inhabitants, however, saw no dramatic shift from the seventeenth to eighteenth centuries in the reception of wives' petitions based on adultery and desertion. The proportion of wives petitioning and their success rates on those grounds remained remarkably constant.[13] The structural stability of Connecticut divorce policy was due

11. Weisberg, " 'Under Greet Temptations Heer,' " *Feminist Studies,* II (1975), 186–189; Lyle Koehler, *A Search for Power: The "Weaker Sex" in Seventeenth-Century New England* (Urbana, Ill., 1980), 152–153 and appendix 1.

12. Cott, "Divorce in Massachusetts," *WMQ,* XXXIII (1976), 587n, 599–608. See also her "Eighteenth-Century Family and Social Life Revealed in the Massachusetts Divorce Records," *Journal of Social History,* X (1976–1977), 20–43.

Both Massachusetts and Rhode Island considered divorce petitions without a unified divorce code until 1786 and 1798, respectively. For Rhode Island, see George Elliott Howard, *A History of Matrimonial Institutions . . .* (Chicago, 1904), II, 360–366; and Sheldon S. Cohen, "The Broken Bond: Divorce in Providence County, 1749–1809," *Rhode Island History,* XLIV (1985), 67–79. For New Hampshire, see Cohen, "What Man Hath Put Asunder: Divorce in New Hampshire, 1681–1784," *Historical New Hampshire,* XLI (1986), 118–141.

13. Note that Connecticut and New Haven residents did not advance adultery charges through divorce petitions before 1672 (see Appendix 1). In that year, with the first outright adultery prosecution in which the confessing pair (John Slead and Abigail Betts) were ordered whipped and branded but not executed, colony residents could be satisfied that a husband charging his spouse with adultery (or vice versa) would no longer hold "her Life . . . in . . . [his] hand" (Joint deposition of Samuel and Hepsiba Dibble [May 26, 1669], Rex v. Israel Dibble and Deborah Bartlett, Samuel Wyllys Papers, 62, CSL). In the same month, the General Court

in large part to its loyalty to a 1667 statute that fixed the permissible grounds for divorce without regard to the sex of the petitioner. Evidence of "adultery, fraudulent contract, or willfull desertion for three years with totall neglect of duty" earned the innocent spouse a full divorce. Unlike Massachusetts, Connecticut throughout the eighteenth century granted only divorces a vinculo, eschewing bed-and-board separations that Puritan reformers had denounced as "a mere popish invention." Securer as a charter colony than post-1691 Massachusetts Bay with its charter-cum-royal governor, Connecticut chose to retain certain Puritan legalisms far longer than any other English-speaking jurisdiction.[14]

The emphasis on divorces a vinculo and the requirement of only three years to establish desertion made Connecticut's divorce policy the most liberal in New England and, indeed, in the English-speaking world. Whereas the British Parliament and the governor and Council of Massachusetts each allowed fewer than 150 marital separations between 1670 and 1799, Connecticut magistrates considered and granted nearly 1,000 divorce petitions.[15] With a few exceptions in the seventeenth cen-

---

removed adultery from the capital list (John D. Cushing, ed., *The Earliest Laws of the New Haven and Connecticut Colonies, 1639–1673* [Wilmington, Del., 1977], 76–77, 83–84). A similar shift occurred in other New England colonies around this time. See Koehler, *Search for Power,* 147; and John M. Murrin, "Magistrates, Sinners, and a Precarious Liberty: Trial by Jury in Seventeenth-Century New England," in David D. Hall et al., eds., *Saints and Revolutionaries: Essays on Early American History* (New York, 1984), 190–191.

14. For the full text of the 1667 statute, see *PR*, II, 328. The 1656 Code for New Haven Colony provided for divorce on the grounds of male impotence predating marriage, of adultery, and of desertion; for the latter two, the lawmakers cited Mat. 19:9 and 1 Cor. 7:15 (*NHCR*, I, 586, II, 479). During the period in which New Haven and Connecticut were separate colonies, the latter did not pass a statute on divorce, but it heard and granted divorce petitions case by case. Except for a clause contained within a 1717 bigamy act that clarified policy for spouses of those lost at sea (*PR*, VI, 27), no amendments were made to the Connecticut divorce statute until 1797.

"Popish invention": Stone, *Road to Divorce,* 302.

Zephaniah Swift, reviewing Connecticut's laws in 1795, explained that the courts and the legislature, except in one "special" instance, had avoided granting divorces a mensa et thoro, because these placed separated spouses under an "irresistible temptation to the commission of adultery, unless they possess more frigidity, or more virtue than usually falls to the share of human beings" (*System of Laws,* I, 193). The one exception was the bed-and-board divorce granted to Susanna Strong in 1791 (*PRS*, VII, 282).

15. Stone, *Family, Sex, and Marriage,* 37–41; Stone, *Road to Divorce,* chap. 10; Cott, "Divorce in Massachusetts," *WMQ,* XXXIII (1976), 586–614. The 1,000 figure for

tury and again in the 1790s, all of these were divorce decrees that omitted arrangements for property division or child custody. Implicit in Connecticut's handling of divorce was the understanding that, when a wife proved a successful petitioner, she would retain one-third of the marital property, as if her husband had died intestate. But when a wife was cast as the guilty party, she had no legal claims to any property or support from her former husband.

Not hedged in by restrictive grounds, petitioners in Connecticut encountered a less intimidating and burdensome divorce process than supplicants elsewhere. Instead of traveling to the legislative sessions, Connecticut residents could with much less cost and effort petition the Superior Court, which convened semiannually at each county seat. Because of this easier access to the primary court of jurisdiction and because of the three-year desertion clause, women constituted a far larger proportion of divorce petitioners in Connecticut than in either eighteenth-century England or Massachusetts. Moreover, their petitions were rarely denied.

Most divorce petitioners in Connecticut saw their requests granted by the judges with a minimum of fuss. In a typical case, the fact of the husband's desertion and nonsupport for three years was corroborated by several witnesses, such as neighbors and kin of the couple; the husband, long gone from the colony, had no interest in contesting the decree. Undoubtedly, the initial episode of estrangement or adultery often caused families acute embarrassment and shame. One man complained that his marital troubles had "become a Towne talk," and another noted that his wife's perfidy "was known In the Day of It I Suppose to most part of the Cuntrey."[16] But the divorce itself usually proved anticlimactic.

Connecticut, 1670–1799, is based on the 37 divorces granted by the Court of Assistants and the General Court, 1670–1710 (see Appendix 1); the 123 divorces granted by that court, 1711–1749, according to a list made by Benjamin Trumbull in 1788 (Sheldon S. Cohen, " 'To Parts of the World Unknown': Divorce in Connecticut, 1750–1797," *Canadian Review of American Studies,* XI [1980], 277); Cohen's count of 839 petitions before the Superior Court, 1750–1797, assuming at least an 80% success rate (275); and the 31 divorces granted by the General Assembly, 1711–1799. I estimate that the Superior Court granted about 70 divorces statewide in 1798 and 1799. All of these data yield a count of roughly 930 divorces granted in 18th-century Connecticut, which may be an undercount.

16. Petition of Hugh Mackey (May 1682), Conn. Archives, Crimes and Misdemeanors, 1st Ser., III, 217b; "A True Abreviate of the Case of Richard Edwards," III, 235a.

Yet on occasion husbands used the petitioning process to urge the judges to establish "precedentiall" limits to a wife's manueverability within a troubled marriage.[17] When a wife left her husband's household because of cruel treatment or irreconcilable differences, husbands tended to adopt the speech of outraged propertyowners: they demanded their spouses be returned to them or that they be rid of such "Disloyal" and "obstinate" dependents. In seventeenth-century Connecticut, judges more often than not refused to grant men's petitions in these situations of estrangement, explicitly insisting that the couples be reconciled on loving terms and implicitly suggesting that the husband was partly or largely to blame. After 1710, when the Superior Court set aside the more informal, case-by-case approach of its Puritan predecessors, it became clear that men's petitions based on a wife's desertion would be received sympathetically. If an estranged wife protested the justice of her husband's plea for a divorce, her reasoning was invariably rejected. If a mistreated wife petitioned in her own right for a divorce based solely on cruelty grounds, the Connecticut magistrates balked. Although the jurisdiction's relatively generous divorce policy operated as protective legislation for abandoned wives, eighteenth-century judges drew the line at sending any signal that might encourage wifely independence.

Contested divorce cases in eighteenth-century Connecticut reveal that the legacy of Puritan reformers did not include dismantling the edifice of coverture that guaranteed a husband's power to dominate. Although seventeenth-century Puritan sermons advanced the vision of marriage as partnership between interdependent, mutually respecting adults, the divorce policy that grew out of Puritan foundations and crystallized in the early eighteenth century was structured so that it would in no way undermine the common law's customary definition of the balance of power between husbands and wives. In New England as well as England, entering into marriage meant that the husband owned his wife's labor and controlled her property; he enjoyed wide discretion to punish her corporally; and he could collect damages from any person who injured or seduced her.[18] Finally, he alone could determine the

17. This was the word Hugh Mackey used in his 1682 petition.

18. Puritan sermons: Carol F. Karlsen, *The Devil in the Shape of a Woman: Witchcraft in Colonial New England* (New York, 1987), 162–173; Edmund S. Morgan, *The Puritan Family: Religion and Domestic Relations in Seventeenth-Century New England* (New York, 1966), chap. 2.

For New Haven examples of men's suing over bodily injury to a daughter or wife,

family's domicile, its livelihood, the size and nature of its debts, and ultimately the ways in which the children would be raised. Husbandly desertion entailed a man's abdication of these powers. In contrast, the wife's role was defined in terms of neither legal power nor property rights. Legally she had no veto over her husband's decisions, and she could not collect damages from her husband's mistress.[19] In the eyes of the law, her duty as a wife was to provide services: household management, primary care of children, sexual access to her body. Wifely desertion was a woman's withdrawal of these services, an act that contravened her marital vow of obedience.

The Connnecticut divorce policy that took its full shape in the early eighteenth century not only defined desertion in differing ways for husbands and wives, but it sidestepped interfering with any of the attributes of patriarchal marriage. A long-suffering wife could be freed from a husband who utterly neglected his familial responsibilities, but a woman who challenged her spouse's decisions, no matter how abusive his behavior, received no relief from the divorce law. Behind the reluctance to admit cruelty to the list of grounds was an unwillingness to cede to women a significant measure of power in determining the limits to male authority in marriage. Generated in a culture in which woman's destiny was equated with wifehood and motherhood and in which women were assumed to be inferior to men, Connecticut's record shows that the granting of divorces was shadowed by the fear of independent wives.

———

Certain patterns characterized Connecticut's divorce caseload consistently throughout the seventeenth and eighteenth centuries. Notable among these were the rarity of denied petitions, the availability of divorce on adultery grounds to women as well as men, and, finally, the proclivity of husbands for selecting inflammatory language to describe the misdeeds of deserting or cuckolding wives. However, there were subtle differences between seventeenth- and eighteenth-century judicial

———

see William Edwards v. Joseph Perkins (June 1668), NHCC, I, 13, 18, 20; Samuel Hemingway v. Nathaniel Finch (June 1694), I, 220; Jonathan Crampton v. Nathaniel Bishop (Jan. 1775), NHCC Files, dr. 59; John Spaulding v. Ezra Curtis (Dec. 1788), dr. 81.

19. Keith Thomas explores the "deeply entrenched idea that woman's chastity was not her own to dispose of" in "The Double Standard," *Journal of the History of Ideas*, XX (1959), 209–216 (quote on 212).

attitudes toward divorce. Seventeenth-century judges manifested a distinctive tendency to see divorce decrees as a means of both preventing sin and regrouping abandoned spouses into stable, male-headed family units. (For a complete list of divorce petitions submitted to the courts of Connecticut and New Haven colonies before 1711, see Appendix 1). To New England's founders, instable households were a sure sign of social disorder. Their receptivity to divorce was of a piece with not only their legislation requiring young unmarried men to live with families rather than in group households but also their prosecutions of spouses who lived apart from mates left behind in England.[20] Lone husbands or wives, it was believed, were subject to intense temptations to enter into extramarital sexual liaisons — sins that would cause God to frown on New England's holy experiment. If clandestine marriages, widespread bigamy, and unpunished adultery were to characterize the young colonies, disaster might ensue.

Faced with scattered instances of abandoned spouses, seventeenth-century magistrates forged practical, ad hoc remedies (including specific property and custody settlements) that sometimes flew in the face of received legal traditions. Less concerned about flagrant departures from the canon and common law than their eighteenth-century counterparts, Puritan magistrates allowed divorces to proceed with a transparency that would disappear in later decades. In other words, their desire to see estranged spouses who still lived in the area either reconciled or placed beyond the dangers of adultery and poverty outweighed any sense of obligation to follow procedural proprieties. From the twin impulses of watching over the security of families and deemphasizing male tyranny flowed an early divorce policy that was surprisingly receptive to women's voices. Thus divorce joined a string of legal actions — debt, fornication, rape — that betrayed the seventeenth-century system's openness to women's concerns and claims, an openness that would largely disappear after the turn of the century.

One aspect of the transparency of the seventeenth-century divorce process in Connecticut is that the documents and claims submitted by seventeenth-century divorce petitioners frequently captured the acts of self-divorce that were not uncommon in the era. Admitting his desertion

20. Morgan, *The Puritan Family*, 39, 145–146. For early New Haven rules and cases against young men living alone, see *NHCR*, I, 70; *NHTR*, I, 370–371, II, 186; NHCC, I, 139. Orders for spouses to return to distant mates are found at NHCC, I, 248, 254, 257, II, 161–162, 211, 215. Prosecutions in both areas petered out after 1700.

TABLE 4
Divorce Cases: New Haven Colony (1639–1666) and Connecticut Colony (1639–1710)

	Granted	Denied	Mooted/ No Action	Unknown	Total
Women Filing					
Desertion	23	1	0	3	27
Adultery	2	0	0	0	2
Desertion and adultery	5	0	0	0	5
Fraudulent contract	3	0	1	0	4
Other	2	1	1[a]	0	4
Total	35	2	2	3	42
Men Filing					
Desertion	4	2	0	0	6
Adultery	2	1[a]	0	0	3
Desertion and adultery	2	1	1	0	4
Fraudulent contract	0	1	1	0	2
Total	8	5	2	0	15

[a]These cases were first deferred or denied by the Court of Assistants; then, in a second step, a separate petition for divorce was submitted to the General Assembly, where the divorce was granted. Thus these petitions are also counted in the Granted column and are represented as two separate cases (as are any other repeated petitions) in the Total column.

Sources: PR, I–V; *NHCR*, II; Conn. Archives, Crimes and Misdemeanors, 1st Ser., I, III; Samuel Wyllys Papers (1632–1709), CSL; *Recs. Ct. of Assts.*, Lacy transcript, I, II; Early General Records, LVI (1663–1665), R.G. 1, CSL.

and adultery, Zachary Dibble had two men witness his letter to his wife Sarah announcing "untoo all to [w]home [It] may . . . Concerne that I doe freely And willingly upon Serious Consideration discharge and disowne you as a wife." Describing himself as "formerly Called your husband," Dibble added that he hoped "to Receive a positive anser . . . unto the same purpose" from Sarah — who had already retaken her maiden name. Not all self-separating spouses could resort to written declarations. Many chose emphatic oral renunciations aimed to reach spouse and community and delivered either at the moment of departure or when an inquiring hometown resident sought them out in a distant city.[21]

Occasionally the passion of spousal enmity colored the act of disowning: on the verge of deserting, David Sage, Jr., boasted to neighbors that "he would Leave" his wife "and give her Rope Enough to hang her Self." In a malevolent twist to the typical renunciation formula, William Reynolds delivered a threat that revealed his understanding of the criteria for divorce. As he left his New Haven family for a final time, Reynolds warned that he would "send . . . [Elizabeth] a letter once in 3 yeares to binde her from marrying while he lived." (On a previous occasion, Reynolds had "curst and swore in a terrible manner" and declared "That if he could get . . . [his wife] away he would Either breake her heart or Else he would sell her.")[22] Others parted on more generous terms, sharing an implicit understanding that both should be free to "take their courses" and remarry. Colonial judges were not averse to granting a divorce even

21. Dibble case: Conn. Archives, Crimes and Misdemeanors, 1st Ser., III, 214. For emphatic oral renunciations, see Joanna Pember's divorce (Oct. 1687), PR, III, 23; Testimony of Samuel Curcum (May 1703), Divorce case of Abigail Crow, Conn. Archives, Crimes and Misdemeanors, 1st Ser., III, 268. In one of three letters that Ruth Gutsell wrote her spouse from Rhode Island where she had fled from a marriage without love, she declared "I am well Contented to be at . . . [this] distance from you. . . . I never intend to have anything to do with you as my husband and therefor desire this may be our farwell" (Apr. 13, 1683, Conn. Archives, Crimes and Misdemeanors, 1st Ser., III, 224). See the renunciation couched in legal vocabulary in merchant Richard Edward's petition, III, 235c, 238b.

22. Joint deposition of Philip Goff and Naomi Goff, Divorce case of Marie Sage (1703–1705), Crimes and Misdemeanors, 1st Ser., III, 278; Testimony of Joseph Tuttle (Oct. 13, 1701), and Joint deposition of Mercy and Ebenezer Frost, Divorce case of Elizabeth Reynolds, III, 264–265. To prove desertion, wives needed to demonstrate that for at least three years they had received from their husband no visits or letters pledging support or his return. For a similar case to the Reynoldses', see divorce granted to Elizabeth Sedgwick, Recs. Ct. of Assts., Lacy transcript, I, 54–55.

if they learned that both spouses wanted one.[23] As long as evidence of one spouse's desertion, adultery, or impotence had not been fabricated, the magistrates would be able to identify a guilty party, and collusion — at least in the strict legal sense — would be held at bay.

In the interest of forestalling cases of persistent adultery, Connecticut judges in the early colonial period proved willing to overlook the sexual lapses of abandoned spouses. In four cases between 1669 and 1702, the Court of Assistants granted divorces to spouses (three women and one man) whom proof, confession, or rumor showed had committed adultery after being deserted. In the most blatant example, the bench in 1701 convicted Elizabeth Reynolds and ordered her severely whipped for bearing a child by William Hoadley during the time her husband was absent. One year later found the same judges agreeing with the logic of Elizabeth's plea for a divorce: she looked upon it as in "both [her] Duty and Intrest to use all Lawfull . . . meanes to prevent further Sin and Sorrow." Elizabeth's divorce decree included the standard phrase that she now was at "Libertie to marry with any meet and Suitable person." Soon local authorities approved her union with her lover, despite the fact that such a marriage was in direct contravention of the canon law principle that barred a convicted adulterer from marrying his or her paramour.[24] The ad hoc remedies forged for Elizabeth Reynolds and others show that, as late as 1702, Connecticut magistrates thought less in terms of English law than of biblical injunction: "To avoide fornication, let everie man have his wife, and let everie woman have her owne housband" (1 Cor. 7:2).

Perhaps the most doleful cry over the sexual vulnerability of deserted

---

23. I have rephrased Robert Jarrad's statement that he "wished . . . [his wife] to take her course" (Divorce case of Elizabeth Jarrad [Oct. 1674], *Recs. Ct. of Assts.*, Lacy transcript, I, 55).

As an example of both parties' wanting divorce, Marie Babbitt, notified of her husband's pending divorce hearing, told the serving officer "that they [the court] Might doe what they pleased" (Divorce case of Erasmus Babbitt [May 1700], Conn. Archives, Crimes and Misdemeanors, 1st Ser., III, 260). Over time, renunciations came to serve as partial proof of desertion. See the case of Jonathan Jennings (May 1709), III, 280–282.

24. *Recs. Ct. of Assts.*, Lacy transcript, I, 358–359, II, 396; Jacobus, *FANH*, 631. See also the Divorce case of Elizabeth Jarrad (Oct. 1674), *Recs. Ct. of Assts.*, Lacy transcript, I, 56; and the divorce granted to Mary Barns (May 1669), I, 12. For English ecclesiastical rules, see R. H. Helmholz, *Marriage Litigation in Medieval England* (Cambridge, 1974), 94–97.

spouses came from the wealthy Hartford merchant Richard Edwards in 1691. Faced with a contrary and mentally ill wife who refused to sleep with him and praised other men to his face, Edwards rued the fact that he had already "Dishonour[ed] . . . God" by yielding to his "own Naughty Hart" and pleaded that he "Bee Extricated out of those many and Dredfull Temtations to sin Against God, which Continuing . . . I Doe unavoydabley Lye under." He underscored the point with poetical flourish: "Neither is my Strength the Strength of Stones, nor My flesh of Brass, Alwayes to Bare sutch things." Despite his admission to sexual indiscretions, Edwards got his divorce on the grounds that his wife's neglect of her marital duties and her cruel rejection of him amounted to desertion.[25]

Since the flirtations or liaisons by these deserted or jilted spouses were not precipitants but consequences of abandonment, granting them permission to remarry did not threaten the basic framework of fault divorce that most Protestant reformers supported. However, the authorities' response to Ebenezer Hill's situation in 1692 indicates that some New England leaders were prepared in unusual cases to unite adulterous couples even if the action contravened the customary pattern of rewarding only the innocent spouse with the option of remarriage.[26] Thirty-six-year-old Hill had been convicted in county court of having an extramarital affair with and a child by young Abigail Wooden. A few months later, Hill's wife, Mercy, persuaded the higher bench to give her a divorce, partly relying on the contention that a reconciliation was impossible. "If either his words or actions may be beleived," she said of her husband, he "Intends Still to adhere to that person with whom he hath had such

<hr>

25. Divorce petition of Richard Edwards to the General Assembly (undated), Conn. Archives, Crimes and Misdemeanors, 1st Ser., III, 238; *PR*, IV, 52–53, 59. The late 17th century was also a time of legal experimentation in non-Puritan colonies; in New York, where a smattering of divorces were allowed up to 1675, one divorced woman suspected of adultery before the divorce was explicitly permitted to remarry (Matteo Spalletta, "Divorce in Colonial New York," *New-York Historical Society Quarterly*, XXXIX [1955], 430–431).

26. In Connecticut, the ban on remarriage for the guilty party in divorce cases was never made explicit in the lawbooks or divorce decrees. However, it was strongly implied by the formula of divorce decrees that declared the innocent, petitioning party "single and unmarried" or discharged from his or her previous bonds of matrimony (SCR, II, 15, VI, [unpaginated], Sept. 1734 session, Divorce granted to Sarah Maltby). On the debates in England whether such remarriage should be explicitly banned or permitted, see Stone, *Road to Divorce*, 302–308, 335–339.

unlawfull fellowship." Not atypically, Mercy resumed use of her maiden name and remarried within a year. What is extraordinary is that when the divorced Ebenezer Hill and his lover appeared "in open Court" and "desired . . . to be marryed," the governor stepped forward and performed the ceremony.[27] In the next century, the ethic of preventing sin through ad hoc remedies such as the Hill-Wooden marriage faded. Secular authorities would not knowingly sanction the marriage of a guilty party in a divorce case.

The seventeenth-century bench responded concretely to deserted wives who had been left with small children and little property, forced to shift for themselves and depend on "the charity of freinds and neighbours." Knowing that women alone had practically no means of securing an adequate family livelihood and angered at the irresponsibility of absconding husbands, the magistrates sought to stabilize at the moment of the divorce decree the economic situation of what they hoped would only temporarily be a female-headed household. For example, when the court set Mary Browne "at liberty . . . to be marryed to any other man If shee see cause so to doe," they further ordered "that the remaynder of estate left in her posession be to her use and [the] childrens." Within seven months, thirty-two-year-old Mary married a local widower.[28]

With such property orders, the judges were often merely preserving the portion of clothes and modest property that a woman had brought into the marriage or preventing the further drainage of meager household necessaries to creditors. In divorce cases following a man's notorious adultery, however, the judges felt free to exceed the customary arrangement that entitled an innocent, divorced wife to one-third of the marital estate.[29] After convicting David Ensign of carrying on a long

27. Divorce case of Mercy Hill (May 1692), *Recs. Ct. of Assts.,* Lacy transcript, I, 183; Conn. Archives, Crimes and Misdemeanors, 1st Ser., III, 240; NHCC, I, 201; Jacobus, *FANH,* 336; Rex v. Ebenezer Hill (Nov. 1691), NHCC, I, 193. For the marriage, NHCC, I, 199. There is no evidence that family connections, public roles, or wealth influenced either the governor to favor Hill or, later, the magistrates to favor his ex-wife in a custody dispute (see below, this chapter).

28. *Recs. Ct. of Assts.,* Lacy transcript, I, 53–54; Jacobus, *FANH,* 346.

29. For judges' preservation of some portion of a small estate for a woman who had earned a divorce, see the Divorce granted to Elizabeth Sedgwick (Oct. 1674), *Recs. Ct. of Assts.,* Lacy transcript, I, 54–55; Divorce granted to Bridget Baxter (May 1662), *PR,* I, 37–39. Hannah Hall in her March 1730/1 petition referred to "the Custom and usage" of granting to the innocent wife "all that estate real or personal

affair with a neighbor's wife, the court granted Mehitable Ensign's request for a divorce and also directed, first, that her husband's personal estate be "equally divided" between them and, second, that Mehitable not be "Mollested" or removed from the house she then lived in.[30] In denying a man access to and the ability to sell his own homestead (property to which he held title), seventeenth-century judges delivered a sharp, punishing rebuke to male adulterers. The early authorities also demonstrated that they were less worried than later jurists about infringing on traditional masculine prerogatives when a moral issue was at stake.

In the area of child custody, seventeenth-century Connecticut judges showed a similar independence from common law tradition. The 1676 and 1692 divorce cases of Elizabeth Rogers and Mercy Hill were probably the first American cases in which courts granted custody to the mother. We can see these two cases as Puritan foreshadowings of the early-nineteenth-century appellate rulings that launched the "tender years" doctrine (fit mothers should have custody of young children) and that announced to the world that American family law would modify patriarchal constructs well in advance of British law.[31] Recoiling with horror from John Rogers's heretical renunciation of the Puritan way and his mistreatment of his wife Elizabeth, the General Court sanctioned Elizabeth's taking their children to live with her father and granted her a divorce. One year later, Elizabeth (now using her maiden name) petitioned the Assembly again, this time asking "that she might have her children continued with her and brought up by her and not with John Rogers, he being so hettridox in his opinion and practice." The deputies not only agreed that the children should "be brought up and nurtured

---

that" she brought into the marriage "that is not spent or disposed of" (Divorce petition of Hannah Hall, NHSC Files, dr. 716).

For confirmation of the practice of assigning a divorced women, if the aggrieved party, her thirds, see Swift, *System of Laws*, I, 192–193.

30. Divorce case of Mehitable Ensign (Oct. 1682), *Recs. Ct. of Assts.*, Lacy transcript, I, 118. For a similar prohibition against a divorced, adulterous husband's entering his own house, see the Divorce case of Mercy Hill (May 1692), I, 183, and NHCC, I, 201.

31. Jamil S. Zainaldin, "The Emergence of a Modern American Family Law: Child Custody, Adoption, and the Courts, 1796–1851," *Northwestern University Law Review*, LXXIII (1979), 1038–1089; Grossberg, *Governing the Hearth*, 234–250.

by" Elizabeth and her father "in admonition and fear of the Lord," but they ordered the "vile" Rogers to pay annual child support.[32]

Almost twenty years later, the Court of Assistants sat in judgment of the divorce petition brought by Mercy Hill against her adulterous husband Ebenezer—a situation less highly charged than the Rogers case, but one that involved a husband's serious moral breach nonetheless. Discovering that Ebenezer's remaining property consisted of one-quarter of an acre with a "small and unfinished Dwelling house," one cow, one swine, and "Some few necessaries," the judges instructed Mercy upon her divorce to keep this estate "in her hands . . . for the bringing up of her Children, and for their benefitt after her decease." Two months later Mercy was forced to come before the town magistrates because Ebenezer had "taken and detained her Child Hannah Hill against hers the mothers Consent." The authorities left no doubt about who was to have custody of thirteen-year-old Hannah and seven-year-old Mary. They ordered Hill to return Hannah "to be and remane under the care and Charge of her said Mother. And . . . Hill was further enjoined upon [risk] of Contempt of Authority to Refraine [from] Comeing to the house of the said Mercy and that he meddle not with the estate or Children."[33]

Seventeenth-century magistrates appear to have issued explicit orders in contested custody cases only when they perceived the guilty divorced parent, father or mother, as incapable of raising children in a properly religious and moral household.[34] In practice, the judges knew that nearly all deserted wives who won divorces would retain de facto custody

32. Although the General Court reserved the right to change the custody order, there is no record that it ever did so. For the Rogers divorce and related lawsuits, see *Recs. Ct. of Assts.*, Lacy transcript, I, 60–61, 72; *PR*, II, 292, 326; Conn. Archives, Crimes and Misdemeanors, 1st Ser., I, 73–79.

33. Divorce case of Mercy Hill (May 1692), *Recs. Ct. of Assts.*, Lacy transcript, I, 183; Conn. Archives, Crimes and Misdemeanors, 1st Ser., III, 240–241; Jacobus, *FANH*, 741. For the July 1692 custody order, see NHCC, I, 201.

34. Learning of the scandalous ménage à trois in which John Betts, his wife, and her lover had shared a household for some time, the higher court ordered the lovers punished for adultery and granted John Betts a divorce. It also instructed Betts to "take and keep" the eldest child "and dispose of the same so as it may be well educated and brought up in the fear of the lord." The *other* children of the household, whom Betts now denied fathering, were allowed to remain with their mother, whom authorities presumably saw as hopelessly degenerate. *Recs. Ct. of Assts.*, Lacy transcript, I, 37–39.

of any minor children of the marriage, since absconded husbands usually made no parental claims. Thus several divorced women apprenticed their children with local authorities' approval.[35] Most such arrangements proceeded smoothly, but occasionally the wastrel father returned or attempted from afar to alter the terms of the indenture. Susanna Hodge, divorced in 1692, found herself one year later embroiled in litigation because she and her ex-husband in Rhode Island had bound their daughter out to two different Connecticut men. Susanna Hodge's explanation of her action to the judges echoed with the mix of parental authority and feminine hesitation that must have characterized the responses of many deserted wives whose state was once described as being "worse than a widow." After consulting with the selectmen, Susanna recounted, she made the decision to put out her daughter, "as I am the mother of the Child and nextly to take Caer when the father had diserted." In this case, the courts upheld the mother's placement of the child over the father's arrangement. However, without consistent criteria for allocating custody, women like Susanna Hodge would continue to face the never-ending agony of uncertainty over their children's ultimate fate.[36]

What is striking about the handful of seventeenth-century court orders stipulating property settlements and child custody after divorce is the authorities' elevation of individual moral behavior over traditional patriarchal rights as a standard for judgment. In the Hodge, Hill, Rog-

35. For example, see the apprenticing of Mary Browne's children: Divorce case of Mary Browne (Oct. 1674), ibid., I, 53–54; John and Mary Clark v. John Smith, Jr. (June 1683), NHCC, I, 137. See also the apprenticeship arrangements and divorce case of Frances Goreing (Oct. 1685), *Recs. Ct. of Assts.*, Lacy transcript, I, 132–133, 146.

36. For the Hodges: see Divorce case of Susanna Hodge (May 1692), *Recs. Ct. of Assts.*, Lacy transcript, I, 183; Joseph Butler v. Samuel Collins, I, 190–191: Conn. Archives, Private Controversies, 1st Ser., IV, 123–131. For a deserting husband who threatened to make his own arrangements to bind out a daughter he left behind, see Divorce case of Elizabeth Jarrad (Oct. 1674), *Recs. Ct. of Assts.*, Lacy transcript, I, 55–56.

Child custody became a regular, official part of Connecticut divorce proceedings only with an 1837 amendment to the divorce statute; see *The Public Statute Laws of the State of Connecticut* (Hartford, 1839), 187. In the 1711–1789 period, at least among New Haven County cases, no divorce order broached the custody issue. For a father's 1734 suit to recover damages when his estranged wife took their nine-year-old daughter with her, see Alison Duncan Hirsch, "The Thrall Divorce Case: A Family Crisis in Eighteenth-Century Connecticut," *Women and History*, no. 4 (1982), 56–57.

ers, Ensign, and Brown cases, magistrates abrogated men's customary rights to control marital property and exercise absolute custody because their sinfulness or aggressive actions were perceived as egregious and dangerous. If judges had continued in this way after the 1690s, as the frequency of divorce rose, new, more equitable criteria for assessing the property needs of abandoned wives and the custody qualifications of separated spouses might have taken hold. That Connecticut judges after 1700 pulled back from their ad hoc approach to divorce cases was part of their retreat from the legacy of Puritan legal reform to the more rigid confines of English common law rules.[37] Whether the retreat came about partly because of a fear of encouraging wifely independence or solely because of broad political and cultural trends encouraging anglicization of the law, the result was a reinforcement of patriarchal authority and male property rights.

The most direct gauge of the limits of any divorce policy is those petitions that fail. Connecticut judges in the pre-1711 period denied seven requests not so much because they found the evidence faulty but because the petitioner was asking for a divorce under unusual or controversial circumstances. In all cases, the allegedly guilty spouse had not left the region and was in a position to contest the process. Sarah Whitecus discovered in 1704 that a divorce petition might be blocked if the judges believed that the offending spouse was "distracted" (mentally ill) and thus not responsible for his or her actions. In the next century the bench tended to lean in the opposite direction in such cases, granting the petitioner — especially a husband — a divorce for spousal infidelity even when the guilty party was arguably insane and would have no means of support after the divorce.[38]

Seventeenth-century magistrates, but not their eighteenth-century successors, decided to draw the line when asked by husbands to expand

37. Lawrence Stone demonstrates that uncontested in England until the mid-18th century was "the patriarchal view" that the father "had an absolute right to entire and untrammelled control over his children until they reached the age of maturity," no matter how egregious had been his own immorality or cruelty in relation to his wife (*Road to Divorce*, 170–173 [quote on 170]).

38. Whitecus case: *Recs. Ct. of Assts.*, Lacy transcript, II, 443. In contrast, Richard Edwards and Marie Sage won divorces after carefully documenting family members' and neighbors' opinions that their spouses' distraction developed only *after* they had willfully abandoned the marriage.

On infidelity and insanity in the 18th century, see the discussion of the 1758 Brockway case below, this chapter.

the concept of fraudulent contract to include a wife's premarital conception of a child by another man. Both Thomas Olmstead and John Ventrous claimed that their wives' concealment of pregnancy constituted a
fraudulent cover-up of an impediment to marriage. But rather than
arguing that female virginity was requisite to marital union, the two men
protested that loving cohabitation and sexual relations were now impossible with women "so debauched" or "so Contaminated." In an era when
out-of-wedlock births were still relatively rare, Olmstead and Ventrous
hoped they could avoid maintaining both "bastard" children and wives
whose "evill misdemeanor[s]" rang, Ventrous imagined, "the wholl
Country over." The judges admitted to having "great Difficulty" with
these cases, but in the end they refused to grant the petitions and urged
the outraged husbands "to make up the breach" and "live . . . in love and
peace" with their wives.[39] Reconciliation would ensure that the community would not become liable to support a woman who, by proper husbandly discipline, might best learn the biblical strictures of obedience
and fidelity.

The type of case that most commonly engendered "apprehensions"
and hesitation among seventeenth- and early-eighteenth-century judges
was that of a husband claiming his wife had deserted. In such petitions,
men's outrage and continuing frustration with their inability to control
women's behavior surfaced quite vividly. But in this first stage of Connecticut's divorce history, magistrates were not always swayed by husbands' diatribes against wives' disobedience. Of six pre-1711 cases based
solely on wifely desertion, three were denied by the bench, and two
others were granted only after a panel of local clergy reached consensus
that the evidence warranted a divorce. Apparently, judges were ready to
believe that wives who sought shelter with nearby family or neighbors
would not have left their spouses without good reason. Rather than act as
a reflexive reinforcer of absolute male authority when a petitioner like

39. Both men based their arguments on Matt. 19:9. Martha Olmstead admitted
the child was "not her husbands" and explained that a married man "came to me
when I was aSleep and had the advantage of me." Divorce case of Thomas Olmstead
(May 1687), *Recs. Ct. of Assts.*, Lacy transcript, I, 151, 155; Conn. Archives, Crimes
and Misdemeanors, 1st Ser., III, 228–234; Divorce case of John Ventrous (May
1694), *Recs. Ct. of Assts.*, Lacy transcript, I, 207–208; Conn. Archives, Crimes and
Misdemeanors, 1st Ser., III, 256–258. Sheldon S. Cohen claims that six Connecticut
men between 1750 and 1798 (all in counties other than New Haven) won divorces
on the grounds that their bride was pregnant by another man ("Divorce in Connecticut," *Canadian Review of American Studies*, XI [1980], 283).

James Wakeley demanded the Court "have his wife . . . sent to him" or "grant him a Bill of divorce," the bench chose the milder position of mediation, nudging fuming husbands to reform their tempestuous or arrogant behavior so as to persuade their wives that a reconciliation would meet both their interests.[40]

The judges' reluctance to buttress traditional male prerogatives in these contested cases is striking. Fifteen years before petitioning for divorce in 1676, James Wakeley had moved to Rhode Island, evidently fleeing a capital charge for witchcraft. Although he claimed that his wife Alice had abrogated her marital vows by refusing to join him, Alice proved to the court's satisfaction that James had engaged in a prenuptial agreement not to remove her from her dwelling in Wethersfield without her consent. Confronted by the facts that this couple had lived apart for fifteen years and that both parties were now asking for "freedome . . . from our former Bond," the bench announced that it saw no grounds to grant either petition and, furthermore, no cause "so to compell . . . [Alice] to remove" to Rhode Island. Even though a reconciliation was unlikely between the Wakeleys — and indeed, never took place — the court left "the matter with both the parties to agree together and to attend their duty each towards one and other."[41]

In a case twenty years later that lacked the element of a prenuptial agreement, the court chose to enforce the husband's right of cohabita-

---

40. *Recs. Ct. of Assts.*, Lacy transcript, I, 64, 155 ("apprehensions"). Disposition was far easier when the wife had left with a man or could be counted as an open adulterer. For example, see Divorce case of Thomas Gutsell (1683), Conn. Archives, Crimes and Misdemeanors, 1st Ser., III, 223–226, and *Recs. Ct. of Assts.*, Lacy transcript, I, 123; and Divorce case of Jonathan Jennings (1709), *Recs. Ct. of Assts.*, Lacy transcript, II, 647–648, and Conn. Archives, Crimes and Misdemeanors, 1st Ser., III, 279–282. The only open-and-shut case was that of Robert Wade, whose wife in England had disowned him and refused to join him in the New World (*PR,* I, 301). For councils of ministers, see the divorces granted to Richard Edwards (1691), Conn. Archives, Crimes and Misdemeanors, 1st Ser., III, 235–239; and Erasmus Babbitt (1700), *Recs. Ct. of Assts.*, Lacy transcript, I, 321, 332–333.

41. As a wealthy widow marrying Wakeley, Alice was careful to keep control over her sizable properties, which permitted her the independence that so few colonial wives could afford. For the full documentation of the divorce case and a lawsuit that followed Alice's death, see *Recs. Ct. of Assts.*, Lacy transcript, I, 64–65, 89, 159; Conn. Archives, Private Controversies, 1st Ser., I, 251–253, Crimes and Misdemeanors, 1st Ser., III, 215–216. For biographies of James Wakeley and the widow Boosey, whom he married in 1652, see John Putnam Demos, *Entertaining Satan: Witchcraft and the Culture of Early New England* (New York, 1982), 353–355.

tion while denying him the divorce he claimed he had earned. Husbands requesting divorces from deserting wives were expected to demonstrate they had made good faith efforts at reconciliation, and, by Joseph Ingram's account, he had bent over backwards during nine years of separation: "I have gone with a sloop to fetch her, I have been with horse and man . . ., [and] I have sent many messengers. . . . But no wayes nor meanes will prevail." The judges saw the situation differently: rather than acceding to Ingram's demand for a divorce, they ordered the marshal to deliver his wife and son to him in Saybrook (the charge to be paid out of the woman's estate), and there Ingram was "require[d] to receive and entertain them Curteously, and they to give due Obedience to him."[42]

The case most emblematic of the seventeenth-century judicial approach to wife desertions that resulted from serious marital disagreement was Hugh Mackey's 1682 divorce suit. In the legal tangles that extended through the Mackeys' estrangement and even beyond Hugh's death, men in authority at all levels of the court system distanced themselves from Mackey's pose as an outraged, ill-used husband. Hugh Mackey tried hard to make his situation a test case that would smooth the path for husbands to divorce and disinherit disobedient wives, yet he was rebuffed at every stage.

In his May 1682 divorce petition Mackey raised flimsy adultery charges against his wife Alice and made the unproven claim that she had beaten and abused him before her recent decision to flee his house (taking all the goods she had there "and something more," he fumed). But most galling were Alice's ungovernability and her defiant actions seeking refuge in the nearby household of a man of higher status and submitting complaints about Hugh's behavior to local authorities. "She hath Cast off the Subjection which is due by the marige Covenant from the wife to the husband, [as] appear[s] . . . in her refusing to yeld obedience to my lawful apointments," Hugh proclaimed. Ignoring the statutory requirement of three years' desertion, he argued that "surely" divorce was warranted "much more" when a wife deserted than when a husband absconded. After cataloging his wife's crimes — abuse, disobedience, desertion, conceiving a child in adultery, defaming him as impotent — Mackey delivered this parting salvo: "Honoured Gentlemen, I am . . . loath to be Trampled under my wives feet, and this case will be

42. Divorce case of Joseph Ingram (Oct. 1695), *Recs. Ct. of Assts.*, Lacy transcript, I, 228–229, and Conn. Archives, Crimes and Misdemeanors, 1st Ser., III, 259.

precedentiall, if these abuses will be allowed, we may say . . . If the case of the man be so with his wife, surely it is not good to marry."[43]

The gentlemen on the bench suspected that both Hugh and Alice had misbehaved, but not seriously enough at this juncture to warrant a divorce. They ordered Hugh "to receive his wife, and Cohabit. . . . Loveingly and peaceably," but they also warned Alice to "carry herself becoming a wife to him, and be diligent in her place for the comfort of them both." Further, the judges forbade Hugh to pursue his scheme to convey his sixteen-acre home lot to a male friend so as to "Cut off" his wife from her dower at his death. Indeed, Hugh's failure to "provide for her Maintenance according to his Estate" might have been at the root of this couple's dissension.[44]

Two months later Hugh Mackey appeared to be partially vindicated when a troubled Alice confessed before the governor that she had committed adultery with one John O'Neal. In the end neither O'Neal (who soon fled) nor Alice (who was perhaps excused for what some saw as her "simplicity") stood trial for adultery. But one would imagine that the adultery confession provided the ideal moment for the revival of Hugh's divorce plea. Instead, illness and eventually death intervened: by the spring of 1684 a close associate of the lately deceased Mackey was suing to prevent the widowed Alice from collecting her thirds. Again, the courts rejected the sweeping claim of the aggrieved surrogate husband: "The Fate of religion and the welfare of all men seems to be Concerned," he pontificated, if "an adulteresse Unreconciled to Her Husband hath [any] . . . right title or claim to his estate." Alice survived the debacle of her union with Mackey not only to retain possession of Hugh's estate but also to remarry.[45]

---

43. Divorce petition of Hugh Mackey (May 1682), Conn. Archives, Crimes and Misdemeanors, 1st Ser., III, 217. Mackey's summation was deliberately echoing Matt. 19:10 *and* a phrase heard often in colonial courts on contempt of authority charges. Alice's complaints, along with what was possibly a separate divorce plea from her, or any document offering her version of events, do not survive in the files.

44. *Recs. Ct. of Assts.,* Lacy transcript, I, 111. Suspecting that Hugh might "refuse" to receive his wife, the judges recommended that overseers be appointed to manage Mackey's estate to ensure that Alice was properly supported.

45. For the adultery confession and Alice's subsequent childbirth, see Conn. Archives, Crimes and Misdemeanors, 1st Ser., III, 218–222, and Private Controversies, 1st Ser., II, 115, 118. Hugh Mackey died sometime between June 1682 and April 1684. As late as May 1684, Mackey's designated heir "concieve[d] according to my

Personal bias perhaps influenced the authorities' unsympathetic treatment of Hugh Mackey. He was not English, but most probably a Scotsman; he chose to marry a recently freed indentured servant; he even called himself "a sorry fellow" and admitted to being disaffected from some of his fellow townsmen. But more important to the magistrates' reasoning was their concern that Alice Mackey be properly cared for—that she not become a "Charge...upon the Town" because of the actions of an obstinate, irresponsible husband.[46] Faced with contested cases in which wives had "deserted" to protest ill-treatment, seventeenth-century judges declined to fulfill the divorce fantasies of petulant husbands, emphasizing instead reconciliation and mutual toleration. Rather than rule reflexively in favor of male privilege, early magistrates imbued their decrees with a skepticism regarding husbands' claims to righteousness—a skepticism surely born of the Puritan emphasis on human depravity. When a man had not skipped town and his wife had not violated the marriage covenant in an outrageous manner, reconciliation rather than divorce was seen as the response that would preserve the social order.[47] In the next century, the meaning that authorities assigned to a wife's act of estrangement changed radically, and with the shift to scrutinizing and punishing women's shows of independence came a marked judicial commitment to making husbands' rights more absolute.

---

best Information that the matter of adultery and divorce is still depending in Court" (Petition of Theophilus Sherman, Private Controversies, 1st Ser., II, 115).

For the failed legal appeal of the probate settlement of Mackey's estate, see *Recs. Ct. of Assts.*, Lacy transcript, I, 132, and Conn. Archives, Private Controversies, 1st Ser., II, 115–121. By spring 1684 Alice appeared in the records as Alice Cook, thus presumably had remarried, unless she was resuming a previous surname.

46. Divorce petition of Hugh Mackey, Conn. Archives, Crimes and Misdemeanors, 1st Ser., III, 217; *Recs. Ct. of Assts.*, Lacy transcript, I, 111. In some respects, the Mackey case resembles the later Thrall divorce case analyzed by Hirsch ("Thrall Divorce Case," *Women and History*, no. 4 [1982], 43–75). What Linda Kerber writes of the Thrall case applies to the Mackeys' plight: to the magistrates "equal fault" on the part of both spouses "seemed to justify [consigning them] to continued misery" (*Women of the Republic*, 173).

47. Note that judges in the early period were quick to rule against utterly defiant wives—women who left the colony as open adulterers. See Divorce case of John Fish (Oct. 1680), *Recs. Ct. of Assts.*, Lacy transcript, I, 89, and Wyllys Papers, 74–75; Divorce case of Thomas Long, *Recs. Ct. of Assts.*, Lacy transcript, I, 104–105; Divorce petition of Thomas Gutsell (undated [1683]), Conn. Archives, Crimes and Misdemeanors, 1st Ser., III, 223.

In 1788 the Reverend Benjamin Trumbull of North Haven complained that Connecticut residents could obtain divorces with such "great facility" that soon there would "be few or no marriages without divorce." Trumbull worried that, if spouses could sunder their unions with very little penalty, then vice would proliferate, and the fate of the young nation would be imperiled. Although no radical, the jurist Zephaniah Swift painted a far more glowing portrait of how the state's divorce law had functioned through the past century. Judges and lawmakers, he asserted, had "wisely steered between . . . extremes," granting divorces for "substantial reasons only." Consequently, Swift believed that "a greater share of domestic felicity [is] enjoyed . . . in this state" than in any other.[48] Behind the comments of both men lay an awareness that the volume of divorces granted had risen dramatically since the early 1700s and that Connecticut now stood out from all other American jurisdictions in the generosity of its divorce policy. But despite the worries of Trumbull and other conservative reformers that Connecticut courts had been too indulgent with petitioners, eighteenth-century judges actually proved reluctant to expand women's leverage in securing "domestic felicity" by approving suits on cruelty grounds.

When the Court of Assistants was replaced in 1711 by a Superior Court that rode circuit, holding sessions in each county seat twice a year, the judicial personnel changed very little, and divorce petitioners would have noticed no immediate shifts beyond the convenience of a shorter journey to court. Yet petitions for divorce were still such an infrequent phenomenon that the process inspired a tone of awestruck trepidation in some female petitioners. Witness the extra pains that Sarah Welsher took not just in decorating her 1723 petition with a frame of pen-and-inked arches and flowers but also in assuming an excessively deferential pose as a "poor afflicted Handmaid" in "my Honoured fathers[']" "magazine of Justice" (see Plate 6). In the seventy years prior to Welsher's petition, only nine New Haven–area residents had come forward to press for a divorce.[49] In

48. Benjamin Trumbull, *An Appeal to the Public, Especially to the Learned, with Respect to the Unlawfulness of Divorces, in All Cases, excepting those of Incontinency* (New Haven, 1788), 45, 49; Swift, *System of Laws*, I, 191–192. For the simultaneous campaign by New Haven ministers to restrict Connecticut's divorce policy, see Kerber, *Women of the Republic*, 178–180.

49. Petition of Sarah Welsher (Sept. 1723), NHSC Files, dr. 716. The number of New Haven County petitions might have been slightly higher, as the residences of several petitioners went unrecorded; see Appendix 1.

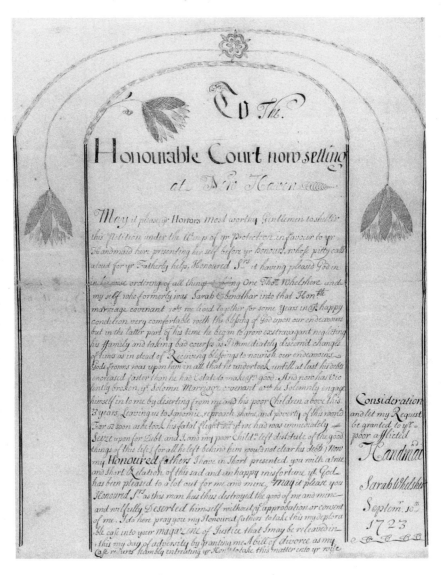

PLATE 6. Divorce Petition. *Of Sarah Welsher, Sept. 10, 1723. New Haven County Superior Court, Papers by Subject, Divorce, dr. 716, R.G. 3. Courtesy of the Connecticut State Library*

the 1710s and 1720s a divorce petition came before the bench at its New Haven sessions only every three or four years.

The prospect of a divorce hearing, along with the spiral of stories each such hearing must have generated, became less of a rarity after 1730. In that decade in New Haven County the frequency of divorce petitions

TABLE 5

Divorce Petitions to the Superior Court from Residents
of New Haven County, 1711–1789

	Women Filing	Men Filing	No. of Petitions
1711–1729	5 (83%)	1 (17%)	6
1730–1749	23 (82%)	5 (18%)	28
1750–1769	15 (60%)	10 (40%)	25
1770–1789	52 (70%)	22 (30%)	74
Overall	95 (71%)	38 (29%)	133

Sources: SCR; NHSC Files, dr. 716, CSL.

shot up nearly fivefold and then held steady until 1770. The justices heard an average of 1.3 requests per year for the four decades following 1730 (see Table 5).[50] Since most of the petitions continued to be brought by women, something or somebody was convincing more wives in broken marriages that they should seek relief. Before the emergence of a professional bar in Connecticut, women often noted that they had come into court only after receiving advice from "some friends" or "being Informed by some Persons of worth that the Law of this Colony is full, and Clear to give Relief." By the 1730s the lawyers who congregated at each county and Superior Court session stood ready to instruct a troubled wife on "her Right by the Law."[51] The bar, then, was the most likely catalyst for the early-eighteenth-century rise in petitions.

A second spurt of increase in divorce petitions occurred in the 1770s and 1780s in jurisdictions across New England. In New Haven County

50. There is as yet no modern, comprehensive, statistical study of divorces requested and granted in 18th-century Connecticut. Sheldon S. Cohen's analysis of 839 petitions lodged before the Superior Court from all counties, 1750–1797, lacks tables that would facilitate appraisals of change over time in volume of petitions, sex of petitioners, and grounds claimed ("Divorce in Connecticut," *Canadian Review of American Studies,* XI [1980], 275–293).

51. Divorce case of Rebecca Smith (1665), Conn. Archives, Crimes and Misdemeanors, 1st Ser., III, 196; Divorce petition of Marie Bennett (1703), III, 269; Divorce petition of Abigail Crow (1703), III, 266. See also the Divorce petition of Frances Hall (1705), III, 278.

not only did the Superior Court caseload triple, but five county residents sought relief from the General Assembly. The spurts by which the population seeking divorce grew in the 1730s, 1770s, and 1780s meant that between the 1720s and the 1780s, a period in which the county population increased by a factor of slightly more than four, the population seeking divorce grew by a factor of more than twenty-one.[52] Moreover, Connecticut petitioners showed themselves more assured in pursuing the divorce process to a successful outcome: in the 1770–1789 years the success rate rose to 92 percent chiefly because fewer petitions were withdrawn or found deficient.

Wartime conditions, rising expectations for companionate marriage, and a new consciousness that tyrants, whether kings or husbands, could be justifiably jettisoned—all might have contributed to the increased willingness of spouses to leave unhappy marriages or petition for divorce. Through the expanded print culture of the new Republic, middle-class Americans were exposed to a steady stream of magazine essays and sermons that stressed the "similarity of sentiments," tenderness, and true friendship that should exist between husband and wife. In 1788 one Connecticut woman eager to divorce her tyrannical second husband encapsulated this new rhetoric of bourgeois marital bliss by underscoring the "reciprocal kindness and mutual affection" that she had experienced with her first spouse.[53] While the expectation that husbands treat their wives with discretion and delicacy might have legitimated divorce in the eyes of many women along with their kin and legal advisers, middle-class husbands, too, demonstrated a new interest in using legal divorce rather than self-separation to end marriages. After decades of witnessing women make the most effective use of the law, men who had a stake in their community—property and children they did not

52. Without any reliable count of marriages, it is not possible to establish divorce rates (proportion of marriages ending in divorce) for early Connecticut. Sheldon S. Cohen calculates Connecticut divorces per 1,000 popuation for 1750–1797. He finds an annual average of .062 per 1,000 population for 1750–1762, increasing to .17 in the 1786–1797 years, with the greatest growth occurring just after the Revolutionary war (Cohen, "Divorce in Connecticut," *Canadian Review of American Studies,* XI [1980], 287–288).

53. Ibid., 288–289; Kerber, *Women of the Republic,* 163–164; Cott, "Divorce in Massachusetts," *WMQ,* XXXIII (1976), 593–594, 605–606, 613–614; Jan Lewis, "The Republican Wife: Virtue and Seduction in the Early Republic," *WMQ,* XLIV (1987), 696, 707, 710 ("sentiments" quotation); Divorce petition of Abigail Strong, Jan. 4, 1788, Conn. Archives, Lotteries and Divorces, 1st Ser., 296.

TABLE 6

Grounds Claimed: Divorce Petitions to the
New Haven County Superior Court, 1711–1789

	Women Filing		Men Filing		No. of Petitions
Desertion	64	(67%)	20	(53%)	84
Adultery	13	(14%)	12	(32%)	25
Desertion and adultery	6	(6%)	3	(8%)	9
Fraudulent contract	4	(4%)	2	(5%)	6
Lost at sea	7	(7%)	0	(0%)	7
Unknown	1	(1%)	1	(3%)	2
Overall	95	(100%)	38	(100%)	133

Note: The tables count each petition submitted, and thus the four men and two women petitioning twice are counted twice.

Sources: SCR; NHSC Files, dr. 716, CSL.

wish to abandon — began to take advantage of the remedy (see Table 5). For men of the middling ranks, suing for divorce rather than walking away had become an acceptable strategy.[54]

As the divorce caseload expanded over the course of the eighteenth century, the limits of the law for women emerged in sharper relief. Although abandoned and jilted wives were authorized to seek divorce, women who endured physical and mental abuse from husbands faced a quandary. No New Haven County woman even presented the Superior Court with a petition based solely on cruelty. Although the General Assembly as a court of equity was seen as sympathetic to distressed peti-

54. In the 1750–1789 decades, husbands' petitions jumped to 32% of the New Haven County caseload from their share of 18% in the previous 40-year period. Linda Kerber makes a similar observation on men's suing, that the class mix of petitioners might have shifted over the 18th century toward a higher proportion of propertied couples (*Women of the Republic*, 166, 180). Since nonlegal records capture many marital breakups that never led to formal divorce, it is dangerous to assume a correspondence between wives' behavior and the stories told by divorce petitions. Men's receptivity to the idea of suing for divorce might have been influenced by their observation of the high success rate of divorce petitioners or by increased contact with attorneys.

tioners who could not meet the statutory divorce grounds, before 1786 only one cruelty-based petition, Mary Larkham's 1753 plea, succeeded.[55] Women with experiences of abuse that fell short of the drama and lurid detail of the Larkham case neither had the temerity nor received the necessary counsel to bring divorce petitions based solely on cruelty to the courts.[56] By discouraging petitions on cruelty grounds, lawyers and judges signaled their discomfort with intervening in marital disputes resting on a husband's exercise of authority. Such cases differed significantly from women's pleas based on desertion and adultery—scenarios in which husbands had in essence opted out of the marriage, abdicating their prime marital responsibilities of economic support and fidelity. By walking out, these men unilaterally transferred their patriarchal authority over their household dependents to the state. In contrast, wives who petitioned for divorce on cruelty grounds were asking the state to inspect the way in which a man governed his family and to declare illegitimate certain actions over which the husband had traditionally in English law been given wide discretion.

Few wives who suffered beatings pursued the one legal process open to them: suing out a peace bond against their husband. Whereas in the seventeenth century abusive Connecticut husbands had been fined or even whipped, in the eighteenth the criminal procedure entailed binding the man on his good behavior between two county court sessions. Only nine wife-abuse complaints came before the New Haven County bench in the eighty years following 1710, and in all nine instances the

55. In a very rare move, in October 1766 the Assembly, after some hesitation, in effect upheld the 1762 separation agreement between Elizabeth and Thomas Marshall of Torrington. The agreement allowed Elizabeth to "live by her self" with a specified annual maintenance from Thomas. The Assembly twice ordered Thomas, who was in arrears, to make the payments. Elizabeth had suffered from repeated "inhuman, cruel, and barbarous Usage," including beatings while she was pregnant. The file papers include not only the written separation agreement and bond but also much revealing testimony by neighbors on how both spouses justified their increasing refusal of duties and how they together sought the advice of a Litchfield man (probably a justice of the peace or lawyer) "whether their was any Law or Rule whereby they Might [Live apart]." See the Case of Elizabeth Marshall, Conn. Archives, Lotteries and Divorces, 1st Ser., 167–185, and *PR*, XII, 520, 621.

56. For example, Sarah Tharp left home after constant threats of violence from her husband, yet she never brought an abuse complaint or a divorce plea to the courts (Testimony of Mary Howard, in Divorce papers of Daniel Tharp [Feb. 1752/3], NHSC Files, dr. 716). Rather, her allegedly abusive husband won the divorce.

husband was discharged once the initial term of his bond was up, since no witnesses (including his wife) appeared to testify that his miscarriage had persisted.[57] In some cases, the complaint might have functioned to rally neighbors and local officials to keep a strict daily watch over the troubled household, thus temporarily sparing the wife the more dramatic episodes of abuse. But peace bonds offered no lasting security to the wife. Indeed, for most wives the disincentives for filing a complaint against husbands with whom they continued to live must have been compelling: the difficulty of proving cruelty; the likelihood that their husbands, unrepentant in court, would punish them privately after the court hearing; and, finally, the shame brought upon one's family by such a public affair.[58]

The paucity of wife-abuse cases in eighteenth-century Connecticut shows that the forces discouraging women's complaints stemmed not merely from the colony's divorce policy but from the general culture, in both its Puritan and its English sources. Puritan divines spoke in rather awestruck tones of the stoicism and quiescence of particular pious women they knew who endured their spouses' recurrent wrath and abuse but never publicized their mistreatment. Thus to the Puritan mind, female submission to a husband's brutal correction could be a model for Christian resignation to earthly woes.[59] Moreover, for most women of English descent, economic dependence on their husbands, along with the "sense of fear, guilt, and helplessness" bred in a patriarchal culture, made public complaining inconceivable. Socialized to accept their dependence on men, many women were psychologically, not just materially, handcuffed to vain hopes that their husband's behavior would improve.[60]

---

57. In 17th century: Rex v. Ebenezer Brown (Nov. 1668), NHCC, I, 18–19; Rex v. William Roberts (Nov. 1700), II, 40, 51. For citations to the nine cases after 1710 and a partial profile of the couples, see Cornelia Hughes Dayton, "Women before the Bar: Gender, Law, and Society in Connecticut, 1710–1790" (Ph.D. diss., Princeton University, 1986), 298. Two of the women eventually won divorces on grounds other than cruelty.

58. Only one husband admitted guilt (Rex v. William Bassett [Nov. 1756], NHCC, V, 104, and NHCC Files, dr. 27).

59. Martha Saxton, "Puritan Women's Moral Authority: Seeds of a Critical Tradition," paper presented to the Annual Meeting of the Organization of American Historians, Anaheim, Calif., Apr. 15–18, 1993.

60. Stone, *Road to Divorce,* 198–201 (quote on 199). One of the best portraits of women's options in the face of abuse is Margaret Hunt, "Wife Beating, Domesticity, and Women's Independence in Eighteenth-Century London," *Gender and History,* IV (1992), 10–33.

Denied not just the option of divorce but also an effective criminal procedure, abused women in early Connecticut adopted one of three strategies: submitting passively to recurrent abuse, working to make their husband's life so miserable that he would provide legitimate grounds for divorce by deserting or committing adultery, or leaving home.[61] This last action, women were aware, meant courting the risk of being accounted a deserting wife and thus the guilty party to a broken marriage. The stakes in being judged the offender in a divorce suit were much higher for women than for men. When a husband won a divorce, he kept all the marital property. When a woman was declared the injured party, she could claim only the equivalent of a widow's dower, or one-third, of her husband's estate. Thus when a husband was judged at fault in a divorce case, he retained legal access to most of his material assets, but a wife who deserted or eloped could recover no more than what she carried with her. When we consider the scarcity of situations in which a lone woman could earn a living and the glare of suspicion she would attract if she fled to a town where she was unknown, we begin to glimpse the web of dependence in which early American women were caught. Only women with extraordinary fortitude or access to unusual resources could afford to cast themselves as willful deserters.

The divorce case of Hannah and John Merriman not only illustrates the conditions that allowed some women to walk out of intolerable marriages, but it also points toward the ways in which wifely protest over male governance would be depicted in eighteenth-century New England culture. Throughout the five-year battle of competing petitions from each of the estranged Merrimans, John insisted that his was a test case. He warned the magistrates that if they found that his "unkind Carriage" toward Hannah justified her desertion, then "the way is plainly laid open for every Rebellious wife to take [flight?] at the least offence, despise their husbands, and break the bonds of Marriage." Worried that Connecticut was already acquiring a reputation for handing out divorces "on very trivial matters" especially to the "foolish [female] sex," the Supe-

61. Anna Teal had solid evidence of wife-abuse, but she received a divorce on adultery grounds (Divorce case of Anna Teal [Feb. 1770], NHSC Files, dr. 716, and Complaint of Anna Teal [Nov. 1768], NHCC, VII, 139–140). For additional cases in which abuse was mentioned, see the Petitions of Sarah Brown (1738/9), Philena Dutton (Aug. 1772), Mary McFarnel (Aug. 1778), and Lowly Dexter (Aug. 1789), NHSC Files, dr. 716.

rior Court judges wrestled with the complex issues raised in the Merriman case, but their final ruling served to rebuke all women who declined to submit to husbandly browbeating and threats.[62]

In 1711 Captain John Merriman, a fifty-one-year-old widower with eight children living under his roof in Wallingford, married for the third time. He brought his new bride, the recently widowed Hannah Newberry, to Wallingford from her home forty miles away in Windsor, accompanied by her four young children. In this new and crowded household, an atmosphere of contentiousness immediately arose. John wished to retract his consent to a jointure he had signed before the marriage, a settlement that allowed Hannah to keep some of her property and set forth financial provisions for the bringing up of her children. Hannah refused to alter the agreement without arbitration or outside advice. When she finally took her case to some neighbors, John retaliated by spreading public reports that his wife was a "carnall" unbeliever, a "Lyar," and "the most wicked of all women." Hannah later recounted that most upsetting to her was the discovery that she had married a man "Generally" of "quarrelling discontented frame." She claimed that John frequently rose out of bed at night and walked "about the Room Striking upon the wall and bedstead," "saying he was an undone man" and acting "in Such a frantick and raveing manner that" she lay "trembling in Expectation" that she would be "murdred or maimed."[63]

If all could agree that the prenuptial document was the chief "bone of Contention" between Hannah and John, both spouses had other serious grievances. Hannah asserted that her life in Wallingford was made "very uncomfortable" because Merriman expected "exceeding hard service" from her, even though during courtship he had often promised that he wanted Hannah not "for any Labour but to be a companion to him to oversee his family." Hannah found the motherly supervision role denied her when John set "his children against me in saying I should Ruine them." Her feelings of isolation and resentment over her husband's "Jealous," even paranoid watchfulness must have complicated her rela-

62. Petition to the General Assembly (May 8, 1718), Conn. Archives, Lotteries and Divorces, 2d Ser., I, 124; Sargent Bush, Jr., ed., "The Journal of Madam [Sarah Kemble] Knight [1704]," in William L. Andrews, ed., *Journeys in New Worlds: Early American Women's Narratives* (Madison, Wis., 1990), 105.

63. Hannah Merriman's Grievances (undated) and Divorce petition of Hannah Merriman to the Superior Court (undated), NHSC Files, dr. 716.

tions with her stepchildren. Three of John's sons reported that Hannah often pined for the "pleasant company that she used to injoy" in Windsor and declared that she could not tolerate living "thus like a hermitt." Hannah attributed her desperation to John's never-failing rule of setting "a watch over mee if absent himselfe" and, upon his return, examining the watchers (probably his children) as to "who had bene there and what we eat [ate] and drank and what I had bene doing" while he was away.[64]

John's strategy was to portray Hannah as a prickly, independent-minded, sharp-tongued, ungodly woman who was unwilling to devote herself to the most obvious tasks of domestic management. Justifying his change of heart over the prenuptial agreement, Merriman charged that Hannah had "overreached" him in setting its terms and that she had "Spoile[d] his Credit" by divulging their disagreement to neighbors. Moreover, he persuaded his sons and a niece to testify that Hannah "took little or no care of the concerns of the family." She neglected, for example, to make use of Merriman's "considerable dary" to provide the household with butter and cheese. Further, she was in their opinion "as cross and untoward as . . . a woman could well be," of "a disquieted, discontented frame of spirit, . . . very prone to Rail on [Merriman] . . . to his face and behind his Back," often calling him "a Judas, a traytor, a monkey." Finally, Merriman's witnesses offered the bathetic picture of the family patriarch sitting in his house "on the Lords days between the meetings" trying to read "good books" (one was John Flavel's *Signs of Grace*) with "tears Runing down his Cheeks" because Hannah allowed her children to "play about [and] make . . . great Noise" and because she was as full "of her untord, frothy and worldly talk . . . on the Sabbath . . . as on other dayes."[65]

Three years into the marriage, Hannah followed through on her frequent threat to go "home again." In July 1713 she took her children and returned to her first husband's property in Windsor. "For my part," she declared, "I should count my Life more happy to bare the disgrace of a prisoners Life then the Life i have Lived with him." John Merriman's first reaction was one of anger and outrage: within a year he went to the governor and Council to insist "on it . . . either to have my wife Return'd

64. Deposition of Nathaniel Royce (Mar. 19, 1717), Hannah Merriman's Grievances, Joint deposition of George, Israel, and John Merriman, Jr. (undated), ibid.

65. Deposition of Nathaniel Royce (Mar., 19, 1717) and undated Divorce petition of Hannah Merriman, Deposition of Elizabeth Bidwell (undated), and Joint deposition of George, Israel, and John Merriman (undated), ibid.

to me: or to have my freedom from her." He quickly learned that he would have to wait three years and prove that he had made good faith efforts to reconcile with his estranged spouse.[66] Consequently, he used "all due means that could be . . . devised" to reclaim Hannah, including thirteen or more visits to Windsor by himself or an agent and letters in which he offered to put out some of his children and hire an "Elderly widow" who would be "good company" to Hannah and who might watch for misbehavior on John's part. Two years after the separation John wrote asking for a final answer from Hannah: "I . . . Request . . . that you without delay Return to me, who am your husband in the covenant of god, and subject yourself to me in all the duties of a wife." Hannah later explained why she had turned down these entreaties: "His temper seems to mee to be such that I have noe great hopes of amendment, . . . [and] I can truly say I find very Little truth to his promises." She concluded allegorically, quoting the prophet Jeremiah: "The Ethiopian cant change his skin nor the Leopard his spots."[67]

Twice in 1717 the Superior Court set aside time to hear the parties argue over John's formal petition for a divorce on the grounds of his wife's desertion since 1713. Hannah submitted not only a counterpetition requesting that she be granted the divorce but also a two-page list of grievances hinting that she had fled unspeakable abuses by John ("some not fit to write nor modesty allow mee to speak"). By this time, the judges had learned that both John and Hannah had behaved in unsavory ways since their separation. In unwomanly fashion, Hannah had twice resisted complying with warrants to bring her before the court, thus demonstrating yet again her taste for following her own lead. Captain Merriman had attracted attention as a loudmouth and a troublemaker in two communities. First, he was hauled into Hartford County Court and fined (on his confession) for spreading the "traducing and vilifying" reports around Windsor "that his wife was a whoare and that the Justices of this town and [others] . . . ware naught [had sex] whith her." One year later, Merriman was fined for slanderously bruiting it about in his own town

66. Joint deposition of George Merriman et al. and Hannah Merriman's Grievances, ibid. Hannah used the prison metaphor at three other points in her documented response to the marital breakup. George recounted his early efforts in his Divorce petition dated Sept. 11, 1716, ibid.

67. John Hamlin's Request to the Elders of Hartford and New Haven (June 25, 1717); John Merriman to Hannah Merriman, June 1714; John Merriman to Hannah Merriman, Apr. 20, 1715; Hannah Merriman's Grievances: ibid.

of Wallingford that he had had sexual relations with a local widow — a woman who eventually became his fourth wife.[68] Finally, the Superior Court heard direct testimony from three Windsor residents about Merriman's temper. John had told them "that if his wife did anything to hinder him and he could not gett a bill of divorce he would have her home and chain her up: to his bed foot if there be any Chain in Wallingford that will hold her." Male householders in Wallingford must have had Merriman's obstreperous behavior in mind when they unseated the fifty-five-year-old in 1716 from his long-held elected positions as an Assembly delegate and militia captain.[69]

While knowledge of John's and Hannah's reputations in their hometowns could have influenced the judges, they kept their focus on the central legal issue: Who should be counted the deserter? Hannah, for "wickedly" departing from her husband and "obstinately" refusing to return to him? Or John, for turning their married life into one of such "bitterness, anxiety," and circumscription that Hannah was compelled by the duty of self-preservation to withdraw? In her petition to the court, Hannah divulged her guess that she would lose the contest over who would be deemed the innocent party, for she admitted, "I have confessed wilful desertion and cannot make full proof of my inocency and sufferings but by my own testimony and my daughters." Nonetheless, early in the separation Hannah had gone to the trouble of procuring a learned man (a minister? a lawyer?) to draw up "Some Considerations touching Wedlock." The author cited the argument of the eminent Puritan, Dr. William Ames, who had written that the man who "by hard usage and cruel treatment" drove his wife away ought "to be esteemed

68. Hannah Merriman's Grievances, Warrant for Hannah Merriman (Jan. 30, 1716/7), ibid. See also Conn. Archives, Crimes and Misdemeanors, 1st Ser., III, 293. The April 1715 Hartford County case against Merriman is documented in Conn. Archives, Crimes and Misdemeanors, 1st Ser., II, 95, and Records of the Hartford County Court, I, 378, CSL. Rex v. Capt. John Merriman (Apr. and Nov. 1716), NHCC, I, 64, 76.

69. Joint deposition of Thomas Moore et al. (Feb. 14, 1716/7), NHSC Files, dr. 716. (The final "if" clause in quotation was inserted with a caret in the original.) Merriman was elected a deputy from Wallingford almost continually from October 1697 through May 1715. He was replaced as captain of the west side trainband by Joseph Doolittle in May 1716 (PR, V, 347, 549). For the General Assembly's 1732 refusal to commission William Thrall as militia captain after his wife deserted him in a gesture of protest, see Hirsch, "Thrall Divorce Case," Women and History, no. 4 (1982), 50.

the Desertor." God's ordinance of marriage became a mockery when made into "a bond to hold the injured person in perpetuall Slavery, prison, and affliction during the whole life."[70] At John's request, the Superior Court canvassed thirteen ministers of Hartford and New Haven County churches. The divines agreed in principle that the man who provoked his wife into leaving home should be deemed the guilty party. However, since Hannah had not articulated "any Lawfull or Just Reason for . . . absenting herself," she ought to be accounted the deserter.[71]

Surprisingly, despite the endorsement of John's position by so many local divines and despite Hannah's vague charges of abuse — charges that fell far short of establishing severe physical cruelty — the Superior Court announced in October 1717 that it found insufficient cause to grant John's plea for a divorce.[72] Neither did it order Hannah to return to her husband. Caught between new pressures to issue narrow, lawyerly rulings and the seventeenth-century judicial mode that drew on local knowledge to fashion ad hoc remedies, caught between an invitation to send a punishing warning signal to rebellious wives and their own older policy of refusing to reward feuding couples with divorces, the judges appeared paralyzed.

It took the intervention of the General Assembly to nudge the Superior Court into taking a clear stand on the Merriman case. In May 1718 Merriman, casting himself as "your miserable and distressed petitioner," asked three things of his former colleagues in the legislature: to grant him a bill of divorce themselves, to declare the Superior Court's dismissal of his case "Erronious," and to establish "for the future" that "Such Wilfull desertion" by a wife would "be duly punished." Instead of exercising their role as a court of equity, the deputies and assistants passed an act recommending that the Superior Court once again con-

---

70. Warrant for Hannah Merriman (Jan. 30, 1716/7); Hamlin's Request to the Elders; "Some Ten Considerations" signed by E.T. (Nov. 13, 1713); Hannah Merriman to the Superior Court (Oct. 10, 1717): NHSC Files, dr. 716. The key Ames passage from his *Cases of Conscience* was paraphrased by ministers responding to a contested 1730s Windsor, Conn., case (Hirsch, "Thrall Divorce Case," *Women and History*, no. 4 [1982], 56).

71. Reply of the Hartford clergy (undated); Resolve of the New Haven County clergy (July 17, 1717); John Hamlin's Request to the Elders (June 25, 1717): NHSC Files, dr. 716. See also the opinion of the Reverend Joseph Moss (Derby, July 12, 1717) contained within the sheets of the joint statement by the New Haven ministers.

72. SCR, I, 252, 292, 318.

sider the case. In doing so they must have transmitted a strong message in favor of Merriman to the magistrates. For in October 1718 at their New Haven session, the Superior Court took up the challenge offered them by John Read, Merriman's lawyer, to establish "a fatal president" and granted John his long-fought-for divorce. The bench implicitly endorsed Read's position that the proper test in such contested cases should be whether a cantankerous husband's actions would cause "a reasonable woman" to fear for her life.[73] In the judges' final analysis, Hannah Newberry Merriman failed to qualify as a reasonable woman.

The Merriman precedent indeed proved fatal for the chances of eighteenth-century Connecticut wives who withdrew from husbands' abusive and tyrannical authority. Over the next eighty years, only one woman, Katherine Witter, used a claim of cruelty to convince the Superior Court that she deserved a divorce; in that case, the husband's abusive treatment consisted of, not repeated beatings, but rather his murder of his infant and two relatives after he fell into suicidal depression. Even though the legislature considered occasional divorce petitions from abused wives and granted Mary Larkham's 1753 plea, it was not until the last thirteen years of the century that the two houses granted several petitions that relied solely on evidence of serious physical abuse. And not until 1843 did Connecticut lawmakers amend the divorce statute to authorize the Superior Court to grant divorces on the grounds of "habitual intemperance, or intolerable cruelty."[74]

73. Petition of John Merriman (May 8, 1718), Conn. Archives, Lotteries and Divorces, 2d Ser., I, 124–125; SCR, II, 15; John Read, "Plea for Capt. Merriman" (undated), NHSC Files, dr. 716. Read added that "reasonable Evidence" of violent treatment — such as the wife's successful prosecution of an abuse complaint before local officials — was also needed.

74. *The Revised Statutes of the State of Connecticut* (Hartford, 1849), 274. I am indebted to Jerome Nadelhaft for supplying the 1843 date. For a summary of the English and American case law between 1790 and the 1840s, see Robert L. Griswold, "The Evolution of the Doctrine of Mental Cruelty in Victorian American Divorce, 1790–1900," *Journal of Social History*, XX (1986–1987), 127–130.

Sheldon S. Cohen states that Katherine Witter's divorce granted by the Superior Court at its Norwich session in March 1782 was based on cruelty grounds (" 'To Parts of the World Unknown': The Circumstances of Divorce in Connecticut, 1750–1797," *Canadian Review of American Studies*, XI [1980] 286). However, a close reading of related documents reveals that the case rested on the murders and a finding of Elisha Witter's insanity. Suffering suddenly from depressive and suicidal thoughts, Elisha had one night fallen into a homicidal rage; his wife escaped, but his infant, his sister, and her infant lay dead. By the time the judges granted Katherine a divorce

While Hannah Merriman's failure to cast John as the "Desertor" placed her in the company of other eighteenth-century wives who felt compelled to leave intolerable marriages, her fate after the divorce highlights how atypical her situation was. First, Hannah did not face the painful prospect of parting with her children. In the Merriman case, no children resulted from the union between Hannah and John, and John made no motion to prevent the departure of the Newberry children who had been, after all, central to much of the dissension in the marriage. Second, in losing a contested divorce, Hannah was not rendered propertyless. The decree affected neither her right to the one hundred pounds in personal estate that her first husband had left her outright nor her access to sizable properties in Windsor left in her control until the Newberry children came of age. Upon her self-separation in 1713, Hannah returned to the Newberry homestead, removed the tenants she had previously installed, and lived off a substantial annual income. As if symbolically to deny that the failed marriage with Merriman had ever taken place, she took back the distinguished surname of Newberry. Received back in Windsor as a major landowner and important community figure, Hannah was accorded a pew in the "forefront galery" of the meetinghouse when it was reseated in 1722. Whereas her first husband had died in 1710 possessed of an estate valued at nine hundred pounds, Hannah died in 1749 worth almost five thousand pounds; in a climate of spiraling inflation, Hannah had managed to retain and even enhance her standing among the wealthiest segment of Connecticut society.[75]

---

from her insane husband (whom she believed "not Likely Ever to Recover"), a trial jury had acquitted Elisha of murder by finding him "to have been non compos mentis when he perpetrated the Deed." See Divorce petition of Katherine Witter (originally submitted to the October 1781 General Assembly), New London County Superior Court Files, box 126, CSL; Rex v. Elisha Witter (Sept. 1781), SCR, XXII, 378; manuscript notes on the Witter case in an anonymous hand, evidently penned in 1781, Thomas Fitch, *A Proclamation . . . for the Observation of the Sabbath* (New London, 1757), Proclamations of the Governors, R.G. 5, CSL, verso of sheet between sheets 34 and 35. I was led to this unusual source by a 1947 note inserted by Margery Case in Georgia Cooper Washburn, comp., Mabel Thacher Rosemary Washburn, ed., *Witter Genealogy: Descendants of William Witter of Swampscott, Massachusetts, 1639–1659* (New York, 1929), at 30–31, at CSL.

75. Hartford Probate District Estate Papers, Estate of Benjamin Newberry (1709/10), 3890, Estate of Hannah Newberry (1749/50), 3894; CSL; Henry Reed Stiles, *The History and Genealogies of Ancient Windsor, Connecticut* (Hartford, 1891–1892), I, 564; Bruce C. Daniels, "Money-Value Definitions of Economic Classes in

Given her independent, prosperous life after her marriage to Merriman, it may seem that Hannah Newberry won in the divorce stand-off.[76] Of course, women whose husbands sought and were granted divorces after an estrangement did gain in that they were rid of any legal ties to a dreaded or hated man. But only a tiny fraction of Connecticut wives had the luxury of choosing to desert. Divorce papers record the cases of fifteen New Haven County women besides Hannah Merriman who left their husbands in the 1710–1790 period. By walking out without inviting adultery charges, these women earned the epithet of deserters while their husbands won divorces. A profile of the sixteen confirms that a woman who rejected her husband's governance needed an unusual set of resources—separate wealth, a secure place to go to, sympathetic family or friends, confidence that she could manage independently, and a fierce resolve.[77]

All of the husbands in these cases knew exactly where their wives had gone; at least two-thirds of the women had returned to their former homes. Notably, seven of them besides Hannah Merriman had been married before. Thus they brought the example of a previous husband to measure against the behavior of the second. Moreover, these women could harken back to the experience of widowhood, a period of life in which they had shouldered the duties of an independent householder and managed on their own. Intriguingly, at least nine of the women hailed from outside New Haven County, a fact indicating that they had moved considerable distances from their parents' or former husband's homes to marry the men they eventually left. Those distances might of course have been part and parcel of the strife plaguing these marriages, or the absence of the woman's kin could have meant that mediation efforts failed. But the Merriman case authorizes us to presume that often the very distance between the two communities gave the "deserting" wife a glimmer of hope that she might reestablish herself in a sympa-

---

Colonial Connecticut, 1700–1776," *Histoire Sociale—Social History*, VIII (1974), 346–352.

76. Indeed, in her original plea to the Superior Court for a divorce, Hannah concluded, after conceding the likelihood that John's petition would be granted, "Let it be don one way or other" (Divorce petition of Hannah Merriman [undated], NHSC Files, dr. 716).

77. The profile encompasses the wives of 14 men who won divorces for desertion (2 petitioned twice) and 2 whose cases were continued but never explicitly granted or denied.

thetic setting, rather than be continually subjected to gossip, scrutiny, and scorn.

The atypical resources available to women who dared to walk out of marriages and the numerical imbalance between men and women who deserted underscore how restricted women's mobility was in the early modern world in contrast to men's. The laws put up practically no disincentives to flight for men who were poor and seriously discontented with their wives or family lives. In this society with no system of identification papers and a growing landless male labor force, a man could easily adopt the guise of a single person, and an alias if need be, and find work, adventure, and often a new wife in strange environs. Absconding husbands occasionally managed to settle and remarry in the next county without detection. A more classic form of abandonment was shipping as crew on a voyage to the West Indies — hardly a choice open to a lone woman. Women who withdrew in disguise and disappeared into "parts unknown" did so only as elopers, under the protection of a man and posing as his wife.[78] Men could escape their past, then, whereas lone women could not. Mobility, defined as the power to create new identities and maintain at least minimal subsistence while encountering strange environments and unknown people, was open only to men in seventeenth- and eighteenth-century New England.

The desertion cases not only dramatize the structural social conditions that cast marriage as a prison for many women, but they also reveal the tensions that could arise over women's work within marriage. Like Hannah Merriman, Elizabeth Morgan believed that her husband Theophilus had treated her as a drudge, quite beneath her station. Walking out of the marriage, Elizabeth announced to kin and neighbors that she "would not Return, for She had ben his Slave long enough already." Although she broadcast far and wide her terms for reconciliation (that Theophilus apologize for "his past faults and buy her a Negro wench"), Elizabeth was never satisfied by her spouse's promises to "Hire what help

78. For men's remarriages nearby, see Petitions of Mary Gardiner (1740) and Lydia Tucker (1783), NHSC Files, dr. 716. For a sampling of men who shipped to the Caribbean, see the Petitions of Chloe Bull (1770) and Ruth Roberts, a free black (1773), ibid. On wives' disappearing, see the Divorce papers of John Fowler (1733/4), Andrew Leet (1769), and Benjamin Morris (1786), ibid. Only one deserting New Haven County wife is described as shedding husband and children to lose herself in the "dissolute" life of New York City (Divorce papers of David Humphreville [1762 and 1764], ibid.).

he Could" so that she should not have to "wet" her hands "to Wash or anything of that nature." Perhaps Elizabeth Morgan was lazy, or perhaps the Rhode Island household in which she grew up relied on slaves for the drudgework. In any event, the central disagreement between the Morgans reveals what one mid-eighteenth-century woman aspiring to gentility sought: freedom from all laundering and from never-ending rounds of unassisted household labor.[79]

George Dudley's neighbors and apprentices were scandalized that Dudley's wife often refused to prepare "Breackfast, Dinner, or Supper" for her clothier husband and his workers, forcing him to fetch in a neighborhood woman or do the cooking himself. A woman's refusal to cook was seen as a serious act of disobedience and a transgression of her marriage vows; if it became a pattern, the woman's eschewing meal preparation was tantamount to desertion. Thus, while a husband's desertion consisted of nonsupport and an unexplained withdrawal of his presence as household head for three years, the signs of a wife's desertion were her withholding of those special "Offices" she provided in her husband's bed and at his board. Hence Samuel Horton's lament over his spouse's insistence that she never would again cohabit with him "nor do for him the Least Trifle." Eighteenth-century women who attempted to rewrite the implicit marital contract that obliged wives to be resourceful cooks or household managers ran the risk of finding themselves hounded or literally "Turned . . . out of Doors."[80]

While Hannah Merriman's path to divorce was an escape route few women could afford to tread, as a separated and ultimately divorced woman Hannah took one action that echoed the actions of many sim-

79. Depositions of Jeremiah Dowd (undated), Samuel Willcocks (Feb. 18, 1742/3), and Ebenezer Bishop (Mar. 30, 1743), in Divorce papers of Theophilus Morgan (1742/3), ibid. Thirty-seven years old when Elizabeth left him, Theophilus had not yet acquired the dignity he would later in life: 11 years after his divorce, he had become a militia captain and begun sporadic service as a deputy (*PR*, X, 196, 486, and see *PR*, XI, XII). When he died in 1766, he left a clear estate of £991 to his second wife, one son from his first marriage, and three sons from his second. The estate included a silver hilted sword, engraved silver tablespoons, a mill, and three farmsteads (Guilford Probate District Estate Papers, unnumbered, CSL).

80. Depositions of Ezra Kimberly (May 6, 1786) and Clarinda Grannis (May 5, 1786), in Divorce papers of George Dudley (1786), Conn. Archives, Lotteries and Divorces, 1st Ser., 249, 255; Petitions of John Dudley (1785) and Samuel Horton (1765), NHSC Files, dr. 716. Turned out of doors: Deposition of Mary Hooker, in Divorce papers of Theophilus Morgan (1742/3), dr. 716. For another such incident, see Hirsch, "Thrall Divorce Case," *Women and History*, no. 4 (1982), 49–50.

ilarly situated women before and after her. By reverting to her maiden or previous surname, even a woman with few material resources could shape her own identity and force her community to recognize aloud the death of a marriage. Long before the legislature passed an amendment in 1848 authorizing the Superior Court to permit name changes to married women who won divorces, Connecticut women were shedding their husband's last name after a marriage broke up or a divorce was officially granted. Starting with Sarah Dibble in 1672, colonywide pre-1711 divorce records reveal at least seven women who, in the wake of separation or divorce, used or were referred to by a surname other than their ex-husband's. Among eighteenth-century New Haven County petitioners, nineteen identified themselves to the court with both their husband's and their own former surnames. At least two of these women actually remarried under their maiden name, and land records show another using her maiden name on conveyances several years after her divorce.[81] Although the majority of divorcing women found it more convenient to continue to use their married surname, the presence of a significant number who insisted on renaming themselves offers a glimpse into one way in which a small subset of colonial women could gain psychological solace in a move that was not always motivated by property or social considerations.

Another telling use of language that emerges from the divorce records revolves around anger. Addressing a male judiciary, husbands petitioning for divorce gave themselves license to express a level of vexation and

81. In some cases a combination of the married and maiden names was used, as in Sarah Dibble's petition signature, "Sary dible alias Wetherbury" (Divorce petition [May 1672], Conn. Archives, Crimes and Misdemeanors, 1st Ser., III, 212). The Dibble case is described above. Further instances before 1711 involved the following women, listed here with the year of their divorce case: Elizabeth Rogers (1676), Alice Mackey (1682), Ruth Gutsell (1683), Rebecca Collins (1685), Mercy Hill (1692), and Marie Sage (1705).

Lydia Brockett, née Lydia Elcock, won a divorce from Benjamin Brockett in the August 1738 New Haven session of the Superior Court, and town records show that one month later Captain Yale married her "under her maiden name" to Samuel Lathrop (Jacobus, *FANH*, 324; Barbour Collection of Connecticut Vital Records, volume for Wallingford, CSL). I have found similar evidence for Guilford resident Submit Cockard (Aug. 1773 divorce), who married Andrew Leet, who had won a divorce in 1769. Elizabeth Armstrong née Doolittle (divorced by the Feb. 1748/9 Superior Court at New Haven) used her two names in a 1749 conveyance and only her maiden name in a 1753 deed (Wallingford Land Records [microfilm], XI, 523, 533, CSL).

moral outrage that was almost entirely absent from women's divorce petitions. For example, when it came to adultery, no New Haven County husband failed to condemn his wife's behavior as wicked or perverse or "very indecent." In contrast, women suing for divorce on the same grounds typically used euphemistic, muted language to refer to their husband's infidelity.[82] Male anger over deserting wives played on the image of the scold. Although New Englanders had ceased prosecuting women as scolds in the 1690s, divorce records demonstrate that the idea exerted a powerful hold over the ways in which judges assessed blame in contested cases. By painting their wives as headstrong, obstinate, "Brawling," and profane, John Merriman and Theophilus Morgan, for example, successfully shifted the focus away from their own behavior to the qualities of their wives. Once depicted as a shrew and a scold, a wife could be disqualified from the ranks of reasonable women whose charges of abuse might be credited. By denouncing their wives as ill-tempered and brawling, prosperous householders like Merriman and Morgan also drew on well-established traditions representing lower-class women as particularly rude and contentious; the association functioned to strip their wives of the veneer of respectability.[83] In siding with husbands like Merriman and Morgan, the Connecticut Superior Court echoed the approach to contested cruelty cases taken in the English ecclesiastical courts. There, a wife's plea of cruelty was not viewed favorably "unless it appears

82. Divorce petitions of Eliphalet Luddington (1786) and Pennock Howd (1786), NHSC Files, dr. 716. For a more extended discussion of the language of men's and women's adultery-based petitions, see Dayton, "Women before the Bar," 339–341.

83. Robert L. Griswold demonstrates that this winnowing out of undeserving scolds — women "of high, bold, masculine spirit" — from virtuous wives was characteristic of 19th-century judicial thinking, even as cruelty became one of the most frequently used grounds of divorce. Particularly after 1850, the distinction merged with notions of class so that judges dismissed the divorce petitions of lower-class women claiming abuse with the logic that such women lacked the refinement, sensibility, and delicacy that would enable them to feel abused and in turn never to provoke abuse (Griswold, "Evolution of the Doctrine of Mental Cruelty," *Journal of Social History*, XX [1986–1987], esp. 129, 134). See also the discussion of husbands' "disciplining" wives in Christine Stansell, *City of Women: Sex and Class in New York, 1789–1860* (New York, 1986), 78–83.

For insightful analysis of the prosecution of nonelite women as scolds in England, see David Underdown, "The Taming of the Scold: The Enforcement of Patriarchal Authority in Early Modern England," in Anthony Fletcher and John Stevenson, eds., *Order and Disorder in Early Modern England* (Cambridge, 1985), 116–136, esp. 120.

that she is a person of good temper and has always behaved well and dutifully to her husband." Thus, in the eyes of the canon law, a woman's bad temper canceled out any legal ramifications that her husband's resort to violence might have had.[84]

The image of the scold proved most useful to husbands saddled with wives who suffered from serious mental illness. Whereas seventeenth-century magistrates had posited distraction as a bar to divorce, the eighteenth-century bench could be swayed by a husband's argument that his spouse's irrational behavior stemmed from a deceitful and rebellious nature. The emblematic case for New Haven County was Samuel Brockway's 1758 suit. The parties joined issue over whether Samuel deserved a divorce for his wife Margaret's "heinous" adultery with a black man (which she did not deny, having given birth to a mulatto child) — or whether the divorce should be denied because of Samuel's cruel treatment of Margaret and because she was "a poor Crazed Creature," too mentally disturbed to be held accountable for her actions.[85]

Twenty-six neighbors and acquaintances of the Brockways lined up and took sides. On the one hand, eleven deposed that, ever since the couple moved into town, they had judged Margaret to be distracted and that Samuel himself had always esteemed her so, "while of late he says that she is possessed." A deacon, the son of a physician who spent much of his time "doctering distracted persons," confirmed the seriousness of her illness. Another neighbor explained that Margaret did not have "the use of her Reason at least half of her time." Some neighbors added that they had seen clear signs of Samuel's beating his wife. One woman recounted that Margaret had recently run away, intending to kill herself,

84. Taylor v. Taylor (1755), quoted in Stone, *Road to Divorce*, 203. Margaret Hunt makes a similar point about the necessity for English wives seeking separations to construct themselves as mild-tempered, affable, dutiful, and passive when confronted with violence ("Wife Beating, Domesticity, and Women's Independence," *Gender and History*, IV [1992], 24). Jane Neill Kamensky offers an apt summary of the English cultural norm for marital relations: "Men's non-violence was contingent upon women's silence" ("Governing the Tongue: Speech and Society in Early New England" [Ph.D. diss., Yale University, 1993], 27). On the preoccupation of Renaissance literature with the domineering wife and her punishment, see Linda Woodbridge, *Women and the English Renaissance: Literature and the Nature of Womankind, 1540–1620* (Urbana, Ill., 1984), 189–223.

85. Petition of Samuel Brockway and Joint deposition of Mr. John Warner, Jr., and Sarah Warner (Aug. 30, 1758), in Divorce papers of Samuel Brockway (1758–1759), NHSC Files, dr. 716.

and had lain out under a fence all night, to be found the next day by a search party.[86]

On the other hand, fifteen acquaintances testified as Samuel's witnesses. Some reported that Margaret "Generaly [appears] to Knew What she Does" and "will give a Rational answer." Others claimed to have observed that her fits and raving were "Deceit and Hypocrisy," occurring only in her husband's presence. Further, they described her as "very cross and Contrary to every Body," turbulent, and "of very bad behavior." Worst of all, she was "Rebelus" and "has Ben very unprofitable and Distructive" toward her husband, behavior that Deacon Moses Blackly believed sprang "not from a Liteheadednes but from a Spiteful Spirit."[87]

The circumstances surrounding Margaret's liaison with Lot, the black man who lived in the Brockway household, are unclear. While some of the neighbors thought that Margaret had been raped, others understood that, immediately after having consensual sexual relations with Lot, she had told her husband, whereupon he had forgiven her and had continued to have sex with her (which, if true, should have barred a divorce on adultery grounds). Margaret herself gave conflicting accounts: sometimes she speculated that Samuel had bought the "Negro for that purpose"; sometimes she claimed that one night in a fit she had "prostituted her Body" to Lot; at other times she exclaimed that she would do it again with witnesses present so "that she Mite get rid of her Husband."[88]

Repelled no doubt by Margaret Brockway's defiant attitude toward her adultery, the Superior Court magistrates, after a second hearing of the case, granted Samuel a divorce. The justices remained silent in the face of a recommendation from some of the Brockways' neighbors that Samuel be made to "give Bond for her maintenance."[89] One wonders

86. Joint deposition of Samuel and Elizabeth Curtis (Aug. 30, 1758), Deposition of Deacon John Warner (Aug. 30, 1758), Deposition of Elizabeth Barnes (Aug. 30, 1758), Joint deposition of Mary and Lucy Pond (Aug. 30, 1758), and Deposition of Timothy Pond (Aug. 30, 1758), ibid.

87. Joint deposition of Capt. Phineas Royce, Mr. Jonathan Cook, and Lydia Barnes (Aug. 25, 1758), Deposition of Hannah Cook (Aug. 25, 1758), Deposition of the Reverend Samuel Newell (Aug. 30, 1758), Deposition of Lt. Josiah Lewis (Aug. 30, 1758), and Deposition of Moses Blackley (Feb. 26, 1759), ibid. Women made up fewer than a third of Samuel's deponents ($N = 4$ of 15) in contrast to nearly one-half of Margaret's ($N = 5$ of 11).

88. Depositions of Elizabeth Barnes (Aug. 30, 1758) and John Warner, Jr. (Aug. 30, 1758), Deposition of Elizabeth Barnes (Aug. 25, 1758), ibid.

89. Deposition of Moses Foot et al. (Feb. 26, 1759), ibid.

how poor Margaret Brockway, whether scold or madwoman, ended her days.

Whatever had occurred in the Brockway household, Samuel Brockway procured a divorce because he successfully portrayed his wife as a willfully disobedient woman whose quixotic and outrageous behavior was inexcusable. Faced with women who claimed to deserve a divorce or offered reasons (as did Margaret Brockway) to block a divorce, eighteenth-century judges sorted petitioning wives into two types: dutiful helpmeets and defiant shrews. The enforcers of Connecticut's divorce policy were eager to protect the former type, women like Jane Fisk and Elizabeth Sedgwick who adopted the rhetorical pose of being loath to give up their wifely duties. Fisk's spouse had removed himself only as far as the next county, but, since he "refused utterly to let *her* live with *him*," Jane complained to the court that she was "by his Conduct . . . wholly deprived of performing any of the Duties of a Wife." Reviewing the many years of her husband's self-imposed estrangement, Elizabeth Sedgwick called the bench's attention to her "sundry offers and Invitations . . . [to] cohabit with him in any place and to comply with him in any low condition in conjunction to provide necessaries for a subsistance." By stressing their willingness to serve their spouses under *any* circumstances, Sedgwick and Fisk marked their distance from contentious and independent-minded wives like Hannah Merriman, who dared to set limits on the housewifery duties she would perform, or like Elizabeth Morgan, who declared she would reconcile with her husband only if "he should maintain her as She pleas'd, and where she pleas'd." Aware of what would attract the judges' sympathy, Hannah Merriman at one point in her petitions attempted to draw on the ideal of wifely virtue — meekness, patience, utter avoidance of expressing anger, Christian fortitude in the face of tribulation. "I can truly say I did endeavour to the utmost," she wrote, to "Gain" her discontented husband's confidence "by a kind and Respectfull Carriage to him." Yet the image of a submissive wife was not the one that stuck to Hannah, as we know. Instead, the judges based their ruling on the image of the woman who had declared at one juncture in the troubled marriage: "I never was tyed to one man, nor never will be, and I will change my Diate in a little Time."[90]

90. Petition of Jane Fisk (1783), ibid.; Divorce petition of Elizabeth Sedgwick (Oct. 1674), *Recs. Ct. of Assts.*, Lacy transcript, I, 54–55; Deposition of Jeremiah Dowd, in Divorce papers of Theophilus Morgan (1743); Hannah Merriman's Grievances (undated), and Joint deposition of George, Israel, and John Merriman, Jr. (undated), in Divorce papers of John Merriman (1718), NHSC Files, dr. 716.

Constructed as scolds, women like Hannah Merriman and Elizabeth Morgan provided eighteenth-century judges with a justification for denying relief to women who claimed they had been ill-treated. Whether actually contentious in character or not, all women who demanded that their husbands' abusive behavior be scrutinized raised the specter of independent, rebellious wives.[91] To have granted divorces routinely on cruelty grounds would have opened the petitioning process to disorderly and perhaps deceitful wives, thus destabilizing the asymmetric power relation between spouses that was seen as crucial to the social order. Conversely, a system that offered divorce to women who successfully depicted themselves as obedient and dutiful wives ultimately reinforced husbandly authority by reprimanding only those men who abdicated their role as governor.[92]

———

The eighteenth-century consensus among the male legal fraternity that women could not be trusted with cruelty complaints drew some of its strength from trends in print culture. By the 1750s and 1760s New England printers showed a newfound penchant for including in their newspapers stories, poems, and jokes about nagging, spendthrift, and deceitful wives — many of which were borrowed directly from the London newssheets. An essay like "A Bachelor's Reasons against Matrimony" or a poem that facetiously claimed of cuckolding wives, "Few Houses are without 'em," would never have been tolerated by the magistrates who controlled seventeenth-century New England presses, given the Puritan concern to portray marriage as a positive good for both men and

91. Jonathan Sheppard, a successful Windham County petitioner, noted that his wife "would often purposely oppose the order and Government of his family" (Sept. 1763 petition). The Sheppard case is similar to the Merriman case in that the spouses told diametrically opposing stories, both sued for divorce, the wife charged cruelty, and the husband won on a second attempt. See the cases of Jonathan Sheppard (Sept. 1763 and Sept. 1764) and Love Sheppard (Mar. 1761), SCR, XVIII, 105, 273, and Windham County Superior Court Files, box 336, CSL.

92. For similar formulations, see Hunt, "Wife Beating, Domesticity, and Women's Independence," *Gender and History*, IV (1992), 16, 24; and Woodbridge, *Women and the English Renaissance*, 197–199. Woodbridge points out that, since male-headed households symbolized a well-governed polity, an underlying fear among male commentators was that shrewish, domineering wives, "armed with governing skills acquired in their households, . . . might advance into the political arena" (197).

women.[93] The circulation of this satiric, antimatrimonial lore among the urban, commercial elites who took out newspaper subscriptions could have served to reinforce existing disdainful attitudes against women who complained within marriage.[94] Indeed, the anglicization of the entertainment content of New England newspapers resonated with the turn taken early in the eighteenth century by the Connecticut magistrates sitting in judgment of divorce petitions. Despite their implementation of Christendom's most generous divorce policy, eighteenth-century justices rejected the ad hoc approaches of their seventeenth-century counterparts — approaches that had at times abrogated men's absolute common law rights to child custody or access to an estranged wife's services.

In standardizing their responses to divorce pleas after the creation of the Superior Court in 1711, Connecticut judges chose a number of paths that reinforced patriarchal authority. By siding with John Merriman, they both underlined their fear that rebellion in wives might become epidemic and discouraged women in the following decades from basing divorce petitions on cruelty charges. By permitting divorces to men who discovered their brides to be pregnant by another man, the justices upheld the urgency of making paternal bloodlines certain and fueled a strain in popular culture that cast women as deceitful. By ceasing to endorse court-ordered transfers of children or property to women who won divorces, the justices distanced themselves from the Puritan willingness to penalize husbands who had demonstrated extreme immorality or irresponsibility.

93. *Connecticut Journal* (New Haven), Nov. 27, 1767, Feb. 26, 1768; Cornelia Hughes Dayton, "Satire and Sensationalism: The Emergence of Misogyny in Mid-Eighteenth-Century New England Newspapers and Almanacs," paper presented to the New England Seminar in American History, Worcester, Mass., Nov. 15, 1991. For a *Spectator*-style fictional exchange of letters satirizing an unhappy couple and their relatives but stressing that the young bride should avoid any upbraiding of her peevish, intemperate husband and should use meekness, patience, coquetry, and charity to reclaim and reform him, see Feb. 16, Mar. 23, and Apr. 13, 1770.

On Puritan prescriptions regarding marriage, see Karlsen, *Devil in the Shape of a Woman*, chap. 5; and Powell, *English Domestic Relations,* chap. 5.

94. Margaret Hunt observes that Addison and Steele and their imitators stressed that the most common cause of marital discord was the talkative, gadding, extravagant, independent-minded wife who was "constantly seeking ways to undermine her husband's legitimate authority" ("Wife Beating, Domesticity, and Women's Independence," *Gender and History*, IV [1992], 26).

At the same time that Connecticut's precocious divorce policy consistently offered a significant remedy for abandoned wives, the history of the policy's enforcement points to three distinct stages in the region's ideological stance toward power relations within marriage. In the seventeenth century, magistrates faced with warring or estranged spouses decreed mediation and reconciliation rather than legitimating male demands to be rid of uppity wives. In the eighty years after 1710, as many more Connecticut residents sought divorces, justices proved ready to view wifely desertion more categorically from the husband's point of view. The reward of divorce went only to women who would pose as dutiful Bathshebas whose proffered services were rejected by restless or philandering husbands. Wives who challenged their husband's methods of household governance were penalized or silenced. The rampart raised to suppress cruelty complaints began to crumble at the very end of the century, when a trickle of women bypassed regular divorce procedures to convince the legislature that a husband's resort to severe physical cruelty should cast him as the deserter.

The fact that a liberal divorce regime could resist cruelty cases for such a long period underscores the defensiveness against independent wives that was central to Puritan and English concepts of marriage upon which early New England policies were founded. Beginning in the 1790s, that resistance was finally breached under the influence of sentimentalism, changing views of male and female capacities for virtue, and budding temperance and humanitarian reform movements.[95] Once material conditions and ideological reconfigurations had located middle-class women firmly within an elaborated domestic sphere, the cruelty-based complaints of dutiful wives could be read, not as bids for female independence, but rather as appeals to judicial compassion and to society's interest in winnowing out dangerous tyrants from the ranks of husbands. A new era of judicial patriarchy had begun.

95. Bloch, "Gendered Meanings of Virtue," *Signs,* XIII (1987–1988), 37–58; Barker-Benfield, *The Culture of Sensibility.* For women's initial, sporadic benevolent efforts outside the home, see Anne Marie Filiaci, "Raising the Republic: American Women in the Public Sphere, 1750–1800" (Ph.D. diss., SUNY-Buffalo, 1982). For evolving definitions of cruelty in Britain and the United States, see Stone, *Road to Divorce,* 203–206; Myra C. Glenn, *Campaigns against Corporal Punishment: Prisoners, Sailors, Women, and Children in Antebellum America* (Albany, N.Y., 1984), chap. 4; and Griswold, "Evolution of the Doctrine of Mental Cruelty," *Journal of Social History,* XX (1986–1987), 127–148.

4

Consensual Sex

THE EIGHTEENTH-CENTURY DOUBLE STANDARD

In 1722 Sarah Hine, an eighteen-year-old living with her parents in Milford, bore a child whom she named Martha. Late in the year, Sarah and a local man, twenty-two-year-old Joseph Nettleton, were presented to the county court for the "sin of Fornication" by two local grand jurors, men appointed to ferret out illegal goings-on in their town. In court Sarah confessed her guilt and paid her fine. Although she never wavered in her insistence that Joseph was her child's father, naming him both in the throes of childbirth and on oath before magistrates, the trial jury of twelve local men accepted Nettleton's plea of not guilty to the fornication charge. Immediately following the verdict, however, the bench, in accordance with the Connecticut statute against "Bastardy," declared Joseph to be the infant girl's "reputed father," a ruling that enabled them to charge him with contributing half of the child's maintenance until she reached the age of four. Nettleton appealed the maintenance judgment to the Superior Court, before which he argued, in effect, the illogic of being acquitted of fornication yet made responsible for the consequences—a "bastard" child. The higher court, which rarely heard such appeals, reversed the county court ruling and exempted Nettleton from contributing to Martha's upkeep.

Sarah Hine's abandonment by her lover and her brush with the law echoed the experiences of many young women in New England during the colonial period. What makes the case extraordinary is not only Nettleton's appeal but also Sarah's subsequent petition to the highest court in the colony, the General Assembly. There she claimed that she had been doubly "undone," first by the duplicity of Joseph, who seduced her by "falsehoods, flaterries and Dissembleations," failing afterwards to marry her, and second, by the Superior Court judgment, which cut her off "from any . . . help . . . from the said Joseph." Sarah's strategy was to impress on the lawmakers that punishment in her case had been meted out contrary to long-held Puritan models of pious, communal behavior. She observed that in court she had "pleaded gilty as justly with shame she ought," whereas Joseph "pleaded not guilty (as justly he ought not)." While petitioning on behalf of "the innosent child that through *his* means is brought in to the world," Hine portrayed herself as "unworthy," deserving "no pity or Compation of god or man."[1] In stark contrast, Joseph's behavior marked him as both the aggressive male seducer preying on female weakness and the unrepentant sinner.

The lawmakers heeded Sarah's fervent plea "that he that is Equall with her in Transgration . . . not go wholy unpunished." Both houses voted to restore the legal decision mandating maintenance payments from Nettleton. Although the votes upheld the rules that had governed fornication and paternity cases for more than five decades, Sarah's struggle with three levels of the judicial system foreshadowed the unraveling of the old system. Given the impossibility of ascertaining paternity, Connecticut lawgivers in 1672 had enacted a statute adopting the English rule that a woman's "constant accusation" of one man was legally sufficient to convict him of fornication and make him liable as a parent.[2] Joseph Nettleton's fight against that rule, even though it was

1. My emphasis. Documentation of the case is found in NHCC, III, 160–167; NHCC Files, drawer 6; SCR, III, Sept. 1723 New Haven session; NHSC Files, dr. 324; and Connecticut Archives, Private Controversies, 2d Ser., XIV, 60–62. In a similar, simultaneous case, Alice Rothbottom submitted a petition like Hine's to the May 1724 General Assembly after the Superior Court reversed a maintenance order against the man she named. Rothbottom had recently moved to Rhode Island, and she withdrew her petition. It echoed Hine's at key points, suggesting that the same lawyer drafted both (1st Ser., II, 385).

2. John D. Cushing, ed., *The Earliest Laws of the New Haven and Connecticut Colonies, 1639–1673* (Wilmington, Del., 1977), 80. Under these conditions, the accused man was to be adjudged "the reputed Father . . . , notwithstanding his denyal" *unless* he

ultimately unsuccessful, signaled a growing discomfort among legal officials over the lack of procedural safeguards for men charged with paternity. Their unease reflected a sea change in New England culture. In the
seventeenth century, a young man brought face-to-face with his lover
and suspicious neighbors in court usually owned up to paternity. At the
village level, neighbors were not plagued by doubt about who had fathered an out-of-wedlock child, because they could gauge who had been
"keeping company" with whom and who could be relied on to tell the
truth. Magistrates and grand jurymen rarely let a case go by in which the
reputed father was not identified and held accountable. But after 1701
no accused white man perceived the traditional path of confession as
coinciding with his self-interest. And by 1745, grand jurors in towns
across the region ceased prosecuting men for out-of-wedlock births.
Sarah Hine in 1723 had warned against the trend that became a matter
of public record by midcentury: a prosecutorial double standard for
sexual behavior.[3]

The most dramatic watershed for the regulation of sexual behavior
occurred in the 1740s. In Connecticut, legal authorities largely gave up
on insisting that the county court be the actual site for the censure of
fornicators. Prosecutions of newly married couples fell off sharply, and
reputed fathers were pursued only at the initiative of unwed mothers
and their families. Single women who became pregnant were permitted
to confess and receive their sentence before a local justice of the peace;
however, their names and crimes were still called out before the audience gathered for county court sessions. By midcentury, new attitudes
on the part of legal officers and the middling men of property — who as
complainants, jurors, and witnesses were the backbone of the legal system — had pushed aside the Puritan obsession with pressuring all sinners
to acknowledge immoral behavior in the most public setting possible.

---

produced sufficient "pleas" and circumstances to convince the court of his innocence. A similar statute, lengthier in its text, was passed in the Massachusetts Bay
Colony in 1668, but, unlike the Connecticut law, it stated explicitly that a reputed
father was to "be liable to" maintenance charges only, not "to other punishment"
(*The Colonial Laws of Massachusetts* [Boston, 1889], 257).

3. Laurel Thatcher Ulrich, *A Midwife's Tale: The Life of Martha Ballard, Based on Her
Diary, 1785–1812* (New York, 1990), 149; Hendrik Hartog, "The Public Law of a
County Court: Judicial Government in Eighteenth Century Massachusetts," *Ameri-
can Journal of Legal History*, XX (1976), 300; Paul D. Marsella, *Crime and Community in
Early Massachusetts: Essex County, 1700–1785* (Acton, Mass., 1990), 20.

Gradually, the regulation of moral behavior was withdrawn from the purview of the community-embodied-in-the-court and lodged in the more informal and amorphous setting of family and neighborhood.[4]

Women's courtroom experiences as defendants charged with sexual misconduct provide an important counterpoint to the images we have gleaned of widows suing over debt or abandoned wives petitioning for divorce. In New Haven County, while about 150 women were involved directly in divorce proceedings and more than 1,300 women litigated over debt between 1670 and 1790, about 625 women, mostly in their twenties, appeared in court to answer for illicit sexual relations. For the most part, they were the daughters of propertied yeomen. In New Haven as in the rest of New England, fornication was by far the largest category of criminal cases on the county court docket from about 1690 until 1770.[5]

The pervasiveness of premarital sex meant that for many young women a summons to appear to answer fornication charges was their first, and sometimes their only, contact with the county court. At first glance, the criminal process seems to have been humiliating, one to which a pregnant single woman could only submit passively. But women like Sarah Hine who had the support of their families learned to manipulate the legal system to make the best of a bad situation. Simply threatening to name the child's father before the local magistrate could prove sufficient leverage for extracting private maintenance payments from the young man. Such strategic use of the courts did not work for every-

4. It is very difficult for historians to gauge to what degree concern over premarital sex lessened among the general populace in the late 18th century. In contrast to an earlier literature implying that interest waned in sexual regulation, Laurel Thatcher Ulrich has argued that "powerful" "mechanisms of control" continued to operate locally and informally — outside the court system (*A Midwife's Tale*, 148–149).

5. The figure of 625 reflects the number of appearances by women for fornication, lascivious carriage, adultery, and incest; thus individuals who repeated are counted more than once.

On the predominance of fornication in 17th-century courts, see Robert West Roetger, "Order and Disorder in Early Connecticut: New Haven, 1639–1701" (Ph.D. diss., University of New Hampshire, 1982), chap. 3. Of the 514 criminal cases before the New Haven County Court between 1710 and 1750, 353 (69%) were fornication prosecutions. For the first time, in the 1770s another category of crimes — violence and contempt — matched the proportion of fornication cases, at 31%. For Middlesex Co., Mass., see Marsella, *Crime and Community*, 14, 18.

one, however. If a woman had been raped by an acquaintance, if her lover had fled the colony, or if her parents were dead, far away, poor, or of ill repute, her experience at the bar could be difficult and bitter: reprimanded, pushed farther toward a marginal existence perhaps by multifold costs, she would see no commensurate measures meted out to her sexual partner.

Most of all, the history of prosecutions for illicit sex illuminates the ways in which the sexual system — the prescribed and coded precepts for male and female sexual behavior — was undergoing restructuring in the eighteenth century. Although the feminine ideal of a chaste, ever-resisting Pamela took hold in all corners of the Anglo-American world, the transformation emerged in sharpest relief in the New England colonies. Only there had dissenting Protestants established a seventeenth-century society that departed in significant respects from the double sexual standard deeply embedded in early modern English culture.[6] But as men began to disdain the Puritan call for confession and as judges and jurors adopted stricter standards of proof for determining guilt in premarital sex cases, women came to stand alone in their adherence to the language and posture of repentant sinners. In the 1750s and 1760s the calculus of accountability for sexual transgressions had shifted to suggest that women bore almost the entire responsibility for guarding female chastity. In the face of such an entrenched double standard, men of the middling and elite ranks who were fathers, jurors, and judges grew uncomfortable with exposing daughters of respectable families to the stigma of a fornication confession. Amid public controversy over fornication proceedings, the range of women prosecuted narrowed in large part to marginal figures — poor women, domestic servants, women in interracial relationships, women who repeatedly bore children without marrying.

In the 1790s came the final act in the privatization and decriminalization of fornication: county court judges, without any statutory prompting, ceased to include fornication cases as a matter of the criminal record, allowing individual justices of the peace to receive pregnant single women, not as criminals and confessors, but as complainants in threatened paternity suits.[7] Thus, just as changes in the economy handed women a marginal presence in civil litigation by 1775, so the demise of

6. Keith Thomas, "The Double Standard," *Journal of the History of Ideas*, XX (1959), 195–216.

7. For details on the new registrationlike process, see n. 132, below.

regulating sexual misdemeanors at the county court level meant that the large numbers of women who had once been called into court as witnesses and criminal defendants were nowhere to be seen as the century came to a close.

————

Wiliam Gouge was not alone among Puritan divines when he complained in 1622 of "the liberty" taken by many courting adults after betrothal "to know their spouse, as if they were married." To Gouge, indulgence in sexual intercourse by engaged couples before the marriage ceremony proper was "an unwarrantable and dishonest practice." English Puritans criticized the ecclesiastical and lay courts for their uneven and often indifferent enforcement of fornication and bastardy laws. For reasons that historians do not fully comprehend, premarital pregnancy and out-of-wedlock births were not only common phenomena in villages across the British Isles and Europe in the early modern period, but they also rose steadily in Britain and the colonies throughout the eighteenth century. Traditionally, the middling and lower classes in many regions blinked at premarital sex (if the couple married) and resigned themselves to the disappointment of a daughter's bearing an out-of-wedlock child (if they could afford to maintain the infant). In England church courts initiated disciplinary proceedings against fornicators only in spotty fashion. Common law courts, after nudging from Parliament, sent to the workhouse some unwed mothers whose children would otherwise become parish charges. Although concern over poor relief certainly drove the majority of prosecutions, seventeenth-century English justices used their discretionary powers to incarcerate *both* poverty-stricken and economically sufficient women while sparing convicted fathers such punishment.[8] In this pattern, we find a precursor to

8. William Gouge, *Of Domesticall Duties* (London, 1622), 198–199; Peter Laslett et al., eds., *Bastardy and Its Comparative History: Studies in the History of Illegitimacy and Marital Nonconformism in Britain, France, Germany, Sweden, North America, Jamaica, and Japan* (Cambridge, Mass., 1980); Daniel Scott Smith and Michael S. Hindus, "Premarital Pregnancy in America, 1640–1971: An Overview and Interpretation," *Journal of Interdisciplinary History*, V (1974–1975), 537–570.

Local practices in England varied widely according to the individual justice, court, and parish. In one of the most detailed studies for the early 1600s, Walter J. King concludes that 80% of unwed parents were never pursued by secular officials, because the costs of incarceration outweighed the expenses of poor relief. Private

the Sarah Hine case: two forces — queasiness over the standards of proof that determined paternity and a double standard that held women to blame for what authorities perceived as widespread promiscuity — combined to yield differential punishments for men and women.

Determined to establish earthly communities that were acceptable in God's eyes, the founders of the New England colonies made the detection and punishment of crime an imperative. In step with the Cromwellian regime across the Atlantic, the fledgling Puritan governments in the New World did away with church courts, uniting the prosecution of immorality with other offenses under the aegis of secular magistrates. These righteous men, it was believed, would be far more effective and systematic in their efforts to root out sin than church officials in England.[9] Legislators for New Haven Colony and the united Connecticut Colony that succeeded it passed criminal statutes against a wide range of illicit sexual activities and related behavior that they considered pernicious. Young people could be fined ten shillings or sentenced to the stocks for "nightwalking" — that is, convening in groups after nine in the evening "in the Street" without parental consent. A young man convicted of "inveagl[ing] . . . the affections of any Maide . . . whether it be by speech, writing, message, company-keeping, . . . [or] gifts" would forfeit two pounds.[10] The more serious misdemeanors of fornication and lascivious carriage (sexual "dalliance" where intercourse could not be proven) regularly brought severe whipping or steep fines. Adultery carried the death sentence until 1672, when the punishment was reduced

---

agreements between unwed parents to share maintenance costs were enforced by orders from individual justices of the peace. See King, "Punishment for Bastardy in Early Seventeenth-Century England," *Albion*, X (1978), 130–151.

9. The English ecclesiastical courts were also unpopular because of their history of persecuting nonconformists, including Puritans. See Gail Sussman Marcus, " 'Due Execution of the Generall Rules of Righteousnesse': Criminal Procedure in New Haven Town and Colony, 1638–1658," in David. D. Hall et al., eds., *Saints and Revolutionaries: Essays on Early American History* (New York, 1984), 99–100; and Edgar J. McManus, *Law and Liberty in Early New England: Criminal Justice and Due Process, 1620–1692* (Amherst, Mass., 1993), 12–14. Individual New England churches could discipline only their members, a process that required a public confession before the congregation.

10. See the New Haven Colony Code of 1656 in *NHCR*, II, 600. For an extensive examination of youths' illicit night meetings, see Roger Thompson, *Sex in Middlesex: Popular Mores in a Massachusetts County, 1649–1699* (Amherst, Mass., 1986), 83–96.

to severe whipping and the lifelong shaming penalties of being branded with an *A* and forced to wear a halter. Three men were hanged for bestiality and two for sodomy in New Haven Colony.[11]

In the eighteenth century, the wide range of laws against illicit sexual practices remained on the books (and a statute against bawdyhouses was added), but prosecutions for nightwalking or inveigling maids disappeared from the county court dockets while judges and jurors became more circumspect than their Puritan predecessors about handing out capital or corporal punishments for the most serious crimes involving consensual sex—bestiality and adultery—where definitive proof so often seemed elusive. Indeed, a closer look at how Connecticut communities and authorities handled adultery, the one crime of passion between consenting adults to be prosecuted in the spotlight of the higher court, provides an important perspective on how the double standard was woven into the fabric of early New England culture.[12]

———

Unlike fornication proceedings, which came, only over time, to punish women more severely than men for consensual sex, a double standard

11. The three bestiality cases ending in hanging were against George Spencer (1642), Walter Robinson (1655), and William Potter (1662), *NHCR*, I, 62–69, 70–73, II, 132–133, 440–443. Two other men were found guilty of this crime and sentenced to severe whipping in the Colony period (I, 295–296, II, 223–224, 293). After Connecticut and New Haven united, the higher court records, 1666–1789, reveal that eight men were prosecuted for bestiality (one in 1674 and the rest in the 1700s). One never appeared for arraignment, four saw the charges dismissed, one was acquitted, and two were found guilty (one escaped, and one suffered the sentence of severe whipping). In 1799, surprisingly, the Superior Court sentenced 83-year-old Gideon Washburn to hang for the crime.

Three sodomy cases appear in records and chronicles of colonial Connecticut and New Haven: William Plaine's 1646 trial and execution for sodomy and teaching masturbation, John Knight's 1655 trial leading to his execution (the charges included a range of sexual misbehaviors), and the 1677 sodomy conviction of Nicholas Sension, ending in a sentence of severe whipping and shaming in the gallows (John Winthrop, *The History of New England from 1630 to 1649*, ed. James Savage, 2 vols. [Boston, 1825–1826], II, 265; *NHCR*, II, 137–139; *Recs. Ct. of Assts.*, Lacy transcript, I, 67–68; Conn. Archives, Crimes and Misdemeanors, 1st Ser., I, 85–102). For a general discussion, see Richard Godbeer, "'The Cry of Sodom': Discourse, Intercourse, and Desire in Colonial New England," *WMQ*, LII (1995), 259–286.

12. Although incest could fall into the category of consensual sex, most colonial cases argue for its treatment as coercion and child abuse. See the discussion below in Chapter 5.

was inscribed into the law of adultery in Connecticut from its earliest codes into the nineteenth century. Long past the intensely Puritan seventeenth century, the statute clung to the Old Testament's restrictive definition of adultery as an act committed with a married woman. Thus a married woman who engaged in any extramarital affair was subject (along with her lover) to the statute's punishment, whereas a married man who had an affair with a single woman or a widow would not be legally accounted an adulterer, but would be liable only to the fines and possible child support imposed on fornicators. Throughout the colonial period, authorities' decisions on how to prosecute adultery reflected additional disadvantages for women. New Englanders carried over from their English heritage a special horror of female adulterers—a horror that stemmed from a legal system premised on transmission of property through paternal bloodlines. Such a system enshrined the same twin concerns that haunted Mosaic law: anger over wifely disobedience and fear that a wife's indiscretions could deprive a man of his rightful, biological heirs or divert property from true sons.[13] In Connecticut indictments, inflammatory, denunciatory language was directed primarily at cuckolding wives and rarely at adulterous husbands. Desire Brown, who gave "her voluntary consent" to sexual relations with Andrew Burr, was thus "Guilty of the *odias* crime of Adultery." The elaborately worded indictment against Mary Smith emphasized (where the indictment of her married lover did not) that by her "Abominable, and detestable Sin of Adultery" she had violated "the sacred bonds of Matrimony wherein She Still is bound and Oblidged unto her said husband William."[14] Freighted with cultural tendencies to see adultery in women as far more heinous and unforgivable than in men, Connecticut residents pursued adulterers as criminals selectively and unevenly, rarely placing both lovers together at the whipping post as recipients of public rebuke.

In the early decades of settlement, when we might expect to find the magistrates assiduously prosecuting adulterers for "poluteing the land" and punishing married women and their lovers equally, we find instead two patterns that would persist well into the eighteenth century. First,

13. Thomas, "The Double Standard," *Journal of the History of Ideas*, XX (1959), 195–216; Carol F. Karlsen, *The Devil in the Shape of a Woman: Witchcraft in Colonial New England* (New York, 1987), 168–169.

14. My emphasis. Rex v. Desire Brown, SCR, XIX; Feb. 1766 New Haven session, and NHSC Files, dr. 330; Rex v. Mary Smith, Early General Records, LVIII (Records of Court of Assistants and Superior Court), 373–374, R.G. 1, CSL. See the discussion of the rhetoric on female adultery in divorce petitions in Chapter 3, above.

during the period in which adultery was capital, authorities and witnesses alike usually backed off from charging defendants explicitly with the full act. If the charges enumerated "uncleanness," "unlawfull familiarity," or lascivious carriage, then the convicted adult could be fined, whipped, or shamed—but not executed. Second, men and women suspected of adultery often faced discrepant outcomes and penalties. This became clear especially for the period after 1672, when adultery became noncapital.[15] Before that time, two executions for adultery occurred for the jurisdictions that encompassed Connecticut and New Haven. In 1650, a person or couple unidentified by name went to the gallows at New Haven, but no trial records remain detailing the case. In 1668 Ruth Briggs was almost certainly the woman who the Reverend Simon Bradstreet reported was hanged in Connecticut for "adultery and infanticide."[16] As a defiant, disorderly, marginal woman whose dalliances, dissembling, and assertive speech had plagued New Haveners for years, Briggs conformed to one type of woman who would attract prosecution for adultery in the decades to come. If the unidentified person executed for adultery in 1650 was a woman, then a pattern of reserving the most spectacular of punishments for female and not male transgressors of the Seventh Commandment was established early in Connecticut.

That women were judged more deserving of harsh punishment was borne out in most of the cases considered by the judges of the Court of

15. "Poluteing": Rex v. John Stead and Abigail Betts (Oct. 1672), *Recs. Ct. of Assts.*, Lacy transcript, I, 37–38. Lyle Koehler's finding that early-17th-century magistrates often held men who were suspected adulterers more accountable than the women they visited (*A Search for Power: The "Weaker Sex" in Seventeenth-Century New England* [Urbana, Ill., 1980], 75) is reflected in Connecticut only in local courts' handling of lascivious carriage, not in the higher court's caseload. See the discussion below.

For noncapital convictions, see Rex v. Mary Benfield (May 18, 1666), *Recs. Ct. of Assts.*, Lacy transcript, I, 2; Rex v. Hannah Hackleton (May 18, 1666), I, 3; Rex v. Ruth Briggs (Dec. 1665), *NHTR*, II, 161; Rex v. Elizabeth Butler (Mar. 1666/7), II, 201.

In May 1672, the General Court had asked the governor and Council to make a new law for adultery (*PR*, II, 179); that law took effect with the code of laws approved by the General Court at its October 1672 session (*PR*, II, 190; Cushing, ed., *Earliest Laws of New Haven and Connecticut*, 76–77). The new punishment—whipping, branding, and haltering—was meted out for the first time to Stead and Betts.

16. *PR*, I, 32; Koehler, *Search for Power*, 162 n. 40; "Bradstreet's Journal, 1664–83," *New England Historical and Genealogical Register*, IX (1855), 44. Documents for the 1668 proceeding against Ruth Briggs are found in Conn. Archives, Crimes and Misdemeanors, 1st Ser., I, 32–33. Note that Koehler lists Briggs's hanging as distinct from the one noted by Bradstreet, mistakenly, I believe (*Search for Power*, 471).

Assistants between 1666 and 1710.[17] Mary Benfield and Elizabeth Reynolds each received severe whippings while their lovers (unmarried men) were ordered only to pay child support and, in one case, a fine. Hannah Hackleton's lover owned that he had slept with her, but the authorities did not move to prosecute or punish him at her side. In an unusual turn of events, when David Ensign, a married man, was arraigned and convicted alone for persistently keeping company with another man's wife (she had fled), the court refrained from inflicting a penalty on his body but chose instead to hold his property hostage (by demanding a four-hundred-pound bond for future good behavior) and strip him of his adult political identity (by revoking his status as a freeman and voter).[18] No other case illustrates quite so deftly that, while a woman's body served as a vessel both for the proof and penalty of her crime, the most appropriate locus for a male transgressor's punishment was his worldly status.

Delivering its sentence in the 1681 Ensign case, the bench underscored the difficulty of proving that adultery had occurred — of finding out, as they phrased it, "such Notorious Wickedness, notwithstanding all care Used."[19] Of nineteen individuals prosecuted between 1711 and 1790, juries found the evidence against six, three men and three women, persuasive enough to convict. However, in only one case did a married

17. In these years 12 individuals were prosecuted for adultery or adulterous carriage: 8 in couples, 2 women alone, and 2 men alone. Three of the women were charged with other serious crimes (such as infanticide or witchcraft) besides adultery. All 6 women were punished, by either severe whipping (4), hanging (1), or shaming in the stocks; only 2 women saw their male partner receive equal punishment.

18. Rex v. Mary Benfield and Deliverance Blackman (May 18, 1666), *Recs. Ct. of Assts.*, Lacy transcript, I, 2; Rex v. Elizabeth Reynolds and William Hoadley (Oct. 1701), I, 358–359; Examination of Hannah Hackleton and Henry Frost (Mar. 31, 1664), Conn. Archives, Crimes and Misdemeanors, 1st Ser., I, 7.

Ensign was simultaneously charged with the "dangerous and very offensive" deed of spreading false reports of the King's death. Rex v. David Ensign (May 1681), *Recs. Ct. of Assts.*, Lacy transcript, I, 96–98. The husband of Ensign's lover won a divorce on the grounds of his wife's adultery at the Dec. 15, 1681, Court of Assistants: Thomas Long v. Sarah Long, I, 104–105.

19. Rex v. David Ensign (May 1681), *Recs. Ct. of Assts.*, Lacy transcripts, I, 97. For a similar point, see Keith Thomas, "The Puritans and Adultery: The Act of 1650 Reconsidered," in Donald Pennington and Keith Thomas, eds., *Puritans and Revolutionaries: Essays in Seventeenth-Century History Presented to Christopher Hill* (New York, 1982), 279–280.

woman and her lover face the same punishment: twin guilty verdicts and the statutory penalty of lashes, branding, and the order to wear a halter forever. Flight, delaying tactics, and the disappearance of witnesses thwarted many prosecutorial efforts. In the eighteenth century, the bias toward conceiving of adultery as a female crime manifested itself not so much in punishments meted out as in who was haled before the bar. In the seventy years prior to 1780, five couples and six women without their partners, but no lone men, faced charges.[20] Although none of the cases against the women who were charged alone ended in conviction, the process of singling out a woman to appear before the bar—whether because she was pregnant during a husband's long absence or because her lover could not be identified or found—was stigmatizing and often financially costly for the defendants. That Nathaniel Brown colluded in his wife Desire's failure to appear for her 1766 trial indicates the lengths that many were willing to take to avoid adultery prosecutions even if they were likely to end in acquittal.[21]

The outcomes in what must have been a much-discussed case, that against John Guy and Mary Smith, show that status difference and a woman's decision to shield her lover could lead to a legal result that negated the man's sexual transgression. In mid-September 1714 two

20. Man and woman receiving same punishment: Rex v. John Cooper and Margaret Jacobs (Mar. 1727/8), SCR, VII, 63–64. Low status was not a factor in this outcome, since Cooper was a sergeant and the son of a corporal and former deputy and Jacobs was married to a native son (Jacobus, FANH, 451, 936).

Files reveal that, at a minimum, four men and three women whom local authorities moved to arrest on adultery charges between 1711 and 1790 successfully evaded initial arrest or failed to appear for arraignment or trial.

Outcomes for the six cases against lone women were: one discharged by proclamation, two dismissed when the king's attorney declared there was no foundation for an indictment, two acquitted by trial juries, and one no appearance. In the 1780s, for reasons that are unclear, prosecutors for the first time in a century brought charges against three men without their married lovers.

21. Desire Brown was informed against by two grand jurors who on Sept. 9, 1765, presented her and Andrew Burr (who fled the arrest warrant) for having "Carnal Knowledge" two days before "at New Haven" (Rex v. Desire Brown, SCR, XIX [unpaginated]: New Haven County Superior Court Session for February 1766, and NHSC Files, dr. 330). In a contrasting case, a husband informed on his wife and garnered at the same Superior Court session both a divorce and the spectacle of seeing his spouse convicted and ordered to be whipped, branded, and made to wear a halter and forfeit £73 of her estate to pay court costs (Rex v. Miriam Leavitt [Sept. 1750], SCR, X, 155–156, and Hartford Co. Superior Court Files, box 89, CSL).

New Haven grand jurors alerted "the Gentlemen in Civil Authority" that it was "commonly reported that one Mary Smith . . . is with child and that her husband has been absent from her a year or years." Within a few days, Mary, the child and wife of poor mariners, was brought before two justices and asked, "Who is the father of the child that you go with?" She responded that the child was conceived when her husband, William Smith, visited in the previous January, lodging with her "Two nights and a day" at "Mr Guys house when he was gone to Boston." Mary had then been serving as housekeeper to John Guy, a prominent trader. Since other servants living in Guy's house at the time testified they had never seen William Smith or been aware that he had visited, Mary was, after some procedural delays, bound over to appear before the next Superior Court. When a grand jury impaneled in March heard the oral testimony and depositions in the case, they returned indictments against both Smith and Guy.[22]

While Smith showed up for her March trial, Guy evaded arrest, and the authorities put off his trial until September. The evidence against them (as it survives in the files) was of two sorts. Most damning was the testimony of Hannah Butler, who had "Lodged in a lower Room" of "Mr Guys house" in the winter of 1713 when Mary Smith "kept the hous." From the chamber over her own room, Hannah heard such "noises of the bedsted and their voices talking together often in the dead time of the night" that she did "verily believe" that Guy and Smith "ordinarily lodged together in the same bed" and had "Carnall knowledge of One another"—"So far as Such A matter can be Conjectured from such Circumstances," Hannah added. (The silence in all the depositions concerning Guy's wife Anna suggests that she was away in this period or living with their one child in a second homestead in Branford.)[23]

A second strand of evidence came from deponents who recounted a litany of more recent compromising activities—"playing together," "kissing," lying "in naked bed together in the day time"—and conversations between John Guy and Mary Smith, all occurring in the houses of Mary's father and brothers in East Haven. Joshua Hotchkiss saw Guy take one of Mary's young children in his arms and kiss it; "then said Mary said

22. The documentation for the cases is found in Rex v. Mary Smith (1715), Early General Records, LVIII (Recs. Ct. of Assts. and Sup. Ct.), 373–374, and NHSC Files, dr. 323; NHCC, III, 47; Rex v. John Guy (1718), SCR, II, 57, and NHSC Files, dr. 323.

23. The documents that accompany the Guy and Smith cases fail to make clear in what town "Mr Guys house," where the alleged adultery took place, was located.

to said Guy wonder how you can be as cruell as to leave the children, for you know it is you[r] child and the other too, and said Guy said if I did not know that you had to do with some other man, I should believe the children were mine." On another occasion Guy responded somewhat differently: Mrs. Mindwell Jones recalled that in front of her late one night Guy "said to Mary Smith you are a fatt Slutt and a Cold bedfellow" and proceeded to brag to Mrs. Jones that "he had Lain with her [meaning Mary Smith] 40 times." Mrs. Jones replied "no wonder She hath Gotten 2 Children If you have Lain with her 40 times." Mary then chimed in, saying to Guy, "If they be yours why dont you take them and maintain them: Guy answerd So I would, but you are such a proud Slutt you wont Let me."[24]

At her trial, Mary pleaded not guilty, but the jury found against her, and the bench declared the sentence: she was to be whipped "on the Naked Body 25 stripes," to be "stigmatized or burnt on the forehead with the letter A on a hot iron, and that she wear a halter about her neck, on the outside of her Garments, during her abode in this Colony."[25]

By September, but probably months earlier, John Guy had "run away" to Shelter Island on Long Island Sound. His wife Anna submitted a divorce petition to the Superior Court dated September 13, 1715, alleging that John's perfidious act of adultery with Mary Smith (who "has been Convicted . . . and punished after her deserts," Anna emphasized) "fully" appeared in "the testimonys and evidences . . . of the whole matter [still remaining] before this Court." The bench never took any action on this petition, so Anna must have decided to drop her suit. In March 1718/9 Guy was finally brought "by a Special Warrant" before the Connecticut Superior Court; he pleaded not guilty and, despite the prior conviction of Mary Smith, was so found by the jury. Before the bench that term Guy might have argued, as he had in an earlier letter to the court from his island exile after hearing of Mary Smith's conviction, that he found it

> very astonishing, that capital crimes should be throughly proved, and
> . . . punished, upon bare presumption, whereas both the Civil law, and
> the Common law of England by statuts or precedents, are entirely

24. Depositions of Hannah Butler (dated Mar. 10, 1714/5) and Mindwell Jones (dated Jan. 7, 1714/5), in Rex v. John Guy (1718), Deposition of Joshua Hotchkiss, in Rex v. Mary Smith (1715), NHSC Files, dr. 323.

25. Rex v. Mary Smith (1715), Early General Records, LVIII (Recs. Ct. of Assts. and Sup. Ct.), 373–374.

without any such appointment or precedent. Did Innocent Railery, diverting embraces or posturs, lying in or upon a bed, naked or Covered, prove adultery, there would but few escape being Criminal.

More likely the jurymen were swayed by the written statement of "Mary Smith alias Velt" (evidently Mary had remarried since 1715) insisting "as I ever said that the children born of my body wair my husbones and said John Gye Is not gilty of Adultery with me."[26]

John Guy's acquittal suggests that prominent men could shape their destinies in a courtroom drama perhaps by suborning witnesses or merely by intimidating deferential jurors dependent on the sole shopkeeper and chief moneylender in town. Although Guy died a wealthy man, he lived out his life in Branford ever conscious that his branded, former lover and a daughter who bore his name ("Sarah Smith alias Guy") were struggling to make a living in nearby New Haven.[27] Yet the stigma of adultery more readily attached itself, in both the literal and the

26. Anna Guy's Divorce petition, in Divorce papers of Anna Guy, NHSC Files, dr. 716; John Guy's letter to the Superior Court (dated Oct. 15, 1715), and Deposition of Mary Smith alias Velt (undated), Rex v. John Guy (1718), dr. 323. By July 1716 Anna Guy was acting by her husband's written power of attorney in the New Haven County Court as his agent to collect from his many debtors (John's Power of attorney to Anna was copied out in NHCC, III, 69).

27. Guilford District Probate Court Records, II, 391 (microfilm); New Haven District Probate Court Records, V, 479 (microfilm), CSL. Mary Smith remained in New Haven, remarried, and got into trouble with authorities in 1728; see the latter case described below, Chapter 6. Depositions located in the file papers for the 1718 Guy trial date from 1715—the time slated for the joint trial of Mary and John. Perhaps Guy, three years later, procured witnesses willing to come into court and impugn those written, three-year-old testimonies.

Race was evidently a key factor leading to different verdicts in the adultery trials of Abigail Clark and free black Zebulon Potter. In February 1771 Potter was found guilty and sentenced to the statutory punishment, but Clark's trial was mysteriously delayed for three years. In the meantime, while she was out on bail, her husband divorced her. Her 1774 trial ended in acquittal, despite her bearing a "mulatto" child in November 1770. Without surviving depositions, we cannot know what tactics were used by Clark's defense—perhaps a rape charge or an insanity defense. What is clear is that a white woman, despite a tainted reputation, maneuvered to evade an adultery conviction, but a free black man had no resources to ward off a speedy trial and the pain of branding, whipping, and wearing a halter. Rex v. Zebulon Potter, SCR, XX (unpaginated): February 1771 New Haven session, and NHSC Files, dr. 332; Rex v. Abigail Clark, SCR, XXI (unpaginated): February 1774 New Haven session, and NHSC Files, dr. 333.

discursive senses, to women than to men. Although Connecticut officials often declined to prosecute adultery cases that came to light through divorce trials or local rumor, the known results of those cases that were prosecuted reveal a vivid gender imbalance: at least nine women condemned as adulterers suffered severe corporal punishment, mutilation, or (in one or two cases) hanging, whereas only four men met with similar punishments. In a patrilineal society that insisted on women's subordination and obedience to men in marriage, this particular double standard—one revolving around exemplary public punishments for adultery—was perhaps inevitable.

While adultery was cast as a woman's crime, bigamy emerged as the prosecutorial sand trap for male transgressors. Straying husbands were singled out for the spectacle of whipping and branding, not for simple adultery, but only when they took their affairs one step further and arranged to be married bigamously to their lovers. The Connecticut Act against Polygamy and Unchastity authorized that the adultery punishment be applied to undivorced persons convicted of remarrying in the colony while their spouse was alive. Given that authorities used this law to pursue men more often than women, five male bigamists (and no women) were sent to the whipping post for lashes, branding, and haltering between 1755 and 1790.[28] From an arithmetic perspective, these five men balanced out the surfeit of women punished corporally for adultery. But, more importantly, these five again signal the double standard at work: they came to the whipping post, not because of sexual philandering during marriage, but because they had abandoned their roles as provider, protector, and governor of a household, leaving the possibility that their neglected wives and children might become a drain on town resources.

When illicit sex was removed from the marriage context, early New Englanders, at least in the early decades of settlement, were more open toward treating the man as the more culpable partner. Rather than the continual pattern of reacting with a special disdain toward female adulterers that linked New England with early modern England, Puritans on this side of the Atlantic broke decisively with Anglican attitudes when

---

28. Seven of the eight men prosecuted alone during this period were brought to the bar after 1772. This clustering of bigamy cases against men in the 1770s and 1780s paralleled a spate of legislative divorce decrees against violent husbands (see Chaper 3, above)—twin developments that signaled the emergence of a public concern over neglectful, intemperate, and abusive husbands.

faced with the sin of premarital sex. Far from static, the history of fornication proceedings at the county court level revolved around, first, the
suppression and, then, the emergence of the double sexual standard.

––––––––

During the Colony period of New Haven's history, magistrates and ordinary residents alike demonstrated remarkable rigor and evenhanded-
ness in the way they treated men and women who engaged in illicit
premarital affairs or flirtations. The language used by the bench in 1642
to condemn the first couple tried for fornication in the colony reveals
the central precepts that guided such cases for the next twenty years.
Samuel Hotchkiss and Elizabeth Cleverly, "haveing . . . sinfully and wickedly defiled each other with filthy dalliance and uncleane passages, by
which they have both made themselves unfitt for any other," should be
not only publicly whipped, the magistrates declared, but also given permission to marry as they requested. The court's treatment of Samuel and
Elizabeth followed from passages in Exodus and Deuteronomy while the
metaphors of pollution that permeated magisterial discussions of sex
cases had their source in the exhortations of the prophets and apostles.
New Haven settlers proved their "hatred of the sinn" to God when they
administered whippings, and in each case they prayed that it would
"please God to bless these stripes to worke out this sinnfull folly."[29]

The Colony period was not only the era of whippings for fornicators; it
was also the era of confessions. The bench was able both to convict nearly
all sexual transgressors and to mete out equal punishment to men and
women because it succeeded in persuading miscreants of *both* sexes to
confess.[30] As David Hall notes, the ritual of confession lay at the heart of

29. *NHCR,* I, 77–78, 435, II, 138. The authorities were loath to force marriage on
unwilling or unlikely couples. In only three of nine cases in which marriage could
have been ordered did the town or colony magistrates so order.

The 1656 New Haven Code summarized laws that the colony had passed since
1639. The code's fornication clause (*NHCR,* II, 590) cited Deut. 22:28–29 and
Exod. 22:16–17, both of which enjoined marriage. Other nearby passages prescribe
stoning, for which the New Englanders substituted whipping. The metaphors of
uncleanness, filth, and defilement appear throughout the Geneva and King James
translations in reference to illicit sex.

30. The caseload for noncapital, illicit consensual sexual relations in the New
Haven Colony and town courts, 1639–1669, comprised 15 fornication cases (involving 4 married couples, 1 wife alone, and 10 unmarried couples) and 13 lascivious
carriage cases or episodes (involving 14 men and 14 women prosecuted in clusters of

Puritan New England culture. If one believed that God detected all secret crimes and that in his eyes guiltiness would be doubled if a sinner lied, then it made sense to respond to the magistrates' strenuous examination with eventual confession and ultimately to submit oneself to the pain of the lash. Recalcitrance, denial, and laughing "in the face of the court" could only be signs of a person's predestined damnation.[31] The price of living under a government that promised to usher in a truly righteous human society, then, was a commitment to the notion that the battle against sin would be waged through neighborly watchfulness, truth telling, and repentance.

The Puritan emphasis on avoiding carnal temptation appears to have carried great weight among early New Haven residents. Only twenty-eight cases of illicit consensual sex reached the colony and town courts in a period in which the population ebbed and flowed but never exceeded twenty-five hundred souls.[32] Birth records reveal very few incidents of prenuptial pregnancy or out-of-wedlock births that did not catch the magistrates' attention. The talk among New Haven women in July 1649 demonstrates just how novel the discovery of a pregnant young woman among them was that summer. Speaking about pregnant Rebecca Turner, Goodwife Charles was overheard to lament "what a sad thing it was"; she went on to insinuate (wrongly, it turned out) that though she wished "ther was no more in the town in" Rebecca's condi-

---

various sizes). Of 29 fornication defendants, 24 confessed, and 3 denied the charges; in the remaining 2 instances, the defendant's final stance is not given. Among the 28 lascivious carriage defendants, 12 are recorded as offering full or partial confessions and 4 as denying the charges or refusing to confess; the responses of 12 are not clearly delineated. Gail Sussman Marcus, in surveying the whole criminal caseload in the colony and town courts, 1639–1658, found that only 14 of 201 trials did not end in conviction. Further, "of the 137 tried and the 129 convicted before 1658 whose pleas are known," 118 confessed ("'Due Execution of the Rules of Righteousnesse,'" in Hall et al., eds., *Saints and Revolutionaries*, 127, 132).

Besides a complete gap in colony records from December 1649 to May 1653, the records of the colony's Court of Magistrates are missing from April 1644 to 1653.

31. David D. Hall, *Worlds of Wonder, Days of Judgment: Popular Religious Belief in Early New England* (New York, 1989), 172, 176; John Williams, *Warnings to the Unclean: In a Discourse . . . Preacht at Springfield . . . August 25th. 1698, at the Execution of Sarah Smith* (Boston, 1699), 26. For a Dutch man who laughed at his escapades before the court, see *NHTR*, II, 68.

32. For the Colony period, I define a case as a proceeding in which magistrates tried persons alleged to have participated in a single incident; thus, one, two, or three individuals might be tried at once, in a single case.

tion, she thought "ther was a maide that satt neere her at meeting that did barnish [grow plump] apace." While neighborhood women like Goody Charles were always on the lookout for courtships gone awry, it would be another five decades before New Haveners found it believable that more than one out-of-wedlock child might be born in the town in the space of a year.[33] The scarcity of sexual transgressors in the early decades prompted one young couple to take an extraordinary measure to cover up the woman's premarital pregnancy by a man other than her intended. In 1654 John Richardson took his betrothed, Martha, to the Boston area, where she delivered a child and they were married. Rumors caught up with them on their return to New Haven Colony, they were haled into court, and there John admitted that they had taken their journey "to avoyde the shame" and "stopp reproach."[34]

Suffering reproach and publicly accounting for one's sin were un-avoidable in the colony along the Quinnipiac, as Martha Richardson discovered. Because she was pregnant again by the time she was sen-tenced, Martha was fined the very large sum of ten pounds in lieu of whipping. No man was punished with her, because she could not name the father of her first child. In contrast, in the remaining fourteen for-nication cases that came before them, New Haven Colony magistrates were able to identify both partners. Cajoling confessions out of the women and all but three of the men, the judges felt the evidence was sufficient to convict two of the accused men despite their denials.

With practically all men and women who were brought to trial confess-ing guilt, punishment was the one remaining area of discretion in which the secular authorities could signal their attitudes toward male and fe-male culpability. When initially announcing the sentence in fornication cases involving couples, the magistrates adhered as scrupulously as possi-

33. R. W. Roetger, "The Transformation of Sexual Morality in 'Puritan' New England: Evidence from New Haven Court Records, 1639–1698," *Canadian Review of American Studies*, XV (1984), 254. Even in the 1690s, there were only three years (1691, 1696, and 1699) in which as many as three children were born out of wed-lock. For similar low ratios in some early Massachusetts towns, see Smith and Hindus, "Premarital Pregnancy," *Journal of Interdisciplinary History*, V (1974–1975), 561–564; and Roger Thompson, *Sex in Middlesex*, 12–13. A reading of Donald Lines Jacobus's reliable three-volume genealogy of New Haven families (*FANH*) yields no out-of-wedlock births that did not result in court cases before 1715.

On Goodwife Charles, see the slander suit brought against Henry Peck, *NHCR*, I, 478.

34. *NHCR*, II, 122–123.

ble to the standard of equal punishment for each partner. However, they often found themselves agreeing to pleas for a lesser punishment, such as a fine, for the woman — usually justified by her "bodily weakness" (due often to pregnancy). Thus, even though the magistrates repeatedly restated their principle that each convicted fornicator, man or woman, deserved corporal punishment, in practice they more often than not sanctioned the man's receiving a harsher sentence.[35] Once the judges had shifted to imposing fines in the majority of cases, it was not unusual for a husband to receive a larger fine than his wife.[36] In Jacob Melyn's case, he deserved the extra punishment not just because it was his second sexual offense but more because "his wife alleged" that he had "draw[n] her to sin" by insisting that the "speech of Christ to the woman taken in adultry [in] John 8" applied only to "a married woman," but, he said, "it was noe sin in single persons"![37]

The magistrates' tendency to punish men as the "prime movers" in illicit premarital sex emerged more pointedly in prosecutions for "lascivious carriage" or "filthy dalliance."[38] This type of charge involved a range of acts between unmarried and unbetrothed couples that fell short of proven intercourse and included kissing, embracing, and delib-

35. Ibid., 136, 202; *NHTR*, II, 184–185, 193.

36. The final sentences handed down to the 29 fornication defendants are as shown.

		Whipping Reduced to Fine		Fine and Shaming		Fine Only	
	Whipping						
	Men	Women	Men	Women	Men	Women	Men	Women
1642–1655	6	3	0	3	1	2	0	0
1656–1668	3	2	1	1	0	1	3	3

If we compare the punishments received by men and women prosecuted *as couples*, in 5 cases each partner received the same sentence while in 8 cases the man endured a more severe penalty. The one exception involved differential status: here the woman (a servant) was whipped, and the man (a sergeant and recent widower) was dismissed with a 40s. fine (*NHCR*, II, 263–268, 289–290). For similar harsh treatment of low-status women, see Karlsen, *Devil in the Shape of a Woman*, 199–200.

37. For the Melyn case, see *NHTR*, II, 11–12; for others in which men received higher fines, see 193; *NHCR*, II, 201–202; and two aberrant post-1670 cases: Rex v. William and Sarah Abernathy (June 1674), NHCC, I, 76, and Rex v. Thomas and Abigail Barnes (June 1692), I, 199.

38. The lascivious carriage cases analyzed here are only those that involved apparently consensual relationships; I have omitted prosecutions of single individuals that involved speech or outright coercion.

erately or privately spending time in a bedchamber together. The sawyer William Harding was expelled from the colony for his repeated sexual advances toward "divers young girls." In two cases in 1640 and 1642 New Haven magistrates prosecuted and sentenced to be whipped only the men who had engaged in "sinful dalliance," not the women, although they were identified.[39] After 1642 the notion that men were often more blamable for illicit sex persisted in prosecutions for lascivious carriage. Although young women were summoned for trial along with their male partners, in eight of eleven cases the bench found reason to impose a harsher sentence on the man. With such decrees the first generation of New England leaders signaled their sympathy for one corollary of the general cultural belief in men's superior capacity for self-control: if men were indeed more rational and women's weaknesses made them less able to resist sexual temptation, then the chief onus for succumbing to lust was men's.[40]

Fornication "is that which the Holy Ghost brands with the name of folly," Governor Eaton and his fellow judges warned one young couple. "Without repentanc," the sin would shut them "out of the kingdome of heaven." Folly was a word the magistrates flung at both women and men, just as malefactors of either sex might have committed "a hainious filthyness" or "a horrible fact." While the colony authorities did not confine their most impassioned condemnations to one sex, they did portray the nature of men's and women's lapses differently. What marked a woman

39. *NHCR*, I, 38, 77, 81. These cases reflected the same pattern followed by Massachusetts judges from 1630 through the early 1640s. See Karlsen, *Devil in the Shape of a Woman*, 194–195; and David Hackett Fischer, *Albion's Seed: Four British Folkways in America* (New York, 1989), 89. Note also that as late as 1670 the Court of Assistants banished one Jacob Lucinah for his "Lascivious dalience and wanton carriages and profers to severall women" without reprimanding the women (*Recs. Ct. of Assts.*, Lacy transcript, I, 24).

40. It might also have been that magistrates in those early years of settlement were more understanding of women who found themselves pressured or coerced into sex. Taught to defer and to be pleasing, young women often could not summon the courage to call out or fight off their seducer (*NHCR*, II, 266; *NHTR*, II, 183–185; Laurel Thatcher Ulrich, *Good Wives: Image and Reality in the Lives of Women in Northern New England, 1650–1750* [New York, 1982], chap. 5). In effect, New England magistrates in this early period often approached lascivious carriage cases as if they were attempted rape incidents: they severely punished the man and sometimes declined to bring charges against the woman.

as guilty of "the great sin" of fornication in the magistrates' view was her failure to call out, to resist with force and clamor, to reject the man's assurances that he would do her no harm.[41] When a man "was by the power of temptation and corruption in his owne heart overcome," he failed to restrain his carnal appetites. The woman's availability, her efforts to please him or show her affections, or, in unusual cases, her deliberate speech and carriage "enflame[d] his lust." Although the woman's supposed consent distinguished these cases from incidents the magistrates recognized as rape, the syntax utilized by both the elite and laypeople to describe what men did in fornication scenes differed little from their depictions of coerced sex. Even on the few occasions when the woman might have been "the first Tempter," the man "had the use of her body." Was it the physical act of penetration, the resonance of biblical phrases, or the unexamined adoption of customary English folkways that prompted early New Haveners to speak of men coming to and making love to maids, and never the reverse?[42]

Yet women were not seen as completely passive. Eaton and his compeers discounted two stories of women who claimed to have been asleep during intercourse. They could not imagine a woman's conceiving "without some knowledg, consent and delight in the acting thereof." The magistrates would not countenance one woman's vague story of abuse by an unknown man told long after the fact. No, she had doubtless "two much complyed," thus rendering herself a "knowne" (knowing) fornicator, which for a woman meant becoming the vessel for her suitor's seed, the conduit for his sexual desire — desire that was "filthy" because it expended itself outside the vows of marriage.[43]

41. *NHCR*, I, 435, II, 135, 136, 266; *NHTR*, I, 498, 499, 507. Rebecca Potter interpreted her suitor's promise "that he would doe her noe wrong" to mean that she "should not be with Child and soe it would not be knowne, etc." (*NHTR*, II, 183–184).

42. Temptation and lust: *NHCR*, II, 201–202; *NHTR*, I, 499. At no time in the early New Haven records does a speaker refer to a woman's lust.

"First tempter: *NHTR*, II, 498–499. For similar findings, see Roetger, "Transformation of Sexual Morality," *Canadian Review of American Studies*, XV (1984), 253–254; and Koehler, *Search for Power*, 73–74.

"Making love": in a 1662 case, both the defendant and the court used the phrase "he made love to her" (Rex v. John Frost, *NHCR*, II, 466, and Records of New Haven Colony, IB, 331, CSL).

43. *NHCR*, II, 123, 138.

Mary Clark's case provides perhaps the most striking indication of New Haveners' tendency to think of the male partner as the chief actor and enticer in sex. Mary was no more than fifteen when she yielded to the "corrupting . . . defyling wayes" of John Knight, "wherby a filthy disposition [was] . . . wrought in her." Granted, Knight was one of the most "corrupt" men that New Haven leaders encountered. He was hanged in 1655 for his crimes of sodomy, profanity, and lying and for his incorrigibly sinful nature — probably just a few days after Mary was ordered severely whipped for complying with him. The magistrates' reasoning with respect to Mary Clark shows that they often, if not in all cases, perceived the man's lust to have been transferred to his partner through the initial sex act. As John Gillis has explained, early modern men and women viewed the boundaries between persons as porous: bodily fluids such as those transmitted in intercourse could profoundly affect not just the *body* of a man's lover but also her heart and mind. Clark, by letting her guard down with a notorious reprobate and by concealing their relations, had absorbed the unclean spirit of her seducer and gone on, predictably, to engage in "filthy miscarriages" with another man.[44]

If fornication in the mind's eye of the colonist was the sin "wherin men show their brutishness" and women demonstrate folly by relenting, female culpability was measured in complex ways.[45] In statutes and sermons the Puritan fathers warned men and women alike against external conditions that could draw them into sin — nightwalking, keeping bad company, ignoring parental advice. But magistrates in the course of examining suspects directed scrutiny and admonitions concerning these factors primarily at women.

A host of small signs aggravated a woman's guilt in the magistrates' eyes: walking out at night with men whom their parents or master and mistress had specifically warned them against, consenting to sex without showing interest in securing a pledge of marriage, lying to the older women of the neighborhood who served as local arbiters of courtships and female sexuality. What alarmed the magistrates particularly was to

44. *NHCR*, II, 138–139; John R. Gillis, "From Ritual to Romance: Toward an Alternative History of Love," in Carol Z. Stearns and Peter N. Stearns, eds., *Emotion and Social Change: Toward a New Psychohistory* (New York, 1988), 90, 93.

45. *NHCR*, I, 435; Ulrich, *Good Wives*, 97; Koehler, *Search for Power*, 73 (citing methods of restraint aimed at men).

find themselves confronted with transgressing women who were church members, "had godly parents," enjoyed the best education and religious instruction, or previously had walked in "the light."[46] The privileges and status of these young women led to high expectations for their pious conduct and aggravated the sin of their fall into fornication or dalliance. To the bench such a woman was "a sad object" because she represented the potential conflation of the virtuous daughter of Zion with "a common Harlot." In this intensely Puritan era, the multifaceted scrutiny of young women's conduct operated alongside concerted efforts to hold their male partners accountable as well. After the New Haven Colony passed out of existence, the fathers of government, laboring in a less godly climate, would search for new frameworks designed to regulate youthful sexual relations.[47]

Between 1639 and 1666, the colony magistrates failed to convict only one man prosecuted for fornication, Sergeant John Baldwin. Disappointed that Baldwin refused to confess "as he ought," the colony court was unable to prove fornication and paternity charges against him in 1658. The judges assessed Baldwin's accuser, Bethia Hawes, as "a loose, vaine wench," not the sort who could be expected to avoid nightwalking, fabrications, and dangerous flirtations. However distasteful they found Bethia's character, the New Haven magistrates, in a gesture that underscored the uniqueness of their regime, proclaimed their hope that

46. Walking out at night: *NHTR*, I, 451, 461, 499, II, 65–71. Consenting easily: *NHCR*, II, 265; *NHTR*, I, 507; note the obverse case of Hannah Spencer, who began a marriage treaty with her lover the morning after they had sex on an overnight sea voyage (*NHCR*, II, 134–136). Lying to older women: *NHCR*, I, 265; Ulrich, *Good Wives*, 98–103. Church members: *NHTR*, I, 8–9, 461, II, 69, 71, 183.

47. *NHTR*, I, 507, II, 9, 183. No similar lamentations over dashed expectations were voiced with regard to the men charged. The logic of admonishing higher-status women for their aggravated sins parallels that of holding men, perceived as the more rational sex, more accountable than women.

Perhaps the discrepancy in tone reflects the fact that sons of eminent leaders were slightly less likely to appear on fornication and dalliance charges than leaders' daughters. Of the 29 women charged with either crime, 5 had officeholding fathers (for example, militia sergeants, deputies, judges).

In contrast, only 3 of the 28 men prosecuted can be linked definitively to higher-status fathers. Although 5 of the 14 men charged with lascivious carriage were outsiders of some kind (such as the two Dutch Melyn brothers), the bulk of the 14 fornication defendants were young men who married and became permanent, settled members of New Haven.

Bethia's severe whipping would be "a warning to any that have had sinfull familiarity with her."[48]

As a warning intended for *men* rather than women, as a jolting physical act that had the power to reach into men's hearts and compel them to confess and reform, Bethia's lashes reminded her fellow sinners of all ranks and sexes that they lived under a government that would not tolerate sexual license in men. A severe reprimand was the lot of any soul who dared to express such "unclean" thinking as Goodwife Bayley did. Twice she justified a male's predatory sexual behavior with this logic: "What would you have the man doe[?] [I]f his owne wife was weake, he must have some body." For three short decades jests and stories built around the approval of male philandering were limited to a few seamen, outlivers, and "scoffers" at religion. The question that guided the magistrates' final disposition of fornicators—whether the fallen woman should "be Corporally punished as he that was companion with her in sin" — would soon be replaced by its opposite.[49]

––––––––

In 1666, Connecticut having absorbed New Haven Colony, the landmass comprising the towns of New Haven, Branford, Milford, Guilford, Wallingford, and Derby became New Haven County. In June a quorum of justices appointed to the county court convened for the first time. Although among the justices were several men who had presided over town and colony courts before the union, gone was the rigorous Puritan jurisprudence that had made adjudication in New Haven Colony unique. Juries were now impaneled, and witnesses and criminal defendants put to oath. And yet judicial discretion was still immense, and Puritan understandings of sin continued to shape laws and enforcement. As it always had been, fornication was punishable by "enjoyning to Marriage, or fine, or Corporal punishment, or all, or any of these, as the Court . . . shall judge most agreeable to the Word of God." In its new Code of Laws Connecticut included, in emulation of Massachusetts and English provi-

48. *NHCR*, II, 263–268, 289–291. The whipping was administered in Milford, Bethia's town.

49. *NHTR*, I, 246, II, 8; 2 Pet. 3:3 ("scoffers"). A lusty male dog occasioned Bayley's second refrain excusing the male's carnal voraciousness. For a man who condoned fornication on his vessel and bragged about his role to seamen after, see William Benfield's behavior, *NHCR*, II, 134–136.

TABLE 7

Fornication Prosecutions of Married Persons,
New Haven County Court, 1670–1789

	Husband and Wife	Wife Only	Proportion of All Decadal Fornication Cases (Couples and Singles)
1670–1679	5	0	71%[a]
1680–1689	6	0	60
1690–1699	24	0	60
1700–1709	23	0	77
1710–1719	23	0	58
1720–1729	74	0	73
1730–1739	107	0	88
1740–1749	44	2	69
1750–1759	26	4	59
1760–1769	31	0	48
1770–1779	3	0	17
1780–1789	0	0	
Overall	366	6	67%

[a] Decadal proportions in Tables 7 and 8 total 100%.

Source: New Haven County Court Records and Files, 1666–1790, CSL.

sions, the "bastardy" provision that, as we saw at the beginning of this chapter, Joseph Nettleton challenged in 1723.[50]

These two laws stayed on the books into the nineteenth century, and they governed the disposition of the 554 criminal cases and the 48 paternity suits in the new county that came before the county court between 1666 and 1790 (see Tables 7 and 8 for the criminal caseload and Table 9 for paternity suits). Despite unchanging statutory guidelines, the county

50. For fornication, compare the Connecticut Code of 1672 (Cushing, ed., *Earliest Laws of New Haven and Connecticut,* 100), quoted here, to the 1656 New Haven Code (ibid., 32) and Connecticut Colony's Code of 1650 (*PR,* I, 527). Bastardy: Cushing, ed., *Earliest Laws of New Haven and Connecticut,* 80. The new code was passed by the legislature and became effective in October 1672, but it was not printed until 1673.

TABLE 8

Fornication Prosecutions of Single Persons,
New Haven County Court, 1670–1789

	Single Woman and Man Paired[a]	Single Woman Alone	Man Alone	Total Cases	Proportion of All Decadal Fornication Cases
1670–1679	1	1	0	2	29%
1680–1689	4	0	0	4	40
1690–1699	4	9	3	16	40
1700–1709	3	2	2	7	23
1710–1719	8	8	0	16	41
1720–1729	13	13	1	27	27
1730–1739	5	10	0	15	12
1740–1749	2	19	0	21	31
1750–1759	0	22	0	22	42
1760–1769	0	34	0	34	52
1770–1779	2[b]	13	0	15	83
1780–1789	1	2	0	3	100
Overall	43	133	6	182	33%

[a]Each case represents two defendants.
[b]Interracial couple prosecuted twice.
Source: New Haven County Court Records and Files, 1666–1790, CSL.

court's approach to the crime of fornication and the problem of single motherhood went through three quite different stages. To understand why Sarah Hine had to take her case all the way to the General Assembly and why women began bringing civil paternity suits in the 1740s, we need to follow the county magistrates as they attempted to fashion an effective legal system amid changing popular attitudes toward sin, sex, and community.

During the first twenty-four years of the county court's existence, fornication cases followed the patterns set in the Colony period in several respects. Miscreants were haled before the bar at a slow, uneven pace. That the bench heard an average of .85 cases per year in the 1670–1689 period suggests that premarital pregnancy and illegitimacy rates remained strikingly low. During one eleven-year period (1676–1687) no prosecutions against single persons found their way onto the docket. When a premarital pregnancy was spotted and the woman charged, she was in all but one instance called to account along with her husband or the man she named as the child's father.[51] Only when Hannah Terrill named a man living outside the county's jurisdiction did a woman appear alone for trial. Thus until 1690, at least at the initial prosecutorial stage, communities and magistrates alike supported a system under which a couple not married by the time their child was born would be dealt with together before the county court. Finally, the court clerk occasionally recorded confessions from repentant malefactors, men as well as women, that echo the rich language of sorrow and self-abasement that was demanded of New Haveners by their first leaders. As late as 1689, young John Clark in pleading guilty for himself and his wife told the justices that "he desired to be humbled for it while he lived . . . ; though his heart was naught yet he hoped the lord would doe him good by it."[52]

What distinguished the county court's early handling of fornication from that of the New Haven Colony's legal regime was the abandonment of whipping. Colony magistrates had begun to back off from a universal policy of sentencing to the lash in the mid-1650s, but after 1670 the bench gave almost all convicted fornicators the choice between whipping and paying a fine.[53] Practically all convicted whites chose the fine, cajoling parents or friends to put up the security pledging timely payment. The first sentencing of a black man, in 1688, set the pattern that New Haven judges would follow for all five "negroes" brought before

51. The records give no hint whether these women appeared at first voluntarily or by grand jury presentment.

52. Rex v. Hannah Terrill (June 1671), NHCC, I, 35, 44 (Hannah named a man from Rye); Clark: I, 175. Few file papers survive for the pre-1710 period, and the record books document much less of defendants' language than do the town court and colony records for 1640–1666.

53. Note that R. W. Roetger's analysis of this shift differs from mine in the way in which it counts cases ("Transformation of Sexual Morality," *Canadian Review of American Studies*, XV [1984], 251–252). The judges were initially defensive about their new policy of offering fines as an alternative to whipping: a five-pound fine, they insisted in the 1670 case of Hannah Terrill, was "a just punishment of her wickedness" (NHCC, I, 35).

them in the next two decades: after Toney, a "negro servant," confessed to fornication with a white servant, he was sentenced to receive twenty stripes.[54] Since corporal punishment was no longer routinely applied to all whites in fornication cases, the image of a black man or woman at the whipping post became yet another device dramatizing the social and legal distance that early Americans wished to put between themselves and Africans. And 1670 becomes the juncture at which New Haveners finally gave up the ideal of submitting themselves to the biblical penalties of the lash and requisite marriage that Samuel Hotchkiss and Elizabeth Cleverly had borne in 1642.

Post-1670 fornication prosecutions departed from New Haven tradition in one other procedural sense. The bench extended a newfound sympathy to newly married women: in most cases the husband appeared alone in county court, making excuses that his wife or their infant was ill and thus she was "incapable" of appearing according to summons. For the most part the justices accepted the wife's absence and allowed her spouse to pay a lump-sum fine for them both. Magisterial leniency depended on their receiving word that the woman had already made a proper confession of her sin alongside her husband in the pretrial hearing before a local justice of the peace.[55] By demoting the site of a wife's public confession to a local court, by assessing couples with a standard lump-sum fine, and by jettisoning the language of defilement along with admonishments tailored to each case, the bench ushered in an era in which fornication committed by persons who later married was distinguished from sex that led to an out-of-wedlock birth. Furthermore, the practice of excusing wives from public appearances and letting husbands stand in for them suggested that women, once married, need not be held accountable as individuals for their actions. Judges' decisions to

54. NHCC, I, 35, sheets sewn in between 164 and 165. Toney was also ordered to pay maintenance, although it is unclear whether the court intended his master to make the weekly payments, or Toney himself if he were a free man earning wages. Between 1710 and 1770, no New Haven County fornication cases involved non-whites.

55. Wives appeared in only 3 of 11 cases in the 1670–1689 years. The practice of excusing wives from appearing persisted, but it was not sanctioned by statute or by the appellate court. In October 1700, the Court of Assistants voided the fornication judgment and fine against a New London woman because she had not been brought before the county court to answer the charges and receive sentence in person (*Recs. Ct. of Assts.*, Lacy transcript, I, 335–336).

make blanket exceptions to seventeenth-century policy thus reinforced women's political subordination and invisibility before the law.

Although premarital fornication was treated in a more routine fashion after 1670, it was by no means decriminalized at this time: the penalty carried quite a sting, since until the 1690s the standard fine remained the hefty sum of five pounds—the equivalent of one milk cow or an acre of meadow.[56] The de facto policy of fining only husbands in the county courtroom was not so much a rejection of the double standard as it was a convenient gesture that underscored who held the reins of authority—and the purse strings—in each newly formed household. Taken together, the shifts to whipping only blacks and to excusing newly married wives of yeomen from court appearances signal the earliest intrusions of embourgeoisement into the realm of sexual regulation. Both changes served to privatize and shield the physical body of middling whites from public chastisement.

In the Colony period, whippings, warnings couched in dramatic biblical phrases, and couplings that precipitated a marriage performed in court had blurred the line between trials of married couples and trials of still-single pairs. After 1670, with the theatricality drained from the court appearance of married persons, the spotlight of community talk and spectator interest on court days turned on the cases of unwed parents. Such couples had doubly lapsed, first in succumbing to sexual temptation and second in not obeying the biblical and community assumption that such persons should marry. Before 1690, the court heard the first five cases that could have been adjudicated under the bastardy law of 1672. The statute was applied in only one case, however, since its test for paternity (which grew out of England's search for ways to cope with the poor) rested on the assumption that the man would deny the charge. Three men—Adam Baldry, Joseph Russell, and the black servant Toney—confessed to the bench, albeit only after they had been haled before authorities on their lover's accusation. With a confession in hand, the bench, operating increasingly under the color of English common law court procedures rather than posing as the oracle of communal will, could apply Connecticut's fornication law to the man, selecting a punishment it felt was appropriate. Toney was whipped; Baldry, an apprentice, agreed to serve an extra five years in order to reimburse his

56. Jackson Turner Main, "The Distribution of Property in Colonial Connecticut," in James Kirby Martin, ed., *The Human Dimensions of Nation Making: Essays on Colonial and Revolutionary America* (Madison, Wis., 1976), 101.

mistress for paying his fine and maintenance share; and Russell, after the law was read to him aloud in court, agreed to marry his lover and pay a fine.[57] A fourth man was not so willing to abide by Puritan expectations: eighteen-year-old John Tuttle fled temporarily when Abigail Humiston, nine years his senior, named him as father of her child. The court interpreted his evasion of prosecution as a denial of the charges and applied the bastardy statute. Tuttle was ordered to make maintenance payments to Abigail until the child was eight years old, but criminal charges against him were not pursued.[58]

The 1670–1690 decades proved to be the last gasp for convictions based on men's confessions. Like many initially evasive men before him, Joseph Russell had to be coaxed to confess by judges and bystanders in the 1687 courtroom. "After much labouring with him for conviction and oweing the truth both by the court and others of his friends and relations, he did confesse and owne that what the said Jane Blackman had charged and accused him with was true." Russell was the next-to-last single man who was white to confess to fornication in the New Haven County Court. Clergyman John Williams bore witness to the trend, even if he did not identify its gendered dimension. In a 1698 sermon, Williams recounted: "Time was when the accusations of conscience made [fornicators] tremble," but many now "commit this Sin . . . without remorse."[59] Despite the cooling of young men's Puritan zeal, grand jurors and magistrates until the 1730s would continue to bring neighborhood men up on both fornication and bastardy charges. These efforts, combined with the growing legal tactics tried by accused men, turned selected fornication proceedings into prolonged courtroom battles.

57. Rex v. Elisabeth Ling and Adam Baldry (Nov. 1675), NHCC, I, 88; Rex v. Jane Blackman and Joseph Russell (Aug. 1687), I, 168. According to the Barbour Collection of Vital Records, volume for New Haven (I, 96), Russell's marriage actually took place in the June before his August trial. It was performed by magistrate William Jones, perhaps at the couple's pretrial hearing.

58. NHCC, I, sheets between 164 and 165 (June 1688 term). About 10 years later Tuttle married Abigail's first cousin in New Haven. See I, 170, 222, 224, for continuing orders governing the child. In the fifth case, charges were dismissed against Thomas Harrison for inadequate proof, because Hannah Swayne could not "positively" account for how she got pregnant beyond noting that she had spent several nights with him (I, 167–168).

59. NHCC, I, 168; Williams, *Warnings to the Unclean,* 23. The last to confess was Thomas Briggs, who confessed after a "private conference" with his lover in the courtroom in January 1700/1 (Rex v. Briggs and Elizabeth Matthews, NHCC, II, 49).

The pattern of fornication prosecutions in New Haven County shifted abruptly in the 1690s. Not only did the number of charges against newly married couples for prenuptial pregnancy quadruple in that decade, but for the first time a significant number of unwed mothers were convicted while no charges were filed against their sexual partners. These two patterns continued to dominate the criminal docket until 1740. Prosecutions of husbands and wives peaked in the 1730s at 107 cases (Table 7). Between 1690 and 1740, only 33 of the 75 single women prosecuted saw the man they named pursued at the county court level (Table 8). At the same time that large numbers of men fled fornication charges, those prosecuted used pleas of not guilty, requests for jury trials, and appeals to challenge the traditional processes by which men had been held accountable and punished for fathering out-of-wedlock children. By the 1730s New Haven County magistrates had given up on imposing criminal sanctions on unmarried male fornicators. As fewer and fewer men received court orders to pay child support, more young pregnant women and their families were left to shoulder the costs alone or to cast about for help outside the criminal justice system.[60]

Why the shift in the 1690s? The decade of the witchcraft hysteria in Salem is typically associated with an unusually high degree of social and economic distress, uncertainty over political direction and governance, and loud lamentations over a marked loss of piety in the general populace. But did these trends characterize New Haven? The county court judges, newly commissioned by the Andros regime, sat as a quarter sessions court for four terms in 1688, and it is possible that that experience, along with Connecticut's fear of losing its charter, prompted magistrates to insist on a more rigorous pursuit of fornicators.[61] In the English mode, that meant making an example of "lewd women." But the contexts of the "bastardy problem" in England and New England could not have been more different. In England, unwed mothers were sent to the house

60. Roger Thompson finds that the evasion of men began in Middlesex County, Mass., in the 1670s (*Sex in Middlesex,* 29–30).

Criminal cases gave rise to the following number of maintenance orders against men named reputed fathers: one in the 1670s, two in the 1680s, four in the 1690s, two for the 1700–1709 years, six in the 1710s, nine in the 1720s, two in the 1730s, and one in the 1740s. After 1745, the county court ordered a man to pay child support only in the context of a civil paternity suit brought by the child's mother.

61. The court personnel changed somewhat: the elected governor, Robert Treat, was dropped off, and three new justices sat in 1688 alongside three holdovers.

of correction for one year; most, though not all, were servants who sought employment because they had few or no family resources.[62] In Connecticut the single mothers who were prosecuted more often than not came from middling to prosperous yeoman households. Their fathers paid their daughters' fines and maintained them until they married a few years later.

Although the English concern over controlling births to unmarried poor women might have rubbed off on New England legal authorities, it is more likely that the upsurge in prosecutions in the 1690s was a response to a real increase in the number of premarital pregnancies and out-of-wedlock births. R. W. Roetger calculates that 19 percent of New Haven's brides were pregnant in the 1690s, whereas only 2 percent had been in the 1670s.[63] The increase in premarital sex did not go unobserved by contemporaries. At the close of the seventeenth century, the minister John Williams used the forum of a public hanging to warn against the "prevailing, growing evil" of "Uncleanness." Although "not many . . . have [yet] . . . had Bastards laid to their charge," Williams intoned, youths and servants were increasingly "toying and dallying [wantonly] one with another, foolishly sporting on beds . . . , unreproved" by "Heads of Families." Not only did "such days" call for parents to reinstill discipline at home, but Williams also implored young people to resist the peer pressure that labeled one "a meer laughing stock" or a "silly creature" for refusing to join in the merriment.[64]

The severe Puritan strictures against what was probably an English and European peasant custom of long standing — sexual relations as a condoned aspect of courtship and betrothal — had lost their bite in New England by 1700. Indeed, sex as part of courtship became such an open question in the early eighteenth century that the issue was chosen as the debating topic for a Harvard College club in 1722: students publicly argued, "Whether it be Fornication to lye with one's Sweetheart (after contract) before Marriage?" Moreover, just as attitudes shifted toward what was permissible between betrothed persons, demographic factors heightened the likelihood of out-of-wedlock births. By the end of the seventeenth century, the scarcity of land available to maturing sons,

62. King, "Punishment for Bastardy," *Albion*, X (1978), 130–151 (quote on 133).

63. Roetger, "Transformation of Sexual Morality," *Canadian Review of American Studies*, XV (1984), 254. See also Smith and Hindus, "Premarital Pregnancy," *Journal of Interdisciplinary History*, V (1974–1975), 549–550, 561–564.

64. Williams, *Warnings to the Unclean*, 20, 22, 50.

along with the good health and impressive fertility of New England residents, had produced something of a population crisis. With more young men leaving their natal villages to find work and land, the incidence of failed courtships increased, because lovers were not in a position to marry.[65]

If the rate of premarital pregnancy took off in New Haven County in the late seventeenth century, why did prosecutions climb steadily until the 1730s and then drop off? Birth records show that, after 1740, many children continued to be born within eight months of marriage and, less frequently, that children were born out-of-wedlock, yet no prosecutions ensued. With respect to patterns of prosecution against young married couples, the timing and force with which the Great Awakening struck in the New Haven area may provide an explanation. Although a few county towns felt some effect from a Little Awakening, which spread down the Connecticut River valley from 1734 to 1736, county residents and churches were most profoundly shaken by religious enthusiasm and dissension after the October 1740 visit of the enormously popular Anglican preacher George Whitefield. During the rest of the decade, virtually all of the touring revivalists found responsive audiences in New Haven, and Yale College became a veritable center of revivalism.[66]

The renewed religious intensity manifested itself within the established Congregational churches both through parish schisms over the propriety of enthusiastic preaching and through increases in church membership, notably among unmarried young people.[67] Beginning in the 1690s, Congregational ministers had often come under heavy criticism for insisting on disciplining strayed church members for sins such

65. Debate topic quoted in James D. Hart, *The Popular Book: A History of America's Literary Taste* (New York, 1950), 23.

66. Stephen Nissenbaum, ed., *The Great Awakening at Yale College* (Belmont, Calif., 1972), esp. 1–11. For a more detailed account, see Benjamin Trumbull, *A Complete History of Connecticut, Civil and Ecclesiastical, from the Emigration of Its First Planters . . .* (Hartford, 1797), II, chaps. 7, 8, 12, 13, and 14.

67. No historian has examined the composition of new membership in the Awakening in New Haven County churches. I am assuming that many of them experienced the same sort of influx of communicants 18–20 years old as did the First Congregational Church of Woodbury, a town just to the west of New Haven County. See James Walsh, "The Great Awakening in the First Congregational Church of Woodbury, Connecticut," *WMQ*, XXVIII (1971), 543–567. On criticism of ministers, see Richard L. Bushman, *From Puritan to Yankee: Character and the Social Order in Connecticut, 1690–1765* (New York, 1970), 159–162.

as fornication. The result apparently was that church members' confessions to fornication slowed to a trickle in most parishes in the years preceding the revivals. Throughout the century, grand jurors—in a respectful gesture toward the right against double jeopardy—chose not to present to the county court married couples who had already been disciplined for fornication in their church.[68] Thus in the 1720s and 1730s, local grand jurors might have understood their own action of dramatically increasing presentments as a necessary corrective to the laxity displayed in the churches. Conversely, after 1740, with the renewed commitment of young people to the church, increasing numbers of fornicators in some parishes confessed to their sins and accepted discipline within the church. Married couples would have been especially motivated to do so by the desire to have their first child baptized.[69] With more couples confessing to their congregations after the 1730s, grand jurors' enforcement of the secular laws against premarital fornication became focused more narrowly on the unregenerate.

Part of the explanation for the drop in prosecutions of married couples in the 1740s may be generational. As men born in the 1690s became grand jurors, jurors, and judges, many might have brought to their posts

68. For an argument that the New England colonies established a firmer policy against double jeopardy than held true in England, see McManus, *Law and Liberty in Early New England,* 98. The records of the First Church of Branford show 42 married couples confessing to fornication between 1733 (when the records begin) and 1780. Only 1 of those couples was afterward presented by grand jurors; 2 additional couples confessed in church some months after their criminal cases were completed (Branford First Congregational Church Records, 1687–1821, I, CSL).

69. For links between revivals and rising church discipline cases, see Emil Oberholzer, Jr., *Delinquent Saints: Disciplinary Action in the Early Congregational Churches of Massachusetts* (New York, 1956), 237–238, and appendix; and Henry Bamford Parkes, "Morals and Law Enforcement in Colonial New England," *New England Quarterly,* V (1932), 443–444.

In my own research in extant New Haven County church records, I have found a list of confessions covering the Awakening period for one church, the First Congregational Church of Branford (Records, 1687–1821, I, CSL). Branford's minister from 1732 was Philemon Robbins, a supporter of the revival. Robbins's discipline records show a small number of church members confessing fornication in the 1730s and 1740s (5 and 2, respectively), with increases thereafter: 10 confessions in the 1750s, 12 in the 1760s, 16 in the 1770s, 17 in the 1780s. Conversely, fornication prosecutions of Branford residents in the county court peaked in the 1730s and 1740s (at 15 and 10 respectively) and dwindled away to an average of 1.3 cases for each of the next three decades.

a more entrenched version of the attitude first glimpsed in their parents: the desire to spare respectable men and women the public humiliation of a courtroom reprimand. Grand jurors in New Haven County, however, did not entirely abandon fornication prosecutions of married couples after 1740 as did their counterparts elsewhere in Connecticut and Massachusetts. Until the eve of the Revolution, they continued to present clusters of husbands and wives, although in greatly reduced numbers compared to the peak of the 1730s. Perhaps prosecuted couples were singled out because of their disreputable status, or perhaps grand jurors felt an obligation to make at least token gestures toward upholding New Haven's legacy as the most Puritan of colonies, as an exemplar in morals regulation.[70]

Even though cases against husbands and wives filled the criminal docket in the decades before 1740, the penalties grew even less burdensome. In a 1727 supplement to the fornication statute, the General Assembly lowered the fine for couples to fifty shillings, the amount paid by convicted single persons.[71] As in the 1670–1690 period, wives continued to be excused regularly from a county court appearance. But, in a twist that left wives exposed to special scrutiny, grand jurors, trial jurors, and magistrates displayed a new openness to the idea that the young bride might have had sex with someone other than the man she married, thus justifying exempting the new groom from punishment.

In 1681, the bench had expressed their "great dissatisfaction" when a husband for the first time denied his wife's admission of their premarital

---

70. For jurisdictions where prosecutions of married couples nearly disappeared from county courts after the 1730s, see Windham County Court Records, CSL; Christine Leigh Heyrman, *Commerce and Culture: The Maritime Communities of Colonial Massachusetts, 1690–1750* (New York, 1984), 384; Hartog, "Public Law of a County Court," *American Journal of Legal History*, XX (1976), 300; Marsella, *Crime and Community*, 20, table 5; and Henry Bamford Parkes, "Morals and Law Enforcement in Colonial New England," *New England Quarterly*, V (1932), 442–443. For a dissent from this periodization, see William E. Nelson, "Emerging Notions of Modern Criminal Law in the Revolutionary Era: An Historical Perspective," *New York University Law Review*, XLII (1967), 453n.

71. *Acts and Laws of His Majesties Colony of Connecticut in New England — Passed by the General Assembly, May 1716 to May 1749* (1750; rpt., Hartford, 1919), 341. The fine was thus equivalent to 12 bushels of corn or half the price of a milk cow. See Main, "Distribution of Property in Colonial Connecticut," in Martin, ed., *Human Dimensions of Nation Making*, 101–102.

coupling.[72] However, after the turn of the century, magistrates grew more self-conscious about following proper common law trial procedures. In fornication cases, the New Haven justices now put aside the personal knowledge and attitudes that had led them to dismiss husbands' separate claims of not guilty. Between 1700 and 1730, four married men were granted jury trials because they insisted on their own innocence while their wives confessed to their joint guilt; in three such instances the husbands won acquittals.[73] This new wrinkle in premarital fornication prosecutions was taken to its ultimate stage in the 1740s and 1750s when six new brides were prosecuted alone; the authorities maintained silence on who they assumed the women's partners had been (Table 7).[74] In casting doubt on the word of some young wives, in allowing newly married men to manipulate the uncertainty over paternity, and in occasionally prosecuting brides without naming their lovers, the magistrates and jurors who sat in judgment over criminal suspects showed themselves to be moving toward the rather illogical tableau by which fornication would be presented to the public as a female crime.[75]

72. Rex v. Miles and Hannah Merwin (Nov. 1681), NHCC, I, 129; the justices ordered Miles to pay five pounds to cover both his fine and his wife's.

73. Rex v. Samuel Johnson, Jr., and Anna (Hotchkiss) (Nov. 1706), NHCC, II, 244, 263; Regina v. Rebeckah Alling, Regina v. Daniel Alling, Regina v. Susanna Hotchkiss, Regina v. Daniel Hotchkiss (all in the Jan. 1712/3 term), II, 403–404; Rex v. Joseph Wooden, Rex v. Sarah Wooden (Nov. 1726), III, 231, and NHCC Files, dr. 6. Surviving records in most of these cases fail to reveal whether the husbands' pleas were based on a denial of paternity or simply on a technicality or prematurity defense in which the wives neglected or refused to join.

74. For one of these cases in which the husband posted bond for his wife's county court appearance, see Rex v. Lucretia Evarts (Nov. 1750), NHCC, IV, 422. No evidence indicates for any of these cases that the husband had either died or temporarily fled. That the Hartford County Sessions Court under the Andros regime prosecuted a wife alone decades before New Haven officials did can be taken as one measure of the distance between Puritan and English approaches to fornication (*Records of the Particular Court of the Colony of Connecticut, Administration of Sir Edmond Andros, Royal Governor, 1687–1688* [Hartford, 1935], 21).

75. The language of several post-1690 presentments indicates that authorities no longer automatically assumed that the husband was the father. Twice in 1739, for example, grand jurors sought the married women's explicit (ultimately unrefuted) statement that the child "was begotten by her husband." Rex v. Stephen and Mary Beecher, Jr. (Apr. 1739), NHCC Files, dr. 11; Rex v. Abraham and Mary Atwater (Apr. 1739), ibid. See also Rex v. Richard and Anna Handy (Nov. 1734), ibid.

The newfound tendency of men to resist fornication charges was particularly marked among the single men accused of fathering out-of-wedlock children. No longer willing to confess and "take shame to themselves," more than half (forty of seventy-five) of the men at risk for prosecution between 1690 and 1740 evaded the legal system altogether (and two more died before being named). Among those summoned before the bar, twenty-one of twenty-two whose pleas are on record pleaded not guilty. Thus, for the first time, New Haven justices were obliged to apply the 1672 statute to a substantial parade of cases. Beginning in 1717, a succession of ten men, including Joseph Nettleton, displayed considerable legal acumen: they demanded jury trials to contest the criminal component of the process. In effect, they used the jury trial to point to the discrepancy between the Massachusetts statute, which explicitly exempted men from punishment beyond maintenance payments, and the Connecticut law, which remained silent whether magistrates could order fines or whipping for convicted men. The success of strategies used by young Connecticut males to rebuff fornication charges in the early eighteenth century sounded the death knell for the older, Puritan-inspired system, which aimed to punish errant men and women side by side.

The men who avoided prosecution fell into three categories. First came the "strangers" and "transients" — men who had ventured or resided beyond county bounds and thus were outside the reach of New Haven's prosecutors. That such men made up 16 percent of fathers named by single women over the five decades suggests the presence of a significant number of temporary or marginal male laborers in New Haven County. As the rural New England labor force came to include more such mobile youths, sexual encounters that failed to result in marriage were bound to increase. Second on the roster of men not prosecuted were locals whom pregnant women identified as their lovers but whom prosecutors chose not to summon on charges. Their reasons for

---

Justice of the peace records for Windsor in Hartford County reveal two cases in which the single woman had married the man she accused by the time of her county court trial. Yet in neither case was the man bound over for trial or called to account by the bench. See Rex v. Lois Porter, Entry for June 22, 1734, Justice of the Peace Records of Roger Wolcott (microfilm), CHS; and Hartford County Court, Record Book, IX, 440, CSL; Rex v. Elizabeth Read, Entry for Jan. 14, 1724/5, Windsor Justice of the Peace Records [of Matthew Allyn] (microfilm), CHS, and Hartford County Court, Record Book, IV, 266, CSL.

not pursuing these men were never explicitly stated. Sometimes the men fled temporarily, as Nathan Smith of Milford did in 1711. When Smith reappeared a few months later, a local magistrate informed the county court that "he could be taken," but no warrant was issued. It is probable that some women, by naming their lover in childbirth and again before a justice of the peace, pressured him into agreeing to make maintenance payments if he refused to enter into marriage.[76] Apprised of such agreements, the local grand jurors and justices opted to prosecute only the single mother — the most visible emblem of the young people's lapse.

Although most New Haven County single mothers continued to name fathers for their children, a third category of men avoided prosecution simply because they went unnamed. In an increasing number of cases justices failed to record whether a woman named anyone.[77] After the 1740s this absence on the record became standard. The records sent by local justices to the court suggest that the magistrates omitted questioning some women about the identity of their sexual partners. This practice could reflect justices' collusion with women who wished to remain silent or who were already collecting maintenance payments. But the trend toward representing women as silent and men as absent clearly signaled the authorities' gradual abandonment of a system under which the county court or even the local magistrate's parlor served as a public forum in which both young men and women were held accountable for their sexual transgressions.

Young men unable to flee or evade prosecution began to seek out

76. On Smith: Samuel Eells to John Alling, Judge of the County Court (n.d., probably between Feb. and May 1712), in Rex v. Abigail Briscoe (April 1712), NHCC Files, dr. 3.

Very occasionally, references to maintenance agreements surface in the case files. Samuel Eells, an assistant, handled one 1722 case as if it were a private prosecution brought by the single mother's father. When Abigail Terrill named fellow townsman Thomas Northrop, Eells reported to the county court that "Northropp was taken by a writ from me and discharged by Mr. Terril as I have been informed for a sum of money" (Rex v. Abigail Terrill [Nov. 1722], ibid., dr. 6). "Mr. Terril" was a very wealthy man (he died in 1727 worth £3,456), but he still felt it appropriate to demand some measure of restitution from young Northrop (New Haven District Probate Court Records, V, 382–383 [microfilm]).

77. There were one such case in the 1710s, four such cases in the 1720s, and five in the 1730s. I distinguish these cases from another five in which women in response to judicial questions refused to name a man. Here, it is clear that the women — whether through fright, confusion, coercion, bribery, or affectionate loyalty — had determined to protect their lover's identity.

lawyers to help them contest fornication charges. Joseph Nettleton retained an attorney, as did at least seven other men who came before the bar.[78] Pleading not guilty could lead to two sorts of trials, either a ruling by the bench or, if requested by the defendant, a jury trial. In the New Haven County Court, judges and trial jurors in the 1690–1740 period moved to adopt the logic of the Massachusetts system: given a man's denial of the charges, he should be criminally punishable *only* if damning evidence existed beyond the woman's accusation. In all but four of twenty-four trials, the male defendant was excused, silently or explicitly, from a criminal fine but was nonetheless declared, as the statute dictated, the "reputed father" and ordered to make maintenance payments.[79] In three cases, jurors clashed with the judges or hesitated over their decision, bringing in a not guilty verdict only on the second or third consideration.[80] Most probably, the men on the bench were insisting on more rigorous standards of proof. At the very least, the trial jurors' uncertainty underscores the 1710s and 1720s as a transitional moment in New Haven's handling of fornication cases.[81]

What was happening? Gradually, in the post-1690 decades, concern over the procedural protections of male defendants was replacing the earlier Puritan emphasis on the collective obligation to atone for sins. Looking back from the vantage point of 1795, jurist Zephaniah Swift pointed out that the 1672 statute, "by admitting the oath of the woman to prove the father of a bastard child, introduces a new mode of proof, which is repugnant to the general rule respecting evidence."[82] This singularity in the fornication law — its reliance on a woman's word — is doubtless what New Haven County lawyers emphasized in their argu-

78. "Council" or attorney's fees as part of court costs are mentioned in five cases taken to juries and three pleaded to the bench.

79. Maintenance payments were calculated at half the lying-in costs and half the standard annual upkeep of a child, to be paid quarterly for four years or for the child's life up to that point. The premise was that the mother or her family (or if they could not pay, the town) was paying the other half of the costs of bringing up the child.

80. In the trials against Benjamin Wooden (Apr. 1716), John Palmer, Jr. (Nov. 1723), and Abraham Stone (Nov. 1728).

81. In New Haven County Court, juries were not used in fornication prosecutions after 1728; the bench overruled a plea by a man sued for paternity in 1773 requesting a jury trial (see Susanna Reed v. James Neal [Dec. 1773], NHCC Files, dr. 56).

82. Zephaniah Swift, *A System of the Laws of the State of Connecticut* (New York, 1972 [orig. publ. Windham, Conn., 1795–1796]), I, 209.

ments before bench and jury. Rather than fine and declare a man a criminal on presumptive evidence from an interested party, male defendants and lawyers began to insist that direct and corroborating evidence of fornication be required for conviction. Like a Hartford County man acting as an attorney for a reputed father in the late seventeenth century, they could have borrowed heavily from the English poor law tradition that explicitly linked "lewd women" with all out-of-wedlock births. The Hartford advocate had invited the judges to reject a procedure by which "the safety of mens names and Estates doe depend [upon] . . . the Bare word of the scandalous," "the accusation of a Naughty woman." Anticipating Swift's repugnance at a mode of proof that empowered women, this anonymous seventeenth-century attorney-in-fact articulated perfectly the rationale behind the decriminalization of fornication for men: "The Law recoyles from findeing the man guilty to all intents upon the womens charge."[83]

Men still might be condemned criminally or specifically targeted for fornication in the 1690–1740 period *if* their sexual transgression was accompanied by aggravating circumstances. Jurors readily pronounced three male defendants guilty. Of two men convicted of fornication with a particular woman, each had, by the time of his trial, married another woman and been presented with her for premarital fornication. In the third case, Elizabeth Painter convinced the judges that she had been forced and thus was innocent; her assailant (a first cousin) was slapped with maintenance and a fifty-shilling fine for "fornication," but he was never prosecuted for rape.[84]

83. Matters of Law pleaded in behalfe of Matthew Woodruff, John Rew v. Woodruff (Oct. 1686 General Assembly), Conn. Archives, Crimes and Misdemeanors, 1st Ser., I, 159.

84. Rex v. John Harpin (Nov. 1719 and Apr. 1720), NHCC, III, 107, 116, and NHCC Files, dr. 6; Rex v. Daniel Francis (Apr. 1724), NHCC, III, 183, and NHCC Files, dr. 11; Rex v. Elizabeth Painter, Rex v. George Clinton (Nov. 1728), NHCC, III, 270–271. In a fourth case, the bench found Henry Williams guilty after he denied the fornication charge. Strong corroborating evidence may explain this ruling. Immediately after the sentence, Williams confessed in court and produced a signed agreement with his lover and her father ensuring his contribution to their child's upkeep. Rex v. Henry Williams (Apr. 1723), NHCC, III, 166.

Twenty-two cases were resolved otherwise: in 5 cases the defendant escaped or the prosecution disappears from the records, 1 man defaulted, 1 man confessed, 2 were discharged before trial, and 13 were tried by the bench. Of those 13, 1 was acquitted at first trial, 1 was found not guilty on review, 1 black servant or slave was

The 1690–1710 decades saw the disappearance of occasional fornication prosecutions singling out the male partner. Men were proceeded
against alone in these years because of the egregious nature of their
conduct: miscegenation, extramarital affairs, and clandestine marriage
all raised red flags for local grand jurors. In this handful of cases, one
woman escaped prosecution because of her "incapacity," and the rest
because of reasons not explicitly stated. Never again, after 1710, would
New Haven County officials commence a fornication case *without* filing
charges against the woman involved.[85]

In the transitional, post-1690 years, single women's experience as
fornication defendants changed very little. As they had in the earlier
decades, women came obediently before both the local magistrates and
the county court to confess guilt. Pregnancy, of course, visibly manifested a woman's offense, so that her only possible defense, besides demonstrating technical mistakes in the process, was to plead rape. Given
these constraints, only a few New Haven County women hazarded not
guilty pleas.[86] By choosing not to contest the charges, the typical defen-

---

ordered whipped (no plea recorded), and 10 were adjudged the reputed fathers and
ordered to pay maintenance.

85. Rex v. Ebenezer Hill (Nov. 1691), NHCC, I, 193, 199: married man convicted
of fornication with a single woman, whipped, sale of property forbidden until the
Court of Assistants granted his wife a divorce with child custody and property settlement; at the June 1692 county court, the governor married Hill and his lover. Rex v.
Cush (Nov. 1692), ibid., 202: confessed to fornication with 19-year-old Mary Potter,
whose father initiated the criminal complaint; Cush, a black slave, was whipped and
ordered to make maintenance payments. Rex v. Nathaniel Finch (Nov. 1694), ibid.,
228: convicted of "incestuous fornication" for secretly marrying his dead wife's
sister, fined five pounds. Rex v. John Tustin (Nov. 1702), ibid., II, 93, 102: charged
with adultery with a married woman who had been abandoned by her husband and
declared "incapable" by her siblings; he was ordered to pay maintenance. Rex v.
Stephen Stone (Mar. 1709/10), ibid., 356: acquitted because of the inconsistency of
woman's charge; reasons why she was not prosecuted at county court level are unclear.

86. Between 1690 and 1740 only four women entered not guilty pleas; all were
tried by the bench. Two women won acquittals on pleas of rape (in 1727 and 1728).
One 21-year-old "acknowledged herself to be the mother of a Child which was a
bastard for ought she knew she being a Singlewoman but pleaded Not Guilty as to
Fornication"; the bench considered "the special pleading" but found her guilty
(Rex v. Elizabeth Wooden [Apr. 1720], NHCC, III, 112). Finally, Abigail Briscoe was
convicted even though she claimed to have been married secretly before her child
was born (Rex v. Briscoe [May 1712], ibid., II, 392, and NHCC Files, dr. 1). The court

dant rationally acknowledged the weight of evidence against her and avoided the additional exposure of a prolonged trial. Moreover, women's tendency to confess had an important symbolic role: by their persistent willingness to assume the mantle of repentant sinner in the decades after the intensity of the Puritan experiment in the New World had faded, New England women kept alive the Puritan ideal that confession and penance purified the community.[87]

Confession could be a woman's pragmatic means of pressuring her lover to marry her or extracting maintenance payments from him through a court order. Before the 1740s, however, New Haven County records divulge only rare cases in which a pregnant, single woman initiated the complaint and thus invoked criminal proceedings against herself.[88] At least two-thirds of the seventy-five women prosecuted between 1690 and 1740 appeared before the magistrates because they had been summoned or arrested. Prosecutions typically began with the local grand jurors, who singly or collectively submitted to a justice written presentments naming individuals suspected of breaking the laws against fornication.[89] In 1712 Derby's constable articulated the sense of obligation

---

showed its sympathy toward Mary Collins, who "acknowledged herself Materially Guilty, But pleaded Discomposure and offered divers testimonies to shew the same." The bench discharged Collins, requiring only that she pay costs (Rex v. Collins [Apr. 1727], NHCC, III, 242).

87. The contrast in the 18th century between women's persistent confessions and men's refusals to acknowledge and repent in court fits in with the decline in male but not female piety observed in Congregational Church records by Mary Maples Dunn, among others. See her "Saints and Sisters: Congregational and Quaker Women in the Early Colonial Period," *American Quarterly*, XXX (1978), 582–601.

88. In 9 cases women appear to have initiated the proceeding, although they might have done so in anticipation of a grand jury presentment. None ended up marrying the man she named. See the written confession of Hannah Briscoe, who claimed that she came before the "honored Court now in session . . . without compulsion" (Regina v. Hannah Briscoe [Nov. 1711], NHCC Files, dr. 3). In two instances, an outside party (a landlady and the young woman's father) lodged the complaint. Finally, 14 cases appeared before the bench with no notation whether grand jurors or others had prompted the criminal action. I have found only 3 pre-1790 cases in which a single woman initiated the process and succeeded in marrying her lover before their trial.

89. Of the 75 women prosecuted in these five decades, grand jurors presented at least 44. Such women typically appeared before the local magistrate on a summons that he issued after receiving the written presentment. In an additional 6 cases, justices noted that the women appeared only after summons or arrest, thus implying

shared by many men chosen for annual grand jury terms in the early eighteenth century. Forwarding names of suspected fornicators to a county court justice, the constable explained: "There being no grand-juryman in ower town I have thought it my duty to present A breach of lawe commited [here] . . . and due herby make presentment to your worship." The zeal of grand jurors varied from town to town within the county, and in every location eighteenth-century presentments were selective, with officials choosing not to prosecute some women who bore children out of wedlock or soon after marriage.[90] The records offer no clues whether favoritism, bribery, compassion for mitigating circumstances, or simple neglect shaped grand jurors' decisions. What is clear is

---

grand jury involvement. In early-18th-century Connecticut a woman who appeared "voluntarily" before a justice of the peace usually had already been presented but was manuevering to avoid the dreaded scene in which the constable would pound on her father's door, formally read her the charge, and either deliver a summons or escort her directly to the issuing magistrate. For such "voluntary appearances," see the 1730s cases against Susanna Hill and Susanna Cornwell, NHCC Files, dr. 11. For the only New Haven case in which a pregnant woman appeared before a justice of the peace to charge her lover *before* a grand jury presentment, see Rex v. Freelove Bartholomew (Nov. 1738), ibid.

Although grand jurors typically chose to present single women during their last few months of pregnancy, roughly one-fifth of women prosecuted in the 1710s and 1720s were presented *after* childbirth. In the latter cases, grand jurors were acting with firm evidence of an out-of-wedlock birth but without much hope of pressuring the father (if identified) to marry the unwed mother.

90. Rex v. Ebenezer and Hannah Johnson (Jan. 1712/3), NHCC Files, dr. 11. In the 1690–1740 period, the town of New Haven contributed 44% of the county court's fornication caseload (157 cases of 358 where defendant's town is known). Surrounding towns trailed considerably: Milford (13%), Guilford (11%), Wallingford (9%), Branford (8%), and Derby and Durham (5.6% each). Three categories of cases are included in these counts: prosecutions against single women, single men, and married couples. Lacking reliable population figures for these decades, we cannot make firm statements about any town's relative zeal or neglect.

On not prosecuting, see David H. Flaherty, "Law and the Enforcement of Morals in Early America," *Perspectives in American History*, V (1971), 236–242. In Donald Lines Jacobus's extensive and reliable three-volume genealogy of New Haven–area families (*FANH*), for the 1710–1740 period there are four out-of-wedlock births (noted in town birth and church baptism records) for which the mother was never prosecuted. This is assuredly an undercount, since Jacobus's work rarely encompasses families beyond the towns of New Haven and Wallingford. Furthermore, some births were never recorded as the law directed, and some birth records for the area are lost.

that most single women at risk for prosecution experienced the criminal action as a coercive rather than a chosen process.

Yet women rarely faced the criminal proceeding for fornication unsupported by kin. Like Sarah Hine, many a defendant was accompanied to court by her father (or an older brother or uncle if her father was dead); his role at the initial hearing was, not to give testimony, but to post bond for his daughter's appearance at the county court.[91] Unlike the mobile servant girls who typically bore out-of-wedlock children in seventeenth-century England and Virginia, most young unwed mothers in eighteenth-century Connecticut experienced pregnancy and prosecution while members of their parents' households. As one nineteen-year-old Windham County woman put it, "She did not doubt but that if she humbled her self on her Knees to her Father he would take her and her Child home."[92] Pregnancy without marriage confronted young women, not with being thrown out onto the streets, but with a redoubled need for self-effacement before the patriarchal institutions of court and family.

In New Haven County before 1740, no daughter of a judge, justice of the peace, sitting deputy, or assistant had a child out of wedlock.[93] But while men serving in the highest political and legal offices managed to marry off their daughters before an untimely birth sparked village gossip, family heads who held considerable wealth or militia posts often faced a daughter's failed courtship and pregnancy. Thomas Painter of West Haven was first elected ensign of his trainband in 1720 at age fifty. He held that post for eighteen years, during which time *two* of his daughters were haled into court on fornication charges. One-fifth (21 percent) of the single white male and female defendants prosecuted be-

91. The run of file papers surviving from 1710 on allows us to identify who posted bond for criminal defendants. For 46 of the 57 fornication prosecutions of single women between 1710 and 1740, the outcome of posting bond is known. In 65% of those cases, a male relative posted bond (20 fathers, 10 uncles or brothers). In another 9 cases (20%), the woman defendant posted her own bond (usually five pounds). In 6 cases (13%), a man who cannot be readily identified as a relative (and was often probably an employer) posted bond, and in 1 case, the defendant was jailed for lack of sureties.

92. Since the young woman was living in her father's house at the time, she was expressing her faith that her father (an elderly justice of the peace) would not throw her and her child out (Deposition of Abigail Nightingale, Rex v. John Hallowell et al. [Mar. 1747], Windham County Superior Court Files, box 172, CSL).

93. However, two men charged with maintenance were sons of prominent Milford officeholders, men who had served variously as deputy, justice, and assistant.

tween 1670 and 1740 had fathers who held a militia post or died with an estate worth more than five hundred pounds. A smaller proportion (15 percent) of the women can be linked to the lowest ranks: either they were servants with no parents resident in the county, or they inherited minuscule portions from poor parents.[94]

That the young people involved in out-of-wedlock births came predominantly from middling families provides one reason to discount here the notion of a "bastardy-prone sub-society" that has been suggested for England. However, families across the wealth ranks were visited twice by an out-of-wedlock birth: six pairs of sisters were prosecuted in the 1710–1740 decades alone, and for the larger 1670–1740 period at least 40 percent of the women prosecuted had a close kin tie (sibling, first cousin, parent, aunt, or uncle) to another defendant. Such linkages undoubtedly raised eyebrows and intensified parental concern over protecting family honor, but they were not sufficient to brush entire families with the reputation for "whoring." Sarah Hine, for example, saw her sister Lydia prosecuted two years before her own fornication trial, but her four other sisters married without mishap.[95] If a substantial number

94. Known fathers of single persons prosecuted were cross-checked with the *Public Records of Connecticut*, in which all justices of the peace, deputies, assistants, and militia leaders are purportedly listed. Court and probate records sometimes indicate whether a defendant's father held such an office. Of 115 individual white men and women prosecuted, at least 16 (11 women, 5 men) had fathers with leadership posts (one woman's father was a deacon). Surviving probate records are much less complete. Wealth at probate was established for 30 fathers: 8 died worth less than £200 (and 2 were very poor), 7 had estates valued between £200 and £500, and 14 were worth more than £500 (6 of these overlap with identified leaders). For helpful lists of class definitions based on the value of probate inventories and accounting for how money values changed over the decades, see Bruce C. Daniels, "Money-Value Definitions of Economic Classes in Colonial Connecticut, 1700–1776," *Histoire Sociale — Social History*, VII (1974), 346–352, esp. 350–351.

Painter died a prosperous man in 1747; his inventory was assessed at £2,525 (New Haven Probate District, Estate Papers for Thomas Painter [1747], 7763, R.G. 4 [microfilm], CSL).

An example of lowest ranks would be Susanna Hill, whose father died when she was two, leaving to his widow and minor children an estate worth £21 (New Haven Probate District, Estate Papers for Ebenezer Hill [1713/4], 4956, R.G. 4.

95. Susan Woodruff Abbott, comp., *Families of Early Milford, Connecticut* (Baltimore, 1979), 340. Sarah's youngest sister, however, was prosecuted for premarital fornication with her husband, George Terrell, in April 1723.

For a definition of bastard-prone women as those who bear more than one child

of young women had borne frequent out-of-wedlock children and never married, then we could surmise that grand jurors and neighbors would have anticipated illegitimacy in certain families and among certain sorts. Yet only five single women, or 7 percent of those prosecuted before 1740, returned to court as repeaters. Before midcentury, then, premarital fornication and out-of-wedlock births were neither confined to nor associated solely with marginal strata in colonial society.

When a young woman's pregnancy became visible, all family members might be drawn into devising a strategy of response. In communities across New England, this was often the point when marriage banns were published. One Durham father tried to impose on his daughter's lover what must have been the logic of many colonial patriarchs: "I percieve your intimacy . . . hath ben such as nesessetats your . . . being marryed which I [hope] you have concluded upon to cover your folly as much as you can." This father believed that in "such [a] case of defilement . . . to marry" was the "manly" response. Many young men, doubtless often under pressure from *their* parents, heeded such advice and immediately arranged for the wedding. Yet others equated manliness with courting, having sex with several women, and choosing among them. John Harpin, who had married another woman soon after fathering a child with Rebecca Baldwin, was confronted by Rebecca's mother, who asked him, "What do you think your wife will say?" Harpin answered, "It is not so bad because i did it before i was married."[96]

When a young man refused outright to marry his pregnant lover, the woman's family often tried to force the man into an acknowledgment of paternity before witnesses. Two sisters of Bathsheba How (whose father had died six years earlier) cornered Benjamin Robinson one day and charged him with "being guilty of the sin of fornication with our Sister . . . [whereupon] he did acknowledge it and promised to maintain the child." Robinson later denied paternity in court, but the sisters' efforts, along with Bathsheba's constant accusation and an eyewitness to the

---

out of wedlock or who bear only one yet are connected with persons exhibiting sexually irregular behavior, see Peter Laslett, "The Bastardy Prone Sub-Society," in Laslett et al., eds., *Bastardy and Its Comparative History,* 219.

96. Depositions of Nathaniel Sutleif, in Rex v. Daniel Francis (Apr. 1724), NHCC Files, dr. 6 (for a similar case five decades later, see Mary Tuttle v. James Glass [Jan. 1772], dr. 53); Deposition of Rebecca Baldwin, in Rex v. John Harpin (Apr. 1720), dr. 6. Abigail Buel aptly described the typical dilemma of a jilted young woman when she said of her lover, "[He] Denyeth Marrage with me at present" (Buel v. Andrew Fowler [Apr. 1758], dr. 21).

pair's intimacy, ensured that the bench slapped Benjamin with maintenance payments.[97]

Some parents of pregnant women rejected by their lovers adopted the
language of ruin and lamentation. Mistress Baldwin lashed out at John
Harpin with this cry of anguish: "You wretched creature, what have you
don[?] You have undone my girl and i have no more [daughters]."
Another father refused the offer of money rather than marriage from his
daughter's lover, saying bitterly, "All the money . . . in the world [would]
not amend the ruined state of my child."[98] But for these families and the
great majority of those in early-eighteenth-century New England hit by a
failed courtship, the prediction of ruin proved overly dramatic, and the
taint of scandal eventually dissipated. The denouement of Rebecca Baldwin's case was typical of at least half of the single women who bore out-of-
wedlock children in early New Haven County. Eight years after bearing
Harpin's child, Rebecca married, at age twenty-four, a local man who at
the end of his life paid ritual tribute to her as "his well-beloved wife."
Moreover, in the interim Rebecca had the full support of her father: he
accompanied her to court, he doubtless paid her criminal fine, and,
later, when her child was two years old, he appeared in court to declare
that he had received in full the court-mandated child support due from
Harpin. Other New Haven–area yeomen similarly intervened to secure
maintenance payments for the grandchildren born out of wedlock
whom they had agreed to bring up. Evidently, eighteenth-century fathers rarely acted on an impulse to disinherit daughters who bore a child
while unmarried. Rather, they often wrote wills at this point that set aside
part of the homestead and farm income for the unwed mother as long as
she remained single.[99] But bearing a child out of wedlock did not doom

97. Deposition of Elizabeth Penfield and Lydia How, in Rex v. Bathsheba How
(Nov. 1738), ibid., dr. 11. Sary Gare testified that a year earlier she had seen Benjamin and "Bashua" in the upper room of Benjamin's father's house, he "with his
Breeches unbuttoned and" she with her "Garments up" so that her knees were
showing.

98. Deposition of Rebecca Baldwin, in Rex v. John Harpin (Apr. 1720), Deposition of Nathaniel Sutleif, in Rex v. Daniel Francis (Apr. 1724), NHCC Files, dr. 6.

At least two unwed mothers showed their distress by naming their children "Lament" — Mary Rose of Branford (Apr. 1775 paternity suit; Barbour Collection of
Vital Records, volume for Branford, CSL] and Sarah Andrews of Wallingford (she
did not come into court, but her child's 1740 birth is noted in Jacobus, *FANH*, 42).

99. Will of Phineas Baldwin, New Haven District Probate Court Records, X, 182–
183. For Rebecca's father's court appearance, see NHCC, III, 138. For dramatic

New England daughters to a life of dependent spinsterhood. Unlike patterns that pertained in some regions of England, few married the man they named before the authorities as the father of their child. But many managed to marry, although often at an age later than their peers and probably in less advantageous matches than if they had preserved a reputation for chastity.[100]

Because young women's families absorbed the initial costs of bringing up children born out of wedlock, towns in early colonial Connecticut were rarely at risk for maintaining unwed mothers and their offspring. Between 1670 and 1740, only three "bastardy" cases led New Haven County towns to assume financial responsibility for the child. In another handful of cases, towns made careful arrangements to avoid becoming liable.[101] Since the norm required a pregnant woman's family to bear all

---

confirmation of a father who entirely shouldered his daughter's and grandchild's support, see the 1729 Petition of Mary Sturgis and Solomon Sturgis, Conn. Archives, Crimes and Misdemeanors, 1st Ser., III, 137.

For fathers or brothers who received child support payments, see Rex v. Henry Williams (Apr. 1723), NHCC, III, 166; Rex v. Samuel Brown, Jr. (review, Apr. 1725), 203; Rex v. Abigail Terrill (Nov. 1722), NHCC Files, dr. 6. For examples of fathers' provisions for daughters who had borne out-of-wedlock children, see Will of Daniel Terrill (dated Mar. 29, 1727), New Haven District Probate Court Records, V, 382–383; Will of Samuel Bradley (dated Apr. 1, 1757), IX, 88.

100. Mary Beth Norton, *Liberty's Daughters: The Revolutionary Experience of American Women, 1750–1800* (Boston, 1980), 52–53. For England, see Karla Oosterveen and Richard M. Smith, "Bastardy and the Family Reconstitution Studies of Colyton, Aldenham, Alcester, and Hawkshead," in Laslett et al., eds., *Bastardy and Its Comparative History*, 107; and G. R. Quaife, *Wanton Wenches and Wayward Wives: Peasants and Illicit Sex in Early Seventeenth Century England* (New Brunswick, N.J., 1979), 98. Only nine New Haven County unwed mothers involved in fornication or paternity cases in the 1690–1789 period married the man they named in court.

How many unmarried mothers eventually married is uncertain. Of the 146 individual white women eligible to marry after being prosecuted for fornication in New Haven County Court, 65 are known to have married, and 8 more possibly married, making 73 (50%) who probably married. Nineteen (13%) definitely did *not* marry: 7 died within 6 years of prosecution, and 12 lived unmarried at least 13 years. Death dates or marriage records for the remaining 54 (37%) have not been found.

101. The three New Haven County cases were Rex v. John Hill (Nov. 1710), NHCC, II, 368; Rex v. John Hill (Feb. 1713/4), III, 29; Account of charges arising to the Town of Wallingford, Rex v. Elizabeth How and Moses Atwater (Jan. 1732/3), NHCC Files, dr. 11.

For an example of the court's usual approach, note the bench's June 1687 decree after it decided that the paternity charge leveled against a Branford man was uncon-

the expenses, the unwed mother in colonial New England stood not so much for the social disorder engendered by poverty, vagabondage, and "lewdness" as she did for the temporary failure of families to ensure that daughters made a smooth transition from one male-headed household to another. The specter of limited town resources being drained by bastards arose more regularly in the second half of the eighteenth century, when both the number and proportion of single mothers with children potentially chargeable to local relief rolls increased.[102]

The transitional 1690–1740 years saw a double standard inscribed into New Haven County's handling of the crime of fornication because of three developments: pregnant, unmarried women were increasingly permitted to remain silent about the identity of their lovers, men who were named often evaded arrest, and men who were prosecuted deployed legal strategies that eventually persuaded officials to decriminalize fornication for unmarried men. Having ceased imposing fines on single men (but not single women), authorities slacked off in their efforts to pursue reputed fathers. In the 1730s criminal cases resulted in only two maintenance orders, and the last such ruling was handed down in 1745. Thereafter, an unwed mother could not rely on the criminal process to hold publicly accountable the man who had been "Equall with her in Transgration"; instead, it was left to the woman and her family to initiate a civil suit to collect child support.[103] Thus, while New

---

vincing: "[We] must leave the charge and maintenance" of the child "upon . . . Hannah Swayne," its mother (NHCC, I, 167–168). Only if Hannah and her father had been unable to support the child would the town of Branford have been liable.

For an example of a town's arrangement, see Rex v. Alexander Bryan (May 1701, NHCC, II, 55, 102), where the youth's stepfather requested that the child "be putt to some family . . . where . . . the charge of maintaining it [may be] lessened." The bench approved this as long as, first, the child's mother agreed and, second, "due care" was "taken to prevent charge to the town." When the court ordered a man to pay maintenance, it usually required him to post bond to ensure future payments. Although some bonds contained the phrase "and to save the town harmless," most did not.

102. For discussions of the proportion of chargeables to nonchargeables among 17th-century English bastardy caseloads, see King, "Punishment for Bastardy," *Albion*, X (1978), esp. 143–144: and Quaife, *Wanton Wenches*, chaps. 9, 10.

103. The wording of one 1774 presentment illustrated how far the pattern of prosecutions had strayed from the 17th-century model of equal accountability. Damaris Punderson was presented "for Sufforing one Glover Ball" of New Haven on June 3 "to have Carnal knowledge of her body" (justice of the peace record, Rex v.

Haveners manifested a concern to emphasize the moral impropriety of fornication somewhat longer than many other New England jurisdictions, here as elsewhere 1740 marked the point at which authorities turned their backs decisively on the policies of their Puritan forebears.

————

In the last half of the eighteenth century, women labeled indigent, women living temporarily in New Haven County as servants, and women who repeatedly bore children out of wedlock appeared more frequently than ever before on the county court lists of single mothers called to account for fornication. With economic prosperity and commercial expansion came increasing inequalities in wealth, so that New Englanders witnessed a striking rise in the group Douglas Lamar Jones calls the "strolling poor," landless laborers who had no settled residence or steady work. Knowing that many of these potential additions to the poor rolls were single mothers and their children, grand jurors focused their attention on young women in their own towns whose marginal, lower-class status was thought to incline or expose them to unwise, unmonitored sexual liaisons and thus childbearing. In New Haven County, one such woman was Eleanor Davis, "a Stranger" living temporarily in Milford who bore a child out of wedlock in 1745 and was presented for fornication by four of the town's grand jurors. Another Milford resident, widow Rhoda Oviat, marked herself as a disreputable figure in several ways. In 1769, she was cited by the town selectmen as unable to care for herself because of "mismanagement and idle living"; six years later, Oviat was presented for (and confessed to) fornication with Newport, an enslaved black man.[104]

————

Punderson [Nov. 1774], NHCC Files, dr. 58). She was fined 33s. and never married; 26-year-old Glover, never summoned to court, married four years later.

104. Rex v. Eleanor Davis (Apr. 1745), NHCC Files, dr. 18; *PR*, XIII, 331; Rex v. Rhoda Oviat, Rex v. Newport (Jan. 1781), NHCC Files, dr. 66. Oviat and Newport were presented and pleaded guilty before a justice of the peace in April 1775, but the final record of the payment of their fines by their masters was made in the county court record book in early 1781.

Marsella posits that most of Middlesex County's single mothers in this period were transient or poor (*Crime and Community*, 22, 29). On rising transiency, especially among women, see Douglas Lamar Jones, "The Strolling Poor: Transiency in Eighteenth-Century Massachusetts," *Journal of Social History*, VIII, no. 3 (Spring 1975), 28–54; Jones, "Poverty and Vagabondage: The Process of Survival in Eighteenth-Century

At the same time that a noticeable class bias crept into fornication prosecutions, a debate over the future of such cases commenced in the public newssheets and private correspondence that were the domain of the mercantile and professional classes. At one pole of the debate stood evangelicals who wished to return to a single standard akin to that of the seventeenth century — a standard insisting on chastity for both sexes and proper public contrition from all sinners, no matter their social rank. At the other pole were newspaper commentators and middle-class youths themselves who believed that respectable New England sons and daughters ought to be shielded from the stigma of fornication prosecutions. These trends make clear that in the five decades before 1789, the year when fornication cases disappeared from the New Haven County Court, the central issue was for whom premarital sex should be deemed private and off the record legally.

Not all pregnant single women chosen for presentment in the 1740–1790 decades were mobile servants or daughters of impoverished men. Prosecuted along with women like Mary Pierson, whom a justice called "very Poor," were women who inherited generous portions from their fathers and counted militia officers and occasionally deputies among their male kin.[105] Particularly if they came from families with middling resources, unwed mothers at midcentury had little to complain about with respect to court procedure. After 1742, single women presented for fornication were permitted simply to acknowledge their guilt before a local justice and send their fine to the county court, on whose records their compliance was noted. With the depreciation of Connecticut's paper money, a fifty-shilling fine paid in "old tenor" amounted to a trivial payment by the 1740s. Moreover, even though premarital pregnancy rates peaked in New England in the 1760–1780 period, prosecutors did not try to fine all miscreants. Although prosecutions of single women alone reached an all-time high in the 1750s and 1760s (Table 8), birth records show that many more unmarried women in the post-1740

Massachusetts," *New England Historical and Genealogical Register,* CXXXIII (1979), 246–250.

105. Rex v. Mary Sloper (Jan. 1741/2), NHCC Files, dr. 18; Mary had married her lover, Thomas Sloper, after presentment. Lydia Russell (1754), Mary Rose (1775), and Eunice Fulford (1778) are examples of some of the prosecuted women whose fathers and grandfathers were officeholders. For a father's bequest to one single mother (Phebe Crane), see Durham-Middletown Probate District, Estate papers for Henry Crane (1763), reel 733, R.G. 4 (microfilm), CSL.

years bore children without undergoing prosecution than in earlier decades.[106]

Although grand jurors did not make direct statements about why they presented some unwed mothers and not others, one issue, gauging from the most discernible change in prosecution patterns in the post-1740 decades, preoccupied them. Once rare, prosecutions of single women who repeatedly bore out-of-wedlock children became much more visible on the county court's docket. When Jane Lewis of Durham was prosecuted in 1758 for an out-of-wedlock birth, she had borne an earlier child, which Durham grand jurors had ignored. In 1758, but not at her second presentment in 1762, officials compelled Lewis to appear before the county court and ordered her whipped—whether because of her aggravated behavior or her inability to pay a fine is not clear. Saddled with an unfortunate first name, Submit Pierson of Guilford between her late teens and early thirties bore four children and was prosecuted each time.[107] Most repeaters came into court only twice, but presentments of

106. The New Haven County Court also adopted this unwritten policy of excusing appearances toward married couples, thus sitting in judgment over no fornication-related trials except appeals and civil paternity suits.

Being tried before a justice of the peace was still referred to as appearing "in open court," and it could generate a flurry of community talk. For two examples, see Testimony of Samuel Hoit in Joint deposition of Chloe Scrantum et al., Sarah Pierson v. Ichabod Scrantum (Jan. 1746/7), NHCC Files, dr. 18; Ulrich, *Midwife's Tale*, 151, 153.

For the late-18th-century peak in premarital pregnancy, see Smith and Hindus, "Premarital Pregnancy," *Journal of Interdisciplinary History*, IV (1974–1975), 537, 561–564. In what is by no means a comprehensive survey of New Haven County towns in Jacobus (*FANH*) and the Barbour Collection of Vital Records (CSL), 70 women bore out-of-wedlock children between 1740 and 1790 but were never prosecuted.

107. Lewis was the last person whipped for fornication in the county (NHCC, V, 200; Barbour Collection of Vital Records, volume for Durham). Protests over whipping sentences surface sporadically in the Connecticut records. In August 1699, two New Haven men were fined for refusing to whip Mercy Stevens, a repeat fornicator (NHCC, II, 19), and Henry Bamford Parkes reports that "a similar incident occurred in Hartford in 1722" ("Morals and Law Enforcement in Colonial New England," *New England Quarterly*, V [1932], 446).

The sexual connotations we attach to "submit" surely were not as pervasive in the 18th century; in the Puritan naming tradition, girls' names such as Submit and Lowly had common religious meanings, as in "submit to the will of God." Pierson's prosecutions are recorded in the county court record books in November 1751, January 1754, April 1759, and April 1765 (NHCC, IV, 483, 673, V, 236, VI, 143).

such women accounted for one-third of all fornication cases in the two decades when cases against single women peaked.[108] Few of the repeaters had fathers by their side when they appeared before the local magistrate, and none can be traced to a prosperous family. The clustering of cases involving repeaters and low-status women suggests a heightened anxiety at midcentury over what was evidently a growing population of unmarried women for whom domestic service threatened to become a permanent rather than a temporary way of life.[109]

The same anxiety manifested itself in a sudden increase in infanticide prosecutions in Connecticut after 1740. Three-quarters of all infanticide cases heard in pre-1790 Connecticut (nineteen of twenty-five) came after 1740, with the largest cluster (six cases) occurring in the 1750s.[110]

Two of her older sisters bore an out-of-wedlock child each in the 1740s. Submit's father, Sgt. Ephraim Pierson of Guilford, served as her surety in each prosecution until his death in 1761.

108. Overall, in their proportion of individual women prosecuted for fornication, repeaters doubled their presence from 7% (5 of 76 women) in 1670–1739 to 14% (11 of 79) in 1740–1789. In the 1750s and 1760s, 9 of 44 women were repeaters (20%), and their cases accounted for 37% of the fornication caseload (21 of 56 cases). The repeater's case made most famous was that of Franklin's fictional Polly Baker; Baker was probably based on Eleanor Kellogg, a Worcester Co., Mass., woman, prosecuted five times between 1733 and 1745 (Max Hall, *Benjamin Franklin and Polly Baker: The History of a Literary Deception* [Chapel Hill, N.C., 1960], 94–96).

109. The procreative powers of single mothers were deemed a subject for notice and jocularity by newspaper printers, as seen in this italicized item appearing under a Boston headline in the *Connecticut Journal* (New Haven) on July 6, 1770: "We hear from Worcester that at an Inferior Court held there, 4 young women who had been indicted for Fornication, made their appearance at said Court with 8 young children, each having been delivered of twins."

After 1770, as the county court began to abandon its efforts at sexual regulation, the concern over repeaters lessened. Several single women who bore more than one child were prosecuted only once, and others brought paternity suits but were never charged with the crime. Several of these women persisted unmarried in their natal communities, bringing up their children in their father's house and on their own earnings.

110. Pennsylvania's caseload also increased in the late 18th century (G. S. Rowe, "Infanticide, Its Judicial Resolution, and Criminal Code Revision in Early Pennylvania," American Philosophical Society, *Proceedings*, CXXXV [1991], 200–232), whereas prosecutions leveled off or declined in Massachusetts and parts of England (Peter C. Hoffer and N. E. H. Hull, *Murdering Mothers: Infanticide in England and New England, 1558–1803* [New York, 1981], 38–39, 80; J. M. Beattie, *Crime and the Courts in England, 1660–1800* [Princeton, N.J., 1986], 115, 122).

With one exception, eighteenth-century prosecutions involved a single woman who had allegedly concealed her pregnancy and murdered her "bastard" child. These capital cases usually ended in acquittal, but they served to place poor, transient servant women in the public spotlight. The narratives of feckless young women who not only committed the folly of fornication but also took desperate measures to cover up the resulting pregnancy became more familiar than ever before. During the decades of the 1750s and 1760s, Connecticut residents could not only exchange stories about the ten women indicted for infanticide within their colony's bounds; they could also glean from their newspapers frequent reports of single women arrested for the "barbarous" crime in other colonies. Sympathetic representations of "unfortunate" single mothers driven to or unwittingly committing infanticide did not appear in local newspapers until the 1780s. Before that decade newspaper bulletins unambiguously assumed the "inhuman" intent of any women who concealed her pregnancy and refused to seek help in labor from the local "Company of Women."[111] Strikingly, nearly all of the defendants brought to the bar for infanticide after 1740 were of marginal status. Thus, almost entirely exempt from prosecution were daughters and wives of elite and middling householders, among whom *some* efforts to conceal pregnancies must have occurred. Five of the prosecuted women were African or Indian servants or slaves. Scattered evidence indicates that all but one of the single white women were either servants or household helpers boarding with relatives; that their parents were either dead, estranged from them, or living several towns distant; and that they or their kin generally had little property. Without a dowry or a set of protective parents on hand to exercise moral suasion, these women were particularly vulnerable to abandonment by their lovers.[112]

111. In nine sample years between 1755 and 1771, three Connecticut newspapers ran 19 reports on infanticide cases outside the colony. The first sympathetic treatment of infanticide I know of to appear in a southern New England newspaper reported on a Connecticut incident (*Newport Mercury* [R.I.], July 2, 1785; I owe this reference to John Sweet). "Inhuman": *Conn. Journal*, Sept. 21, 1770. "Company of Women": *Conn. Gazette*, June 21, 1755; and see Ulrich, *Good Wives*, 196–201.

112. The one case involving the daughter of a prosperous settler was the 1745 trial and conviction of Elizabeth Shaw of Windham. For a temporarily successful cover-up of an abortion in the family of a justice of the peace, see Cornelia Hughes Dayton, "Taking the Trade: Abortion and Gender Relations in an Eighteenth-Century New England Village," *WMQ*, XLVIII (1991) 19–49. A fuller analysis of the Connecticut infanticide cases is found in Dayton, "Narratives of Infanticide: Chang-

The fear that impoverished, mobile servant women might eventually fall prey to the lure not just of incautious sex but of infanticide was realized in the case of Lucretia Smith. Smith bore her first child in 1753 at age fifteen while boarding in her natal town of New Haven. Described by a local magistrate as "an Indigent Person, a Servant Girl," she was probably already orphaned. Nonetheless, she managed both to collect child support by suing the infant's father, a transient cooper, and to have the fornication case against her dismissed because grand jurors had presented her after the one-year statute of limitations ran out. A decade later, Lucretia's straits were far more desperate. In 1764 she was serving in a New London household, where she secretly gave birth to a daughter, whom she was charged with strangling. Placed under house arrest for three weeks, then indicted and transferred to prison, four months later Lucretia was acquitted of infanticide in Superior Court. However, neither her economic hardships nor her assertiveness in seeking a remedy had evaporated. After languishing for a year in jail unable to pay her large trial costs and failing to attract any householder willing to take her into service, Smith together with her jailer persuaded the legislature "to release her from her long, unhappy and miserabl[e] Confinement."[113]

The anxiety over infanticide reflected in newspaper reports and criminal prosecutions in the 1750s and 1760s may partially explain why fornication presentments of single women peaked in New Haven County in the same decades (Table 8). Many Connecticut residents no longer viewed bastardy and the concealment of an unwanted pregnancy as sins for which women of all ranks needed public chastising. Instead, the most effective use of the legal system, as grand jurors, prosecutors, and witnesses signaled, came in making examples of disorderly and marginal women. One logic behind selective prosecutions that spared most daughters of well-established families was to allow churches and middle-class families to police their own. At midcentury, most grand jurors perhaps understood their mission as largely one of presenting for fornication those women who received little apparent discipline or supervision.

---

ing Configurations of Gender, Race, and Class in Eighteenth-Century New England," paper presented to the Annual Meeting of the Law and Society Association, June 16, 1994, Phoenix, Ariz.

113. Lucretia Smith v. Hugh Ferril (Apr. 1753), NHCC, IV, 602, 723, V, 69, and NHCC Files, dr. 28; Rex v. Lucretia Smith (Nov. 1755), NHCC, V, 40; Rex v. Lucretia Smith (Sept. 1764), SCR, XVIII, 286, and New London County Superior Court Files, dr. F-17; Conn. Archives, Crimes and Misdemeanors, 1st Ser., V, 240–242.

These women, usually transients or servants without dowries, were at the highest risk for the far more serious crime of infanticide. If fornication prosecutions could serve as warnings to low-status women that the gaze of the justice system was on them, then one specter raised by infanticide might be averted — the ultimately rebellious woman freeing herself from sexual restraint and containment within the family.[114]

As fornication prosecutions became more selective, grand jurors who attempted to return to the older pattern of presenting nearly all miscreants found themselves under fire. A prank staged by a large group of New Haven youths can be seen as ushering in an era of public debate over the fate of fornication prosecutions. On the evening of January 30, 1766, residents must have gathered to witness the public protest against a recent, highly unusual acceleration of fornication presentments — an increase out of rhythm with the relatively desultory pace of prosecutions since 1740. The *Connecticut Courant* reported: "Several young People of both Sexes . . . having conceived an extream Dislike to a new Grand-Jury-man for being . . . too rigid, inquisitive and covetous in the Exercise of his Office, last Night the Male Part burnt his Effigy on the Green near the Court-House. Numerous are the Stories told to render him odious." The newspaper had it slightly wrong. Ten months later, seven young men were prosecuted for the deeds done on that January night: they had hanged "upon a Gallows with a Rope . . . and then" burned *two* effigies "habited with Cloathes . . . and Descriptions plainly importing" the two grand jurors being mocked.[115] These officials had dared to contribute to a total of eleven fornication complaints lodged against married couples and single women. Not only was this an unprecedented number of presentments for any single year in the town's history, but it flew in the face of recent trends. The average number of fornication cases against town residents for the years between 1740 and 1765 had been 1.7. Following the furor raised in 1766 against the too "inquisitive" grand jurors, the presentment rate for fornication dropped back to its previously modest level.[116]

114. On the law's role in reinforcing the profile of unmarried mothers as lewd, murderous, and defiant of governance, see Dolan, *Dangerous Familiars,* 127–132.

115. *Connecticut Courant* (Hartford), Feb. 10, 1766; Rex v. Lyman Hitchcock et al. (Nov. 1766), NHCC, VI, 181, 242, and NHCC Files, dr. 45. The five defendants for whom ages are known ranged from 18 to 22.

116. After two years of no fornication presentments, New Haven grand jurors presented four couples and eight single women for 1766. During the rest of the

One year later a former grand juror took his complaint about the current state of fornication prosecutions directly to the pages of Hartford's newspaper, the *Connecticut Courant*. Calling himself "Justice" and informing his readers that he had served "more than once" as a grand juror in his town, the editorialist objected to a recent scene at the Litchfield County Court. There, "two likely looking young women" were arraigned at the bar for fornication, even though each had already made a "humble . . . confession" before her church, "been restor'd to charity in a gospel way," and led "a virtuous, blameless life ever since." Declaring, "I think the grand jurors, in this case wrong—grosely so," Justice pleaded for the alteration of the 1673 fornication statute still on the books. When executed "in its utmost rigor and extent," the statute "exposed" pious young women "before a king's c[ount]y c[our]t" and placed their names "upon lasting record, for the vilest and . . . malicious to make use of at pleasure."[117]

Not only did the man who signed himself Justice speak for many of his grand juror peers who increasingly shielded from prosecution those women they felt to be meritorious, but his comments pointed in one significant direction that future debates over youthful folly and seduction would follow. Rather than protesting a double standard that exempted young men from punishment, Justice implicitly embraced a class test for female culpability. Well-behaved and well-kempt New England daughters who demonstrated a capacity for penitence should be spared the humiliation of being haled before the bar; others who committed the "scandalous sin" with no hope of reformation deserved no such mercy. Justice's comments illuminate how public discourse about fornication had shifted in seventy years. Whereas the exhortatory language of late-seventeenth-century ministers tended to locate iniquity and uncleanness in *all* youths' souls, no matter their sex or family status, printed discussions in the latter half of the eighteenth century often

---

decade, only four single women were presented. Twelve men were appointed to serve as grand jurors in 1765 (*NHTR*, III, 774–775), but records do not indicate which two were the target of the protest. When, at a town meeting on Feb. 3, 1766, the selectmen expressed alarm that, in the absence of courts' meeting for several months, "disorders violences and breaches of Law in this Town" had been growing, they were perhaps thinking of the Jan. 30 incident (ibid., 786).

117. *Conn. Courant*, Oct. 19, 1767. In an aside, the letter writer urged that at the very least such fornication prosecutions should be heard only before a justice of the peace. In the 1760s, evidently the latter practice was unevenly followed across Connecticut.

focused on contrasting female archetypes: "the Harlot . . . [whose] ways lead down to hell" and the marriageable "celestial maid" who "will crown" a man's days "with bliss."[118]

Other critics of local approaches to fornicators in the post-1740 era turned in a different direction. Writing in 1769, "The Memorialist" challenged his audience along with the grand jurors whom he felt were shirking their duty: Why does "this wicked sin [fornication] so often go unpunished?" The author supplied one reason: it often goes "unpunished [when] . . . perpetrated . . . [in] great families."[119] Here the Memorialist was highlighting a common response among mid- to late-eighteenth-century prosperous and high-status families, a response that marked their era off from the Puritan seventeenth century. Rather than urging their children to confess publicly, male household heads often hoped that the attention of grand jurors and church deacons would not be drawn to their daughters' ill-timed conceptions. As one recently married Massachusetts woman told her minister: "Her Family were unwilling it should be known" that she had "had her first Child before it was lawful." Yet since moving to her husband's town, "she had been in great perplexity about" whether she ought to confess to premarital fornication before the congregation.[120] Contrary to what ministers might urge, middling and elite families increasingly claimed the right to keep private the premarital sexual lapses of their young people.

The Memorialist advanced a second approach that countered prevailing trends. He believed it was important to address young men, not just women, when enumerating "the Evils of lewdness." If each Christian man could be persuaded to flee from "every propensity he feels to commit fornication" as he would flee "from the face of a serpent," then there was hope "that a reformation may be attained." Here the Memorialist spoke in the voice of an eighteenth-century evangelical critic — a voice not unlike Jonathan Edwards's. Desiring a return to the ethics of New

118. From a poem printed (or reprinted) ibid., Feb. 8, 1768.

119. Ibid., Feb. 13, 1769.

120. Aug. 11, 1785, Journal for 1785, Diaries of the Rev. Justus Forward of Belchertown, American Antiquarian Society. Mrs. Darling's private conversation with her pastor shows a wife internalizing the notion that her intercourse with her husband before marriage was more her crime than a joint transgression. Note that after 1740 in Middlesex Co., Mass., and New London Co., Conn., when grand jurors chose to pursue premarital pregnancy, they tended to charge only the wife (Marsella, *Crime and Community*, 20, table 5; Hartog, "Public Law of a County Court," *American Journal of Legal History*, XX [1976], 300; New London County Court Records, CSL).

England's first founders, Edwards lamented the inadequacy of cash payments made by men to their pregnant lovers.[121] The *only* fitting reparation from a man who had "taken the liberty to use [a woman] as his wife," Edwards argued, was a sincere pledge of marriage. Bidding to redefine manliness, the pastor of Northampton declared, "Tis utterly unfit [that men] should think to put away at their pleasure, those whom they have seen cause for their pleasure."[122]

Even if New Light clergy across New England used their pulpits to denounce the sexual irresponsibility of many male youths, secular jurisprudential concerns had penetrated the criminal justice system too deeply for magistrates to return to enjoining marriage between an unwed mother and the man she named in childbirth. However, the protests of mid-eighteenth-century evangelicals over the double standard and the general declension in morals would be taken up by female moral reformers in the 1820s and 1830s. Through their branches in New York City, New Haven, and towns throughout rural New England, these early collective women's associations launched a campaign against a legal and ethical system that allowed men to go unpunished for seducing and abandoning young women. Public pressure, the middle-class reformers realized, could be more effectively applied through the courageous decisions of individual women and families than through the courts. If women in polite society were willing to name publicly, even in print, the known rakes in their communities and forbid these men their houses and parlors, then suitors would be forced to cease their predatory behavior.[123] But in the eighteenth century, women's remedies for a pros-

121. *Conn. Courant,* Feb. 13, 1769. One dimension of clerical distress focused on young men's lying about their sexual escapades. For an example, see Laurel Thatcher Ulrich, "Psalm-tunes, Periwigs, and Bastards: Ministerial Authority in Early Eighteenth Century Durham," *Historical New Hampshire,* XXXVI (1981), 255–279.

122. Kathryn Kish Sklar, "Culture versus Economics: A Case of Fornication in Northampton in the 1740's," University of Michigan, *Papers in Women's Studies,* 1978, 45. Edwards made his arguments before a regional council of clergymen to which a prominent young member of his church, Elisha Hawley, had appealed his August 1748 excommunication for refusing to marry his pregnant lover, a woman of similar status. The council rejected Edwards's reasoning and ruled that whether a man married a woman he had impregnated should "be left to . . . his own conscience" (ibid., 36). For another useful summary of the case, see Patricia J. Tracy, *Jonathan Edwards, Pastor: Religion and Society in Eighteenth-Century Northampton* (New York, 1980), 164–166.

123. See Carroll Smith-Rosenberg, "Beauty, the Beast, and the Militant Woman: A Case Study in Sex Roles and Social Stress in Jacksonian America," in Smith-Rosen-

ecutorial policy that failed to pursue fathers of out-of-wedlock children lay, not in collective action, but in strategies hammered out by individual women, their families, and legal counsel. Just as a selection process marked the decisions of grand jurors, so too did pregnant, single women choose among an array of possible responses to their plight.

New Haven was perhaps a unique jurisdiction in New England in its early policy of allowing unwed mothers to sue their lovers for child support *even if* the woman had not confessed and been punished for the crime of fornication.[124] Between 1720 and 1790, thirty-nine paternity suits that were clearly dissassociated from criminal prosecutions appeared on the county court's dockets (see Tables 9 and 10). What is curious is that, although the women prosecuted for fornication in these decades had the option of suing their lover, very few did so.[125] Thus,

---

berg, *Disorderly Conduct: Visions of Gender in Victorian America* (New York, 1985), 109–128. When the New Haven Auxiliary of the Female Reform Society was formed in 1835, the members wrote for inclusion in the Society's journal, the *Advocate*. "The recent development of facts shows that in this city, . . . iniquity abounds; the sin of licentiousness prevails to an alarming extent." The New Haven branch reported a membership of 130 by 1836, and in the same year another auxiliary was formed in Wallingford. See the *Advocate*, I, no. 12 (December 1835), 1, 95, II, no. 2 (February 1836), 10–12, 13, 16.

124. Thus, Hendrik Hartog finds that in Middlesex Co., Mass., prosecutions of women were tied to paternity suits. Until 1795, only if an unmarried mother voluntarily made a confession of her guilt before a local magistrate could she then sue the reputed father for child support ("Public Law of a County Court," *American Journal of Legal History*, XX [1976], 300–303). Hartog's finding that in all cases someone — either the woman prosecuted or the man sued — was bound to save the town harmless does not appear to have been followed in New Haven County.

Whether any other Connecticut counties followed New Haven in permitting freestanding paternity suits awaits further research. A sampling of the New London County Court records for 1744 and 1749 shows no paternity suits where the woman had not also confessed. On the other hand, Justice of the Peace Matthew Talcott of Middletown (Hartford Co.) recorded four cases (in 1763, 1764, and 1771) of women bringing paternity suits — women from whom he did not require a criminal confession and fine (Justice of the Peace Records of Matthew Talcott [microfilm], CHS).

125. Some unwed mothers, of course, must have succeeded in extracting maintenance payments privately from their lovers. Two earlier cases are listed with the criminal cases yet appear to be paternity suits pursued by single women, but possibly they commenced with the woman's confession before a local justice of the peace, after which her prosecution was dropped. The cases against these two men disappear from the records without conclusion too, suggesting out-of-court settlements. I have

TABLE 9

Paternity Suits in New Haven County Court, 1720–1789

	Suit by Mother Who Is Not Prosecuted	Suit by Mother Who Is Prosecuted[a]	Suit Brought by Town[b]	Total Suits
1720–1729	1	0	0	1
1730–1739	1	0	0	1
1740–1749	4	2	0	6
1750–1759	9	2	1	12
1760–1769	5	4	0	9
1770–1779	14	1	1	16
1780–1789	3	0	0	3
Total	37	9	2	48

[a]In at least five of these cases, grand jurors lodged presentment several months after the woman initiated her suit.

[b]In these cases, the mother was not prosecuted.

Source: New Haven County Court Records and Files, 1666–1789, CSL.

three quite separate populations of single mothers could be found scattered throughout the county's villages and outlying farmsteads: those who avoided any contact with a criminal or civil proceeding; those who were presented by grand jurors, confessed, and paid the thirty-three-shilling fine; and those who initiated a lawsuit and hired attorneys in the hopes of winning a maintenance order from the bench.

In the middle of October 1743, eighteen-year-old Mary Smith bore a child in the house of her father, Enos Smith of Wallingford. Three weeks later, during her lying in, she requested or her parents arranged for the local justice of the peace to come to their house so that Mary could file a paternity complaint against Wallingford resident Samuel Tyler. On the same day, a "Court for Tryal of Small causes" was held in the Smith dwelling — perhaps in the downstairs parlor, or perhaps at Mary's bed-

---

not included them in Table 9. See Rex v. Samuel Adams (Nov. 1726), NHCC, III, 227, and NHCC Files, dr. 6; Rex v. William Chilson (Apr. 1739), NHCC, IV, 4, 27.

TABLE 10

Unmarried Mothers Winning Maintenance
in New Haven County Court, 1670–1789

	Women Prosecuted[a]	Unlinked Paternity Suits	Maintenance Orders	
			Potential Cases	Cases Awarded[b]
1670–1679	2	0	2	1 (50%)
1680–1689	4	0	4	3 (75%)
1690–1699	13	0	13	3 (23%)
1700–1709	5	0	5	1 (20%)
1710–1719	16	0	16	6 (37%)
1720–1729	26	1	27	11 (41%)
1730–1739	15	1	16	2 (12%)
1740–1749	21	4	25	4 (16%)
1750–1759	22	10	32	9 (28%)
1760–1769	34	5	39	5 (13%)
1770–1779	15	15	30	11 (37%)
1780–1789	3	3	6	3 (50%)
Overall	176	39	215	59 (27%)

[a]Nine of these women also initiated paternity suits.

[b]This column does not reflect two maintenance orders that ensued from five pre-1710 cases in which men were prosecuted for fornication although no charges were filed against their female partners.

Sources: New Haven County Court Records and Files, 1666–1789; SCR, NHSC Files, CSL.

side in an upper chamber. Tyler was summoned, and he pleaded not guilty in response to Mary's face-to-face accusation. The magistrate, certifying there was "just cause" for the complaint, required each party to produce bonds for their appearance at the April county court. At the trial, crucial witnesses, such as the midwife and her helpers, would have testified whether Mary had remained constant in her accusation of Samuel. A pair of attorneys for each side argued over technical issues. The bench ruled for Mary: like 72 percent of the forty-six single mothers who brought paternity suits, she won the right to collect one-half of her lying-in costs and weekly or quarterly support payments for the initial years of her child's life.[126]

The relative youth of Mary Smith and other young women who initiated paternity litigation may provide a clue to what prompted families to bring suit. In each decade between 1740 and 1780, women who filed paternity complaints were on average two to six years younger than those who came into court on criminal charges (see Table 11).[127] This contrast suggests that many of the women who sued — along with the fathers and male kin who supported them — anticipated spending several years at home or self-employed before marrying, years in which receiving help toward the child's upkeep might be vital to preserving resources for a dowry (for middling families) or to warding off the humiliation of applying for poor relief.

The paternity suits brought in New Haven County Court between 1740 and 1790 represent the decision of some unwed mothers and their kin to act in the default of criminal justice officers who had in the past pursued putative fathers of children born out of wedlock. In other words, yeomen fathers, and sometimes women who were alone, shouldered the costs and risks of civil litigation in order to blunt the impact of the prosecutorial double standard. In effect, the suits continued in large part the traditional system of community-based justice in which older women — through the midwife's testimony — joined forces with younger women to hold men accountable. The differences were that the issue of paternity now became a matter of the civil, not the criminal, record and

126. Mary Smith v. Samuel Tyler (adjourned Apr. 1744), NHCC, V, 237–238, and NHCC Files, dr. 19. Tyler reviewed his case to the November 1744 court, by which time Mary had married. On a technicality, the bench reversed its previous ruling for Smith, agreeing with Tyler that Mary's husband had not joined properly in the process.

File documents in Mary Smith's case fail to list the witnesses summoned, but records for many 1740–1790 paternity suits indicate that the midwife was called to testify. For a case with extant depositions from the midwife and female attendants, see Dorcas Fulford v. Alling Sage (Apr. 1764), NHCC Files, dr. 32.

127. Since the economic backgrounds of only a minority of women in either group can be traced, distinctive patterns of wealth and social status cannot be discerned. However, ages can be determined for 53% of women's court appearances between 1740 and 1779. No study of age at marriage for 18th-century Connecticut or New Haven County has been conducted to my knowledge. If we assume that out-of-wedlock pregnancies occurred in the context of courtship, the data suggest that age at marriage in general was increasing (Table 11).

TABLE 11

Ages of Women Coming into Court for Fornication Charges
and Paternity Suits, 1740–1779, New Haven County Court

	Women Prosecuted for Fornication				Women Suing for Child Support			
	Age Range	Median	Mean	N	Age Range	Median	Mean	N
1740s	16–26	19	19.9	11	12–22	18	17.5	4
1750s	18–31	23	23.4	14	15–22	19	19.0	7
1760s	17–32	26	26.9	14	17–39	23	24.3	6
1770s	20–42	28	28.9	13	16–30	22	22.6	11

the impetus for combating the double standard now rested with individual laypersons and not with authorities representing their communities.[128] Finally, post-1740 paternity litigation reflected the lag between men's and women's readiness to manipulate legal procedure: women and their kin demonstrated that they had learned suitable strategies to counter the evasions and not guilty pleas young men had employed from the 1690s on while awaiting, as it were, the decriminalization of fornication for white men.

A focus on paternity suits as a remedy assertively pursued by single mothers overlooks the more numerous women who fell into two other categories: first, those who used their naming of a man before the midwife or a magistrate to extract compensation from their lover, whether

128. On midwives, see the discussion of their role in a county in which fornication and paternity suits evolved quite differently, in Ulrich, *Midwife's Tale*, chap. 4, esp. 159. For a richly detailed glimpse of older women's roles in urging a pregnant servant girl to "lay it to the Right," see Mabel Leet v. Charles Hall (Nov. 1778), NHCC Files, dr. 64. For a case in which many women testified to assisting in the childbirth examination, see Dorcas Fulford v. Alling Sage (Apr. 1764), dr. 32.

After 1740, paternity complaints had more of the features of civil than criminal actions: the parties hired attorneys and offered responsive pleadings; the loser could review or appeal; the loose documents were filed under the female complainant's surname and not under *Rex*. However, the suits were often listed as a separate genre of proceeding in the New Haven County Court record books — interspersed with neither the civil or criminal caseloads.

through marriage or private maintenance payments; and, second, those women who by choice or circumstance declined to attempt to collect child support. We will never know how many New England patriarchs like Jeremiah Arnold confronted their daughter's lover and persuaded him to hand over three ten-pound notes in order "to prevent the expense and vexation of a tryal at Law."[129] And since women prosecuted after 1740 were no longer asked to identify their lovers for the record, we lose the ability to gauge how many New Haven–area women named transient or distant men who could not be harassed for compensation. However, the number of such women left without recourse must have been significant, judging from the women who named transient men in the early decades of the century and from the fact that nearly half of the children recorded in town records as born outside marriage between 1740 and 1790 were given the mother's surname — *not* the father's as was customary when the community agreed on his identity.[130]

As the 1700s rolled by, the courting practices of bundling and keeping company through the night evidently became widespread. Betrothal and marriage typically followed sexual relations and even pregnancy. Parents, unable to supervise closely their daughter's sociability and choice of a mate, doubtless breathed sighs of relief when the young man followed custom and agreed to marry.[131] However, if he was already

129. Writ in error (dated Feb. 4, 1788), in Lydia Arnold and Jared Bishop v. Thaddeus Hitchcock (Feb. 1788), NHSC Files, dr. 337. Two fathers successfully pursued their daughters' lovers with separate suits claiming damages for assault and loss of services: Samuel Barker, Esq. v. Joseph Wilford (Apr. 1778), NHCC, VIII, 349, and NHCC Files, dr. 64; and Josiah Pardee v. Elijah Bryant (Nov. 1785), NHCC, IX, 276–277, SCR, XXIV, 369–370, and NHCC Files, dr. 76.

130. For transients named in the 1690–1740 period, see above, this chapter. Of 75 out-of-wedlock births noted in Jacobus (*FANH*) for 1740–1789, 35 children (or 47%) bore the mother's surname, and 40 were given a surname other than hers. Laurel Thatcher Ulrich finds a low proportion of persisting men named by women who delivered out-of-wedlock in late-18th-century Hallowell (*Midwife's Tale*, 157). A few New Haven County women might have brought paternity suits in other counties. For an example of a Windham County woman who successfully sued the estate of her deceased lover, a New Haven physician, see Martha Preston v. David Dutton (June 1727), Windham County Court, Record Book, I, 82.

131. Henry Reed Stiles's contention that public attention to the practice intensified in the 1745–1775 period should be taken seriously (*Bundling: Its Origin, Progress, and Decline in America* [n.p., 1871], 75–80). Example of sermons condemning bundling include: one (undated) among the loose papers of Nathan Fiske of Brookfield, Mass. (Manuscript Sermons, 1757–1799, Fiske Family Papers, American Anti-

married, if their daughter had been raped, or if she had had a liaison
that could disgrace the family name, then parents (particularly if their
economic footing was secure) might think twice about pursuing legal
action that would expose the sordid affair to intensified community
gossip. Whether or not fathers of unwed mothers tried to silence talk
about the matter as far as possible or extracted private payments from
their daughter's lover, clearly after 1740 most families touched by the
temporary crisis of an out-of-wedlock birth opted for the path that would
bring them the least publicity possible and the least judicial intervention. Such choices were not necessarily at odds with the policy of grand
jurors after 1740 of dropping prosecutions of single men and most married couples. After all, many of the unwed mothers' male kin and their
social counterparts constituted the jurors and grand jurors participating
in fornication proceedings. The actions of these New England men both
as family heads and legal officers led toward reducing the community's
role in ensuring that families were well-ordered units, unblemished by
immorality. Such a role for the county court as an embodiment of community had been central to the seventeenth-century Puritan way of life.
By 1790, even the persistently Puritan New Haveners had abandoned
the county court as a major arbiter of moral behavior.[132]

<hr />

quarian Society), and Samuel Hopkins, sermon dated Mar. 11, 1753 (Huntington
Library). See also the comments of a traveler through Connecticut in 1786: Antonio
Pace, ed. and trans., *Luigi Castiglioni's Viaggio: Travels in the United States of North
America, 1785–1787* (Syracuse, N.Y., 1983), 253–254. For an excellent analysis of
courting practices in a late-18th-century town, see Laurel Thatcher Ulrich and Lois
K. Stabler, " 'Girling of It' in Eighteenth-Century New Hampshire," *Dublin Seminar
for New England Folklife*, X (1985), 24–36.

132. Fornication charges against women disappear from the records of the New
Haven County Court after 1788. The surviving justice of the peace records of
Thomas Clark of Derby indicate that, as early as 1779, some Connecticut justices
oversaw an abbreviated complaint process for women and never required the women
who appeared to submit to criminal charges. Between 1779 and 1799, 17 pregnant
single women appeared in a registrationlike procedure before Clark. Each swore to
the identity of the man who fathered the child she bore and stated the date on which
conception had occurred. Most often the matter of record ended there; presumably
the woman and her family used her sworn statement to pursue the man for marriage
or child support. In four instances, the man was summoned before Clark and bound
over to the county court, but only one of these four paternity suits was actually
conducted (Justice of the Peace Records of Thomas Clark, 1777–1803, CSL). This
new system, in which fornication was decriminalized for both men and women,

Ignoring more often than not misdemeanors such as drunkenness and Sabbath breaking that must have occurred with some frequency in colonial Connecticut, the "sober, discreet" men serving as grand jurors in each town made premarital sex (when it resulted in pregnancy) their most frequent presentment. Why this preoccupation with fornication? Partly, grand jurors were heeding Old Testament lessons, which taught that lewd conduct was closer than intoxication in the chain of sins leading to the unpardonable one of renouncing God. In addition, vigorous enforcement of laws against premarital and extramarital sex was obligatory for Puritan regimes that stressed, first, the legitimacy of loving sexual relations only within marriage and, second, the sanctity of marriage as the keystone of the social order.[133] Thus illicit sexual relations threatened not only marriages but also fundamental structures of authority. Finally, an important factor in the pursuit of sexual misconduct was the visibility of the sign that uncovered the sinner: pregnancy. Other common misdemeanors, like failure to attend public worship, were as readily observable to alert grand jurors as an ill-timed pregnancy. But with the latter the sign remained visible for months, triggering a spiral of local talk and speculation beyond what an episode of drunkenness might prompt. To the Puritan mind, such a persisting mark of sin — one that lingered open to the community's and God's witness — demanded a response that led to public punishment and, ideally, public confession.

That the identifying mark of sin showed itself on women's bodies might be expected to be a recipe for punishing women only. But what most distinguished Puritan New England from other English legal jurisdictions was the founders' creation not only of a climate in which, for a time, men and women *alike* confessed to sexual transgressions but also of a legacy by which legal officers would *choose* to prosecute and punish men for fornication into the early eighteenth century. The emergence of a prosecutorial double standard in the later colonial period must be

evidently took hold in some towns *before* 1790. For example, Wallingford justices of the peace forwarded only two prosecutions of single women to the county court between 1730 and 1770; Derby sent its last in 1753. For discussions of the decriminalization of fornication in Massachusetts, see Ulrich, *Midwife's Tale*, chap. 4; and William E. Nelson, *Americanization of the Common Law: The Impact of Legal Change on Massachusetts Society, 1760–1830* (Cambridge, Mass., 1975), 110–111.

133. Williams, *Warnings to the Unclean*, 15, 56–57; Edmund S. Morgan, *The Puritan Family: Religion and Domestic Relations in Seventeenth-Century New England*, rev. ed. (New York, 1966).

understood in the context of the many men who, before 1740, were whipped, fined, and reprimanded for the folly of fornication.

The unraveling of a criminal justice system which held both women and men accountable for the "begetting" of a child out of wedlock began in the 1690s and was complete by 1740. The key shift occurred when the directive to a man to confess "as he ought" no longer came from the magistrates' mouths, but issued only as an unavailing morality tale from single mothers such as Sarah Hine. Indeed, the moment when New Haven jurists accepted the argument that relying on a woman's constant accusation was repugnant to the law, another death knell for the cultural power of Puritan values sounded. What was happening on the criminal side of county court business in the decades around the turn of the century paralleled the trends in civil litigation away from ad hoc remedies and informal pleading. Under the prompting of lawyers, New Haven magistrates and jurors rejected a set of rituals rooted in early modern mentalité and society—truth telling in childbirth, the midwife's testimony, community corroboration of who was keeping company with whom—that had been sufficient for their forefathers to whip or fine men for fornication. In the place of those rituals, the New Haven legal fraternity substituted the rules of evidence increasingly in vogue in eighteenth-century English criminal trials, rules that valued direct eyewitness testimony over hearsay and circumstantial evidence. Men would have to be caught in the act of fornication (a rare eventuality) or pressured into confessing (as was the sole African man prosecuted).[134] By the 1740s, when grand jurors no longer even attempted to pursue men criminally for fathering out-of-wedlock children, the legal system had endorsed a symbolism that equated the pregnant, female body with a woman's sole guilt for the crime.

The reconfiguration of the system of punishing fornication in the mid-eighteenth century coincided with a broad range of cultural sign-

134. In the 18th-century cultural system, whiteness exempted men from confessing to fornication. Tim, "negro servant" of Gideon Platt of Milford, was prosecuted twice (in 1773 and 1775) for fornication along with his lover, a 40-year-old, never-married, white woman, Mercy Morris, whose mother had died insolvent in 1767 and who in 1773 evidently was in the employ of a local widow. On both presentments, the two defendants confessed to fornication before a local justice of the peace (NHCC, VII, 537; NHCC Files, dr. 61).

On the links between the "coming of the lawyers" and "the development of the modern law of evidence," see John H. Langbein, "The Criminal Trial before the Lawyers," *University of Chicago Law Review*, XLV (1978), 306–314.

posts marking new attitudes toward male and female sexuality and accountability. As Laurel Thatcher Ulrich has noted, the New England gentry's taste for portraits of married women with tiny waists, flowing tresses, and décolletage, along with the popular rage for Samuel Richardson's novel *Pamela,* betrayed the simultaneous idealization of women's youthful sexuality and the premium placed on female chastity.[135] One logic that flowed from the story of Pamela matched on a symbolic level the practice of the New Haven County Court: since women had heroic capacities to resist seduction, they alone should be held up for punishment if they succumbed. But middle-class culture at midcentury also harbored a growing sensitivity to class differences, to the lines between genteel and nongenteel, respectable and uncouth. The renewed fear that impoverished, servant women would commit infanticide and the drumbeat of newspaper reports on the disorderly conduct of poor, laboring, Irish, and black women in the cities marked the beginning of an era when carnality, that evil that for centuries had been associated with Woman, came more and more to be represented as the particular failing of lower-class women.[136] New Haven County grand jurors played their part in this ideological work of class polarization by increasingly shielding the daughters of middling and elite families from prosecution and targeting poor women who often had no settled residence, no supportive or intact family, and little chance of marriage or social mobility.

Discourses in print culture and the legal system's responses to real-life seductions mutually reinforced each other to shape changing concepts not just of femininity but also of masculinity. Manliness, to Puritan patriarchs, meant confessing to one's sin and making good on a spoken or implicit pledge to marry one's lover. In the middle decades of the eighteenth century, private correspondence touching on young men's affairs and humorous tales printed in newspapers show the degree to which

135. Ulrich, *Good Wives,* 104–105, 114–117.

136. Karlsen, *Devil in the Shape of a Woman,* 256–257; Christine Stansell, *City of Women: Sex and Class in New York, 1789–1860* (New York, 1986), chap. 1. Note the dichotomy set up in Nathan Fiske's exclamations in his undated sermon on bundling: "Are not Modesty and Chastity the brightest Jewels, the richest Ornaments of a female?" "Alas, what is more odious and contemptible than an immodest and shameless woman!" (Manuscript Sermons, 1757–1799, Fiske Family Papers, American Antiquarian Society).

For examples of newspaper reports, see *Conn. Courant,* July 29, 1765, June 23, 1766, Aug. 17, 1767; *Conn. Gazette,* Aug. 30, 1755, Sept. 28, 1759; *Conn. Journal,* Nov. 13, Dec. 4, 1767, Oct. 19, 1770.

male sexual license was becoming a casual, even a joking matter in New England.

One of the best examples comes from the papers of Robert Treat Paine, a Massachusetts lawyer who intervened in 1763 to explain the predicament of twenty-four-year-old Ephraim Keith, Jr., to his father, a justice of the peace. Young Ephraim, a recent Harvard graduate, was living in Paine's town of Taunton, studying the law, when a paternity suit was initiated against him. Privately, he resolved to flee the legal process and disappear (according to Paine) "anywhere, to the Worlds End, by Land and Sea." On learning this, the older, more knowledgeable attorney's first move was to arrange for Ephraim to "conceal himself" until the affair was settled out of court. Second, Paine felt that the only person to whom the young man owed an apology and a "sincere" pledge of "repentance and future good Behaviour" was his father. The resolution of the temporary crisis was to be entirely a private, familial "Reconcilement." "Officer[s]" and courts were to be avoided.[137]

Third, Paine emphatically underscored one of the prime ways that genteel families had fixed upon to mute the consequences of their sons' sexual activity: "Money answers all Ends," he declared. In this case, the sum paid to the unwed mother of Ephraim's child answered dual ends. It saved a promising youth from the "Utter Ruin" of becoming a "freindless . . . Vagabond," retaining to the colony and to the "honour" of the Keith family a man "well fitted to do good in the World (Notwithstanding this Affair)."[138] Money also served to silence and put in her place the unnamed woman whom Paine implicated as an uppity, grasping representative of the lower classes and entirely unsuitable as a marriage partner for Ephraim.

137. Stephen T. Riley and Edward W. Hanson, eds., *The Papers of Robert Treat Paine,* II (Boston, 1992), 252.

138. Ibid., 252–253. For another cash settlement by an elite family, see Sklar, "Culture vs. Economics: A Case of Fornication," University of Michigan, *Papers in Women's Studies,* 1978, 36–38.

Benjamin Franklin, the anonymous author of the long-lived "Speech of Miss Polly Baker" (first published in England in April 1747), unerringly identified the class differential within the double standard that was at work in 18th-century New England: Polly, reviewing her prosecutions for five out-of-wedlock births, lamented that the first man to seduce and deceive her "is now become a Magistrate" and that her "Betrayer and Undoer . . . should be advanc'd to Honour and Power in the Government" while she is punished "with Stripes and Infamy" (Hall, *Benjamin Franklin and Polly Baker,* 163–164).

What is perhaps most striking about Paine's and young Ephraim's letters on the affair is the satirical tone they adopt in self-conscious emulation of both the learned and playful elements in the culture of English and European gentlemen. Paine's narrative could almost have been lifted from the pages of Fielding:

> In Short, honest Ephraim, yr. Shamefaced, dutiful Son Ephraim is too handsome. A Dighton Girl (Heavens Screen us from the Girls) laid Amorous hands on him, as Joseph's Mistress did on him, but being More good Natured than Joseph She saith he did not resist. And now the fruits of Love begin to make their appearance, She makes her Complaint to a Justice hoping to Scare a poor inoffensive inexperienced Youth into Some disadvantageous Accomodation of the Matter.[139]

Written to appease Ephraim's father, Paine's exploitation of such images as the scheming seductress and the innocent, passive boy is understandable, if rather unconvincing. Young Ephraim's effusive letter of thanks to Paine, penned from "In Secessu long" (in remote seclusion), referred to the incident sportingly, with mock horror and self-pity, and with a touch of braggadocio: "It is needless for me to Describe the Perplexities and Embarrassments I laboured under with a Brace of Bailiffs at my Heels *and all merely for the Peccadillo of begetting my own Likeness.*" It was his "Persecutors" who by their "disingenous Conduct" should be called "inhumane."[140]

Satire, once banned by the Puritans, increasingly pervaded the private letters, colonial newspapers, imported books, and locally produced almanacs that circulated among urban and rural households and taverns. Much of it was at the expense of women, and much of it was blatantly antimatrimonial. Frequent contributions came from anonymous essayists or poets who warned bachelors against marriage, since wives could doom one's life to misery by perpetual scolding and humiliating cuckoldry.[141] In four rhyming lines, a 1769 almanac aphorism managed both to wink at extramarital sex *and* cluck at women's pestiferous voices:

139. Riley and Hanson, eds., *Papers of Paine*, 251. Dighton was the town abutting the southern border of Taunton.

140. Ibid., 254 (my emphasis). Ephraim added that he felt "the persuasive Eloquence" of Paine's letter to his father was "above the Power of Cicero or Demosthenes."

141. *Conn. Journal*, Nov. 27, 1767 (for an essay); Feb. 16, Mar. 13, Apr. 13, 1770 (for an exchange of fictional letters); Feb. 25, 1768 (for a poem). For different

> By your Eye a Mistress chuse,
> By your Ear a Wife.
> That grown plain you may refuse;
> This must last for Life.[142]

With the Puritan founders surely turning in their graves, these were among the many examples offered in print to New Englanders of ways to put down women. Expressed as humor, the bons mots masked the seriousness and persistence of fears that female sexuality and female speech threatened to confound male ambition and civic order.

One item, reprinted from the *London Magazine* in 1740, spoke directly to the controversy over whether men should be punished for sexual activity before marriage. The squib took the form of a facetious comment on what was purportedly a new effort by the king of Prussia to stamp out "Licentiousness." Prussian men of all ranks who "seduce[d] young Girls" would in future "be obliged to marry them" without fail. The London editors waggishly responded: "We . . . prophesy, that [in Prussia] young Girls, instead of being seduced, will soon become the Seducers."[143] Although a law enjoining marriage for men who "defiled" single women had been part of their founding heritage, by 1740 New England newspaper readers, this item suggests, were ready to imagine that attempts to punish or curtail men's youthful sexual experimentation would unleash hordes of manipulative, sexually aggressive women desperate not to become spinsters. With the cessation in the same year of prosecutions against single men for begetting their likenesses, public law, alongside such jokes, taught young men that their sexual irresponsibility was forgivable while it held women to a higher standard of sexual virtue. Whether reading *Pamela* or hearing the most recent account of a female peer who had confessed before the local justice, young women gleaned the lesson that they would preserve their respectability only if

---

versions of the same satirical poem on marriage in various 1777 New England almanacs, see Marion Barber Stowell, *Early American Almanacs: The Colonial Weekday Bible* (New York, 1977), 265, 273. A fuller treatment of the typology of satire and gendered images in print culture is found in Cornelia Hughes Dayton, "Satire and Sensationalism: The Emergence of Misogyny in Mid-Eighteenth-Century New England Newspapers and Almanacs," paper presented to the New England Seminar in American History, Worcester, Mass., Nov. 15, 1991.

142. Nathaniel Ames, *An Astronomical Diary: or, Almanack, for . . . 1769* (New London, [1768]).

143. *Boston Evening-Post*, May 12, 1740.

they resisted the sexual advances of men who had no intention of marrying them. Discomfited over their recognition that many of their daughters were failing that test, New England yeomen waited another fifty years before finally pulling the plug on a system that for a century and a half had held up the forum of the secular courtroom as the proper theater for the acknowledgment of sin and immorality.

5

Rape

THE PROBLEMATICS OF WOMAN'S WORD

A haunting, abbreviated story of curious origins appeared in the *Connecticut Journal* on April 14, 1769: "Yesterday an old Countryman was deposited in Gaol at Norwich, for committing a Rape on one Widow Wickwire, an elderly Woman. . . . We hear he broke one of her Ancles, and bit her Nose very badly."[1] Was it based on an actual incident, or was it a joke? The former seems unlikely, since no arrest warrant or prosecution for sexual assault appears in the New London County Superior or County Court records for the months surrounding April 1769. On the other hand, the Wickwires were an established Norwich family, and there might indeed have been a widow in her seventies or eighties living in part of a homestead, supported by her children and grandchildren. Whether the newspaper item was authentic news or cruel satire, it was part of a trend among New England printers to include for their urban, commercial, elite readers more entertaining stories that might, among other things, offer depictions of the maiming or dismembering of women's bodies.[2]

1. *Connecticut Journal* (New Haven), Apr. 14, 1769.
2. Cornelia Hughes Dayton, "Satire and Sensationalism: The Emergence of Misogyny in Mid-Eighteenth-Century New England Newspapers and Almanacs," paper

By the time of the Wickwire item, the cultural and legal responses of New Englanders to stories of sexual assault had changed markedly since their seventeenth-century beginnings. Before 1700, when almost all sexual assault cases that came to Connecticut courts involved attempted violations of women who knew their assailants, the conviction rate approached 100 percent. Puritan magistrates emphatically articulated their design to "make punishment exemplary" both for men who carried on with such "filthynes and boldnes" and for all those who concealed such crimes. After 1700, the growing reliance of judges on English legal treatises and more rigorous evidentiary standards altered the face of rape prosecutions as it did fornication cases. A woman's general reputation and the details of her behavior at the time of the alleged incident came under heavy scrutiny. As a consequence, the climate for rape charges changed from one in which women's accounts of abuse were greeted with sober respect to one in which women who charged white acquaintances almost invariably saw their accusations discounted or eventually dismissed. Moreover, between 1700 and 1770, the Connecticut court with jurisdiction over rape, unlike its Massachusetts counterpart, did not entertain prosecutions for attempted rape. This failure to indict assailants for anything less than the capital crime of rape undoubtedly discouraged women and their families from reporting assaults.[3]

---

presented to the New England Seminar in American History, Worcester, Mass., Nov. 15, 1991. For examples, see *Connecticut Courant* (Hartford), Jan. 9, 1769 (a fasting girl), Aug. 12, 1765 (an English woman burned at the stake); *Connecticut Gazette* (New Haven), June 21, 1755 (an eloping servant woman thrown from a horse, torn from limb to limb), June 28, 1755 (a battered woman's fatal injuries).

No record books for the New London County Court survive for the mid-18th century, but loose dockets for June 1769 through February 1770 reveal no case plausibly related to the newspaper report (New London County Court Files, box 149, CSL). A jailed man could have escaped from the jail, of course, and eluded detection and thus prosecution in Superior Court. For the Wickwires of Norwich, see Charles Dyer Parkhurst, *Early Families of New London and Vicinity* (Hartford, 1938), XXXI, 141 (copy at CSL).

3. *NHTR*, I, 32. For similar emphatic statements from the bench, see I, 183, and Rex v. Arthur Teague (Aug. 1667), NHCC, I, 12. At times, sexual assault was subsumed under other categories such as lascivious carriage and prosecuted in the county courts.

I use "assault" throughout this chapter in its broad legal sense, thus encompassing *both* threats or attempts to inflict bodily injury *and* the actual application of illegal

Growing popular doubts about capital punishment and, even more significantly, prejudice against nonwhites and outsiders were two further factors shaping patterns of rape prosecutions and convictions in the eighteenth century. Given that rape was a capital crime throughout the seventeenth and eighteenth centuries, juries often declined to return a guilty verdict, and women hesitated to come forward with a charge out of fear that it would take away a man's life. Communities and jurors were better able to validate a woman's rape charge and stomach the idea of a hanging if the alleged assailant were an outsider. Two-thirds of the men indicted on rape-related charges from 1700 to 1790, and all six of those sentenced to hang, were blacks, Indians, foreigners, or transients.

There was only one crime of sexual violence for which Connecticut jurors consistently voted to punish white male residents: "incest," in which a father or father figure was seen as perverting his proper authority by coercing a daughter into sexual relations. No separate criminal category existed for the sexual abuse of children; cases involving child victims were prosecuted either as rape or incest. Even though the latter crime according to its colonial definition presumed the voluntary participation of both partners, in most cases the punishment of the young woman was mitigated in recognition of her forced compliance. Rape was defined in colonial Connecticut, as in England, without reference to the age or marital status of the woman attacked. The capital law in force throughout the 1666–1799 period was direct: "If any Man shall forcibly and without consent Ravish any Maid or Woman, by committing Carnal Copulation with her against her consent, he shall be put to Death, provided prosecution and complaint be made forthwith upon the Rape." As the prosecutions of four child molesters indicate, Connecticut authorities silently followed English practice by encompassing within their understanding of the crime of rape the ravishment of "a woman-child under the age of ten years with or against her will."[4]

---

force; technically, the latter in Anglo-American law is "battery" (*Black's Law Dictionary*, 5th ed. [St. Paul, Minn., 1979], s.v. "assault," "battery").

4. *PR*, I, 77; John D. Cushing, ed., *The Earliest Laws of the New Haven and Connecticut Colonies, 1639–1673* (Wilmington, Del., 1977), 83; Matthew Hale, *Historia Placitorum Coronae: The History of the Pleas of the Crown* (London, 1736), I, 628. Incest was included for the first time in the capital list in the 1672 Code (Cushing, ed., *Earliest Laws of New Haven and Connecticut*, 83). In the pre-1666 period, Connecticut Colony had declared rape a capital crime in 1642, but New Haven Colony in its 1656 Code left the punishment for rape up to the judges' discretion while specifying death for

We know little about the extent of sexual violence in early New England. One author of a study of eighteenth-century Massachusetts rape cases reached the "inescapable" conclusion that, despite underreporting, "many fewer rapes were committed in proportion to the population" in the colonial period than today.[5] That assessment, while almost certainly correct, need not deflect us from inquiring into how both women and men perceived and interpreted male coercion and sexual violence and why it was at times condemned and at other times excused by the legal system. The fundamental shift in early New England came at the beginning of the eighteenth century, when magistrates and community residents let go of the Puritan belief that assailants and victims alike were bound in an ethical pact with both their God and their earthly communities to tell the truth. With the importation into New England legal practice of English suspicion of women's rape charges, the notion that middle-class white men had proprietary rights to women's bodies became more deeply entrenched as an unspoken assumption of gender relations and legal culture.

In ruling on the first case that came before them involving the sexual assault of an adult woman, the New Haven Colony magistrates broadcast two powerful themes that would govern magisterial responses to coercion cases through the 1600s. They underscored not only the seriousness with which they would receive rape charges but also the severe treatment that awaited any woman or man who concealed knowledge of sexual assault. This earliest case involved a woman who would seem to have three strikes against her. First, Goodwife Fancy (whose first name the records never reveal) was a rootless servant who had moved with her husband from colony to colony and from household to household. Second, she had previously been whipped for theft, once in New Haven and twice in Connecticut. Third, as a resident of New Haven in the mid-1670s she failed to report promptly any of a series of attacks against her. However, once the story of her abuse came to light in the spring of 1646, the bench proceeded swiftly to examine and punish the miscreants.

---

sodomy and the abuse of the "unripe vessel of a Girle" (*PR*, I, 77; *NHCR*, I, 577–578).

5. Barbara S. Lindemann, " 'To Ravish and Carnally Know': Rape in Eighteenth-Century Massachusetts," *Signs: Journal of Women in Culture and Society*, X (1984–1985), 72, 81–82.

Under legal regimes in other places and times, a focus on Goody Fancy's character might have deflected attention from and cast doubt on the details of her revelations. But in early New Haven her sworn enumeration of the assaults that came as she went about her duties — gathering pumpkins, fetching wood, catching hens, working in the cellar or in the cowhouse — placed the spotlight on the three men who had "indeavored to satisfie [their] lust" with her. Indeed, it was her principal assailant who, while reflecting on his own fate, anticipated the attitude of the court: he said "he knew . . . that a weomans word would passe before a mans in this case, espetially seeing [that Goody] Fancy . . . said she would take her oath for the truth of her chardge." Since the colony magistrates, fearful that weak mortals would fall into perjury, allowed very few accusers or witnesses to be sworn on oath, their willingness to let Goody Fancy take the oath demonstrates their conviction that she was speaking the truth.[6]

While the hellish parade of secret assaults might have ended for Goodwife Fancy with the 1646 trial, the magistrates did not allow her to leave the courtroom without reprimand. Able to catch only one of her assailants, they sentenced him to a severe whipping. They then addressed a troubling aspect of the case that set an extremely poor example for colony residents: the assaults had occurred over the last two years, and throughout that time Goody Fancy had been persuaded by her husband to hide the incidents from authorities and neighbors.[7] The Fancys — she for concealing her tribulations and he "for his being as it were a pander to his wife" "who should have bin her protector" and "neglecting the timely revealing of" the attacks — were both ordered to be severely whipped.

---

6. *NHCR*, I, 235, 236, 238. For the Fancys' previous clashes with the law, see 89, 229–230.

On the colony courts' policy on oaths, see Gail Sussman Marcus, " 'Due Execution of the Generall Rules of Righteousnesse': Criminal Procedure in New Haven Town and Colony, 1638–1658," in David D. Hall et al., eds., *Saints and Revolutionaries: Essays on Early American History* (New York, 1984), 112–114; and the discussion in Chapter 1, above.

7. Goody Fancy felt compelled to talk publicly about Thomas Robinson's attacks only when Robinson raised a rumor that she had recommenced thieving. Hearing of his charges from a woman who employed her, Fancy "passionatly and in way of revendge took up this proverbiall speech, save one from the gallowes and he will hang you or cutt your throate if he can." Her interlocutor, supposing by these words "some great guilt was concealed and lay hidd, inquired the meaning, and Fancyes wife discovered Robinsons filthynesse and villeny" (*NHCR*, I, 235).

TABLE 12

Sexual Assault Cases in New Haven Colony Courts, 1639–1666,
and Connecticut Colony Courts, 1666–1699

Date, Court	Defendant and Charge	Status and Age of Women	Outcome
Jan. 1641/2 New Haven Col. Ct.	Thomas Badger uncleanness	his master's child — under 7, sex un-specified	whipping and carting about town
Spring 1646 New Haven Col. Ct.	Thomas Robinson Mark Meigs Stephen Metcalf attempted rape	married, ser-vant	—fled —severe whipping —had died
June 1650 New Haven Col. Ct.	Mark Meigs attempted rape	newly married	confessed; severe whipping, pillory-ing
July 1653 New Haven Col. Ct.	Ellis Mew attempted rape	single, servant	whipping
July 1654 New Haven Town Ct.	Joshua Bradley sexual molesta-tion ("filthiness")	girl (age 6)	severe whipping
May 1664 New Haven Town Ct.	an Indian sexual abuse	girl (age 13)	severe whipping, banished to his "own country"
Jan. 1664/5 New Haven Town Ct.	Patrick Morran attempted rape	2 single women (sisters)	found not guilty but "imprudent"
Aug. 1666 New Haven Town Ct.	John Tharp coerced sex	single (age 23)	severe whipping, to pay child sup-port
Aug. 1666 New Haven Town Ct.	William Collins attempted rape	married woman	severe whipping

TABLE 12

Continued

Date, Court	Defendant and Charge	Status and Age of Women	Outcome
Aug. 1667 New Haven Town Ct.	Arthur Teague rape	single, servant	severe whipping, £10 fine
June 1677 New Haven Town Ct.	Roger Camp attempted rape	married woman	severe whipping, £20 bond for good behavior
Oct. 1693 Ct. of Assts.	Daniel Matthews rape — 2 indictments	girl (age 10) girl (age 12)	not guilty pleas; juries find guilty; sentence of hanging

Sources: *NHCR*, I, II; *NHTR*, I, II; NHCC, Records and Files, 1666–1699; *Recs. Ct. of Assts.*, Lacy transcript, I, II.

Thus, in this early exemplary case, Governor Theophilus Eaton and his compeers signaled their insistence that women and others abide by "the mynd of God" in exposing all sexual assaults.[8]

Unlike fornication prosecutions, the shape of which changed noticeably when New Haven Colony merged with its less Puritan neighbor, sexual assault prosecutions retained up until 1700 the tenor and exactitude of the earliest cases. Besides the three men charged by Goodwife Fancy, ten men were prosecuted for attempted rape (all before 1678) and two men for rape (in 1667 and 1693) (see Table 12). All were convicted except for Patrick Moran, whom the New Haven town court acquitted in 1665 but chided for imprudent behavior tending to coercive seduction. The first man sentenced to hang for rape in Connecticut

8. Ibid., 235, 239. Several times Goody Fancy pressed her husband "to complayne to the governor" about the attacks — and at one point announced she would go herself — but he resisted this strategy, perhaps out of fear they would be treated contemptuously and lose their precarious footing in the settlement, perhaps out of a desire to collect money from his wife's assailants (235, 237, 238).

was Daniel Matthews, the "little taylor," who was found guilty of raping two young girls (aged ten and twelve) in 1693.[9] The one nonwhite charged, an Indian who was never named, was whipped and then banished. His expulsion foreshadowed the eighteenth-century pattern in which juries tended to perceive the crime of rape in racial terms and judges doled out far harsher penalties to nonwhites convicted.

The structural characteristics of the seventeenth-century rape caseload suggested a neat conceptual division. Attempted rape came to the courts as something that occurred between a woman and a man she knew; he used enticement and then force, driven by the sinful lusts that raged within him (perhaps because his own wife was barren), and he allowed her (or she managed) to scare or fight him off. In the rare cases defined as rape, not attempted rape, the act was accompanied by lurid threats of violence ("he would splay her," "he would kill her and cutt [her?] in peices and Hang her on that tree") — threats that served to squelch female resistance. Moreover, it was perpetrated by strangers — men who were outsiders and itinerants.[10] Although the reality of women's experience of sexual violence must not have fitted into this apparent dichotomy, by the end of the seventeenth century outright rape had been constructed in the legal realm as an act committed by strangers. This strong association, combined with the abandonment of attempted rape cases by Connecticut prosecutors, would dramatically limit the ways in which women's words would be credited in court in the next century.

What is astonishing about the seventeenth-century Puritan regimes is the way in which they distanced themselves from the skepticism har-

9. On Moran: *NHTR*, II, 122. When one factors in the two men accused by Goodwife Fancy who disappeared before trial, the 16 prosecutions for rape and attempted rape in New Haven and Connecticut colonies up to 1700 yield a conviction rate of 81%.

On Matthews: *Recs. Ct. of Assts.*, Lacy transcript, I, 200–201. Three assistants objected to Matthews's sentence and extended him a temporary reprieve, which was overruled by the Assembly; presumably Matthews was then hanged. See *PR*, IV, 132–133.

10. For an example of the barrenness argument, see *NHTR*, I, 30–32. Quotes: Rex v. Arthur Teague (Aug. 1667), NHCC, I, 12; Testimony of Rebecca Goodrich (dated June 20, 1693), Rex v. Daniel Matthews, Connecticut Archives, Crimes and Misdemeanors, 1st Ser., I, 201, CSL. Both Arthur Teague and Daniel Matthews had aliases, came from outside the county where the assaults occurred, and were unknown to the women they attacked.

bored by the English legal system toward women who brought rape accusations. Instead of hewing to the image of manipulative women who easily cried rape, Governor Eaton of New Haven sought enlightenment from a key biblical passage. His interpretation of Deuteronomy 22 helps us to understand why early New Englanders were predisposed to believe a woman's word. Eaton explained: in "the case of a rape, . . . there is no witnes onely the testimoney of the maid and the effects found upon her; the damsell cryed and there was none to save her: then none but herselfe to testifye, yet that was accepted." Ready to believe that "a young girle [would not] bee so impudent as to charge such a carriage upon a young man when it was not so," Eaton also depended on the broad, probing judicial interrogations so central to his juryless system to expose when an accuser was dissembling or hiding her own complicity. In sexual assault cases, the magistrates focused on the various accounts of the incident itself, not on the previous character or truth-telling habits of the parties. That a young servant girl, Susan Clarke, had been "taken . . . in some untruthes" on other matters did "not prove that she tells untruth" when charging a fellow servant, Ellis Mew, with attempted rape. Conversely, just because Mew had not been caught in falsehoods beforehand, he could very well be, like the biblical figure Gehazi, covering his sin on this occasion.[11]

Indeed, the early New Haven cases tended to indicate that it was men, not women, who had a proclivity for lying. When first examined, Mark Meigs "denied all" but "some foolish speeches, and cariage" to Nathaniel Seeley's wife. Brought to court a second time, however, and confronted "with all the particulares of" Goody Seeley's charges, he "confessed them all." Similarly, Joshua Bradley "owned . . . before the Court" that which "he had impudently denied . . . at first" — sexually abusing a six-year-old girl. Two other convicted men who were never cajoled into confession displeased the judges, one with an assertive protestation of his innocence ("he was as cleare from it as any man in the world, god know his heart"), the other with a baldly self-serving maneuver "to cast aspersions upon" his female accuser. Finally, two married men revealed that they had carried around a powerful incentive to deny their assaults on Goody Fancy: one claimed "if it came to light he should be undone,"

11. *NHTR*, I, 152, 182. On early New Haven's unique examination system, see Marcus, " 'Due Execution of the Rules of Righteousnesse,' " in Hall et al., eds., *Saints and Revolutionaries*, 118–129.

and the other said "he would rather that his life and all goods were gone then that his wife should have knowne of it."[12]

While the early decades of settlement in New Haven were years in which assault complainants could expect their word to be taken over that of their assailants', women were discouraged from exercising control over the social ramifications of assault incidents. Rather, seventeenth-century Puritan culture encouraged women to place the question of how to respond to rape or serious harassment in their husbands' or fathers' hands. Stalked or grabbed by Thomas Robinson, Goody Fancy deflected his immediate advances by evasion, struggling, hollering, and cursing ("Goe and be hanged"). But the next step—whether to confront Robinson, collect money from him, or report him—she left to her husband. In fact, she told her harasser that "her husband knew of his filthy leawd carryadges, . . . therfore" it was up to the two men to "make peace." The disposition of a woman's body also became a matter of negotiation between men in the case involving Mary Pinion. In this 1666 incident, it appears that a small clutch of men got drunk at Ralph Russell's house and that during the carousing Thomas Pinion jestingly offered the newly married William Collins a "Commission" to lie with Pinion's wife "if she would give her Consent." When Collins took this as license to "hunt [Mary] about," telling her he had her spouse's permission, she fought him off and "answered that her husband had noe such power over her as to make her sin."[13] But a woman like Goody Fancy who practiced wifely deference *was* led by her husband into the sin of hiding a foul crime and thus to the whipping post.

Despite the sympathetic hearing extended by the magistrates to most women who complained of sexual assault, not all women's claims of coercion were treated and punished as rape in the 1600s. Occasionally, rape or assault charges were raised in the context of fornication and lascivious carriage prosecutions. The woman who at that juncture claimed she had been forced was at a disadvantage because she had not

12. *NHTR*, I, 31, 220; Rex v. Arthur Teague (Aug. 1667), NHCC, I, 10–12, Rex v. Roger Camp (June 1677), NHCC, I, 103; *NHCR*, I, 235, 238, 239.

13. *NHCR*, I, 234 (Fancy); *NHTR*, II, 182–183 (Pinion). When Robinson, after one year of harassing Goody Fancy, had the audacity to ask her to act as lying-in nurse for his wife, she sent "him unto her husband, and he, considring the weomans neede," consented—thus subjecting his spouse to additional assaults (*NHCR*, I, 234). For another case in which the woman's assailant negotiated with her spouse, see *NHTR*, II, 210–211.

reported the assault to family members or authorities soon after it occurred. Martha Richardson of Stamford was brought before the colony court in 1654 to answer for being pregnant, before her marriage, with a child both she and her husband admitted was not his. Now nineteen months after the incident, she recounted having had a fainting fit in her master's house while two men were present, one of whom she supposed had "abused" her. The bench dismissed this vague story, partly because she had engaged in continual lying about other aspects of her embarrassingly early pregnancy, but mostly because they adhered to the popular notion that a woman who was raped—who had no "delight" in the act—could not conceive. Martha Richardson had conceived and borne a child, and thus she deserved to be "publiquely and seveerly corrected" as a fornicator.[14]

A sexual encounter that took place on a crowded boat overnight provided the judges with an ideal test case for demonstrating to early New Haven residents how the line between coerced and consensual sex should be drawn. When Hannah Spencer and William Ellitt were called into court in 1655 to account for the "uncleane, filthy cariages betwixt them," each gave a different version of what had occurred. Hannah, a young orphan, testified that William had fallen on her in the crowded cabin in the night, "and by degrees got up her coates and had carnall knowledg of her . . . without her consent." Ellitt, who had already earned himself an unsavory reputation in the region, contended there had been two episodes, one at night when he had endeavored to woo Hannah "but could not," and one in the morning when Hannah lay down with him out of sympathy because he was shaking with cold—then she consented to sex, he said. Other passengers in the ship's cabin with Hannah and William had not heard her cry out to protest unwelcome advances, and the next day they overheard the two "[fall] into a . . . treaty of marriage." The court concluded there was "not satisfying evidenc that it was a forced rape, yet . . . it is likely [it] was begun in a way of force though after[wards] her consent might be drawne."[15]

Although the colony magistrates categorized the boating incident in

---

14. *NHCR*, II, 123. The fading tenacity of the no-rape-if-conception theory can be traced through Giles Jacob's works: compare Jacob, *The Modern Justice* . . . , 3d ed. (London, 1720), 350, with Jacob, *A New Law-Dictionary*, 7th ed. (London, 1756), s.v. "rape." See also William Hawkins, *A Treatise of the Pleas of the Crown* . . . , 2d ed. (1724–1726; rpt., New York, 1972), 108.

15. *NHCR*, II, 134–136.

the end as consensual sex—"a great sinn and folly" for which both partners deserved punishment—their recognition that disreputable men like William Ellitt sometimes coerced women testified once again to their willingness to listen to women's stories. On the other hand, the message that the court sent to women in this ruling and in others prosecuted as lascivious carriage was that they would not be excused from responsibility if they in *any* way encouraged or tolerated the dalliance. For example, a predatory man like William Harding might be deemed "not fitt to live among [this] people," but the three women he harassed also deserved punishment for "yielding" to him. The case involving Caleb Horton was only partly resolved when Horton was fined for throwing "three mayds . . . down upon heaps" in a yard, sitting on them, and calling for a passing man "to help him, for he could not serve three at once." At the next court, the young women were summoned and seriously warned that "their carriage was then uncomly," "unseasonable," "mixed with some degree of daliance," and characterized by "too much complyance." Sexual assault crystallized in the magistrates' eyes when a man propositioned, "dogged," and used physical force against a woman without any invitation or encouragement from her. If a woman's response was to flirt, tarry, or quietly submit, then she lost her claim to being free from corrupting sin, and she was perceived to merit some measure of punishment, even though the more aggressive man was typically penalized more severely.[16]

The calculus of culpability shifted when race was an issue. Although all seventeenth-century sexual assault cases but one were against white men, the fornication caseload contains clues that magistrates could conceive of interracial sexual relations only as coercive. In 1691 the county court pointedly declared it would fine but assess no other punishment on two young women "known [to be] persons of weak and Imperfect understandings" who admitted to acts of fornication with Indian Robin. Robin, a servant, had fled to avoid the severe punishment the court undoubtedly would have meted out to him. The judges labeled Robin "that wicked Indian" and made it clear that they could imagine his sexual relations with two young white women only as involving coercion

16. Ibid., 136 (quote); *NHTR*, II, 182–183 (quote from case against William Collins); *NHCR*, I, 81, 84 (Harding was banished in January 1642/3); *NHTR*, I, 455, 461 (Horton). The magistrates used the verb "to dog" in their condemnation of Samuel Ford: *NHTR*, II, 211.

See the discussion of lascivious carriage cases, Chapter 4, above.

on his part and lack of full consent on their part. One year later the small town of New Haven must have been rocked with the news that Sergeant John Potter's daughter Mary had given birth to "a male Child of a Negro Complexion." Mary admitted to her father that, while she was serving in William Rosewell's household, Cush, a black servant there, had committed fornication with her. In an era when women who bore out-of-wedlock children were invariably prosecuted, the fact that authorities never moved to charge or punish Mary implies that they perceived this as a case of coercion. Cush's presumed assault was prosecuted as fornication and not as rape because direct evidence and a prompt complaint were lacking. However, after extracting a confession from Cush in court, the judges registered their alarm by authorizing a more severe whipping than that meted out to white fornicators. The court clerk recorded the sentence in unusually precise detail: the sheriff was to "fasten [Cush] to the place of Execution And then with a sutable Instrument him severely whip upon the naked back not exceeding 40 stripes."[17] The bench had stipulated the maximum number of lashes meted out for *any* crime, and a number far exceeding that given white male fornicators earlier in the century.

––––––––

The profile of sexual assault cases in Connecticut changed markedly as the eighteenth century commenced. The clearest sign of the new climate was the string of defendants acquitted or excused from rape charges—a string that extended through four decades until 1743 when Jack, a black slave, confessed to rape and was sentenced to hang (see Table 13). A second new feature of rape cases lay in the racial composition of the men brought before the bar. Although only one nonwhite had been prosecuted before 1700, during the first fifty years of the eighteenth century six of nine defendants haled before the higher court were black or Indian.

In the realm of procedure, Connecticut authorities also shifted gears. Having articulated a system under which felonies would be tried by a higher court (called the Court of Assistants until 1711, and the Superior Court thereafter), magistrates were careful from the 1693 Matthews case on to submit rape charges to grand juries before proceeding to trial. There was some confusion in these decades about what court level

17. Rex v. Margaret Trowbridge and Rex v. Mary Butler (Nov. 1691), NHCC, I, 194; Rex v. Cush (Nov. 1692), I, 202.

TABLE 13
Rape Prosecutions in the Court of Assistants, 1700–1710,
and the Superior Court, 1711–1790

Term, County	Defendant	Status and Age of Woman	Outcome
Oct. 1706 New Haven	Joseph Mallery	married woman (24)	grand jury: ignoramus
Sept. 1729 New Haven	James, Indian	girl (8)	cleared by proclamation
Sept. 1736 Hartford	John Green	single woman (19?)	not guilty plea; jury: not guilty
Feb. 1736/7 Fairfield	Sam, Negro	girl (6–7)	remanded to county court
Sept. 1743 Hartford	Jack, slave	married woman	guilty plea; sentenced to hang; executed
Feb. 1743/4 Fairfield	Sampson, slave	girl (9)	cleared by proclamation
Mar. 1744/5 Hartford	Pompey, slave	single woman (14)	not guilty plea; jury: not guilty
Feb. 1748/9 New Haven	Cuff, slave	single woman (15)	not guilty plea; jury: guilty; sentence: hanging; executed
Mar. 1749/50 Windham	Solomon Read	single woman (30)	grand jury: ignoramus
Mar. 1755 New London	William Ford	married woman	grand jury: ignoramus
Sept. 1756 New London	Bristo, slave	single woman	[plea not recorded]; sentence: hanging; released by Jan. 1757 Assembly after accuser's recantation

TABLE 13

Continued

Term, County	Defendant	Status and Age of Woman	Outcome
Aug. 1760 Fairfield	Vanskelly Mully	girl (10)	not guilty plea; jury: guilty; sentence: hanging; Assembly: commuted to whipping etc.
Sept. 1761 Hartford	Richard Oliver William McKee	single woman (19)	not guilty pleas; juries: both not guilty
Sept. 1761 Windham	John Fox John Carpenter, Jr. Mary Chub	single woman (18)	men: not guilty pleas; juries: both not guilty. Chub: billa vera; dropped
Oct. 1767 New Haven	Joseph Dudley	married woman (25)	grand jury: ignoramus
Sept. 1770 Hartford	Charles Livingston	married woman (20)	not guilty plea; jury: not guilty
Mar. 1783 Hartford	James Gibson	older woman	not guilty plea; jury: guilty; sentence: hanging; Assembly: commuted to castration
Aug. 1790 New Haven	Joseph Mountain, free black	girl (13)	not guilty plea; jury: guilty; sentence: hanging; executed

Sources: Court of Assistants Records, 1700–1710; Superior Court Records and Files, 1711–1790, CSL.

should have jurisdiction over sexual assault cases that fell short of out-right rape. In 1708 and again in 1737, the higher court remanded to the appropriate county court attempted rape cases that had been forwarded to it by local officials or the county court itself. The refusal of the assis-tants who sat on the higher court to assume responsibility for attempted rape is curious, since in Massachusetts the equivalent court handled both rape and attempted rape charges. Connecticut criminal justice officials might have decided to adhere more closely to the English sys-tem, by which rape was tried at the assizes and lesser assaults at the local quarter sessions.[18]

Just as more rigorous rules of pleading were introduced to civil litiga-tion in the early eighteenth century, so too did expert English legal opinions on rape begin to influence Connecticut proceedings. As bibli-cally inspired approaches receded in importance, Connecticut lawyers and judges relied more heavily on imported law books — and in those, as Barbara Lindemann has pointed out, "the rules of evidence [laid out for rape cases] were weighted for the defendant." In the anglicized legal environment of the early eighteenth century, general attitudes in New England shifted from a tendency to believe a woman's accusation to an inclination to doubt, at least initially, her word. "A Woman's positive Oath of a Rape, without concurring Circumstances," Giles Jacob, the great popularizer of law, wrote, "is seldom credited." Sir Matthew Hale and Sir William Blackstone, two of the most widely cited jurists of the century, named several "concurring circumstances" which would give "greater probability" to the woman's testimony: if she be "of good fame"; "if she presently discovered the offence, and . . . if the party accused fled for it"; if the place were remote, and if the victim when examined by a group of female "inspectors" showed "signs of the in-jury."[19]

18. Lindemann, " 'To Ravish and Carnally Know,' " *Signs*, X (1984–1985), 64; J. M. Beattie, *Crime and the Courts in England, 1660–1800* (Princeton, N.J., 1986), 129–130.

19. Lindemann, " 'To Ravish and Carnally Know,' " *Signs*, X (1984–1985), 68; Jacob, *A New Law-Dictionary*, s.v. "rape"; William Blackstone, *Commentaries on the Laws of England* (1765–1769; rpt., Chicago, 1979), IV, 213; and Hale, *Pleas of the Crown*, I, 633. By the 18th century, the English jurists noted that "no time of limitation" for bringing a rape complaint was fixed; it was up to the jury to assess reasonable promptness according to the circumstances of each case. Many treatise writers noted that the laws of Scotland and Aragon required reporting the assault within 24 hours, but an English statute passed in the reign of Edward I established a 40-day limit.

Behind the enumeration of such tests was a palpable anxiety on the part of male authorities over the possibility that women would falsely accuse men of violent sexual assault. The most resonant statement of this concern came from Hale: "It must be remembred, that [rape] is an accusation easily to be made and hard to be proved, and harder to be defended by the party accused, tho never so innocent." Noting instances of recantations and "malicious" copycat accusations, treatise writers warned jurors that they should form a strong presumption against a woman if: she "be of evil fame"; the complaint were "stale," not timely; "she is wrong in the Description of the Place"; or the location of the alleged attack "were near to inhabitants, or common recourse. . . . when and where it is probable she might be heard by others" if she cried out.[20]

When considering what constituted the act of rape, Connecticut jurists faced an array of contradictory directions from English legal authorities. Some experts, following William Hawkins, insisted that "there must be Penetration *and* Emission to make this Crime." Hale, in contrast, argued that "the least penetration maketh it rape . . . , yea altho there be not *emissio seminis*." Zephaniah Swift, summarizing Connecticut's criminal law in 1796, favored Hale's criteria: "To constitute this crime," Swift wrote, "there must be an actual penetration."[21] The vexed issue of how to gauge the extent of penetration and emission on the basis of a woman's testimony provided trial jurors with yet another rationale for acquittal.

The greatest damper on the apprehension and conviction of accused rapists was undoubtedly the death sentence. The capital nature of the crime contributed to women's hesitation to bring charges forward. Martha Olmstead, telling the story of being raped by a married man many

---

Zephaniah Swift does not mention any particular Connecticut custom or expectation governing prompt complaints (*A System of the Laws of the State of Connecticut* [New York, 1972 (orig. publ. Windham, Conn., 1795–1796)], II, 308–309). On the extensive use of character witnesses in 18th-century criminal trials, see John H. Langbein, "The Criminal Trial before the Lawyers," *University of Chicago Law Review*, XLV (1978), 305.

20. Hale, *Pleas of the Crown*, I, 633, 635; Blackstone, *Commentaries*, IV, 213–215; Jacob, *New Law-Dictionary*, s.v. "rape."

21. Hawkins, *Treatise of Pleas of the Crown*, I, 108 (my emphasis), and Giles Jacob citing Hawkins, in *New Law-Dictionary*, s.v. "rape," and in *Every Man His Own Lawyer . . .*, 7th ed. (New York, 1768), 280; Hale, *Pleas of the Crown*, I, 628; Swift, *System of Laws*, II, 308. For a summary of the conflicting theories and their application in 18th-century English cases, see Edward Hyde East, *A Treatise of the Pleas of the Crown* (Philadelphia, 1806), I, 437–440.

months after the incident, explained that she had never spoken of it to anybody: "I was afrayd Least it would take away his Life." Rape's definition as capital also affected jury behavior, especially as outright rape cases accumulated after 1700. Jury reluctance to convict when a verdict meant hanging was part of a broad trend manifested in felony trials in England in the eighteenth century. There criminal justice officials routinely indicted serious offenders for lesser offenses in order to obtain noncapital convictions.[22]

In Connecticut during the seventy years when Superior Court grand juries mysteriously did not indict on attempted rape charges, jurors, judges, legislators, victims' families, and communities touched by rape all wrestled with the problem of proof in sexual assault cases and became increasingly unwilling to hang convicted defendants. Two black men were executed in the 1740s, but in the hiatus until the next execution in 1790 the legislature agreed to commute the capital sentences of two white defendants. In the 1770s, the Superior Court suddenly began to entertain indictments for attempted rape, perhaps as a concession to the diminishing likelihood of obtaining convictions on full rape counts. By 1796 Zephaniah Swift was urging that rape, and indeed all crimes but murder and treason, be taken off the list of capital crimes and be made punishable by life imprisonment at hard labor.[23] Just as Connecticut residents had grown queasy at the thought of hanging young women for a crime they found despicable — infanticide — in the second half of the century, many elements of the society arrived at a consensus that rejected the taking of a man's life for serious sexual assault.

22. Examination of Martha Olmstead at a Court, July 10, 1686, in Divorce case of Thomas Olmstead (1686), Conn. Archives, Crimes and Misdemeanors, 1st Ser., III, 230. On juries, see Cynthia Herrup, *The Common Peace: Participation and the Criminal Law in Seventeenth-Century England* (New York, 1987); and John H. Langbein, "Shaping the Eighteenth-Century Criminal Trial: A View from the Ryder Sources," *University of Chicago Law Review*, L (1983), 36–55.

23. For the commutations, see the Mully trial (1760), discussed below, and the Assembly's resolve in the case of James Gibson (1783), *PRS*, VII, 124. Richard Gaskins wrongly states that rape was removed along with arson from Connecticut's capital crimes in 1792. See his "Changes in the Criminal Law in Eighteenth-Century Connecticut," *American Journal of Legal History*, XXV (1981), 334, 337. An October 1792 statute made arson, perjury, and *attempted* rape "Newgate" crimes, thus punishable by imprisonment at hard labor (*PRS*, V, 494–495). See also Swift's comments in his *System of Laws*, II, 291–297, 308–311. For parallel trends in Massachusetts, see Lindemann, " 'To Ravish and Carnally Know,' " *Signs*, X (1984–1985), 75.

From 1700 on, the men charged with rape were predominantly outsiders: the twenty included six black slaves, one transient free black, one Indian, and, among the white defendants, one Frenchman captured during the Seven Years' War who was imprisoned in Connecticut, two transient soldiers, a British deserter, and one other man identified as a vagrant (see Table 13). Only seven of the alleged attackers were white men with established residences in Connecticut towns.[24] The eighteenth-century conviction rate for rape defendants was 30 percent: one black slave confessed and was sentenced to hang, and juries convicted two slaves, the transient black man, the British deserter, and the Frenchman. Since the legislature reprieved one of the slaves and commuted the sentences of the two white men, the final result was that three black men were hanged for rape in Connecticut between 1700 and 1791. The remaining defendants were either acquitted by trial juries or dismissed through such pretrial factors as lack of witnesses or an indictment returned "ignoramus."

The eighteen women who claimed to have been raped included four children under the age of eleven, eight "maids" or "spinsters" ranging from thirteen to thirty, and six married women. Two of the wives, one of the adolescents, and one nine-year-old girl made their complaints directly and in person to local officials. In the remaining cases, either the young woman's father or master registered the complaint, or the local grand jurors initiated the inquiry. Most of the complaints were made promptly — either within hours of the alleged incident or a few days thereafter.[25] Whether the alleged attacker was known to the complainant was made clear in only three of the fourteen cases. For example, young Diana Parish knew Cuff, the black slave of a local shoemaker, and Elizabeth Bissell, a single woman, had previously lived in the same household as her alleged attacker, John Green. On the other hand, Mrs. Hannah Andrews, a traveler between Haddam and Middletown, reported

24. In the 1761 case arising from an alleged gang-rape incident, one widow was charged initially with abetting the assault (a crime which carried the death penalty). The prosecution against her was dropped after the two male defendants were acquitted by trial juries. Thus, officially there were 21 defendants in Connecticut rape cases, 1700–1790: 20 men and 1 woman.

25. Eight complaints fall into the category of "prompt": they were made within 5 days of the alleged assault. Five of the eight were made on the day of or the day after the incident. In the three additional cases with surviving dates for both the alleged incident and the initial complaint, we find gaps of 10 days, one month, and three months.

being dragged into the woods and violently attacked by a negro man whom she did not know but whom she identified the next day. Four of the attacks reportedly took place inside — two in the woman's own dwelling house — and five allegedly occurred out-of-doors, usually while the woman was walking or riding alone in the woods or in a secluded spot.

Although the status of the female complainant did not sway juries to acquit or convict in rigid patterns, a few notable tendencies emerge when we compare outcomes in cases involving girls aged ten and under, "maids" or single women, and married women (see Table 14). By a slight margin, the highest conviction rate was obtained when the female complainant was married. Although in some situations a single woman claiming rape did see her assailant convicted, when she charged a white man, particularly an acquaintance or a settled Connecticut resident, juries refused to credit her story. Significantly, six of the seven acquittals in Connecticut rape trials between 1700 and 1790 occurred in cases involving single women. This pattern echoes Barbara Lindemann's finding for Massachusetts of a strikingly lower conviction rate of assailants of single women than for attackers of children or married women.[26]

In some periods and jurisdictions, assuming a pose of passivity and demureness has been shown to have aided a woman's credibility when advancing a rape charge. Examining sexual assault trials in the urban setting of early national New York City, Marybeth Hamilton Arnold concludes that only women who had the visible backing of male kin and who "stressed their helplessness and dependence on men" won convictions. However, in the more rural neighborhoods of eighteenth-century Connecticut, although the support of family members was surely important, women who brought their own complaints to local officials were not treated with undue skepticism.[27] What made women's rape claims believable in the climate of eighteenth-century Connecticut was not so much the complainant's demeanor as her demand for retribution against the illegitimate advances of outsiders.

26. Lindemann, " 'To Ravish and Carnally Know,' " *Signs*, X (1984–1985), 80–81.

27. Marybeth Hamilton Arnold, " 'The Life of a Citizen in the Hands of a Woman': Sexual Assault in New York City, 1790 to 1820," in Kathy Peiss and Christina Simmons, eds., *Passion and Power: Sexuality in History* (Philadelphia, 1989), 48; Beattie, *Crime and the Courts*, 130. Convictions ensued when women brought their own complaint in Rex v. Bristo (Sept. 1756), New London County Superior Court Files, box 13, and State v. James Gibson (March 1783), Hartford County Superior Court Files, dr. 13, CSL.

TABLE 14

Outcome of Rape Cases by Status of Woman Assaulted, 1700–1790

	Age 10 or under	Married	Single (13 or Older)	Total
Remanded to county court	1	0	0	1
Discharged on proclamation	2	0	0	2
Ignoramus	0	3	1	4
Jury: guilty verdict	1	2	3	6
Jury: acquitted	0	1	6	7
Total	4	6	10[a]	20

[a]Ten male defendants allegedly assaulted eight individual women. In each of two incidents, two men were prosecuted for gang-raping a woman.

Source: Court of Assistants Records, 1700–1710; Superior Court Record Books and Files, 1711–1790, CSL.

Whereas we might expect that early New Englanders would find child molestation the most detestable of sexual assaults and one worthy of death, Connecticut authorities manifested a good deal of hesitation over how to secure adequate proof in such cases. The typical evidentiary problems of rape cases were compounded by the issue of the reliability of a child's testimony (and her ability to comprehend the meaning of an oath), by disputes among physicians over the nature of injuries sustained by sexually molested children, and by the victim's tentativeness and confusion in reporting the incident. Two early-eighteenth-century Connecticut cases involving the alleged rape of young girls were dropped in the Superior Court when no witnesses appeared to testify against the accused men, an Indian and a black slave.[28] A third pre-1750 child-rape

28. Rex v. James Indian (1729), SCR, VII (unpaginated): New Haven, June session; Rex v. Sampson (Feb. 1743/4, Fairfield), SCR, XI, 242. In the former case the defendant was originally presented by town grand jurors for "lascivious carriages" to a nine-year-old. Two examining justices, however, believed that the summoned witnesses "charged the prisoner with such facts that in the Judgment of the Law makes it Rape" and bound him over for trial at the Superior Court.

For a fascinating illustration of the reluctance of juries to convict in child-rape cases, see the long excerpts and discussion of Stephen Arrowsmith's case (1678) in

case was remanded to the county court, where the defendant, a black slave, was presented for "Lascivious Carriages toward" a six-year-old "with most gross and aggravating Circumstances."[29] Two sets of circumstances were probably most influential in determining why these cases were not pursued: first, the difficulty of proving penetration and, second, the tendency of parents to negotiate out-of-court settlements recovering damages or guaranteeing the assailant's removal from the area. In the one prosecution that proceeded to trial in Superior Court, ten-year-old Amy Beecher's parents had the satisfaction of witnessing the jury bring in a guilty verdict, yet they soon persuaded the legislature to commute the convicted man's sentence from hanging to whipping and banishment.[30]

Finally, in the 1770s, Connecticut judges and prosecutors resolved on a successful formula for handling cases involving the sexual abuse of children. In 1774 and 1779 indictments were brought for the *attempted* rape of children (a two-year-old and a four-year-old). Lemon, a black slave, confessed to his crime of "breaking open the body" of an Indian girl until "the Blood run out." Henry Bokes, a transient person, was convicted for "Endeavour[ing] to penetrate the private Member of his Body into the Body" of an infant. Lemon and Bokes received the same sentence: standing in the gallows, carting, and a series of whippings at four corners of the marketplace for a total of thirty-nine stripes.[31] Juries,

---

Langbein, "Criminal Trial before Lawyers," *University of Chicago Law Review*, XLV (1978), 291–295.

29. Rex v. Sam, "a Negro Man" (1737), SCR, X, 39, and Fairfield County Court Files, box 180, folder 17. Nathaniel Knapp testified that, "being skilled in surgery," Jane's mother and grandmother asked him to examine the child. He reported that she "was swollen in the Privities and her Smock was bloody" and that he believed it was "true that said Negro had penetrated the Child's Body and acted his will as far as he could."

30. Rex v. Vanskelly Mully, SCR, XVII, 44; Fairfield County Superior Court Files, box 621, CSL; and Conn. Archives, Crimes and Misdemeanors, 1st Ser., V, 144–146. This case is analyzed below.

31. The language of these indictments indicated the prosecutors' attempts to define a noncapital crime while recognizing its reprehensible nature. Both indictments emphasized that the injury to the child had endangered her life. Lemon's bill declared his act "in Violation of the Laws of Reason and Humanity," and Bokes's indictment labeled his crime "a Wicked high-handed and great Misdemeanour." Rex v. Lemon (May 1774, New Haven), SCR, XXI, 204; Rex v. Henry Bokes (Sept. 1779, Windham), XXII, 163–164. Thirty-nine stripes was the highest number or-

freed from the responsibility of relying on a child's word to hang a man, now might have believed child-molesters could receive their just deserts.

The first sign that eighteenth-century rape cases would generate protracted community debate and negotiation came with the 1706 complaint lodged by Thomas Beach on behalf of his twenty-four-year-old wife Sarah against a married New Haven man, Joseph Mallery. Within two days of the alleged assault, Sarah had sought counsel from Assistant John Alling, whereupon she reported to her friends that "she did not Care as Long as Mr. Pierpont [New Haven's minister] and Mr. Alling stood by hur." Sarah's confidence that the religious and secular leaders of her community would support her story reflected women's experience in the seventeenth century. But vindication of her story by way of a conviction was not to happen for Sarah Beach, even though by the rigorous rules of evidence the case for the prosecution initially looked strong. Sarah was able to give a coherent, sworn account of the afternoon on which Mallery pinned her by a fence for three hours, pulled up her clothes, "importund [her] hard," and finally raped her. Moreover, her mother and other female relatives could testify convincingly to Sarah's soreness, fainting, and general incapacity since the incident. In addition, another New Haven woman came forward to describe Mallery's unseemly intrusion into her bedroom one night two years before. Yet within a week of the original complaint, Sarah's male kin reappeared before the local magistrates with news that rendered the case highly problematic. Sarah, they testified, had been "out in [her] head" since losing a baby a few months before. They had gone along with her rape story out of fear that to countermand it would have "put her quite out."[32]

Perhaps out of a concern for preserving Sarah's sense of dignity, her relatives allowed the rape complaint to go before the grand jury in October; by then they referred to the incident as "this sad [and lamentable] accident." Not surprisingly, the jurors returned the bill ignoramus. Be-

---

dered in the 18th-century Connecticut courts for serious criminal offenders; 15 to 20 stripes constituted the average range in Superior Court sentences.

32. Deposition of Daniel Collins (undated), Conn. Archives, Crimes and Misdemeanors, 1st Ser., I, 425; Accusation of Sarah Beach (undated), I, 405; Deposition of Elizabeth Sanford, I, 429; Joint deposition of Elizabeth Sanford and Sarah Beech (Oct. 1706), I, 436; Depositions of Eleazer Beecher and Colin Miles, I, 426–427; Testimony of Elizabeth Hoadly (Sept. 1706), NHCC, II, 236.

sides sharing a consensus that Sarah had been "distracted" "for a considerable time," several eyewitnesses believed that Sarah had tarried willingly, flirting with Mallery and consenting to an indecent "Bout."[33] Whatever the truth, the dilemma of the Beach family as it was acted out in public established a troubling precedent for future rape complaints. If family members might reassess the nature of what had happened when a woman cried rape, then why should jurors being asked to cast votes for the death penalty trust in the stability of a woman's word?

The community's potential role in negotiating the appropriateness of a man's punishment for sexual assault emerged most clearly in the 1760 case against Vanskelly Mully. As the first white man convicted of rape since 1693, Mully presented Connecticut residents with a test of their willingness to hang an outsider, a Frenchman but not an African, for rape. Mully, a French soldier captured at Niagara and brought into Connecticut for imprisonment, had boarded in a series of Fairfield County households. On the morning of August 25, he had drunk "half a pint of Rum" and had "no bretforst [breakfast]" before going out "to keep the birth day of one of his fellow prisoner[s]." Evidently, on his way, at about six in the morning, he spotted ten-year-old Amy Beecher and abused her sexually. On that same day, Amy's father reported the assault, and Mully was apprehended, examined, and jailed to await trial for rape. Ten witnesses traveled to the Superior Court session in Fairfield just a few days later (none of their testimony was recorded). Mully pleaded not guilty, but the trial jury convicted him of rape, and the bench sentenced him to hang on November 4.[34]

One month before his scheduled execution, Mully petitioned the General Assembly to commute his sentence to any punishment — "be it ever so great" — but death. The legislature dispatched a man to Fairfield County to "Get Information Conserning the poor prisoner," and on October 14 it received a report yielding many details of the community's

33. Letter to October 1706 Court of Assistants from Thomas Beach and Thomas Sanford, Sr., Conn. Archives, Crimes and Misdemeanors, 1st Ser., I, 433; Deposition of Dr. John Hill (undated), I, 422; Deposition of John Cooper (June 24, 1766), I, 406. According to Dr. Hill, Sarah's husband, father, and brother moved to declare her distracted out of fear that she was about to be jailed; although it seems farfetched, perhaps Thomas Beach was afraid she would be accused of perjury (a felony) or, more likely, lascivious carriage.

34. The documentation for this case is found at Rex v. Vanskelly Mully, SCR, XVII, 44; Fairfield County Superior Court Files, box 621; and Conn. Archives, Crimes and Misdemeanors, 1st Ser., V, 144–146.

reaction to the case since the August 25 incident. First, several townspeople expressed skepticism with respect to the complaint made by Amy and her family. One man declared that the girl had "Reported such things of others, and he did not Regard her [word]." Others observed her behavior in the days following the complaint and could see "nothing amis in her." She seemed "as Nimble as Ever," and neighbors found it surprising that her parents would allow her to ride horseback and go out in the rain if she were as "hurt as they pretended." Second, a community consensus had been reached that the assault did not involve penetration. The men who had examined Mully after the incident now reported that they "did not think . . . he Ever Entered her body but Supposed that he fumbled ther abouts till he sattisfied him Self." The child's parents agreed with this reassessment, admitting that the child had not been as badly treated as they had at first believed.[35] Finally, Amy's father came forward voluntarily and "manifested a Great Consern for the frenchman and said . . . that he and his wife should be Very Glad if there might be a way found out that his Life might be spared and he have proper puneshment acording to the merit of the offense and not to Come into these parts no more on . . . acount of his daughter for She is so terrefied at the name of him that she trembels at it."

Persuaded by the new physical evidence, by the reluctance of the general community and the victim's family to see Mully hang, and by Mully's postconviction repentant acknowledgment of his "glaringly Sinful" deed, the Assembly voted to commute the death sentence.[36] It ordered that Mully instead be set at the gallows with a halter about his neck for an hour, receive thirty-nine stripes and have one ear cut off, and

---

35. Mully's inspectors based their opinion on "what appeared on his Shirt." Amy's father explained that in retrospect he did not think the child was entered but that Mully "was bisse [busy] there abouts till he sattisfied himself for the child told him that he said to her now you may go but he bruesed her and mead her blead sum." The father added that he now wished he had had "sum Independent persons" search the child "at first, and not his own relations."

36. It is possible that the delegates commuted Mully's sentence partly out of a hope that the path to rehabilitation and conversion lay open to him. Mully claimed in his petition that he had been brought up "wholly deprived of the Bible" and "forbid[den] the Priviledge of Reading or Writing." He further asserted that he had been "Ignorant of the Law of God and Man" respecting rape and its penalty and so had been acting with "no Check or Restraint on his Mind." Fully acknowledging his wicked act, he asked "the Pardon of the said Girl and all Concerned for her: humbly and Earnestly Intended."

finally be banished from the colony. This was a harsh sentence, tailored to reflect the horridness of Mully's abuse of an innocent girl. However, the dialogue between the legislators and the Connecticut community touched by the incident reveals the collective sympathy extended to a doomed white man by the 1760s. Connecticut citizens spoke explicitly of Mully as "the poor prisoner" and of his capital sentence as "the sad consequence" of the rape charge. By extending sympathy to the convicted man as well as to his victim, legislators signaled with this their first commutation decree in a rape case that blacks and whites would be treated differently. In 1749 the Assembly had turned down the petition of Cuff, a slave sentenced to die for rape. The only other commutation they would agree to during the century was in James Gibson's 1783 case, and Gibson was the only white man besides Mully to receive the statutory death sentence.[37]

In the Mallery and Mully cases, what metamorphosed between arrest and final outcome was not so much the word of the central female player as the interpretation of what she had suffered by those situated closest to her. In effect, the voices of Sarah Beach and Amy Beecher were repressed, drowned out by the reconstructions supplied by relatives and neighbors whose consciences were pricked at the thought of hanging a man because a child or a mentally troubled woman might have been abused. In the dramatic scenario played out in 1756 between Hannah Beebe and Bristo, the slave of a New London County minister, the crisis that could arise over the instability of a woman's word took the starkest form possible — that of a recantation. Only after Bristo's trial and conviction did Hannah as the complainant admit that she had fabricated the rape story and conspired to manipulate the proceeding out of self-interest. Here then is a rare case in which we can glimpse, while listening to the testimony unfold, how some eighteenth-century women and men constructed the black man as rapist.

In mid-May 1756, Hannah Beebe of Lyme, a "Maid and Single Woman" of unspecified age, complained that the black slave Bristo had sexually assaulted her four days earlier "in a bye and Secret place." When Bristo first surprised her, Hannah recounted that she had asked him "Who he Was and from Whence he Came." The "Negro Replied that he was the Devill and Came Right from Hell."[38] Hannah demanded

37. The 1790 and 1798 petitions for commutation from two free blacks, Joseph Mountain and Anthony, were also turned down.

38. Bristo was a longtime slave of Lyme's Congregational minister, George Beckwith, and it is difficult to believe that any Lyme resident would not have known him.

to know "what he Wanted of her," and he said he "Wanted to Lie With [her]" and that "Nobody would know it." To that, Hannah virtuously countermanded: "God would know it," upon which Bristo burst out with, "Dam God, their is no other God but a Wooden God." He then, according to Hannah, threw her down on the ground, "discovered his private parts to her," pulled out a knife, and threatened to kill her immediately "if she Did not forbare hallowing [hollering]" and striving. When she refused to be quiet, Bristo "Stopt her Mouth" with a handkerchief, "Blinded her Eyes," and then "Rumaged her private parts upon which Supprise" she "fell into fits." It was later "when she Recovered her Reason" that she deduced "by the Effects Which she felt on her body . . . that he did actually Commit a Rap[e] on her body."[39]

When Hannah's complaint was first heard before local justices, the presiding magistrate decided to prepare an indictment against Bristo (who denied the assault) "for Lascivious Carriage only," as Hannah "was not Clear to sware a rape upon him." But suddenly Hannah changed her testimony and said she could charge Bristo with rape. At the same time, Wait Wright, a mulatto man seen with Bristo on the day of the alleged incident, departed from his previous insistence that Bristo had "never touched" Hannah or even been with her that day. Now in court Wait swore not only that he saw Bristo with Hannah in the place she mentioned, but also "in the very act of which she . . . complained." On the basis of the new evidence offered by Hannah and Wait, an indictment for rape was drawn up. At the September Superior Court session in New London, a trial jury convicted Bristo of rape, and the bench sentenced him to hang.[40]

Within two months of Bristo's trial, Hannah Beebe came before a local justice and "solemnly declared" that her complaint against the slave "Was altogether false and Groundless." The governor then ordered that the execution of Bristo's sentence be suspended until the General Assembly was able to consider the situation. In January 1757 the legislators received a plethora of depositions from Lyme residents. These documents revealed that at least some members of Hannah's community had suspected her story from the beginning. Some believed the story false, because soon after the complaint was made they heard Hannah and her father predict that they could get money from either

39. Rex v. Bristo (Sept. 1756), New London Superior Court Files, box 13.

40. This discussion is based on the papers of the General Assembly found in Conn. Archives, Crimes and Misdemeanors, 1st Ser., V, 47–53.

Bristo's master (by "saving" him) or from "the Court" for the damage done to Hannah's "carrecter" by the alleged assault. Others testified that a certain Thomas Tozzer of East Haddam had interfered at the first hearing of the evidence and persuaded both Hannah and Wait Wright to alter their testimonies. Indeed, several persons had heard Tozzer boast after the hearing that "they would not So much as have whipt him if it had Not bin for me."[41] Hannah herself admitted to one neighbor that "she shold not have Given in such" evidence against Bristo "if she had Not bin Perswaded to it by Thomas Tozer for She knew he was not Gilty of what she had Charged him with."

Tozzer's motivations are unclear. The two most probable explanations are either that he wished to see Bristo severely punished for some indecent behavior short of rape which he had offered to Hannah, or that Tozzer was Hannah's lover (or forcible seducer?), feared she was pregnant, and attempted to frame Bristo. Hannah's recantation also obscures whether any incident at all had occurred between her and the slave. Hannah's parents reported that she had "seemed More easy in her mind" since her "Recantation," and her mother declared that her own evidence given in at the Superior Court trial had been "Mistaken" and she "now Believed those Effects Which she testified about on her Daughters Body did not proceed from said Negroes Being with" Hannah. This rethinking suggests that at the time of charging Bristo, Hannah had been either sexually active or abused by someone or, alternatively, that she had deliberately faked the symptoms. Whatever the young woman's actual situation, the General Assembly was careful to ascertain first that Hannah "was in the free exercise of her reason and understanding" when she "openly and freely Declared . . . Bristo to have been Innocent." The legislators then voted that Bristo be reprieved from the sentence of death and dismissed from jail.

The chameleonlike quality of rape stories such as those aired in the Mallery, Mully, and Bristo cases surely haunted the scenes of other eighteenth-century Connecticut rape proceedings about which the documents are less forthcoming. Fragmentary evidence indicates that, in at

---

41. About the Tozzers several men testified in a later court case that they had "often heard people Say" that "Men were afraid to go into the law with" them "because they thought [they] could get Evidence to help[?] [their] Turn in allmost Every Case" (Joint deposition of David Wells et al. [Mar. 3, 1759], loose document inserted at back of SCR, XVIII).

least two instances, indigent rape defendants had attorneys appointed to defend them.[42] Presumably native Connecticut defendants had more lead time to hire defense counsel who could exploit any inconsistencies or vague elements in the complainant's account and, moreover, search out as witnesses neighbors who were skeptical about the woman's innocent conduct and motivation.

Whether Joseph Dudley, a married Guilford man accused in 1767 of raping young Esther Hand, "his Neighbours Wife," had an attorney is not clear. But as a Connecticut newspaper explained, he was able to cast doubt on his accusers' word: "In the Course of the Examination of the Witnesses," the printer coyly revealed, "*some Things* were made Publick, not much to the *Ravish'd Woman's* Credit, or her Husband's Honor." Esther swore that Dudley had sprung upon her by a fence "where she Stood picking Burys [berries]," but investigators found that the spot was just 35 rods (about 575 feet) from "the house and the shop," with "no obstacles of Bushes between." Not only should Esther's cries have been heard, but four grand jurors later testified that they heard evidence that Dudley was probably never "at the place or near there at the time." Thus the grand jury returned the bill ignoramus, concluding that the "prosecution . . . was set on foot, through a clear mistake or a worse Cause." Afterwards Dudley believed that he caught Esther's husband admitting to neighbors that he was "Glad" to bring the charge "to Ruin [Dudley's] Interest" and wreak hardship on him through a high bill of costs.[43]

Doubts similar to those raised inside and outside the courtroom in Joseph Dudley's case must have been behind the seven trial acquittals and four ignoramus bills that marked the eighteenth-century Connecti-

---

42. The Superior Court "assigned" Thomas Fitch and Samuel Darling "to be of Council for" the slave Cuff at his 1749 trial, but not "till he was called to plead." Looking back, the lawyers wished they had had more time to prepare and to raise objections to the indictment (Petition of Fitch and Darling to the May 1749 Assembly, Conn. Archives, Crimes and Misdemeanors, 1st Ser., IV, 118). Similarly, the transient Briton James Gibson complained in 1783 that neither "he nor his Councel ever had fifteen minutes to enquire or prepare his Defence before his Tryal" (Petition to the May 1783 Assembly, VI, 220).

43. *Conn. Journal*, Oct. 30, 1767; Testimony of Thomas Willcox (dated Oct. 27, 1767), in the file papers for Rex v. Joseph Dudley of Guilford (Oct. 1767), SCR XIX, in the miscellaneous leaves at the back of the volume; Testimony of James Sherman et al. (May 26, 1768), Testimony of Nathaniel Allis and Hannah Allis, Jr. (May 23, 1768), Conn. Archives, Crimes and Misdemeanors, 2d Ser., IV, 112–113.

cut rape caseload (Table 14).[44] In the case of Pompey, the only black man acquitted, the evidence apparently consisted of a fourteen-year-old girl's word that she had been attacked at night while in bed and had "cried out for Healp But no help Came" and the testimony of the married couple who saw her "after She was abused by the Negro."[45] The file papers offer no clues why the jury in this case found the testimonies unconvincing. Similarly, in the two instances of alleged gang rape, the surviving legal documents fail to illuminate the evidentiary problems that might have contributed to the defendants' acquittals.[46] In all ignoramus and acquittal cases the defendant was ordered to pay the costs of his prosecution. The bill, which typically included his upkeep in the county jail for several months between arrest and grand jury inquiry, often proved to be a daunting burden. The slave Pompey's costs amounting to sixty pounds old tenor were paid by his master, but four white defendants were forced to offer their full-time services to a bidder for terms of up to two and a half years to pay off their debts to the legal system.[47] Thus while in the majority of eighteenth-century rape cases the woman's word was not vindicated by the legal outcome, men who might have committed sexually violent acts did not get off scot-free: their lives and fortunes were often seriously disrupted by the capital charge.[48]

44. Three cases ending in acquittal or an ignoramus bill are discussed at length in this chapter: Mallery (1693), Green (1736), and Dudley (1767). For the remaining eight cases, few depositions survive.

45. Rex v. Pompey (Mar. 1744/5, Hartford), SCR, XI, 357, and Hartford County Superior Court Files, box 87. At least one other witness (a woman) was summoned: her testimony is not in the files.

46. The complainants' accounts also do not survive. In the second gang-rape case, three men and a female accomplice — a widow — were named in the original complaint filed by the Windham County king's attorney. However, only two of the men and the woman were held without bail for trial. True indictments were found against all three, but, after juries separately acquitted the two men, the case against the widow was dropped. Rex v. John Carpenter, Jr., John Fox, John Chandler, and Mary Chubb (Sept. 1761), SCR, XVII, 144–145, and Windham County Superior Court Files, box 176, CSL.

47. The four were John Green, Solomon Read, William McKee, and Richard Oliver (see Table 13). John T. Farrell notes that any appearance before the Superior Court "on criminal charges was likely to be ruinously expensive" (Farrell, ed., *The Superior Court Diary of William Samuel Johnson, 1772–1773* . . . [Washington, D.C., 1942], xlv n. 2).

48. Of course, disruption, defeating costs, and public infamy were the lot of most felony defendants; for one example, see the discussion of Lucretia Smith's imprisonment on infanticide charges in Chapter 4, above.

The impossibility of persuading a jury to deliver a guilty verdict against an established white resident in the post-Puritan era dramatizes the difficult situation of young, unmarried women who found themselves coerced by a suitor or assaulted by an acquaintance. The discomfort over relying solely on a woman's accusation to stigmatize men as criminals shaped not only fornication prosecutions in the first half of the eighteenth century but also how incidents of alleged rape and attempted rape were handled. From 1700 to 1770, as we have seen, Connecticut officials declined to hear attempted rape cases in the higher court; rather, sexual violence short of rape was intermittently prosecuted at the county court level under the rubrics of assault and lascivious carriage. When Lydia Clinton complained in 1727 that Moses Tuttle had "pulled her off her saddle" and into the bushes and "endeavored to force her," Tuttle was brought before the New Haven County Court. He confessed and was thereupon sentenced to pay a three-pound fine or receive twenty stripes. When Captain John Logan, a mariner, was witnessed in 1717 "discovering his nakedness" in public and "making some attempts" at a maid, he was bound over for trial at the county court, not the Superior Court. When the king's attorney for Windham County informed against Isaac Willow in 1743 for throwing Margaret Searle, a newly married woman, "Down on the hearth," "forcably" pulling down her clothes, putting "his hand to the most privit part of hir Body," pulling "out the most privit part of his Body," and "Endeavour[ing] to tempt [her] . . . to Adultry," the charge was assault "in a Lascivious Manner," and the venue was the Windham County Court.[49] The colony's policy of assigning such cases to courts of lower jurisdiction and meting out fines as penalties set a patently different tone from the consistency and severity with which male assailants were punished before 1700. In eighteenth-century Connecticut, women had reason to believe that their experiences with sexual harassment and violence would not be treated seriously. Indeed, few such complaints surfaced in the county courts.

That acquaintance rape was often not treated as rape in eighteenth-

---

49. On Tuttle: Rex v. Moses Tuttle (Nov. 1727), NHCC, III, 252, and NHCC Files, drawer 6; Rex v. James Logan (Feb. 1716/7), dr. 3. See also Rex v. Mary Goodritch (Sept. 1700), NHCC, II, 37, and Jacobus, *FANH*, 663. On Willow: Rex v. Isaac Willow (Feb. 1742/3), Windham County Court Files, box 383; Windham County Court Records, V, pt. 2, 255; Barbour Collection of Vital Records, volume for Coventry, CSL. The jury found Willow guilty, and the bench sentenced him to receive 20 lashes. Unable to pay costs of his trial, Willow was assigned as a laborer to a local man for the term of one year.

century New England is illustrated most compellingly in the case of Elizabeth Painter. In September 1728, Painter, a twenty-two-year-old single woman who had lately given birth, came before the New Haven magistrates on the charge of committing fornication with her unmarried cousin, George Clinton. For the first time publicly and under oath, she told the story of being attacked by Clinton on the night "after the thanksgiving the last year" on the road. Clinton, forcing "her hands behind her" and crowding her up against a fence, had proceeded to rape her, even though she had "told him she had Rather he should Dash her braines out and Stamp her into the ground." Later, in the privacy of her parents' house, Elizabeth had accused George to his face of forcing her, and he had responded, "I don't deny it." Neither Elizabeth nor her family, however, entered a complaint against Clinton for sexual assault. When the fornication case reached the county court, the bench accepted Elizabeth's plea of rape and excused her from any penalty. At the same time the magistrates did not see fit to proceed against George except on the criminal charge of fornication. Clinton professed his innocence even to the charge of consensual sex, but the trial jury found him guilty; he was fined and ordered to contribute to the maintenance of Elizabeth's child.

The New Haven authorities probably based their decision not to charge Clinton with rape on the Painters' neglect to file an assault complaint "forthwith." The official failure to pursue the Clinton case, however, flew in the face of further testimony given at the county court trial. Two New Haven women, one married and one Clinton's sister-in-law, came forward to assert that in the past two years George had attempted to rape or seduce each of them.[50] Thus, while some women in Clinton's

50. Rex v. George Clinton (Nov. 1728), NHCC, III, 270–271, and NHCC Files, dr. 6. Two men related to the Painter family through marriage testified that "soon after the matter [had] becom publick" (probably meaning after Elizabeth's pregnancy became visible), they heard her charge Clinton to his face with notorious abuses to her. Thus the story had circulated, at least within the extensive kinship network encompassing the Painters, well before the parties were examined by a magistrate.

Clinton's notorious treatment of women as a young man did not disqualify him from the marriage market: he married twice before middle age. In 1760 Hannah Bingley, the daughter of the married woman who testified in 1728 of Clinton's rape attempt on her, sued Clinton (then about 55 and possibly a widower) for paternity and maintenance of her child born out of wedlock. (This suit disappeared from the records without resolution; Hannah Bingley v. George Clinton [Jan. 1762], NHCC, V, 381.) Clinton died in 1776 in great indebtedness. In contrast, Elizabeth Painter

community apparently felt he was enough of a threat to them and to the general peace to warrant further public warning or prosecution, the male authorities felt he was not the sort of man who deserved to be exposed to a process that could lead to a capital sentence.

Elizabeth Painter was one of two women whose pleas of rape exempted them from punishment for fornication in the New Haven County court.[51] Presumably a scattering of similar rape cases subsumed under fornication prosecutions could be found in the court records of other counties. The failure of these young women to report sexual attacks "forthwith," combined with their willingness to claim rape as a defense when their own innocence and morality were publicly challenged, suggests that the early New England community acknowledged the existence of a certain amount of sexual violence in the relations of young white unmarried men and women. What is striking about such cases is that although a woman's account was accepted by the bench, her partner was punished *as if* their relationship had been consensual. The identification of sexual violence as legally rape became hardest when a white man with locally established roots coerced sex from a woman he knew. To judges, jurors, witnesses, and even the women involved, the line between illegitimate sexual violence and legitimate seduction at those moments was blurred.[52]

If Connecticut prosecutors were generally loath to put white men from established families up on rape charges, when such a case did manage to make its way to a grand jury and on to trial, male jurors hesitated to convict not only because a recantation was an ever-present possibility but also because they found it difficult to believe that an unmarried woman had truly withheld her consent and had not in some fashion invited the man's advance. The well-documented trial of John Green in 1736 provides a glimpse into how difficult it had become for women to cry rape against a neighbor or respectable male citizen.

---

lived to be 80 and remained unmarried, although she inherited considerable land and wealth from her parents. It is not clear in whose household Isaac, Elizabeth's child born in 1728, was brought up.

51. In the second case, again the bench accepted the woman's plea that she had been "forst by Strength of arms." Deborah Corbey was dismissed without paying a fine, but whoever had attacked her months before was not even identified, much less apprehended and charged (Rex v. Deborah Corbey [Nov. 1727], NHCC Files, dr. 6).

52. See the excellent discussions on this point in Laurel Thatcher Ulrich, *Good Wives: Image and Reality in the Lives of Women in Northern New England, 1650–1750* (New York, 1982), chap. 5; and Lindemann, " 'To Ravish and Carnally Know,' " *Signs,* X (1984–1985), 79–80, 82.

Green's accuser was a young single woman, Elizabeth Bissell. Elizabeth's story was that she had been walking from her married sister's house (where she lived) into town to attend "the Publick fast," when Green, an acquaintance, came by on horseback and offered her a ride. Progressing on a little to a small brook, Elizabeth suddenly "mistrusted" John and understood "By his actions and word that He Intended Carnaley to Ly With me." She slipped off the horse and tried to get away, but John followed, took hold of her, and "Told me that He would Git me With Child Before He Left me." Elizabeth recounted that she had resisted "with all my might and Cried for help" and then had sought to persuade John that her brother-in-law "was Coming . . . [any] minutt," but John "stoped my mouth with his Hand" and said "he was not ashamed." He flung her down and she "Was then So spent with Striving" that she could no longer resist, "But was forsed to Submit" so that he had "Carnall Copulation of my Bodey By actuall Penetration of the Same by force contrary to my Will." Afterward John threatened to "Do seven times Worse then He Had yet Don" if she spoke of the incident to anyone. The next day Elizabeth was so "Cripled" that she could scarcely walk, according to her sister and brother-in-law, whom she told merely of a "scuffle" with and "abuse" offered by John Green. But on the following day Elizabeth gave them "a full account" and accused John of raping her.[53]

While the local justice, on examining both John and Elizabeth, declared that there was "strong Suspicion" of John's guilt and committed him to jail without bail, the trial jury at the Superior Court was not willing to legitimate Elizabeth's story. Perhaps this acquittal of a white man was a classic case of jury nullification — where jurors privately agree that the crime was committed but give in a not guilty verdict to register their disapproval of the severe sentence that conviction entailed.[54] Or maybe the jurors truly doubted Elizabeth's story and believed John's version of the incident: that he had indeed given her a ride, stopped at the brook where "she had slipt down" and perhaps hurt herself, and then delivered her to the fast. Green might have also successfully cast

53. Documentation of the Green case is in Rex v. John Green of Windsor (Sept. 1736), SCR, X, 8, and Hartford County Superior Court Files, box 83.

54. For an excellent treatment of this phenomenon, see Thomas Andrew Green, *Verdict according to Conscience: Perspectives on the English Criminal Trial Jury, 1200–1800* (Chicago, 1985). The jurymen might have known that John Green was so impoverished he could not pay the £15 costs of prosecution and so would be assigned into service for about two years.

doubt on the young woman's character; he insinuated that Elizabeth had previously expressed a desire to be seduced by him and that she had spread rumors that they "had been to [too?] Great together." It is likely that in this culture, if a young woman had at any time conveyed a sexual interest in a man, a rape complaint, even if supported by circumstantial evidence, would not result in conviction.[55]

In the three Connecticut cases that culminated in executions we can virtually watch the eighteenth-century public differentiating between an unpersuasive story like Elizabeth Bissell's and stories that conjured up real rapists in the guise of men with black skin. The same white property-holding men who found women's charges against white men unconvincing were able to reach unanimous verdicts on the guilt of black men. In a social and political system that denied blacks and Indians any legitimate sexual access to white women, and in a culture suffused with pejorative images of the black man as heathen, carnal, irrational, crime-prone, and ineducable, jurors could accept the scenario of the black man's resort to violence and the woman's genuine lack of consent.[56]

The prospect of hanging Jack, the slave of a New York City man, convicted of raping Hannah Andrews in Connecticut in 1743, probably posed the least concern among colony residents who followed rape trials. The movement against capital punishment had not yet caught hold on the American side of the Atlantic; and, moreover, Jack was the sole eighteenth-century rape defendant to plead guilty when arraigned before the Superior Court bar. The story that emerged upon his arrest was indeed a "Tragical Scene," as the survivor's husband termed it.[57]

---

55. Note the warning words of Zephaniah Swift: "As the law gives a woman so much power, to subject a man to capital punishment, it ought particularly to be observed, whether the witness has not had a previous controversy with the person accused, so that it is probable that the charge is made from motives of malice and revenge: especially if the witness be a woman of bad fame: for the vindictive spirit of lewd women, has furnished frequent instances of such conduct" (*System of Laws*, II, 309).

56. Winthrop D. Jordan, *White over Black: American Attitudes toward the Negro, 1550–1812* (Chapel Hill, N.C., 1968), esp. 20–24, 32–40, 181–190, 199–205.

57. Hannah's husband petitioned the October 1743 session of the General Assembly to grant him relief for the heavy expenses he had incurred because of his wife's injuries. Andrews gives us a glimpse of the notoriety of rape cases by his statement that the "Tragical Scene" involving his wife "is so well known that the bare mention thereof is Sufficient to renew his Sorrows and move the Compassion of all that hear." Among the items Andrews listed in his expenses were £3 for damage

Alone among early Connecticut rape prosecutions, the case against Jack was littered with witnesses who agreed that "the Barbarous and Cruel Violence of an Inhumane Negro Slave" had "greatly Indanger[ed the victim's] life." According to her prompt complaint, Mrs. Hannah Andrews had been traveling home from a visit to friends and was lost in the woods when Jack, from whom she had asked directions earlier in the day, forced her off her horse and threatened to kill her. He then let her ride on again, but soon forced her down once more, and this time, according to Hannah, "Commanded me to prostrate mySelf Down to him but I refused and Beged for my life." At this point Jack raped her, telling Hannah she "would have a black Bastard." Afterward, Hannah got up to flee, but Jack caught her and beat her with a sapling and a stone until she lost consciousness. Several hours later she woke up and crawled to the road, where her uncle and a party of men found her. The race of the suspect and the brutality of his act, the word of a married woman, her "instant" complaint and identification of Jack the next day, and finally the "full and voluntary" confession of the suspect combined to make this, for the jurors and the general Connecticut community, a clear-cut case of a rape deserving capital punishment.[58]

Six years later, a second case arose against a slave that contained elements nearly as compelling as those in the Hannah Andrews assault narrative. Evidence in the 1749 case against Cuff, a man owned by an East Haven militia captain, was fully aired before the trial jury because

---

done to Hannah's clothes, £18 for "three weeks under the doctor before she came home," and £3 for "the loss of her time after she came home." The Assembly resolved that Andrews should have £30 in bills of old tenor (Conn. Archives, Crimes and Misdemeanors, 1st Ser., IV, 71–73).

58. Rex v. Negro Man named Jack (Sept. 1743, Hartford), SCR, XI, 204, and Hartford County Superior Court Files, box 86. Hannah Andrews's written complaint made the only mention of ejaculation among the surviving documents for the 1700–1790 Connecticut rape cases involving mature women. Hannah reported, "[Jack] threw me down on the Rock and uncovered my Nakedness and I Cried out for help but he with force Did Enter my body with his private part and had as I sopose Emition of his Seed into my body."

There is no evidence that counsel was appointed for Jack at his trial (as was done in Cuff's case in 1749) or that any plea was entered for commuting his sentence. The *Pennsylvania Gazette* (Philadelphia) picked up the story, reporting the defendant's arrest in its July 7, 1743 issue; I am grateful to Sharon Block for bringing this to my attention.

Cuff, provided with a pair of attorneys by the Superior Court, pleaded not guilty.[59] Benjamin Pardee brought the complaint in early October, reporting that on that same day in New Haven the slave Cuff had assaulted and raped fourteen-year-old Diana Parish, an orphan who lived in Pardee's house and served as "an Apprentice Girl." On the following day, all the principal parties and witnesses assembled before four justices of the peace. The centerpiece of the occasion must have been Diana's sworn testimony. She deposed that on the previous day, a Sabbath, she had been walking home "from Meeting alone in a By-Road distant from any House." Cuff came silently up behind her and "violently" caught hold of her. Her recorded testimony continued:

> that she screamed as loud and as long as she could: that the said Cuff said to her you have told Stories about me: that she bid him be gone, but that he still forceably held her, and she Screaming and Striving till she was out of Breath, he threw her down and pulled up her Coats and unbuttoned his Breeches, threatned to kill her if she would not be Still: that he entered her Body with his Private Member; that the whole Time was three quarters of an Hour as near as she could guess, but she was so frighted that she could not tell: that when he had done he told her she might goe.

Jacob Bradley, fifteen years old, picked up the story from there: he testified that he had been riding "in the By-Road from Benjamin Pardee's to East Haven" on October 2, "the Sun being about half an Hour high," when he spotted Cuff and Diana.[60] In retrospect, he said he had been riding "so fast when . . . coming toward them that it was not likely he could hear Diana scream." What Jacob saw first was Cuff "git off from" Diana (who was on the ground) and sit or lean "against the Fence." After a moment, Diana "roll'd over and got up and ran across the Path, and catched up a Stone and said she would kill said Cuff, . . . [who] said to her don't tell any more lies about me; she replied that she would have him hanged." Jacob then took Diana up behind him on his

---

59. The documentation for the case against Cuff (unless otherwise noted) is found in NHSC Files, dr. 327. The record book entries for the New Haven September term at which Cuff was tried are missing.

60. The discrepancy between the time given by Jacob, about 6:30 in the morning, and Diana's reference to her returning "from Meeting" is nowhere explained in the court papers.

horse; he recalled later that "all the way Home" she "cried," "sighed and sobbed" and told him that Cuff "had almost killed her"; he reported also that she had "breathed Short and seemed as if she would faint away."

When Diana and Jacob reached "Home" — Benjamin Pardee's house — Jacob's mother, Mehitable Bradley, was present. Before the justices, she continued her son's narrative. To Mrs. Bradley, Diana had appeared "in a terrible Condition, as if She would fall into Fitts." All the girl could cry out was that Cuff, Captain Tuttle's Negro, "has killed me." Given some "Castor," Diana recovered "a little." At this point, Mrs. Bradley asked the girl "as plain as she could [what had happened] and that said Diana answered her as plain as she could," finally declaring "that said Cuff had forced her." Mrs. Bradley's immediate response was to send for widow Hannah Woodward. Together the matrons searched Diana's body, being "very Particular in their Examination," and concluded that "according to their best Judgment the Body of the said Diana had been entered by Some Man."

In the face of this testimony, Cuff "confessed himself guilty" and was committed to the county jail without bail. Besides Diana Parish and Mehitable and Jacob Bradley, seven additional New Haven residents, four women (including Benjamin Pardee's wife) and three men, were summoned to testify before the February Superior Court. Evidently the bench was anticipating that Cuff would plead not guilty when arraigned, thus necessitating a full rehearsal of the evidence against him.[61] But Cuff's strategic switch to a plea of not guilty was not adequate to save him: his counsel had but "very short time to prepare," and without unusual delay the jury returned a guilty verdict against him.

Three months after being sentenced to hang, Cuff, still in prison, inscribed his shaky mark on a petition addressed to the General Assembly, asking that "the Terrible Sentence of Death" be "Changed into whiping branding transportation or Castration any or all" "so that his miserable (tho to him precious) life" might be spared. Cuff's petition and an accompanying memorial from his attorneys clutched in vain at

---

61. No record survives of oral testimony given in court. One of the men summoned was Jared Ingersoll, then a 27-year-old attorney, later infamous as the New Havener who accepted the post of Stamp Act collector. Possibly, the Superior Court bench assigned attorneys to Cuff because of a sense of unease generated by Jack's 1743 hanging, which was dictated by his guilty plea and his failure to invoke legal arguments to challenge his accuser and indictment.

several arguments: the Deuteronomy prescription of death only if the victim were "betrothed," the two-witness rule, the necessity of having "some good Circumstances besides the womans Evidence," and the unreliability of Diana's evidence because she was "so young a person." Finally, the lawyers made a poignant plea that ran against the grain of their culture: "We cannot see however some may think and talk that the Life of a Slave etc. may be treated other than the Life of another."[62] The two houses of the assembly denied these petitions, and we can assume that Cuff hanged. Yet the efforts made on Cuff's behalf, along with the delay in the execution of the February sentence, indicate that the death sentence for rapists was becoming controversial and disturbing to many in eighteenth-century Connecticut, even when black slaves were cast as the assailants.

Forty years later, Connecticut residents were riveted by the rape trial of a free black wayfarer, Joseph Mountain, and by the publication of a purported autobiography that drew a sensationalized portrait of Mountain as insolence and evil incarnate. Having heard the evidence against Mountain on the charge of raping a thirteen-year-old girl while her sister was forced to watch, "the jury had little hesitation" in bringing in a guilty verdict. After being sentenced to hang, Mountain petitioned the General Assembly for a commuted sentence similar to those given white men previously convicted of rape, Vanskelly Mully in 1760 and James Gibson in 1783.

The jury's quick verdict and the Assembly's refusal to commute the death penalty in Mountain's case stand in marked contrast to Gibson's case of just seven years before. Gibson, a British deserter, had been passing through the state in 1783, when he allegedly came upon an "aged woman" "walking in the Country Road" and raped her. "After doubting and debating a long time," the jurors sent an officer "requesting some advice [from the bench] and that the common Law Books might be sent them. . . . after which, tho' with doubts and reluctance in some, they came into Court and returned the Petr. Guilty." The hesitation of the jurors here was borne out by the Assembly's decision two months later to

---

62. Conn. Archives, Crimes and Misdemeanors, 1st Ser., IV, 118–119. Cuff's lawyers were correct in stating there was no precedent for hanging a man for raping an unmarried or unbetrothed woman. This argument ignored, however, both the English legal treatises and the colony's well-established practice of indicting men for rape without regard to the marital status of their victims.

commute Gibson's death sentence, upon his petition, to castration.[63] By doling out commutations along racial lines, lawmakers sent a clear message that capital punishment, the ultimate expedient for removing a source of pollution from the land, was peculiarly suitable for black men. Perhaps more surprising than the racial double standard is that, by the end of the century, religious and secular leaders had to work hard to justify the death penalty even for the most liminal of "strangers."

In May 1790, Mountain, who had that month arrived from a life of crime in England and on the Continent, had been in the midst of walking from Boston to New York. On the journey he was first arrested in Hartford and whipped for theft. Next he encountered Eunice Thompson and her sister on the road into New Haven. "Intoxication" and a desire to ruin an innocent being had driven him to the "most cruel attack," he is quoted as asserting in his purported autobiography, *Sketches of the Life of Joseph Mountain, a Negro*. Five days before his execution date of October 20, Mountain submitted to the General Assembly a two-page petition, most probably drafted with the help of a lawyer. In it he confessed that "the malignity of a Rape . . . justly subjects the perpetrator to a severe punishment," but, taking a page from Enlightenment thinking, he questioned whether "it would not be as [or more] advantageous to society" if he were confined to hard labor, or sold into slavery out of the state, and the proceeds donated "to the injured girl" — rather than if his life were taken. Almost as an afterthought, Mountain added that the commutation of his sentence would give him time to adequately prepare for death, in other words, to convert and fully repent, tasks of self-improvement he had neglected so far.[64]

Mountain's petition, rejected speedily by both the lower and upper houses, became the springboard for James Dana's execution sermon delivered to a "great concourse" "of all orders and characters" three hours before the hanging. Entitled simply *The Intent of Capital Punishment*, Dana's sermon enumerated several general and particular justifica-

63. Before agreeing on commutation, the two legislative houses tossed back and forth several different votes whether to change the sentence or grant Gibson a new trial as he requested. For documentation of the Gibson case, see SCR, XXXIII, 150–151; Hartford County Superior Court Files, dr. 13; Conn. Archives, Crimes and Misdemeanors, 1st Ser., VI, 220–222; PRS, VII, 124.

64. *Sketches of the Life of Joseph Mountain, a Negro, Who Was Executed at New-Haven, on the 20th Day of October 1790, for a Rape, Committed on the 26th Day of May Last* (New Haven, 1790), 17; Petition of Joseph Mountain (Oct. 15, 1790), Conn. Archives, Crimes and Misdemeanors, 1st Ser., IV, 131.

tions for the death sentence in Mountain's case without ever mentioning the condemned malefactor's race or conceding that Connecticut had not always been consistent in how it chose "to protect female honor from violence."[65]

The aims of capital punishment, Dana proclaimed using standard execution sermon logic, were twofold: "to rid the state of a present nuisance" and to strike deterrent terror into the minds of undetected criminals, youth, and all persons watching. Dana curtly dismissed the alternative punishments — banishment and life imprisonment — as inconsistent with the safety and welfare of innocent citizens. Like Mountain himself, who conceded he had had "every indulgence granted" at his trial in contrast to those he had seen "at Old-Bailey," Dana congratulated Connecticut's lawmakers, who by 1790 had sagely reduced the number of capital crimes to six. Aware that some observers might advocate that rape *not* be on the capital list, Dana carefully emphasized that Mountain's behavior went beyond the pale and that the criminal's self-admitted biography cried out for the satisfaction of God's wrath. To Mountain's sixteen-year record of riotous participation in highway robber gangs in England, Dana responded: "You have merited the punishment you are now to suffer more than twenty times." With Mountain's admission that he had reacted to his assault on Eunice "by insulting her in her distress, [by] boasting of the fact" to neighbors who responded to the girls' "pitiable shrieks," and by being so cocky that he "loitered unconcerned" at the scene, the preacher could hold up incontrovertible proof that the condemned man "had cast off all shame, and even all fear of detection." Finally, Dana could assert that Mountain's case differed from most rape cases in that there had been witnesses: "Seldom is *such* an offence so amply proved."[66]

After Joseph Mountain swung from the gibbet on October 20, 1790, the two pamphlets quoted from above were made available for purchase by New Haven's printers. While James Dana's execution sermon partook of a 110-year-old New England tradition, the other pointed the way toward the popular crime literature of the nineteenth century. The anonymous editor of Mountain's *Sketches* appended a note in which he assured his readers "that the facts [herein] related were taken from the

65. James Dana, *The Intent of Capital Punishment: A Discourse Delivered in the City of New-Haven, October 20, 1790, Being the Day of the Execution of Joseph Mountain, for a Rape* (New Haven, [1790]), 5, 9, 13.

66. Ibid., 5–10, 12, 23, 26; *Sketches of Joseph Mountain*, 17–18.

mouth of the culprit. In no instance has any fact been substantially altered, or in the *least* exaggerated." Instead of the three-page account of the "dying warning" of the malefactor that was a standard part of eighteenth-century printed execution sermons, the first-person account allegedly written by Mountain himself stretched over nineteen pages and offered readers a sprightly chronicle of the convicted man's life from his birth in Philadelphia to free black servants in the household of Samuel Mifflin, to his years as part of the criminal underclass in England, to his arrest and trial in Connecticut. In essence, this new autobiographical genre used a lurid, local crime (rape) as an excuse to deliver picaresque tales of a criminal's progress and to paint a tongue-in-cheek portrait of a self-consciously outrageous personality. Mountain's small gestures toward apologizing for his multifarious taboo-breaking ways (including his three-year marriage to a white woman whose property he exhausted) are far outweighed by his evident glorying in the spotlit role of antihero. From the pulpit, Parson Dana expressed his repulsion that Mountain in telling his life story would boast about and treat as "honourable" his past preeminence, "skill and bravery" as a highwayman and confidence man. To the minister, the most eye-opening sign of the gaping chasm between himself and this "negro" was the distinct possibility that Mountain was "deceiving the world" with a "pretended" history and thus was "mock-[ing] at the most presumptuous sins."[67] For a white readership, the tale's power to shock and titillate was of course enhanced by the advertisement that the brazen narrator was of African descent.

To an observer attuned to the cultural history of early New England, one irony of the presentation of Mountain is that he, a black heathen, many years after the demise of the region's most Puritan regime, relied on the precise wording of Deuteronomy 22 to plead that his sentence was incompatible with the laws of God.[68] In yet another gesture that garnered nothing for the condemned man, his body was represented as author in the launching of a new form of literary transaction: the marketing of a quasi-fictional character and a sensationalist type of storytelling that rewarded the reader by divulging lurid detail and flirting with jocularity rather than by delivering bolts of terror and remorse. At the same time that the legal fraternity was downplaying the crime of rape

---

67. *Sketches of Joseph Mountain*, [20]; Dana, *Intent*, 23, 24, 26.

68. Mountain argued that the biblical law did not specify death when an unmarried, unbetrothed "damsel" was raped. This argument had failed to save Cuff who hanged in 1749; see above.

and resisting its punishment by death when white men were accused, opportunistic authors grabbed the public's attention with fantastical tales that projected the violence and violation of sexual assault onto black men.[69] A final irony is that Eunice Thompson's voice and body were displaced by the focus on the criminal antihero. Unlike most eighteenth-century rape victims, Eunice's words were not treated with distrust: but her own account proved practically irrelevant to the trial and to popular retellings, since eyewitnesses and the identity of the alleged assailant made it clear that a real rape had occurred.[70]

Eunice's passive role stood in part for the shifting fates of female complainants at the hands of the eighteenth-century legal system. As anglicized rules of evidence and attitudes toward women crowded out Puritan ways of ascertaining truth, as jurors grew squeamish over indicting and convicting men — especially local white men — on the basis of a woman's word, it became even more difficult for individual women to imagine any course but remaining silent about acquaintances, employers, and suitors who raped.[71] After a period of some resistance to West-

69. For the evolution of these genres, see Daniel A. Cohen, *Pillars of Salt, Monuments of Grace: New England Crime Literature and the Origins of American Popular Culture, 1674–1860* (New York, 1993). For another picaresque story about an alleged black rapist, see *The Life, and Dying Speech of Arthur, a Negro Man Who Was Executed at Worcester, October 20th 1768, for a Rape Committed on the Body of One Deborah Metcalfe* (Boston, 1768).

70. The text of "the Girles Complaint" and her testimony at the August 1790 Superior Court do not survive (Rex v. Joseph Mountain, SCR, XXVII, 147–148, NHSC Files, dr. 338, and Conn. Archives, Crimes and Misdemeanors, 1st Ser., IV, 130–131).

71. For a similar point on women's silence, see Anna Clark, *Women's Silence, Men's Violence: Sexual Assault in England, 1770–1845* (New York, 1987), 8. Women were also silenced in a related type of legal action that appeared occasionally on the New Haven County Court dockets in the late 18th century. In 1775 and again in 1788, a husband brought a civil suit for large damages against a man whom he claimed had assaulted, beaten, ravished, kidnapped, and then stolen the affections of his wife, precipitating a marital separation and his loss of her services. Jonathan Crampton v. Nathaniel Bishop (Jan. 1775), NHCC Files, dr. 59; Dr. John Spaulding v. Ezra Curtis (Dec. 1788), dr. 81. By importing a version of the English action of criminal conversation into their legal system, New Englanders signaled a deliberate willingness to confuse the issue of a woman's consent: the action denied what was in reality a woman's willful abandonment of her husband by cloaking it in the fiction of forcible rape and taking. For a thorough analysis of criminal conversation in England, see Lawrence Stone, *Road to Divorce: England, 1530–1987* (New York, 1990), chap. 9.

ern traditions of tolerating a certain amount of male sexual license and coercion, New Englanders after 1700 moved to adopt key features that persist in modern-day sexual assault trials: defense attorneys who skeptically scrutinized the woman's accusation, prosecutions that targeted chiefly outsiders and nonwhites, and community attitudes that harbored ambivalence over how rape and attempted rape should be treated. However, of all the categories of crimes involving consensual and coercive sex — fornication, lascivious carriage, adultery, bigamy, rape — there was *one* in which the double standard creeping into the legal and print culture of eighteenth-century New England did not show its face.

———

Neither the earliest laws against incest in Connecticut and New Haven colonies (which carried the death penalty) nor the superseding 1702 law (which prescribed a severe punishment short of death) treated incestuous relationships as if they might involve coercion. In establishing the ban against marriage and sexual relations between men and women in a long list of degrees of consanguinity, the lawmakers prescribed the same penalty for "every man and woman": severe whipping, shaming on the gallows, and the wearing of an *I* on their clothing. The 1702 statute presumed that both parties had engaged in the illicit sexual relation knowingly and freely.[72] However, despite the seemingly equal treatment promised by the laws, in the smattering of father-daughter incest cases that arose in the pre-1790 period judges consistently handed over sentences that acknowledged the special culpability of the father.

In the two incest cases to come before the higher court before 1710, the magistrates followed the Puritan patterns of meting out corporal punishment unflinchingly and using whippings to warn women against complying with male lust. Thus female incest victims were whipped, but the men who pressured them into the "abominable" crime were treated even more harshly (see Table 15). Small though the pre-1790 incest caseload was, the near 100 percent conviction rate and severe punishment of men serve as a foil to outcomes in other criminal prosecutions involving sexual misconduct. Incest was the *only* sexual crime for which white men pleaded not guilty in vain. Respectable standing in the community did not mitigate the cases against white men, but instead made the crime more heinous in the eyes of the authorities. A man's commis-

72. "An Act to Prevent Incestuous Marriages," in *Acts and Laws, of His Majesties Colony of Connecticut in New-England* (New London, 1715), 74–75.

TABLE 15
Incest Prosecutions in Connecticut, 1666–1789

Date	Defendants	Kin Relation	Outcome
Oct. 1672	Thomas Rood	father	guilty plea; hanged
	Sarah Rood	daughter	guilty plea; 2 severe whippings
May 1703	Thomas Hall	stepfather	not guilty plea; whipping, gallows, *I*
	Susanna Hall	wife/mother	not guilty plea; whipping, gallows, *I*
	Hannah Rood	stepdaughter/daughter	guilty plea; severe whipping
May 1703	Joshua Holcomb	brother-in-law (wife's sister)	grand jury: ignoramus
Mar. 1724/5	John Perkins, Jr.	father	not guilty plea; whipping, gallows, *I*
	Sarah Perkins	daughter	not guilty plea; whipping, gallows, *I*; Assembly exempts from all but paying costs
Dec. 1777	Dudley Drake Abigail Holcomb	uncle niece	both: plea in bar ruled insufficient; whipping, gallows, *I*

Note: The sentence set by the 1702 incest statute consisted of one hour on the gallows, a whipping of fewer than 40 lashes, and wearing a woven *I* forever. In the cases with not guilty pleas, juries found the defendants guilty; in the case with a plea in bar, the bench issued judgment.

Source: Records, Court of Assistants, 1666–1710; Superior Court Records and Files, 1711–1789.

sion of incest was abominable not so much for its partaking in illicit sex as for its perversion of the authority entrusted to parents — especially fathers — to ensure the well-being and direct the moral education of dependent children and kin.

Thomas Rood was the only person to be executed for incest in Connecticut's history. Indicted alongside his "reputed" daughter Sarah in 1672, the authorities moved quickly to dispatch Rood once he confessed to his great sin: only ten days elapsed between his trial and his hanging.[73] Although Sarah Rood pleaded guilty when brought before the bar immediately following her father's trial, several assistants on the bench expressed their dissatisfaction with passing a sentence of death on her head. The decision on Sarah was put off until the May 1673 court. There the judges announced that they had taken "notice of a great appearance of force layd up upon her spirit by her father overaweing [her] and . . . [using] bodily striveings . . . which kind of forceing to a person so ignorant and weake in minde . . . doe render her not equally Guilty but that as the fathers fault was much aggravated so the child's is exceedingly mittigated."[74]

Five decades later, the bench's recognition of such mitigating factors would exempt a coerced daughter from all penalties, but in the 1670s mitigation meant that Sarah Rood's life was spared. Because she "yield[ed] to his Temptation" several times after the first assault and concealed the fact, some "due punishment" was called for "that others may heare and feare and do no more such abominable wickednesse." Just as the whipping of a woman fornicator in this era was intended to strike horror into the souls of male seducers, so the Connecticut assis-

---

73. Rex v. Thomas Rood, *Recs. Ct. of Assts.*, Lacy transcript, I, 35–39. With no written statute yet on the books, the Assistants when faced with Rood's case asked the advice of several ministers and the General Court whether incest should carry the death penalty. The answer was in the affirmative. See *PR*, II, 184.

The town vital records list Sarah as the eldest child of Thomas and his wife, Sarah, who died in 1668 and bore her husband nine children in all. It is not clear why the court clerk referred to Sarah once as Thomas's "reputed" daughter, a phrase indicating her paternity was in doubt. For the Rood family, see Barbour Collection of Vital Records, volume for Norwich; *Vital Records of Norwich, 1659–1848* (Hartford, 1913), I, 34.

74. Rex v. Sarah Rood, *Recs. Ct. of Assts.*, Lacy transcript, I, 36, 39, 46 (for the quotation). Sarah was 23 in 1672. She died unmarried in 1713, and her small estate descended to her sister Mary (ibid.; New London Probate District, Estate Papers for Sarah Rood [1713] [microfilm], CSL).

tants meant the two severe whippings they ordered for Sarah Rood, one in Hartford and one in her home town, to warn not simply women who might comply but also men who like Thomas Rood might transform their "parentall authority" into "Tiranicall abuse."[75]

Although the scandal of incest infrequently diverted early Connecticut denizens, when a public trial became the talk of the town its central element was likely to be a riveting, sorrowful story told by an adolescent woman. In 1703 that woman was Hannah Rood (no relation to Sarah of the 1673 case). Spurred perhaps by her husband, newly married Hannah sparked an incest investigation by appearing before a local justice to acknowledge that her premaritally conceived baby was fathered, not by her spouse, but by her stepfather, Thomas Hall. After Hall had married her widowed mother, Hannah had served "as a drudge sometime in one house and sometime in another [until] at last . . . [she] was brought home." There, Hannah recounted, her mother importuned her to sleep with her stepfather, arguing "it was no sin [rather] it was my fathers comande which i ought to obay." Her stepfather importuned Hannah by first threatening to "box hir ears" and then declaring that "he was prophet priest and king and if i did not obaye him i would resist the motion of the holy goste." Testifying to a shocking scene, Hannah contended that she had resisted with many arguments, but in the end her mother, being stronger, managed to pull "part of my clothes off," "theay got me into the bedd," and "my mother held me by the hand whilst my father did abuse me and had his will of me."[76]

Once Hannah's mother, Susanna Hall, admitted "that shee was instrumentall of forcing her Daughter . . . to lye with . . . her husband," all three were bound over to answer for their crimes at the May 1703 Court of Assistants. As in the 1673 incest case, the bench tried the more adult actors first. Thomas and Susanna Hall both entered not guilty pleas, requested jury trials, and were found guilty. The full rigor of the new incest law was carried out on the pair on May 29: they were placed side by side for an hour on the gallows with a rope about their necks (doubtless suffering pelting and insults from the crowd), then were severely whipped, and from that moment on were required "to wear a Capitall I of two Inches

---

75. *Recs. Ct. of Assts.*, Lacy transcript, I, 46. The phrase "due punishment" was used in a similar case: Rex v. Hannah Rood, *Recs. Ct. of Assts.*, Lacy transcript, II, 419. See the discussion of whipping in the fornication case of Bethia Hawes in Chapter 4, above.

76. Conn. Archives, Crimes and Misdemeanors, 1st Ser., I, 325.

long . . . Cutt in Cloth of a Contrary Colour . . . , sewed on thy upper Garment . . . [or arm or back] in open view."[77]

Whereas Thomas and Susanna Hall would wear the appliquéd stigmata of incest for life, Hannah would not. She appeared before the bar after her abusive guardians, offering "the honered corte" a long, written confession and account of her ordeal. Appended to her story of how the abuse began was a classic portrait of the mental state of an incest survivor. "I can truly say i was so grived and tormented in my minde i knew not what to doe. I went to one house and to another and to a third thinking to declare my grife to them but when i cam thear theay being strangers to me i had not power to speake but [did] sit downe and cry, as my nibours have often taken notis of."[78]

Soon Hannah lapsed into a nearly incapacitating depression, which was broken only when George Rood asked her to marry him, and suddenly she could imagine the prospect of cutting all ties of obligation with her stepfather's household. Hannah's full confession was meant in part to persuade the judges to forgo punishing her "as if it wear a sin by me wilfully comited." In keeping with their treatment of Sarah Rood thirty years earlier, the assistants acknowledged Hannah's smaller role in the crime by exempting her from the shaming hour on the gallows and from the lifelong wearing of an *I*. But at the same time they underscored "her great guilt" in "Concealing [the sinne of Incest] for So long" by ordering Hannah to submit to a severe whipping.[79] The solemnity of the magistrates' announcement of Hannah's punishment underscores that their primary goal was to jolt miscreants and onlookers into living God-fearing lives, not to repair the self-esteem of abused women.

The Hall and Rood cases were perhaps superseded in Connecticut residents' historical imagination by the equally engrossing story of the Perkins family. In February 1724/5, local grand jurors presented John

77. *Recs. Ct. of Assts.*, Lacy transcript, II, 412–415, 417–418 (417 for the sentence). By 1702, Thomas and Susanna had several children of their own, born from at least 1688 into the 1690s. At his 1727 death, Thomas's immediate family refused administration of his estate, Susanna "Considering my Infirmities," and two grandchildren "Considering our Incapassity to manage in such afair." After debts, Thomas's estate amounted to £31 of personal property. *Vital Records of Norwich*, I, 39; New London Probate District, Estate Papers for Thomas Hall (1727), 2379 (microfilm).

78. Conn. Archives, Crimes and Misdemeanors, 1st Ser., I, 325.

79. Ibid.; *Recs. Ct. of Assts.*, Lacy transcript, II, 417–419.

Perkins, then forty-six years old with a second wife still living, and Sarah, his only daughter by his first wife, for "carnally knowing" each other at specific places in the past month.[80] On examination, nineteen-year-old Sarah "acknowledged that her father has been want to sollicit her to lie carnally with him, and the reason why her father sent her away this winter from his house was because she would not complie with him." Sarah had been living in the houses of Samuel Chatterton and Richard Sperry over the winter, and various members of those men's families recounted that John Perkins would come almost every day and sit on his daughter's bed, comporting himself toward Sarah "with a lascivious air," and often commanding that she take long walks with him. Mrs. Chatterton remembered that Sarah "seemed vehemently to dislike it, as if she were going among rattlesnakes and often hinted as if her father was wont to sollicite her and as it were drive her to uncleaness with him." Before the justices, Sarah admitted she had been guilty of the crime with her father at these times and others, but that "she always opposed him by arguments, and was never willing to comply with him, and that he has been want to kick and strike her for her noncomplyance, and that he has threatened her he would have her hand cut off for being a disobedient child and to disinherit her and to have her stoned to death for her not falling in with his motions."[81] Despite Sarah's confession, John Perkins resolutely maintained his innocence.

When the case came up for trial before the Superior Court two weeks later, the grand jury returned a bill of indictment against the father and daughter pair. Before the bar, both defendants pleaded not guilty. The jury brought in a verdict of guilty against them, and the bench sentenced them according to the statute: John was to stand on the gallows and be

80. Perkins's first wife was Sarah Warner; she died in 1705 when young Sarah was only four months old. Perkins married one year later, and his second wife, Elizabeth, bore him 10 healthy children, the last of whom was born in May 1726 — and thus conceived in about August 1725. See Jacobus, *FANH*, 1420–1425.

81. Grand jury presentment, justice of peace examination dated Feb. 19, 1724/5, in Rex v. John Perkins, Jr., and Sarah Perkins (Mar. 1724/5), NHSC Files, dr. 324. Elizabeth Chatterton, a matron of 51 years, recounted that she had watched John and Sarah "through the crack of the door" in the Chattertons' house and that John's "deportment towards her [Sarah] was unchast and unseemly and confirmed her in her suspicions of his lewdness with his said daughter and filled her with disquietment."

whipped twenty stripes on March 10, and Sarah was to undergo this punishment (but only ten stripes) on an appointed day in June. They were both to wear a stitched *I* on their garments forever.[82]

The execution of Sarah's sentence was delayed, perhaps deliberately, and she petitioned the May 1725 General Assembly for remission or commutation. In her "humble" memorial, Sarah described herself as "Bereaved of my natural Mother, and . . . [now in effect] Destitute of my natural father" and thus in need of a hearing "before this assembly (as fathers of the Commonwealth)." Although she had "never sought to hide" her sin but had always confessed it "after it was made publick," Sarah explained that she had pleaded not guilty in the trial "through the advice of those who Knew better than I and I thought I Did my Duty therein, but If I Erred . . . I am very sorry for it." She also voiced her guilt at not having "Sooner" made her sin "publick": "But how Difficult is it to withstand the authority of A father, and So far to Destroy him that was the Instrument of Giving being to me." Finally, she elaborated on the various forms of her resistance to her father's demands — she had argued with him that it was a sin, she had tried to escape — yet in the end "he would proceed in the manner of A force, I Still opposing him with words and utmost of my Strength, But . . . his Strength . . . was greater than mine." Both legislative houses, observing that Sarah had "made a penitent Confession" of her crime and "manifested great sorrow . . . for the same . . . all the time of Tryall," concluded that, as she had been "unnaturally . . . forced thereto by her fathers sovereign authority" (though she "grossly" misconstrued the "Paternall authority . . . over her"), she should be released from all penalties except paying costs.[83]

The compromises with the statute's rigorous language arrived at in the Rood, Hall, and Perkins cases could have set the tone for father-daughter incest cases that occasionally came before the county courts. In the one such case to come before the New Haven County Court, the bench (without a jury trial) found James Benton, Jr., guilty of lascivious

82. SCR, V, 53–60. On the day the sentence was announced, John was called three times but failed to appear. The bench ordered that his £200 appearance bond be declared forfeit. Thus the father in this case probably escaped the physical and shaming penalties and paid for his crime by giving up £200 worth of property. He evidently did not flee the area for long, because his estate was probated and distributed among his heirs in an orderly fashion a few years after his death in 1749.

83. Conn. Archives, Crimes and Misdemeanors, 1st Ser., III, 42–43. Here Sarah Perkins (and her lawyers) displayed a probable cognizance of the Connecticut incest precedents: both Sarah Rood and Hannah Rood had confessed in court.

carriage with his daughter "in a high Degree attended with many Aggravating Circumstances" and sentenced him to be whipped thirty-five stripes. James had pleaded not guilty, but his twenty-year-old daughter Rosilla confessed to lascivious behavior with her father, and the court ordered her to pay only a five-pound fine. Although Rosilla's account of her father's behavior toward her does not survive, we can safely assume that evidence or presumption of his coercion and her confession and penitence determined her milder, noncorporal punishment.[84]

The one other incest indictment to come before Connecticut's Superior Court before 1790 involved an uncle and niece who not only had "Carnal Knowledge and Copulation with Each Other" but also had cohabited as "husband and wife" for many months. In this 1777 case, the bench rejected as "insufficient" the defendants' plea that the girl's mother was her paramour's half, not full, sister. No plea of coercion was made, and thus the justices must have believed they were making an example of an incestuous couple indulging consensually in "their own Unnatural and Abominable Lust" when they sentenced both defendants to stand on the gallows, be whipped twenty stripes, and "forever" wear a letter *I*.[85]

84. Rex v. James Benton Jr. and Rosilla Benton of Guilford (Jan. 1769), NHCC, VII, 164, and NHCC Files, dr. 45. On sentencing, James was whipped and then jailed again until April, when he was assigned into service to pay his £10 costs. Rosilla on the other hand simply "gave [in] her note." James's punishment was reported in the *Providence Gazette; and Country Journal,* on Mar. 4, 1769; I am indebted to Sharon Block for this reference.

In 1723 a mother and her 19-year-old son were prosecuted for lascivious carriage, having been seen several times in the winter "lying in the naked bed together" in the room they rented. Although the defendants argued they innocently shared the bed "not undresst," the trial jury found them guilty, and the bench fined them 20s. Given the common practice of sharing beds in cramped quarters, the prosecution suggests the existence of a taboo against a lone parent and an adolescent child of the opposite sex sharing a bed. The woman's husband was not reported dead until 1730 but was apparently absent throughout the 1720s. Rex v. Rebecca Luddington, Rex v. James Luddington (Apr. 1723), NHCC, III, 164, and NHCC Files, dr. 6. For fuller speculation on this case, see Cornelia Hughes Dayton, "Women before the Bar: Gender, Law, and Society in Connecticut, 1710–1790" (Ph.D. diss., Princeton Univ., 1986), 144–146. For a much earlier case in which both the mother and son (of unspecified age) were whipped for "lyeing in the same bed . . . severall times," see Rex v. Mary Osborn and Ephraim Osborn (June 1674), New London County Court Records, III, 67, CSL.

85. Rex v. Dudley Drake and Abigail Holcomb of Windsor (Dec. 1777), SCR, XXII, 8–9; the quoted phrase is from the bill of indictment. A full accounting of the incest

The readiness of justices and jurors to back the Puritan rhetoric of "abominable" sinfulness with convictions in the few incest cases that entered the legal system stands in marked contrast to their hesitation over indicting and convicting suspects in other categories of sexual crimes where the evidence most often consisted of the woman's word against the man's.[86] Furthermore, the sentencing pattern in father-daughter incest cases forms an intriguing and useful counterpoint to the pattern of allocating blame between men and women who engaged in other types of illicit sex. Evidently in the eyes of the men sitting in judgment in these cases, the role of the young woman caught up in an incest situation was different in two important respects from the perceived role of women involved in adultery and fornication and even in coerced sexual relations with a man unrelated through blood. First, rather than disobedience to a husband or parent, the woman's sexual act represented *obedience* (albeit misplaced) to a proper male figure of authority — her father. Second, the judges in their condemnatory language and their differential treatment of men and the younger women they abused acknowledged that "filthie Lust" motivated only the perverse fathers; the young woman's "lust" was not the cause of her compliance.[87] The only other illicit sexual exchange to which judges and jurors applied the same logic was when they were convinced that a black man or a white stranger had raped a white woman.

In 1798 Timothy Langdon, the minister of the First Church in Danbury, Connecticut, took on the task of preaching on the day appointed for the execution of "Anthony, A Free Negro" for rape. Langdon's text was from Ecclesiastes: "Be not wicked overmuch, why shouldst thou die before thy time?"[88] By the end of the eighteenth century, a consensus had been reached in Connecticut that only black men deserved to die on the gallows for sexual assault. The few white men convicted of raping children or adult women succeeded in obtaining commuted sentences, but

---

caseload in Connecticut's higher courts for 1666–1789 would include the May 1703 prosecution of Joshua Holcomb for incest with his wife's sister: see Table 15.

86. For example, the adjective "abominable" was used in the 1703 indictment of Susanna Hall, *Recs. Ct. of Assts.*, Lacy transcript, II, 413.

87. Ibid., 419 ("filthie lust").

88. Timothy Langdon, *A Sermon, Preached at Danbury, November 8th, A.D. 1798, Being the Day of the Execution of Anthony, a Free Negro* . . . [Danbury, Conn., 1798], [3].

crimes like incest and adultery once labeled so abhorrent that they should bring death were demoted to noncapital felonies. The backing off from convicting and hanging white men for rape reflected in part a larger movement in the West that challenged the rationale behind capital punishment.[89] But it also mirrored and reinforced an increasingly pervasive double sexual standard present in eighteenth-century New England culture. Anglicized legal rules brought with them an altered approach to judging women's complicity in possibly coercive incidents —an approach that highlighted the instability of women's words and prompted many women to not perceive and not report coerced sex as rape. While women in the seventeenth century could take some comfort from the twin facts that their accounts were taken seriously and that almost all accused men were punished, they met with a multifarious set of barriers when bringing assault charges in the eighteenth century. After 1700, the only coercive sexual act for which white men were universally punished was father-daughter incest, and such cases occurred too infrequently to offer women much assurance that excessive male violence would be detected and stopped.

Trends in print culture also might have served to give women pause over the legitimacy of advancing sexual assault charges. In the 1760s it was clear that rape stories were being elevated to a form of entertainment. Accounts of the 1768 trial of Frederick Calvert, seventh Baron Baltimore—who had kidnapped and raped a young milliner, yet was acquitted—were serialized in the *Connecticut Journal* and other New England newspapers.[90] Although midcentury newspapers took care to note when men were arrested for sexually assaulting girls under age twelve, stories in which rape functioned as a joke fanned the culture's ambivalence over the integrity and worth of sexually mature women who suffered attacks.[91]

A June 1769 issue of the *Connecticut Journal* entertained its readers

89. Louis P. Masur, *Rites of Execution: Capital Punishment and the Transformation of American Culture, 1776–1865* (New York, 1989).

90. The story ran in scattered issues of the *Conn. Journal*, from Apr. 15 to June 10, 1768. A pamphlet devoted to the trial issued in 1768 in London by Joseph Gurney was advertised by John Mein in the *Boston Chronicle*, Oct. 12, 1769.

91. My survey of 20 years of issues of nine newspapers (ranging from 1704 to 1770, but concentrated mostly in the 1750s and 1760s) reveals the following breakdown in reports of arrests or trials for rape and attempted rape in the British colonies: seven involving children under 12; two involving adult women; two involving local, married women; and three giving no information on the victim's age or status.

with a report from Cork, Ireland, that featured cross-dressing as disguise and an adventurous plot to foil a seducer. But the story's darker side takes for granted that younger women of respectable families were at the disposal of their male kin and that men might presume to treat them as interchangeable objects. Learning of a seducer's scheme to ravish his sister, a young Irishman "disguised himself in his sister's clothes" and allowed himself to be kidnapped by the villain. Finding himself lodged with the villain's own sister for one night before a priest could be found to perform a clandestine, coerced wedding, the protagonist "realized [the intended injury]" on the hapless girl. The next morning he got away, but "the cheat was discovered, to the great mortification . . . of the intended bridegroom, on whose sister marks of pregnancy soon after appeared. Whereupon bills of indictment were found against the hero of the farce, for which he stood his trial, and was honourably acquitted."[92] That New Englanders in 1769 could laugh at rape (or rape disguised as seduction) as a justifiable revenge indicates how far they had traveled from the utter solemnity of Governor Eaton's biblically instructed bias toward believing women's testimony against sexual assault and punishing male assailants consistently and severely.

92. *Conn. Journal,* June 30, 1769.

6

Slanderous Speech

GENDER AND THE FALL FROM SOCIAL GRACE

"A good character," Zephaniah Swift wrote in 1795, "is the source of some of our highest enjoyments, and the preservation of it from the blast of envy, and the tongue of malice, is one of the most essential benefits we derive from society." The late-eighteenth-century jurist's enunciation of citizens' right to defend themselves from slander echoed the emphasis articulated by New Haven authorities 150 years earlier when they ordered a wealthy townsman to publicly "repaire" the reputation of a newly arrived servant girl whom he had "rashly" impugned. While rhetorical claims that reputation was "next to . . . life" were commonplace throughout the early American period, the ways in which authorities and lay men and women used the courts to punish evil speech changed significantly between 1640 and 1790.[1] As slander and contempt cases

---

1. Zephaniah Swift, *A System of the Laws of the State of Connecticut* (New York, 1972 [orig. publ. Windham, Conn., 1795–1796]), I, 179; Complaint of Hannah Marsh v. Mr. Frances Brewster (Nov. 1645), *NHCR*, I, 180–181; William Jones v. John Lambert (1661), *NHTR*, I, 496. "Evil" as a noun and an adjective appeared frequently in the confessions and rebukes of slanderers in civil and criminal cases throughout the New Haven Colony period; for examples, see *NHTR*, I, 389–390, 416, 486, II, 22; *NHCR*, I, 316, II, 353, 413.

came to occupy an ever smaller corner of the business of New Haven courts in these years, the contours of litigation over speech both reflected and distilled patterns of change apparent in other legal actions such as debt and fornication. Indeed, the story of slander in the seventeenth and eighteenth centuries throws into sharper relief the shifting relationships of white women and men to religious modes of expression, standards of sexual behavior, the expanding economy, and the public space of the courtroom.

Before 1710, the intimate scale of court sessions and the informal methods of pleading permitted by judges meant that women's experience of suing or being sued over insulting speech did not diverge in notable ways from men's experience. Loose charges of sexual misconduct against young men, for example, were deemed just as much "gross slander" as similar charges hurled at young women. Women's initiation of defamatory gossip was perceived as no less potent than men's. In essence, men and women who decided to complain over slander shared similar concerns and aimed their actions at the same audience, the local community. Seventeenth-century men and women "looked upon it as . . . [their] bounden duty to vindicate" their names in court, because their ability to function effectively at the village level had been put at risk by a circulating rumor. Moreover, magistrates and almost all New Haven residents shared a religious understanding of what constituted godly and ungodly speech: slander cases involving men and women alike typically ended with a public apology laced with references to sin and repentance. Although New Haven authorities might have been prompted by biblical examples and early modern English precedent to single women out for prosecution as slanderers and scolds, they chose instead to uphold a largely gender-neutral standard for public speech.[2]

By the early eighteenth century, the New Haven bench formalized and tightened the rules under which an aggrieved man or woman could sue for slander. Ironically, although the flexibility given to plaintiffs to sue over a broad range of injurious words disappeared, eighteenth-century cases tell historians more about the dynamics of speech and reputations than do seventeenth-century cases because plaintiffs' writs survive for the post-1710 period. Following proper common law formulas, the writs are essentially small narratives that paint a before-and-after picture of the plaintiff's financial, social, and psychological state. Most crucially, each writ cited verbatim the allegedly slanderous words and indicated

2. *NHCR,* I, 151; *NHTR,* I, 496.

where and to whom the report had been broadcast. Although most seventeenth-century New Haven adults spread accusatory reports to third parties as warnings, the eighteenth-century writs make clear that women continued to pass on damning information behind the scenes while men often chose to accuse others face-to-face, engaging in competitive bragging. Besides modes of speech, the types of charges that men and women sued over in the 1700s diverged. As the civil caseload mushroomed and county court business became increasingly geared toward new credit relations facilitating a commercializing economy, slander suits shrank in presence and narrowed largely to prosperous men anxious over their reputations for creditworthiness. Thus the community that most slander plaintiffs felt they could reach through a suit was no longer their entire neighborhood or town, but, rather, the network of men active in trade, credit, and debt litigation.

As the nineteenth century neared, litigants became less preoccupied with suing over sexual and moral matters, and women receded from an earlier appearance rate of one in three suits to one in five. Furthermore, from the late seventeenth century on, proportionately fewer and fewer women were cast as slanderers.[3] This trend along with other signs raises two possibilities: that women's words over time came to be seen as not particularly dangerous to men's reputations, and thus no longer of public communal concern, or that women learned to suppress their critical or angry assessments of others' characters. Notable in this regard is the handful of women in each century prosecuted for their unruly tongues and resistance to authorities. The seventeenth-century women who chose the pose of stubborn defiance appealed to individual conscience and a sense of their callings as religious teachers or neighborhood monitors. The few women haled into court for contempt in the 1700s, on the other hand, protested that their seemingly obnoxious conduct was undertaken in necessary defense of family or household obligations. In the heady climate of the Puritan experiment, some women felt licensed to speak out forcefully on religious and public issues — thereby treading on dangerous ground. By the early eighteenth century, even such tenuous public space had been cut off to most New England women. Although church records and women's spiritual memoirs chronicle women's work behind the scenes to influence neighborly relations and church policy,

3. While the balance between plaintiffs and defendants among female parties to slander suits was even in the 1640–1709 period (17 versus 18), plaintiffs predominated in the next eight decades (16 versus 7).

the idea of public leadership roles for gifted women was anathema to the orthodox system. As evangelical culture spread in the mid-eighteenth century, women were among its chief proponents, but they exerted their influence in ways seen as befitting their domestic and familial loyalties.[4]

The lack of concern manifested over outspoken, scolding women in mid- to late-eighteenth-century courts suggests how entrenched habits of silence and deference had become in the socialization of young women in New England. Outside family governance and educational settings, the burgeoning world of print culture, with its frequent images of nagging wives, provided an alternative locus to the courts for monitoring and regulation of women's speech. Just as other legal actions provide windows onto the divergences in women's and men's relationships to economic exchanges and standards of sexual conduct, slander litigation offers yet another gauge of the increasing invisibility of women's activities in the public records and civic theater of early American courtrooms.

From the opening of sessions in 1639 until 1710, New Haven courts heard a total of 115 slander cases, one-third (39) of which involved a woman as complainant or alleged slanderer (see Table 16). In these early decades, civil suits (initiated with a common law writ by the allegedly slandered party) and criminal actions (prosecuted in the name of the king) did not differ much in the sorts of disorderly speech they addressed. One could be sued directly by one's business associate, for example, for calling him a thief and a cheater who was "as unmercyfull as a dogg," *or* the injured party could instead persuade the magistrates to lodge a criminal complaint against the alleged defamer.[5] Although the

4. Laurel Thatcher Ulrich, *Good Wives: Image and Reality in the Lives of Women in Northern New England, 1650–1750* (New York, 1982), chap. 12; Ulrich, " 'Daughters of Liberty': Religious Women in Revolutionary New England," in Ronald Hoffman and Peter J. Albert, eds., *Women in the Age of the American Revolution* (Charlottesville, Va., 1989), 211–243; Barbara E. Lacey, "The World of Hannah Heaton: The Autobiography of an Eighteenth-Century Connecticut Farm Woman," *WMQ*, XLV (1988), 280–304. It is important to recognize that, when New England authorities in the late 17th century reconciled themselves to a policy of de facto toleration toward unorthodox worshipers, arenas for women's religious speech, public interpretation, and leadership did open up under the aegis of Quakers and Baptists. Still, the number of women embracing these dissenting sects was small.

5. John Evance v. John Charles (Feb. 1646/7), *NHCR*, I, 298. Some alleged

TABLE 16

Slander Cases in New Haven Courts, 1639–1789

	Civil			Criminal			Total		
	All	with Women		All	with Women		All	with Women	
	All	N	%	All	N	%	All	N	%
Colony period									
1639–1665[a]	58	16	(28)	22	11	(50)	80	27	(34)
New Haven									
County Court									
1666–1709[b]	29	10	(34)	6	2	(33)	35	12	(34)
1710–1759	33	10	(30)	6	1	(17)	39	11	(28)
1760–1789	47	9	(19)	0	0		47	9	(19)
Overall	167	45	(27)	34	14	(41)	201	59	(29)

[a]Includes 7 civil cases heard in town courts, 1666–1671.

[b]Includes one criminal case prosecuted before town magistrates but recorded in the county court records.

Sources: NHCR, I, II; *NHTR*, I, II; NHCC, Books and Files.

judges sometimes mixed civil and criminal penalties in a single case, in general a criminal conviction ended with the defendant's suffering a reprimand and being required to pay a fine to the appropriate treasury, whereas in a civil suit a defendant found guilty was ordered to pay spec-

---

slander was prosecuted in conjunction with express laws against breaking the peace (such behavior included "reproaching"), defaming the courts and magistrates, and lying (this included publishing a false report "tending to the . . . injury of any particular person"); for such provisions in the 1656 New Haven Colony Code, see ibid., II, 585–586, 598–599. But, in general, New Haven and Connecticut authorities, like their counterparts in 17th-century Massachusetts, proceeded with civil and criminal defamation actions according to their understanding of English practice, even though they broadened the definition of what was slanderous. In Connecticut, the only express law criminalizing defamation was passed in 1708; it set a standard 50s. fine (*PR*, V, 54–55).

ified damages to the plaintiff, in addition to covering the court costs incurred by both parties.[6]

Slander actions apparently registered their most visible presence ever in North American caseloads in the earliest decades of white settlement. In New Haven in the Colony era (1639–1665), an average of 2.9 suits came before the town and colony courts annually.[7] The frequency of suits at a time when the population of the English settlements was tiny indicates the importance given by both authorities and residents to ascertaining and protecting each individual's reputation. The governor and his colleagues on the bench solemnly entertained complaints over injured reputations from all comers, including youthful servants of suspect or humble origins. Operating without juries and eschewing the common law rules applicable to slander, the colony judges' prime interest was in exposing the truth about character. If an inhabitant uttered reproachful words with "no ground" and "in . . . hast," he or she would be prevailed upon to offer a public acknowledgment sufficient to "repaire . . . [the] Names" of the victims. However, if the speaker could produce witnesses proving that the targeted person had indeed committed the alleged acts, such as stealing a handkerchief or selling unmerchantable shoes, then what began as a slander complaint ended with a judicial reprimand or sentence for theft or cheating.[8]

6. In the 1640s, "fines" in cases that appear to be criminal were ordered to be paid to the defamed party, thus underscoring the near interchangeability of criminal and civil proceedings in the pre-1666 period. For examples, see *NHCR,* I, 257–259, 279, 327.

7. For civil suits, the average was 2 cases per year. Colonial historians often make the claim for the unusual prominence of slander in the 17th-century courts without quantifying the phenomenon, especially by proportion of total court business (John Demos, "Shame and Guilt in Early New England," in Carol Z. Stearns and Peter N. Stearns, eds., *Emotion and Social Change: Toward a New Psychohistory* [New York, 1988], 73; Jane Neill Kamensky, "Governing the Tongue: Speech and Society in Early New England" [Ph.D. diss., Yale University, 1993], 62–63, 71; Helena M. Wall, *Fierce Communion: Family and Community in Early America* [Cambridge, Mass., 1990], 31). Roger Thompson counts 108 actions for *all* types of verbal abuse in Middlesex Co., Mass., courts, 1649–1699 (" 'Holy Watchfulness' and Communal Conformism: The Functions of Defamation in Early New England Communities," *New England Quarterly,* LVI [1983], 504), and Robert St. George counts 856 for Essex Co., Mass., between 1640 and 1680 (" 'Heated' Speech and Literacy in Seventeenth-Century New England," in David D. Hall and David Grayson Allen, eds., *Seventeenth-Century New England* [Boston, 1984], 288–289).

8. Case against Edward Keely et al. (Feb. 1658/9), *NHTR,* I, 390; Youngs v. Budd

The earliest cases reveal not only the speed with which a person's reputation could be harmed in the small New World outposts of English society but also some of the techniques that Governor Theophilus Eaton used to create an aura of magisterial infallibility. The colony bench insisted on maintaining a strict line between rulers and ruled. If an inhabitant presumed to offer a private opinion on what punishment a sinner deserved or even to predict the magistrates' ruling in a criminal case, he was promptly chastised. In 1648, the bench told William Wooden that his prognostication that a man would be banished "was none of his worke." Some years later, William Bassett and his wife individually apologized for their breach of a biblical rule in acting as busybodies "medling with that which did not Concerne" them: they had criticized the man appointed to be executioner, and implicitly the sentence, in a sensational buggery case.[9]

Colony magistrates drew slander defendants like the Bassetts on a path toward identifying how each had been "out of her way and [did] breake rule in receiving a reproach against a neighbour . . . [and] spreading of it."[10] Even in civil litigation in Puritan New Haven, slander was understood as an evil and a sin—a departure from God's ways. In making confessions, those who had used rash words asked for God's help in enabling them "to be more watchfull for the time to come." Repenting slanderers also sought absolution by articulating the precise biblical rule that their speech had contravened. Henry Tomlinson, for example, listed his breaches of the Fifth, Sixth, and Ninth Commandments and the rule that "enjoynes him to live peacably with all men."[11] Early New Haveners thought of slander and contempt particularly in the context of Leviticus 19:15–18, passages that established the ethics of neighborly relations. Spreading rumors of a person's wrongdoing was "evil," because the godly way instructed Christians first to speak privately with the person under suspicion, then to take matter to the authorities only if evildoing had occurred and the miscreant refused to confess.[12]

The circulation of evil reports was worrisome not just because of the

(May 1661), *NHCR*, II, 431; Dickerman v. Wheadon (Aug. 1661), *NHTR*, I, 486. On producing witnesses, see *NHCR*, I, 51, 180–181, 301, 345–353; *NHTR*, I, 455.

9. *NHCR*, I, 339, 399; *NHTR*, I, 527–528, II, 1.

10. Fuller and wife v. Newman and wife (1649), *NHCR*, I, 476.

11. *NHTR*, II, 1; *NHCR*, II, 368. For other biblical rules mentioned, including Isaiah 53 "Latter End" and Matthew 18, see *NHCR*, II, 274; *NHTR*, I, 503, II, 1.

12. See *NHCR*, I, 184, II, 440, on speaking privately.

fragility of reputations in the wilderness setting but also because the loosening of tongues signaled the devil might be making strides there. Susanna Man, a servant who had passed her theft off as the deed of another servant, confessed "shc had slaundered him, and said thatt God had given her over to the Devill to make her lye."[13] Repeatedly, men who humbled themselves for behaving contemptuously to the magistrates explained that "God left" them in those moments. Such incidents included a man who announced that "he would have justice in another place . . . if not here," and another who publicly slurred the bench with the claim that one "had as good be bitt with a mad dog as snapt at by [such] a company of fooles." The magistrates declared these insults tantamount to "neglecting the imadge of God in magistrats." So closely was the image of an ever-present God bound to Puritans' ways of monitoring their own speech that the standard expectation for civil and criminal defendants alike was that they would "fall under" — submit to God's rules for neighborly conversation and acquiesce in the guidance of the magistrates.[14]

Although the great majority of convicted slanderers were required to pay a fine or damages for their misdeed, injured parties and mediators believed that a formal apology went the furthest toward repairing a maligned name. Some complainants made this preference clear by refusing to accept damages assessed by the bench. Richard Malbone, a retired judge and deputy, announced in court "that he would not inrich himselfe in this way," and on other occasions plaintiffs "professed . . . it is not his estate they seeke, but a reformation and the cleering of their names." The judges often found themselves prodding the defendant to publish "an acknowledgment suteing the case," which meant a speech retracting all unproven slanders, expressing adequate repentance, and addressing those groups who had heard the original "evil" report. For example, Hannah Fuller "desired to be cleared *where* she was wronged," just as Goodwife Beckly witnessed her detractor tender an apology, as ordered, "in the presence of their neighboures." The acknowledgment thus was calibrated to fit the specific crime of misspeech. Sometimes the judges closed the case once the injured party was satisfied; at other times

13. Ibid., I, 51. See also II, 274.

14. Ibid., II, 271; *NHTR*, II, 134. The judges chided drunken and combative William East for currently going "under the divell as his keeper" and acting "as if he were an atheist" "given up of God to satisfie his sensual appetites" (*NHCR*, II, 311–313). For examples of "falling under," see *NHCR*, I, 248, 475; *NHTR*, I, 210.

they made clear that an apology was "short of what the case required, not reaching to the healing of her name so farr as" was possible.[15]

Men and women in New Haven Colony's tiny settlements sued over a wide range of insults, not all of which fitted within the strict common law categories of actionable slander (see Table 17). However, colony residents did not take advantage of the judges' permissive definition of slander to complain about a host of sexual slurs. The scarcity of such suits underscores what appears to have been a low incidence of illicit sexual activity, especially in the decades before 1690. Even more notable, women initiated suits much more often for nonsexual charges than for attacks on their chastity.[16] During the Colony period, and indeed throughout the seventeenth century, sexual slander constituted the same proportion of men's suits as women's suits, and in their awards judges registered the general climate of emphatic disapproval of male misbehavior. When John Fish of Stratford falsely accused two men of sexually harassing his sister-in-law, the bench rebuked him for laying "a gross slander," indeed a "high and heavy" charge, on both young men. In the 1640s, even the faintest hint of sexual impropriety could garner substantial damages for a defamed woman or man. Three men were ordered to make payments of ten and twenty shillings to servant Margaret Cadwell for spreading a report that one of them had "fownd her plyable" and "could have don what he listed with her." Goody Fuller suffered when neighbors gossiped that she had entertained a young man while her husband was away: the court required her slanderers to pay the Fullers five pounds in damages. Conversely, when the magistrates dis-

---

15. Refusing damages: *NHCR*, I, 258–259, II, 226. See also II, 413; *NHTR*, I, 364, 390. Apparently in some cases the "damage" charge covered only the court costs. See Caffinch v. Fowler (1646/7), *NHCR*, I, 278.

On acknowledgment: Fuller and wife v. Newman and wife (July 1649), *NHCR*, I, 475–476 (my emphasis); Beckly and wife v. Frances Hitchcock (1659), *NHTR*, I, 414.

Closing the case: Complaint against John Seckett (Aug. 1641), *NHCR*, I, 56, II, 354; *NHTR*, I, 126.

Insufficient apology: *NHCR*, I, 476. See also *NHTR*, I, 414. Jane Kamensky documents many similar examples from Essex Co., Mass., of the "proportionate justice" meted out in misspeaking cases ("Governing the Tongue," 407–421).

16. Combining the criminal and civil suits in which women were allegedly slandered in New Haven courts, 1640–1709, sexual misconduct figured in only 7 of 36 (19%) cases for which the charges are known. In contrast, sexual slander comprised 62.5% of civil cases brought by women in the 1710–1789 period.

TABLE 17
Primary Slanders in Civil Suits in New Haven Courts, 1639–1709

| | Object/Plaintiff | | |
Slander	Men	Women	Total
Sexual Slander			
Adultery	1	0	1
Fornication	1	1	2
Siring/bearing bastard	1	1	2
Lascivious carriage	6	1	7
False courtship	1	0	1
Buggery (implied)	1	0	1
Rape	1	0	1
Total	12	3	15
Nonsexual Slander			
Drunkenness	1	1	2
Witchcraft	2	3	5
Scolding/slandering	2	1	3
Illegal entertaining	0	1	1
Lying	8	1	9
Perjury/forgery	5	1	6
Theft	18	1	19
Cheating	5	0	5
Being bad neighbor	2	0	2
Other	9	1	10
Total	52	10	62
Unknown	12	4	16
Grand total	76	17	93

Note: In six cases, two individuals sued jointly over allegedly slanderous words aimed explicitly at both of them; the cases thus are counted twice.

Sources: NHCR, I, II; *NHTR,* I, II; NHCC, Books and Files.

covered that the allegedly slanderous report raised against James Hayward was true — he had indeed behaved in a "very false harted" fashion
in courting a maid in the Bay Colony — they decreed he should "beare
his owne shame."[17] In all of these cases, rumors of misconduct that fell
short of fornication or even lascivious carriage were taken seriously and
investigated promptly by the authorities.

But early New Haveners manifested far more sensitivity over and proclivity for rash accusations that involved such betrayals as stealing or
lying. Theft was the most common type of charge sued over: these suits
were almost entirely brought by men, and the words sued over typically
contained strong insinuations that the thief was engaged in some form
of cheating or oppression. Thus the epithet "thief" was bruited about
when a man borrowed a boat or tools without permission or temporarily
misplaced bushels of malt he had pledged to deliver to a purchaser.[18]
Most slander cases that rested on charges of theft, then, grew out of
men's fears that they would no longer be trusted in the dense networks
of exchange among villages that sustained family livelihood in early New
England. The second most frequent category of slander cases, those
revolving around imputations of lying and perjury, reflected a similar
preoccupation with maintaining a reputation for accuracy and honesty
— a crucial form of credit in a localized, memory economy.[19]

Slander plaintiffs in the earliest decades of settlement articulated several concerns related to the importance of being regarded as a good
neighbor and community member. These concerns failed to reappear in
the caseload of the next century.[20] The first illuminates one aspect of

17. Fish (1655): *NHCR*, II, 150–151; the judges ordered Fish to pay each man five
pounds. Caldwell: ibid., I, 327–328. Fuller: ibid., I, 473–476. Goody Fuller of this
1649 suit was the former Hannah Marsh, who had complained when called a "slut
and Billingsgate slutt" just after her arrival in 1645; see the case cited in n. 1, above.
Haywood: ibid., I, 339, 399.

18. Joseph Tuttle and Eleazer Peck v. John Morris (Jan. 1670/1), *NHTR*, II, 274–
275; Samuel Hotchkiss v. Christopher Todd (May 1658), I, 351. See also James Mills
v. John Thompson (May 1658), *NHCR*, II, 248.

19. One of the next-largest categories — witchcraft — included three cases, in
1653, 1654, and 1689, in which women were called "witch" (*NHCR*, II, 29–36, 77–
89, 122; NHCC, I, 172) and two (1657 and 1666) in which men were accused of
either bewitching livestock or doing the devil's work (*NHCR*, II, 224–226; *NHTR*, I,
317–318, II, 163–164).

20. The one exception was the lone witchcraft-based slander suit brought by
widow Elizabeth Gould in 1742 (Gould v. Chittenden, NHCC, IV, 135–148; SCR, XI,
193.

what it meant to be manly in the New World Puritan communities: two male householders went to the trouble of suing over slander when they were accused of being bad neighbors. All we know of the slur leveled at Goodman Johnson is that it suggested he was an "uncomfortable neighbour," but the invective aimed at John Conklin "before a great part of the traine band" survives in detail: Conklin "was a neighboure not fitt for an Indian to live by" because he took advantage of his near neighbors' sickness to kill one of their hogs. Along with their obligation to govern effectively a household of dependents, good men were expected to be accommodating and generous toward their neighbors. Yeomen family heads accused of parsimony and cantankerousness in their neighborhoods felt they could not afford to let such an image persist.[21]

Other insults threatening one's legitimacy as a community member were keenly felt by both men and women. Several seventeenth-century suits arose when the morals of church members were challenged; judges believed that church members deserved relatively high damages considering "the censure" such a charge as lying, if "proved," "might have brought upon" the slandered person.[22] Finally, three women and two men used slander suits to ward off the most damaging suspicion of all: neighborhood fears that they practiced witchcraft. William Meaker won an apology from a neighbor, Thomas Mullener, who had performed tests on his dying pigs to discover whether they were bewitched by Meaker. Mullener, in fact, was thought to have such a loose, unreformed tongue that the authorities considered banishing him. Yet taking the initiative to sue could redound to the plaintiff: rather than receive an apology, Elizabeth Godman was admonished against going "to folkes houses in a rayling manner," one of the activities that had caused nine town residents to call her a witch. In Godman's case, the imputation of witchcraft continued to haunt her: she was never formally tried yet never fully cleared. Despite the near absence of witchcraft trials in seventeenth-century New Haven, the slander caseload confirms that witchcraft stories circulated and that much was at stake for those who spoke as accusers and those who were seen to speak like witches.[23]

21. *NHTR*, II, 36; *NHCR*, II, 352.

22. "Censure": Thomas Staples v. Roger Ludlow (May 1654), *NHCR*, II, 122. For slander cases touching on church membership issues, see Hayward v. Wooden (1647), *NHCR*, I, 339–341, 397–399; Law v. Mead (1656), II, 166; Beckly and wife v. Frances Hitchcock (Sept. 1659), *NHTR*, I, 414; and Rex v. Jeremiah Johnson (Sept. 1662), II, 8, 22.

23. Meaker v. Mullener: *NHCR*, II, 224–226; *NHTR*, I, 317–318. Godman: *NHCR*,

Examining how status, age, and gender entered into the dynamic tension between alleged slanderer and target offers some clues to the patterned ways in which men and women expressed anger in the seventeenth century. It is not possible to ascertain age for most slander litigants before 1670, but in the 1640s–1660s, as in the 1700s, most adversaries were probably of similar ages. When significant age gaps are found, however, they can reveal which members of society felt license to lash out at nonpeers and which restrained themselves or found their speech ignored.

Slander and contempt cases in the Colony period and in the following decades manifested a trend that persisted into the eighteenth century: youthful, low-status men, but no women at all, dared to speak out against prominent public officials or higher-status persons.[24] In the 1640s, for example, two young men spread reports around town and "in other plantations" that the Reverend Mr. John Davenport had lied about the Delaware trade. Edward Parker, a resident in his twenties, charged former magistrate Richard Malbone with dereliction of duty and ill-treatment of the seamen who worked for him. In 1678, thirty-seven-year-old Samuel Cook accused a commissioner twice his age of stealing for himself and for his son-in-law. Captain Samuel Eells, judge of the county court and speaker of the House at the time, was repeatedly condemned by a junior militia officer for lying in court and being "not fitt for any

---

II, 30–31. For more details on the suspicions against Godman, see Carol F. Karlsen, *The Devil in the Shape of a Woman: Witchcraft in Colonial New England* (New York, 1987), 23, 27–28, 60–61, 125–126. For the other three witchcraft-related slander suits, see Staplies v. Ludlow (May 1654), *NHCR*, II, 77–89, 122; Mallery v. Hotchkiss (Jan. 1665/6), *NHTR*, II, 163–164; Bowden v. Cooke (Nov. 1689), NHCC, I, 172.

24. In the slander caseload, the one woman who commented on public affairs was the wife of a man who soon became a deputy, judge, and corporal (John Cooper): she criticized the morals of a distant community, not a specified public official (Richard Haughton v. Goodwife Cooper [Sept. 1651], *NHTR*, I, 86). As revealed in civil and criminal cases before 1710, women's alleged slanderous speech, whether directed at men or women, did not tend to cluster around one type of insult. In fact, in the 15 cases in which the content of women's words is known, 3 female parties match each of the following categories: women monitoring other women's moral or sexual behavior, women identifying or criticizing men's sexual misconduct, servants accusing others of theft, wives voicing opinions on economic dealings or public affairs, and women trading charges as part of family or neighborhood feuds. As for contempt (which could range from refusing to obey a court order to insulting magistrates to their faces), I count 29 cases in the colony court and at least 11 in the town courts before 1666: only 1 involved a woman defendant.

place in the Government."[25] Even though they might be slapped with a heavy fine, a range of younger men, not just a few aberrant souls, felt entitled to publicly express personal grievances or use public talk to monitor the probity of senior officeholders.

The early New Haven records of male challenges over the deadly serious matter of reputation reflect very little of the narcissistic bravado and face-to-face pugnaciousness that emerged in eighteenth-century lawsuits over slander. Indeed, potentially slanderous talk appears to have been passed around New Haven and surrounding towns, not in direct confrontations, but rather as exchanges among neighbors that constituted a testing process to discern whether a criminal complaint against a suspected liar, thief, or fornicator ought to be made to the authorities.[26] Witness the plight of Henry Peck: in 1649 he circulated a thirdhand rumor that reached his wife insinuating that a maidservant in another household was pregnant by her master. In the process, Peck had found the story "to be but a supposition," and he then deliberately went about reporting "it was so." Nonetheless, the bench in the end sentenced Peck to pay five pounds to the two slandered persons. Thus in the intensely Puritan colony of New Haven, where scoffing and jesting were discouraged in both men and women, defamatory speech circulated for the most part, not as direct confrontation or assertive bragging, but rather as telegraphs from sometimes overzealous partakers in the ethos of neighborly watchfulness.[27]

25. *NHCR*, I, 184, 279. Davenport was the minister in New Haven from 1639 to 1668, when he left for Boston. In addition, during the 1640s three male servants were prosecuted for defaming their mistresses. Cook, Eells: ibid., I, 257–259; NHCC, II, 297.

26. Information on to whom the words were passed emerges for 53 of the 115 pre-1710 cases: in only 8 did the slander defendants (including three women) directly confront their targets; in 6 instances, the words were spoken in court; in the remaining 39, the alleged slanderer spoke to third parties without the targeted person's being present. For the scattered, late-17th-century cases involving aggressive, narcissistic male speech, see *NHTR*, II, 268, 274, and NHCC, I, 137.

Using mostly the Essex Co., Mass., court records, where speech was often recorded verbatim, John Demos suggests such narcissistic attacks abounded in early New England. Unfortunately, he does not attach years to his examples. See Demos, "Shame and Guilt in Early New England," in Stearns and Stearns, eds., *Emotion and Social Change*, 69–85, esp. 74.

27. *NHCR*, I, 478–479. If Peck had been able to produce witnesses to confirm that two local women had originated the report, his damages might have been mitigated or canceled. For rebukes of scoffers and jesters, see I, 246, and *NHTR*, II, 22.

On a few occasions New Haven Colony magistrates explicitly reprimanded a woman for speech that was "uncomely for her sex." Rebuking Hannah Marsh for her "frowardnes and brawling on shipboard," the bench pointedly reminded the young servant "that meeknes is a choise ornament for weomen." The judges used similar language in one of their most dramatic confrontations with a defiant woman. The showcase trial they staged for religious dissident Lucy Brewster ended with the magistrates' declining to banish Brewster, but sentencing her instead to pay a whopping two-hundred-pound fine. Most of the eleven counts against Brewster revolved around "her dislike of the churches proceedings" and her encouraging others to challenge authorities' rulings. During the trial, Brewster exacerbated the charges of profane slander and "uncomely jesting" by appearing "full of speech" and loading "the witnesses with reproach." "She was told meeknesse and modesty would better become her in such a place."[28]

What is surprising is that, beyond this rather tame warning, Governor Eaton and his compeers did not compare Lucy Brewster to stock images of female scolds. Rather, the one biblical figure they held up was "Micaell the Archangell," who, they reminded the courtroom audience, had not dared to use "such rayling landguadge . . . with the Divell, though he had matter enough against him." In reprimanding Frances Hitchcock, the woman whose depiction in early New Haven annals came closer than any other's to that of a scold, the town court resorted to a phrase used twice in the Bible to describe *all* sinners: "These evill carriages of hers" "manifest that the poyson of asps is under her lipps."[29] Confronted with at least three other women charged with aggravated episodes of railing, discontent, and meddling, magistrates in the Colony period refrained from using language that singled out women's tongues for special denunciation. Horrified as they were at any woman who would not keep her place, seventeenth-century authorities typically chose a common vocabulary to persuade women and men away from "high," provoking, "wicked" speech and to reconcile them to their proper station.[30]

28. Marsh: *NHCR,* I, 180–181, 257. Brewster: I, 246, 248, 251. Lucy Brewster was the new widow of one of the wealthiest early settlers of New Haven. For a narrative summary of her trial, see Lilian Handlin, "Dissent in a Small Community," *New England Quarterly,* LVIII (1985), 203–215.

29. *NHCR,* I, 247; *NHTR,* I, 415–416. The phrase is found at Ps. 140:3 and Rom. 3:13.

30. Elizabeth Godman v. Larremore et al. (Aug. 1653), *NHCR,* II, 31. See also the cases against Goodwives Bayley and Lines: *NHTR,* I, 245–247. Compare the judges'

If the men on the bench eschewed outright condemnations of women's unruly tongues, ordinary settlers showed they had not left behind the rich lexicon from which the English drew to describe scolding women. Thomas Langden called Mistress Tuttle "a tattelling woman"; Widow Hitchcock accused Goody Beckly of "pratling" and backbiting (and taunted her husband with the label "scold"); Edward Parker shuddered to think that formidable Lucy Brewster might question him, "for she hath a notable patte[r?]." To call a woman unjustly "a Rayler," one early jury made clear, was "slaunder . . . of a high nature." With their muted language reprimanding outspoken women, and with their damage awards to women unfairly labeled tattlers, the New Haven magistrates discouraged facile links between women and loose tongues. They did not hesitate to chide fellow magistrate Francis Newman for his aggravation of a feud between his wife and Goody Fuller. Newman had first reminded Fuller of "what she was" (he had formerly called her a scold), and then he had threatened her that "if she would not rule her tongue he must have it ruled." Here, the magistrates announced, a man who should have known better "fell short of his duty, both in not pressing the rule [of settling disputes in private] upon his wife, . . . and . . . himselfe instead of speaking healing words did unnecessaryly provoake." Cognizant of the reputation of some New England "plantations" (the fishing villages of Essex County, Massachusetts, for instance) for social disorder that revealed itself by a plague of scolding women, New Haven Colony magistrates might have believed that in their more stable, hierarchical settlements scolds would increase, not out of material conditions (in New Haven few husbands were away long at sea), but out of mimesis — a contagion kindled by the public display of powerful, outspoken women.[31] By focusing on "the rule" of godly speech that was to guide all inhabitants and by *not* encouraging the naming of scolds, colony leaders employed the comforting strategy of denying the potential existence of the most telling portent of hierarchical inversion — unruly women.

characterizations of offensive speech in men and women at *NHCR* I, 473–476, II, 164; *NHTR*, I, 414.

31. *NHTR*, I, 56, 413–414, II, 157–158, *NHCR*, I, 258, 475–476. For analysis of the ungodly conditions in early Marblehead and Gloucester, see Christine Leigh Heyrman, *Commerce and Culture: The Maritime Communities of Colonial Massachusetts, 1690–1750* (New York, 1984). The court records for Essex County show the presence of many more "scolds" than in New Haven Colony (Kamensky, "Governing the Tongue"; St. George, " 'Heated' Speech," in Hall and Allen, eds., *Seventeenth-Century New England*, 275–321).

When the Puritan legal regime of New Haven Colony ceased to exist, conceptions of slander and the importance of reputation did not change so much as the form of the legal action did. Gone were the frequent magisterial interventions urging disputants to govern conversation by biblical rules and to reconcile differences with healing words. After 1665, the procedures for entering a civil action and initiating a criminal complaint became much more distinct. Authorities were less interested in pursuing defamation as a criminal matter, civil litigants were required to specify damages in monetary terms, and the range of insults sued over narrowed to fit common law rules of actionability.[32] No longer were plaintiffs given leeway to define what words were injurious or to consult with the bench over appropriate remedies. The vague charge of being a bad neighbor could not be litigated as slander because it failed to fit within the three categories of charges that the English legal system labeled actionable: behavior proscribed by criminal law, a heinous condition (such as having an infectious disease) that would exclude a person from society, and professional incompetence. Thus if someone charged his neighbor was a fornicator or a thief, if a soldier spread the rumor that his mate was infected with the pox, or if a dissatisfied client called "a tradesman a bankrupt, a physician a quack, or a lawyer a knave," a slander suit would stand.[33]

The availability of juries after union with Connecticut Colony meant that New Haven County residents chose between two principal routes in settling a slander dispute through the courts. A sizable group of plaintiffs used the initiation of a lawsuit to cajole their adversary into settling out of court: thus the suit was withdrawn before trial. When post-1665 litigants in county or town courts chose to continue to trial, they almost always opted for a jury trial. Juries, like the magistrates sitting in summary

32. Only 1 of 41 civil litigants in the colony and town courts, 1640–1662, had named a sum—and then only when asked by the bench "what damages he expected" (James Mills v. John Thompson, "action of defamation in high degree" [May 1658], *NHCR*, II, 248, 250).

33. William Blackstone, *Commentaries on the Laws of England* (1765–1769; rpt., Chicago, 1979), III, 123. If the words did not fit one of these categories, a plaintiff's case would stand only if he or she could make a case that "special damages" had been incurred. For a full discussion of the 18th-century legal treatises on rules for slander litigation, see Cornelia Hughes Dayton, "Women before the Bar: Gender, Law, and Society in Connecticut, 1710–1790" (Ph.D. diss., Princeton University, 1986), 191–193.

judgment in the Colony period, four times out of five gave verdicts for the plaintiff. While a plaintiff who settled privately might extract a full public apology from a slanderer, the mystery in suits taken to trial revolved around what size damage award the jury would name. Consistently over the 1640–1710 period, magistrates and juries with only a few exceptions gave out awards of either five pounds or ten pounds. Despite the fact that some plaintiffs asked for double or ten times the amounts granted, an award of ten pounds was a substantial amount in the early colonial period — equivalent to two or three cows.[34] Those familiar with court tradition could have discerned coded meanings assigned to certain sums, with five pounds going to innocent, respectable citizens who had been maligned, ten pounds reserved for plaintiffs of high rank or who had been smeared with especially damaging charges, and slighting awards of sixpence handed to plaintiffs who had been technically slandered but whose notorious misbehavior had contributed to the dispute.[35]

Resort to lawyerly arguments and objections had crept into some cases as early as the mid-1650s, when a smattering of litigants requested to have an attorney argue their case. The plaintiff's team was generally at advantage because it was difficult in most cases for the defendant's attorney to establish either that the alleged slanderous words had never

34. For three examples of written acknowledgments read in court or publicly, see the following cases from 1674, 1684, and 1692, respectively: NHCC, I, 76, 146, 201–202.

For equivalencies, see Jackson Turner Main, "The Distribution of Property in Colonial Connecticut," in James Kirby Martin, ed., *The Human Dimensions of Nation Making: Essays on Colonial and Revolutionary America* (Madison, Wis., 1976), 101. The New Haven Colony Court handed down one £50 award in February 1646/7 to a former magistrate, John Evance. The town court gave out 8 awards ranging between 10s. and 40s., besides six £5 and £10 awards. In a signal that judicial officials were still sorting out how slander should be assessed in a post-Puritan regime, the bench disagreed with jury verdicts or awards five times in the 1665–1710 period.

35. William Chatterton was awarded the very low sum of sixpence even though the report raised against him by a married serving woman, Grace Mattock, was serious: rape or attempted rape. Perhaps the jurors felt that something improper (but not rape) had happened between them and Chatterton should be humiliated with a pathetically low award for his suspected dalliance while his wife was away and his threatening Grace "that if shee told of it he would knock her of the head and that shee would be hanged" (*NHTR*, II, 257). For another sixpence award in a suit over a woman's reputation as a witch, see Elizabeth Gould v. Benjamin Chittenden (Aug. 1743), SCR, XI, 189–195.

been spoken or that the words were true.[36] Thus an attorney for the plaintiff could earn his fees best by persuading the jury that his client deserved more than "other men ordinarily [received] whose business is of a narrower Compass." For the entire colonial period, men who held public office or who engaged broadly in trade justified and won the largest damage awards. Rooted in local social and economic networks and excluded from formal politics, New England women could have little hope of making large monetary claims based on "the loss of such a name."[37] Indeed, as lawyers became more frequent participants in civil litigation, as public apologies vanished as court-ordered remedies, and as the regulation of moral behavior gradually faded from the agenda of county courts, women would find themselves more and more out of place in slander litigation.

"A woman of no truth," a man "not worth a Groat," "a Lying, Cheating, Knavish Fellow," and a whore "just like her Grandmother" — these are some of the caricatured types who turn up in the angry, denunciatory speech of eighteenth-century slanderers.[38] Since writs survive for almost all eighty cases that came before the county court in the eight decades following 1710, not only can actual fragments of New Englanders' speech be overheard, but aggrieved plaintiffs can also be observed fashioning declarations of their previously unblemished reputations and their now seriously disrupted social lives.[39] We need to imagine, in addition, the invisible hand of lawyers increasingly playing a part in choosing

36. *NHTR*, I, 46, II, 136, 163; *NHCR*, II, 77, 248; Blackstone, *Commentaries*, III, 125.

37. The phrases are from a rare plaintiff's brief, or written summary of arguments, made in defense of a request for £100 in damages, to "you Gentlemen of the Jury": Capt. Samuel Eells v. Miles Merwin (Mar. 1707/8), NHCC Files, dr. 1.

38. Writs: Israel and Abigail Dayton v. Col. Thaddeus Cook (Mar. 1782), ibid., dr. 72; Ebenezer Keeny v. Eliphalet Beecher (Aug. 1762), NHSC Files, dr. 330; Samuel Tyler v. Asa Barns (Apr. 1761), NHCC Files, dr. 36; Mary Hoadley v. Jonathan and Hannah Barker (Nov. 1759), NHCC Files, dr. 24.

39. The plaintiff's declaration of the cause and damages claimed in his or her suit was incorporated into the writ served on the defendant. In New Haven, no printed forms appeared for slander writs in the 18th century; the need to write each writ manually opened the way for plaintiffs and attorneys to pick and choose among conventional phrases and insert idiosyncratic language.

language and formulaic phrases, sometimes quite distinct for male and female plaintiffs, that might persuade judges and jurors to award generous damages. The eighteenth-century writs make clear that the metaphor of the fall from social grace was central to the experience of slander in early New England. Over the century men and women came to express their vulnerability to that fall in significantly different ways.

While initiating a lawsuit to defend one's name might be of great consequence to an individual tradesman or a young woman on the brink of marriage, slander suits in the 1700s failed to increase in proportion to the steadily growing population of New Haven County. Indeed, amid mushrooming debt cases on court dockets, slander receded to near invisibility. Suits over defamation comprised 16 percent of the civil caseload between 1666 and 1675 but only 3 percent by the 1690s. In the first half of the eighteenth century, slander made up only 1 percent of all civil cases, and its share continued to drop thereafter.[40] The changing profiles of who sued and the insults that brought them into court suggest why suing over slander came to seem less satisfactory to many New Englanders over time.

First, suits brought by women declined from one-third of all slander cases in the 1666–1709 years to one-fifth in the 1760–1789 period (Table 16). Even more dramatic was the near disappearance of suits over women's words: women made up 21 percent of seventeenth-century defendants but only 6 percent of the persons sued after 1760. Second, while sexual slander loomed large at the very time that fornication prosecutions peaked — comprising nearly 40 percent of the cases heard between 1710 and 1760 — it accounted for not quite one-fifth of the suits heard between 1760 and 1790.[41] Sexual insults became particularly irrelevant for male plaintiffs, declining from one-quarter to fewer than one-eighth of men's suits.

Finally, while the bulk of charges traded between men in seventeenth-century slander disputes focused on trustworthiness in the context of a barter-based, local agrarian economy, defamatory slurs traded by men

40. See the similar figures for Plymouth Co., Mass.: William E. Nelson, *Dispute and Conflict Resolution in Plymouth County, Massachusetts, 1725–1825* (Chapel Hill, N.C., 1981), 23–24, 159 n. 64.

41. These percentages reflect suits for which the charges are documented; see Table 18. All sexual charges but one aimed at women focused on premarital affairs, whereas nearly all the accusations against men involved adultery. Female plaintiffs claimed they had been targeted with sexual slurs as frequently by men as by women while men almost exclusively named other men as their accusers in such cases.

later in the eighteenth century involved credit in business in a different sense. After 1760 men sued mostly in response to charges of bankruptcy or cheating. Thus they were suing to protect their standing in the expanding commercial economy in which credit relations were increasingly cash-infused and impersonal (see Table 18). Sometimes the speaker addressed a man's creditors directly: Jonathan Collins told a crowd on a New Haven court day, "I have sued Daniel Mckey at this Cort but I am sorrey I Did not Etach him for there will be nothing Left.... I Advize you and all he owes too to get it imeadatly or you will lose — for he owes more than he is worth." Other men who were called bankrupts suffered because their slanderer had used nearly every conceivable phrase ("He is not worth a Groat, he is not worth a penny: he is not able to pay his Debts, And he is Broake") or because it had been said that his alleged insolvency made him "a Laughing Stock for all New Haven." With such attacks on the dependability of men involved in trading, it is no wonder that plaintiffs frequently expressed worries that their "credit [was] ruined" or that "honest and worthy Persons" would "refuse to have any Dealings or Commerce" with them.[42]

Why were private citizens choosing less frequently to sue over slanderous words as the seventeenth century gave way to the eighteenth? Are we to believe that New Englanders ceased or even slowed in their tendencies to insult and spread malicious stories about one another? It might have been that, as the local community through its grand jurors began to slacken in its pursuit of philanderers, drunkards, and revilers, village denizens who before had used gossip and even slander to identify such transgressors now abandoned that effort. Even if sexual slander continued to be bandied about, potential male plaintiffs might have felt free to ignore such charges because, after 1740, grand jurors ceased to prosecute and punish young men for fathering children out of wedlock. What is plain is that the sorts of slanderous speech touching on what we today would think of as a person's *private* behavior and character — illicit sexual conduct and drunkenness, for example — were litigated only rarely after 1760. Middling to prosperous families in the more densely populated, increasingly commercial towns of late-eighteenth-century New England had evidently come to see a slander suit over such charges,

42. MacKey v. Collins (Nov. 1784), NHCC Files, dr. 74; Keeny v. Beecher (Aug. 1762), Eliphalet Beecher v. Ebenezer and Elizabeth Keeny (Aug. 1762), NHSC Files, dr. 330; Scrantom v. Benton (Apr. 1768), NHCC Files, dr. 45; Beecher v. Caldwell (Apr. 1761), NHCC Files, dr. 30.

TABLE 18

Primary Slanders in Civil Suits in the New Haven County Court,
1710–1789

| Slander | Object/Plaintiff | | | | |
| | 1710–1759 | | 1760–1789 | | |
	Men	Women	Men	Women	Total
Sexual Slander					
Cuckoldry	1	0	0	0	1
Whoremastery	3	0	0	0	3
Pox (venereal disease)	1	0	1	0	2
Adultery	0	0	1	1	2
Fornication	0	0	1	3	4
Siring/bearing bastard	1	1	1	0	3
Lascivious carriage	0	5	0	0	5
Total	6	6	4	4	20
Nonsexual Slander					
Drunkenness	2	0	0	0	2
Witchcraft	0	1	0	0	1
Treason	0	0	1	0	1
Lying	0	0	0	1	1
Perjury	2	1	9	1	13
Forgery/counterfeiting	1	0	0	0	1
Theft	7	1	7	1	16
Bankruptcy/cheating	3	0	11	0	14
Incompetence	0	0	1	0	1
Other	1	0	3	0	4
Total	16	3	32	3	54
Unknown	2	0	4	0	6
Grand total	24	9	40	7	80

Source: NHCC, Record Books and Files.

not as a remedy, but as a humiliating public event and an infringement on their privacy.[43]

Indeed, the most important shift in the relationship between slander suits and society may be the one most invisible to us: the changing nature of the "community" to whom the news of the slander and its effectual retraction mattered. In the seventeenth and early eighteenth centuries, the relevant community was the plaintiff's town and its residents, with most of whom the plaintiff was connected in multilayered relationships encompassing trade, kinship, neighborliness, town politics, and church membership. By the eve of the Revolution, as Bruce Mann has argued, these relationships had splintered so that a person's connection to a fellow townsman tended to be one-dimensional.[44] The community most concerned in post-1760 slander suits, given their preoccupation with business reputation, was no longer the entire town, but the network of men active in trade and credit. Fittingly, and perhaps not so coincidentally, this was the community most likely to endorse the concrete and symbolic importance of money as a means of defending reputation and settling disputes.

For New England women in the late eighteenth century, availing themselves of the "benefits" of the courts to preserve "a good character . . . from . . . the tongue of malice" had become a daunting and not particularly efficacious exercise. In contrast to a formal public apology, a cash payment in a slander suit was doubtless seen by many families as an inadequate response to unethical attacks on a woman's reputation.[45] But even for those women and their kin ready to accept the secular link between a ten-pound damage award and reparation of one's good name, the changed nature of the county court's business and prime constituency made a slander case there less compelling than it had been in the

---

43. Plaintiffs' lack of success was not the reason why slander suits declined in proportion to the population, at least after 1750. Between 1710 and 1750, many suits failed because the plaintiff's declaration was found to be insufficient. But after midcentury, plaintiffs and their attorneys proved adept at formulating documents that could not be objected to on grounds of technicalities or failure to allege actionable words or special damages. The 17th-century pattern of a sizable number of parties settling out of court continued through the 1750s and then disappeared until the 1780s. A slightly higher proportion of the female plaintiffs than all plaintiffs (44% compared to 38%) won their suits outright in court.

44. Bruce H. Mann, *Neighbors and Strangers: Law and Community in Early Connecticut* (Chapel Hill, N.C., 1987).

45. "Tongue of malice": Swift, *System of Laws*, I, 179.

previous century. By the mid-eighteenth century, men initiated slander litigation when damaging information on their creditworthiness reached potential creditors and economic partners "not . . . acquainted" with them or their general "conversation among men."[46] Maintaining a good character in the world of men outside their own neighborhood and town became more and more critical for propertied male householders in the commercializing economy. Women, on the other hand, with their more circumscribed networks of friends and economic activities, were likely to have less need to sue for slander in county court, since a false tale about them would be quickly investigated and discounted by acquaintances.

Under certain circumstances, however, a woman's reputation could have been seriously harmed by persistent rumors: if she sought a marriage partner outside local bounds; if she engaged in an enterprise that depended on a steady stream of clients or a reliable employer; if she were a stranger in town, or not native-born, so that the community had little knowledge of her past.[47] The predominance of sexual accusations among eighteenth-century slander suits brought by women, especially unmarried women, confirms that, as the colonial period progressed, a woman's honor rested almost entirely on her sexual reputation — at least among those for whom a county court suit mattered. Further, several New Haven slander suits brought by widows and orphaned single female boarders serve as reminders of the peculiar vulnerability of status that could pertain to a woman whose place in a male-governed household was uncertain or impermanent. As affairs of households became more privatized, as neighbors could no longer monitor or be certain what occurred within doors, single women who moved about from house to house, and from town to town, seemingly without consistent supervision, sparked unease. As we have seen, such women, who were typically associated with the lower sort and whose only prospect for attaining respectability was through successful courtship, were most vulnerable in the middle decades of the century to fornication prosecutions and suspicion of infanticide. Now we learn that they were also vulnerable to certain kinds of slanderous stories. Thus the court records throw into relief a few individual efforts — backed to some degree by community gossip and

46. Deposition of Jehiel Royce (Feb. 22, 1762), in Samuel Tyler v. Asa Barns (Feb. 1762), NHSC Files, dr. 330.

47. For examples of the latter two situations, see Robert and Ruth Fairchild v. John Wise (Apr. 1775), NHCC, VIII, 146, and Henry and Jemima Carmer v. Samuel and Mary Wilkinson (Nov. 1718), III, 94–95.

censure — to rebuke and control women whose deviance stemmed just as much from their lack of a properly dependent place within a male-headed household as from their particular behavior.[48]

Hannah Sanford was probably in her middle or late twenties when she brought her suit against Jedediah Andrews in 1748.[49] She was presently resident in New Haven, living in the household of her married brother and doing odd jobs in the neighborhood, such as tending the sick. Possibly orphaned, she had lived in "Several Parishes and Towns" in both Fairfield and New Haven counties in the previous ten years. In May and again in September 1747 Andrews, who had just recently married for a second time, told some of his neighbors about an incident involving Hannah and himself that had occurred in December 1745. Jedediah, then recently widowed, had come home very late one night; on that same day Hannah was at his house tending his children and his sick housekeeper. Andrews "got Sum refreshment," "striped to his shirt," went to his bed, and found Hannah already there. It is not clear whether Hannah ever disputed these basic points of Andrews's story.[50] What she objected to as slander were the tone, the insinuations, and the ridiculing details with which Andrews embellished the tale in his several tellings of it.

Of all the oral speech acts recorded in the New Haven slander cases, Jedediah Andrews's came the closest to resembling a lampooning libel, a sensational story that through its indulgent use of ridicule betrayed the

---

48. Interestingly, the profile that David Underdown draws of women likely to be prosecuted as scolds in 17th-century England corresponds exactly to the subset of female slander plaintiffs I have described here: women of "low status" — "women who were poor, social outcasts, widows or otherwise lacking in the protection of a family, or newcomers to their community" ("The Taming of the Scold: The Enforcement of Patriarchal Authority in Early Modern England," in Anthony Fletcher and John Stevenson, eds., *Order and Disorder in Early Modern England* [Cambridge, 1985], 120).

49. The documentation for this case is found in NHCC Files (Jan. 1747/8), dr. 19; NHSC Files (1749), dr. 327; and Conn. Archives, Private Controversies, 1st Ser., IV, 121, 133–143.

50. Deposition of Patience Horton (Feb. 13, 1748/9), NHSC Files, dr. 327; Deposition of James Sherman (May 9, 1749), Conn. Archives, Private Controversies, 1st Ser., IV, 139. Two jurors who sat on the only jury to hear this case later reported that they had *not* "found by the Evidence" the fact alleged by Andrews — that Hannah had "of her one accord" gone into the defendant's bed knowing it to be his bed (Testimony of George Clark 2nd and Caleb Smith [May 1, 1749], IV, 142).

falsity, or at least the great exaggeration, of its charges. Although the tale partook of sexual bragging, Andrews's yarn was curiously anticlimactic. In some versions of the story, Jedediah contended that he had played the virtuous (or disdainful) man: he had come innocently to bed, discovered who was there, and done "no more" before leaving the bed, dressing, and spending the night by the fire.[51] The subtext here was that he had rejected Hannah because he found her (as any man would, he implied) undesirable. In other versions, Andrews reported that, curious to find out "if it was the Devil" or "what it was" in bed with him, he "began at her head and felt down to her feet and did as much as he was amind to," finding in the process "two dryed things" like "old tobackow pouches." The rejection took a different form, however, in the version of Andrews's speech that was cited in Hannah Sanford's writ (a version that Andrews once admitted was "Indiscreet" but never denied). There Jedediah declared that after feeling Hannah all over, he got on top of her, was "Ready to Enter her bodie," but "then asked her if Shee was willing." When she replied that she "had Rather Nott," Jedediah "Did Nott Enter her."[52]

The plaintiff and her kin had a ready explanation for what would prompt Jedediah to fabricate such a sensational story imputing to Hannah immodest (if ultimately recalcitrant) conduct. Although Hannah lived with her brother and sister-in-law in New Haven, she was "sundry times before and after" the death of Andrews's first wife asked to help at his house. By the time of the December 1745 incident central to Andrews's tale, Hannah was, according to her sister-in-law, very loath to go when importuned by Jedediah. Andrews had previously let it be known that "if he desired to be in aney gals company and they refused it: that he would do the turn for them": he would tell such stories about them that they should "never be in Credit any more." And, indeed, Hannah's relatives reported, a few nights after Hannah had tended at the Andrews household, Jedediah came by, "pretending to Court" Hannah. When she "would not be in his Company," he "went away in a very grait raige." This, the Sanfords concluded, is what "maid [Andrews] . . . tel baudry stories about . . . Hannah."[53]

51. Jedediah Andrews's Petition to the General Assembly (Oct. 2, 1749), Conn. Archives, Private Controversies, 1st Ser., IV, 133.

52. Deposition of James Sherman (May 9, 1749), ibid., 139; Deposition of Patience Horton (Feb. 13, 1748/9), NHSC Files, dr. 327; Sanford v. Andrews (1748), NHCC Files, dr. 19 (writ).

53. Deposition of Esther Sanford (Feb. 13, 1748/9), NHSC Files, dr. 327; Joint

Where the Sanfords' version of events was a story about sexual harassment, Andrews's rebuttal painted the tableau of the eligible widower
entrapped by a "light Cariaged girl." His niece-housekeeper testified
that Hannah had "signified" to her that she thought "she should have
my uncle [in marriage]." Moreover, Andrews persuaded two married
couples from New Haven to depose that Hannah "put her Self in the way
of Jedediah Andrews in the time of his widowhood and that she had a
desier to have him as it apeard to them by her Conduct."[54] As for Jedediah's own attitude in the same period, he told the legislature that he
"was Weary of her," that it was "the Woman [who] was thus first in the
Transgression," and that they should regard Hannah as "highly faulty
Shameful and fraudulously Immodest to Lye in Wait" for "your unwary
Petitioner." Finally, Andrews argued that Hannah's behavior toward him
and her general reputation "among the Young People" meant that "She
had not that Caracter to be hurt and defamed."[55]

Hannah evidently was the type of young woman who attracted suspicion in each town she lived in.[56] Townspeople's skepticism about her
character probably served to make Jedediah Andrews's version of events
plausible to those who did not know Hannah well and to prevent the
Sanfords from effectively squelching the story before a lawsuit was
needed. The community, after all, served as a crucial third party in
slander incidents such as this one, not just in its role as audience but also
in its role as *creator* of the legal injury. Even before witnesses and jurors
played their official roles in court as representatives of community, the
community members faced the choice of entirely discounting Jedediah

---

deposition of Esther and Stephen Sanford (May 9, 1749), Conn. Archives, Private
Controversies, 1st Ser., IV, 138.

54. Deposition of Lydia Northrop (May 11, 1749), Conn. Archives, Private Controversies, 1st Ser., IV, 135; Joint deposition of Samuel Alling et al. (May 11, 1749),
136. In a secondary approach, Andrews argued that, when he had "dismissed"
Sanford from tending his family, she "took Umbrage (and from Nothing Else)"
began to frequent his house and "Ingratiate herself with his Children" (Petition to
the General Assembly dated Mar. 8, 1748/9, 121).

55. Andrews's Petitions (Mar. 8, 1748/9, Oct. 2, 1749), ibid., 121, 133. Andrews
also held himself blameless for speaking out about Hannah: he was "in no wise guilty
of" acting out of "Malice Envy and Revenge," he told the Assembly, but had been
"induced and bad[?] into the Discourse about her by the Designs, Device, and
Artifice of her Brother (Seeking as your Petitioner apprehends, to Ensnare and
expose him to an action[)]" (121).

56. For example, see Joint deposition of George Clinton and Esther Washbond
(May 11, 1749), ibid., 137.

Andrews's reiterated tale or permitting the report to alter their esteem for and relations with Hannah Sanford.

When Hannah and Jedediah presented their two versions in court, however, Andrews lost on each of five occasions.[57] His technical objections to the writ were insufficient, his speech against Hannah revealed him to be an insolent blusterer, and his witnesses evidently were neither as persuasive nor as numerous as Hannah's. Two men from the jury that awarded Hannah damages in the case's last round in the Superior Court testified when Andrews renewed the case before the Assembly. Asked by Andrews "Whether the Jewry took the Carecter" of Hannah Sanford to "Stand Good notwithstanding the Evidences alleged against her," the jurors "replyd they took it to Stand Good." And when Andrews tried to claim that he had found new evidence to prove Hannah's loose character, she responded by putting the issue before the members of her church. In May 1749, a full two years after Jedediah Andrews began to circulate his sensational story about Hannah, Benjamin Woodbridge, the minister for Amity, recorded "the sentiments" and "Recommendation" of the church "in Regard" to Hannah:

> We have Looked upon her as a person harmles in her Life, one that minded the best things and walked agreeable to her profession: we had never Known or Looked upon her as a person vicious in her practice or scandalous in her Life and Conversation or So much as heard any such thing of her till the Scandalous Report that Come from Jedidiah Andrews and She is still in full Communion with us.[58]

One of the most striking features of the dispute is Jedediah's persistence in trying to overturn the court decisions in favor of Hannah, or at least to obtain relief from what he argued were unfair damages. Part of the explanation is a factor that, in interpreting most lawsuits, we can rarely discern—Jedediah Andrews's personality. Just four years after Andrews brought his final petition to protest the outcome of the slander suit, his wife Elizabeth took the desperate action of bringing a complaint

57. The suit was heard twice by the New Haven County Court before being appealed to the Superior Court and the General Assembly. It elicited the testimony of at least 30 persons.

58. Both the jurors' testimony (dated May 1, 1749) and the church recommendation (dated May 11, 1749) are found in Conn. Archives, Private Controversies, 1st Ser., IV, 140, 142. The recommendation was drawn up by the Reverend Mr. Woodbridge and then "Read to the Church after a publick Lecture."

of abuse against him. She reported that her husband had "for a long Time past used and abused her very cruelly," sometimes throwing her down on the floor and stamping on her body, threatening to kill her with his knife, cursing and warning "that he would send her Soul to Hell," and finally turning her "out of Doors." In 1753, Elizabeth concluded that Jedediah, in "his wicked and vicious Way of Living . . . seems to be given up to all Manner of Evil and wholly void of the Fear of God."[59] It may well be that six years earlier, when Andrews told his satiric, lascivious tale about Hannah Sanford, the community already had an inkling of his vicious temperament. If indeed Andrews had a recurring tendency to abuse women, his aggressive unrepentance in the Sanford case reveals that he depended on two sources for exoneration: the authority of a man's word or version of events over a woman's, and the casting of the woman as "first in transgression." In the case of Hannah Sanford, Andrews's strategy of manipulating the stereotype of the immodest, calculating girl drew its potency from the society's general policy of punishing young single women alone for sexual transgressions.

That Andrews lost his bid and that Sanford's damages were upheld demonstrates that the double standard was not all-pervasive: New England communities in the eighteenth century *did* recognize and impose limits on men's sexual exploits and bragging, and they *would* act to guard the reputation of a woman whom the majority believed had been unjustly maligned. The role played by the double standard was in creating a climate in which certain men like Jedediah Andrews assumed the license to ruin a young woman's reputation through a tall tale and, further, in which certain unattached young women like Hannah Sanford, whether through their flirtatious behavior or their uncertain status, attracted enough suspicion to make misconduct charges plausible and to necessitate a lawsuit. Sanford paid a high price for the eventually successful outcome of her efforts: she endured the frequent retelling in courtrooms of a sexually explicit and satiric story about herself over a period of two years, and she put herself and her relatives at risk for the large bill of costs run up in the critical enlistment of a large number of witnesses to testify in her favor.[60]

59. Rex v. Jedediah Andrews (Nov. 1753), NHCC Files, dr. 27. At the time of Elizabeth's complaint (August 1753), she had been married to Andrews for seven years, and they had a five-month-old baby and a two-year-old son.

60. When Andrews's petition was finally negatived by the General Assembly in May 1750, the costs had mounted up to more than £40 (whether old or new tenor is

Clearly, the greatest danger in a slander episode for women like Hannah Sanford resided in its potential to displace them from social acceptance and community networks. In Sanford's case, the chief worry was that she would never marry. In the wake of Jedediah's storytelling, Sanford claimed that she had been "utterly Neglected by Young men of fasion and Credit who used to Court her for marriage." For Roxanna Frisbie, suing over slander in 1781, the focus of her complaint needed to be trained on her ability to transact "her Business and Affairs." Frisbie was the only female plaintiff in the New Haven slander cases to be identified as plying a trade. During three months in 1780 the twenty-three-year-old had "kept a School" in her home town of Branford, during which time a Branford man had begun to spread rumors that she stole from the men in whose households she boarded. Poor and orphaned, Roxanna could retain a place in the community only by boarding with other families.[61] The business of keeping a school for a young woman was interchangeable with other seasonal and intermittent wagework, such as sewing, tending, and housekeeping. Thus to be charged with repeated stealing from the families with whom she dwelt was a very serious matter: it threatened to dislodge her from the community entirely.

Hannah Sanford's and Roxanna Frisbie's cases are unusual in that the young women, while not bereft of kin, had no parents supervising their employment or legal strategies. Parents defending family honor played a central role in a series of slander cases brought by New Haven County women who saw their marriage chances threatened. The level of prosperity and social prestige that a woman could hope to achieve in her adult life was determined by the man she married in her youth; a good match could mean a step up in the social ranks for a family of modest origin. Eighteen-year-old Eunice Heaton sued in part because a particular young man "of good fame and Credit" had "forsaken her Company and Conversation" on account of the charge of fornication laid to her.

---

not noted): *PR*, IX, 544. In her analysis of the role of gossip and defamation in villages in early modern England, Susan Dwyer Amussen comes to several of the same conclusions drawn in this paragraph; see her essay, "Feminin/masculin: Le genre dans l'Angleterre de l'epoque moderne," *Annales: Economies, sociétés, civilisations*, XL (1985), 271, 273, 282.

61. Sanford v. Andrews (Jan. 1747/8), NHCC Files, dr. 19 (writ); Roxanna Frisbie v. Samuel Hoadley (Jan. 1781), dr. 66. There are no marriages recorded for either Sanford or Frisbie in county records. Frisbie had lost her father at the age of 3 and her mother at 16.

Molly Hoadley's father brought three suits on her behalf against a wide-ranging panoply of cousins who had spread salacious stories about Molly.[62] Hoadley was clearly using the glaring public nature of sensational slander trials to score points in a bitter family feud. But that some yeoman families would take on the cost and risk of these suits suggests a genuine fear of being associated with families known to include "whoring" women who produced illegitimate children in successive generations. Despite the prevalence of premarital fornication, there might indeed have been a segment of society—one that remains indistinct to us—concerned to differentiate itself from the sort it perceived to be less than respectable.

Sensational sexual detail might have been another factor propelling families to submit their cases for a woman's good name to a jury. Parents and newly married couples did not bother to sue when rumors circulated about a young woman's routine sexual relations with her husband before marriage. But talk charging that a woman had had sex at a very young age or carried on a liaison with "a negro" and covered it up was deemed highly dangerous. Jemima Carmer was slurred as a "whore" because she "had a bastard child at 14 years of age." The label "Negro Whore" stuck to newly married Mary Lewis when the story got around that she "had to do with a Negro and was carried to the Post for it and was stripped to be Whipp'd and She then declar'd that she was with child by the said Negro and that screen'd her." One of the stories circulated about eighteen-year-old Molly Hoadley shared in the sort of deadpan, satirical reportage that Jedediah Andrews had indulged in when weaving tales at Hannah Sanford's expense. Molly's cousin told "diverse" persons a story in two parts. First, she recounted, her brother Samuel had slept in the same bed with the two young cousins and that night he had "Shug'd" Molly. Afterward, "Mo[ll] Came to me and ask'd if I thought She was with Child, She told me he didn't put it in above an Inch."[63]

Not only did the young New Haven women who sued over sexual slander win awards, but most of them married soon after their suits were

62. Eunice Heaton v. John Cotter (Feb. 1755), NHSC Files, dr. 329 (writ). Heaton won a £10 award. For the three suits brought in the name of Mary Hoadley, see NHCC, V, 148, 243.

63. Henry and Jemima Carmer v. Samuel and Mary Wilkinson (Nov. 1718), NHCC Files, dr. 1 (writ); Jacob and Mary Lewis v. Moses and Mary Blakeslee (Nov. 1780), dr. 66 (writ); Mary Hoadley v. Lucy Barker (Nov. 1747), dr. 24. The *OED* gives the following meaning for the verb *shug*: "To force one's way, shove in"; *shug* was a variant of *shog*, a verb which meant "to shake."

resolved. For a handful of county families, then, a costly defamation case over salacious words had proven effective in clearing the family name and ratifying a young woman's place in her community. In contrast, women who sued over nonsexual slander were not only less able to detail concretely the nature of their losses, but they also chose not to litigate insults that touched directly on their economic activities and competency. Although men often sued because they had been charged with cheating or incompetence at their trade or profession, no women did so. Moreover, women were prompted to sue when *men* accused them of theft, perjury, or witchcraft, not when other women did so. Yet disputes undoubtedly arose between women and the female neighbors with whom they traded. Evidently these disputes did not engender the types of spiraling interpersonal conflict that we have imagined lay behind slander suits. Damning words growing out of economic disputes were aimed at those persons who represented the basic unit of production in the society—male heads of household.

When impugned in ways that would damage their ability to operate in the rural economy, women addressed the injury more obliquely than did men, revealing a distinctly female understanding of how credit was gained and lost. Men suing over such charges as bankruptcy or theft made direct claims that their "Credit [was] ruined" and that they had "lost the Advantages of those gains and profits" that their good reputations had made possible.[64] In contrast, women whose trustworthiness was attacked made no reference to "Credit" as it related to one's ability to finance purchases and accumulate wealth. Instead, they located their losses in the realm of social intercourse. Widow Elizabeth Gould, for example, insisted that the slanderous words spoken against her in 1742 (an accusation of witchcraft) threatened "to Deprive her of the Society, Traffic, and both pleasant and Necessary Converse of her Neighbours" and inhabitants of her parish. Here, Gould neatly blended a portrait of losses in the social realm with a fleeting acknowledgment of the damage done to her economic dealings ("Traffic") so vital to her livelihood. Forty years later, Abigail Dayton, having been called "a Thief and a Lyer," asserted that not only her "good name" was "greatly hurt" but that she was also "in danger of loosing the favour, friendship and Fellowship of . . . her friends and acquaintance." In this case, the formula of loss drawn up by the plaintiff's lawyer denied that Abigail had any economic

---

64. Nathan Scrantom v. Silas Benton (Apr. 1768), ibid., dr. 45 (writ); Stephen Howell, Jr. v. John Eliot et al. (Aug. 1748), NHSC Files, dr. 16 (writ).

power or agency within her household or community that could suffer damage.[65]

What distinguished women's from men's descriptions of the disruption that nonsexual slander portended in their lives was the absence of a vocabulary that acknowledged the important role played by women's work and the female economy in the economic prosperity of every household. If a New England housewife found herself deserted by the female friends who throughout the seasons bartered, baked, spun, and tended with her, she would be severely hampered in her ability to fulfill the supportive, wifely role of domestic household manager — a role essential to her husband's own ability to "gain great profits" at his calling. As another mark of the invisibility of women's work in public documents, the conventional phrases of these writs herald the creeping acceptance of a sensibility that sentimentalized and mystified women's role in the household.[66]

Words uttered in anger, phrases penned in ridicule: these are the central artifacts remaining to us of those acts of communication that New Englanders perceived as slanderous. The details of eighteenth-century writs often reveal a speaker's pose, tone, and intent and thus illuminate important differences in how men and women used gossip and slander. Most intriguing is the age gap between male and female defendants. For the eighteenth-century cases, the median age for male defendants (with known ages) was thirty-six while for women it was forty-nine. Whereas not one of the female defendants had spoken out against a person older than herself, at least twelve male defendants were young men who had spoken against an older man (by eight to thirty-four years). For these young men, spreading charges of cheating or bankruptcy might have been a way of expressing envy at an elder's power and resources or frustration at one's own lack of advancement. More broadly, in their aggressiveness these youths called attention to their exclusively male right to participate in public affairs; in essence they were laying claim to a share in older men's power. The absence of suits between young women and older adults might disguise the fact that youthful women engaged in critical or angry talk about their elders and were either simply ignored or chastised with-

65. Elizabeth Gould v. Benjamin Chittenden (Apr. 1742), NHCC Files, dr. 15 (writ); Israel and Abigail Dayton v. Thaddeus Cook (Mar. 1782), dr. 72 (writ).

66. For an argument that women's work was increasingly devalued after the late 17th century in the northern colonies, see Jeanne Boydston, *Home and Work: Housework, Wages, and the Ideology of Labor in the Early Republic* (New York, 1990).

out recourse to a lawsuit. However, it is worth considering an alternative explanation: although young men were not entirely intimidated from challenging or insulting their male elders, young women in eighteenth-century New England might have generally abided by the social taboo against expressing such disrespect.[67] After all, their culture offered them no models or concepts that legitimated their giving voice to desires for power or autonomy in their lives — the sorts of desires that lay behind young men's expressions of anger, grievance, and competition.

The eighteenth-century New Haven cases reveal two further notable divergences in the styles and modes of speech used by the men and women who were cast as slanderers. First, although one-third of the men made their accusations to the plaintiff's face, none of the female defendants used this technique. Second, more than a third of the men — but again none of the women — added some phrase to their accusation that drew attention back to themselves and particularly to their boldness in speaking out publicly. Some of these phrases were small shows of bravado that served to imbue the scene with heightened drama. Traveling along the road with Daniel Barker and other men, Samuel Pond told Barker that he, Pond, had "been as far into" Barker's wife as Barker ever had been and confirmed it by "wishing if it were not all true" he would "not go one Rod further" down the road. Elihu Hall, a colonel and former justice of the peace, publicly accused an older man, William Carter, in words that echoed a judicial sentence: "You are a thief and a Robber and deserve to be hanged; . . . I dare to publish it to the world, and don't care who hears me say so."[68]

A few men used a gesture to make the target of their anger unmistakable. In a Guilford tavern, "warm discourse" broke out between an itinerant peddler, Joseph Parmenter, and townsman William Leet, who was negotiating to buy a horsewhip from Parmenter. Leet became convinced that the peddler had slyly pocketed some money Leet had put out on the table. Witnesses recalled that, in making the accusation of theft, "Leet put forth his hand and took Parmenter by the face." In another consciously theatrical public performance, one man took another "by the hand" and declared, "Here is the Captain of Amity, this is Amity Cap-

67. For perceptive comments on the gendered patterns of childhood socialization of speech in early New England, see Kamensky, "Governing the Tongue," 32–38.

68. The scene involving Barker and Pond is described in the NHCC Files for both Rex v. Samuel Pond (Apr. 1712), dr. 3, and Barker v. Pond (Apr. 1712), dr. 1. Carter v. Hall (Jan. 1776), dr. 62.

tain" (referring to the man's militia rank) and "he is a perjured Lying Rogue."[69]

Rather than hurling colorful epithets, the slanderers who are revealed in eighteenth-century writs commonly expressed their anger and contempt through such forms as tale-telling, professional criticism, satire, and personal protest.[70] The speaker almost always conveyed his distress through repetition, whether his statement was short and pungent (as in, "That is false what you say[.] It is false What you say"), or a long litany of his target's faults. Some simply used the first person reiteratively to underscore their act of speaking out: "And I will Say, I *Do* Say: I believe [you stole the money]," asserted John Wooden, Jr. The most common phrase appended to accusations took the form of a dare: "And I can prove it," twelve men reportedly said, with one of them adding, "and I challenge him to sew me."[71]

This evidence suggests that men and women in eighteenth-century New England managed personal conflict in quite distinct ways. The impulse to turn a rebuke into a personal contest, and, indeed, explicitly to invite a showdown on issues of proof in the public arena of the court-

69. Deposition of Reliance Bradley (Nov. 12, 1747), in Parmenter v. Leet, ibid., dr. 18; Barnabas Baldwin v. Benjamin Bunnell (Jan. 1752), dr. 20 (writ).

70. Satire, ridicule, and even parody characterized two of the four libels that are included in the post-1710 slander caseload. The "Paper, Callendar [or] Advertisement" posted by three young men to ridicule Stephen Howell read, in part: "Lost or naughtily taken away from Stephen Howell, Jr., of New Haven . . . Merchant, his character or Reputation valued at four pounds Cash old Tenour . . . and whoever Shall overtake said Character and Return the same to the said Howell shall have 13 pence Halfpenny Sterling, Hangmans Wages as a bountiful Reward and no Questions asked" (Howell v. John Eliot et al. [Aug. 1748], NHSC Files, dr. 327). By far the most creative and enterprising libeler, Samuel Royce not only posted his two verses aimed at tavernkeeper Enos Atwater, but he also had his children learn "the obcene Lible" "by Heart" and sing it "whenever the Plaintiff or any of his Family" came into view. The verses were full of veiled allusions to various lawsuits and controversies involving Atwater. The opening verse offers a glimpse of the meter and rhyme pattern that the composer roughly maintained throughout: "There was one Squire Night Cap / a Man of Great Renown / and he is the most Last [Laught] about / of ane a Man in Town" (Atwater v. Royce [Apr. 1775], NHCC Files, dr. 61).

71. Joseph Wilford v. Amos Thompson (Jan. 1785), NHCC Files, dr. 74 (writ). For litanies, see John Alling v. Edward Melloy (Apr. 1760), dr. 30 (writ), and Theophilus Merriman v. Eliakim Hall (Apr. 1775), dr. 60 (writ). For first person and dares, see John Hotchkiss v. John Wooden, Jr. (Aug. 1762), NHSC Files, dr. 330; Baldwin v. Bunnell (Jan. 1752), NHCC Files, dr. 20.

room, appears to have been a distinctly male mode of behavior. Women passed on damning information behind the scenes, rarely choosing to confront their target. They appear less concerned with inflating their own reputations when they put someone else down and thus less engaged in overt competition.[72] According to the writs quoting the speech of women sued for slander in eighteenth-century New Haven County, none had used the second person, as in, "You are a thief"; rather, these women had told their stories or expressed their grievances deliberately to audiences who could challenge and debate the story on the spot and later could relay the information to the target.[73] The closest incident to a direct confrontation involved widow Elizabeth Bishop, who pointed her target out on one occasion to a group gathered in a New Haven street: "There is the man . . . that I Saw have carnel knowledge of old Lidia Monk [in my house one night]."[74] Perhaps women, not accustomed to playing the public role of grand jurors, believed that they could circulate damaging stories within their communities effectively but, nonetheless, without being drawn into further court battles. In other words, women might have used damning words *as if they were gossip* and not a category of speech that made the speaker legally liable. Finally, the female mode of contributing to the community's stock of information about someone's reputation was akin to the dominant pattern seen in seventeenth-century male and female slander defendants who passed on reports to solicit the most truthful version. Tied to the Puritan philosophy of placing communal concerns before personal ones, the persistence of this mode of speech among women reinforces other evidence, drawn from patterns in eighteenth-century debt and fornication cases, illustrating diverging male and female spheres.

In the realm of sexual slander, men's and women's divergent styles reflected their different purposes. Men's accusations of female promis-

---

72. St. George, "'Heated' Speech," in Hall and Allen, eds., *Seventeenth-Century New England,* 308. On men's narcissistic speech, see Demos, "Shame and Guilt in Early New England," in Stearns and Stearns, eds., *Emotion and Social Change,* 73–75.

73. When widow Mehitable Whitehead, "in discourse with" Edward Frisbie and others at a deacon's house, claimed that her peer Micah Palmer (age 45) had wronged her in administering an estate and had "feathered his nest," the company present gave her "some reproof" (Palmer v. Whitehead [Nov. 1716], NHCC Files, dr. 2 [writ]).

74. Joel Tharp v. Elizabeth Bishop (Jan. 1782), NHCC Files, dr. 72 (writ). Bishop repeated the story on several other occasions at which Tharp was neither present nor in sight.

cuity often took the form of bragging about their own sexual performance with a single woman. Jedediah Andrews's tale of finding Hannah Sanford in his bed was a variant of this theme. Nineteen-year-old Samuel Barker's speech was a more straightforward case of a youth showing off, claiming: "I Lay with Moll: Hoadley. I Strip'd her up to the Navel, and Catch'd her private parts." John Cotter (in his late twenties and as yet unmarried) told a married man: "I wonder Eunice Heaton is not with Child, for I have done as much to get her with Child as ever You did to get your wife with Child."[75]

Women, in attacking another woman's sexual reputation, were often spreading cautionary tales about in-laws or newcomers who they feared were disreputable. Forty-nine-year-old Hannah Barker slandered her niece because she was concerned that the teenager's mother, Hannah's sister, had married into a family of "whores." Matron Mary Wilkinson warned a group of "diverse worthy persons" (five women and one man) that whoring, bastardy, and miscegenation were part of the past of Jemima Carmer; Carmer and her husband had just arrived in Milford from New York City.[76] These women were in effect playing out a role that fell to women in traditional village societies: that of keepers of memory and history, especially concerning the sexual lives of women. Where men's use of sexual slander against women reflected their personal concerns — vindictiveness, for example, or insecurity over their own virility and masculine image — women spoke out as the unofficial guardians and judges of female sexuality.[77] A sense of history, then, and an understanding of female reputation as extending beyond self to mothers and daughters, to female ancestors and posterity, informed the sexual slurs traded among women.

Women's avoidance of expressing even limited self-centered rage at male authority figures in the eighteenth century emerges in contempt

75. Mary Hoadley v. Samuel Barker (Nov. 1757), NHCC Files, dr. 24 (writ); Eunice Heaton v. John Cotter (Feb. 1755), NHSC Files, dr. 329 (writ).

76. Mary Hoadley v. Jonathan and Hannah Barker (Nov. 1757), NHCC Files, dr. 24. In the Carmer case, the plaintiffs withdrew the action after the bench ruled that the writ was insufficient, because the words "were spoken as an hearsay and not spoken positively" and thus were not actionable (Henry and Jemima Carmer v. Samuel and Mary Wilkinson [Nov. 1718], dr. 1).

77. On women's gossip as history, see Susan Harding, "Women and Words in a Spanish Village," in Rayna R. Reiter, ed., *Toward an Anthropology of Women* (New York, 1975), 298. For a lucid statement of the role of older women in guarding and controlling female sexuality, see Ulrich, *Good Wives*, chap. 5, esp. 98, 103.

prosecutions. In the thirty or so New Haven County Court cases involving physical resistance to officers or verbal defiance of judges between 1710 and 1790, only two women appeared as active resisters. Unlike seventeenth-century female dissenters such as Anne Hutchinson, Anne Eaton, and Lucy Brewster who argued with judges on the basis of their individual intellectual and religious convictions, New Haven's eighteenth-century women resisters presented authorities with carefully calculated rationalizations of their behavior.[78] These constructions were meant to deflect attention from the woman's autonomous act of defiance to her embeddedness in family obligations and the weaknesses of her sex.

Anglican Susanna Walstone was accused in June 1730 along with her husband Thomas and their four daughters of using "Threatning words, Turbulent behavior, and actual violence" to resist the town rate collectors. Although criminal charges against the pregnant Susanna were dropped, she spearheaded the family's efforts to release Thomas from jail and to seek vindication for their perception that local officers had colluded to see that this Church of England adherent would "get no Justis." "By word of mouth and by writing," Susanna Walstone petitioned authorities at three levels of the legal system for due process. Borrowing from liturgical phrasing, Susanna declared to the General Assembly, "Now Gentelmen . . . I will be bold to say that [this treatment] tis inconsistent with the Rule of the Gospel and the law of the Nation to which we owe our Obedience." Despite her forthright appeal and her persistence, Susanna deliberately used respectful language, cast herself as a concerned wife and mother, and played on her alleged ignorance that the collectors, one with his "formidable great stauf," were officers.[79]

78. The light 18th-century caseload for contempt contrasts with 57 similar prosecutions in the county court between 1666 and 1710 (9 involved women) and at least 40 persons (almost all men) reprimanded before colony and town magistrates during the Colony period.

For a modern interpretation of the Anne Hutchinson affair, see Kamensky, "Governing the Tongue," chap. 3. On the excommunication of Eaton, wife of Governor Theophilus Eaton, see Newman Smyth, ed., "Mrs. Eaton's Trial (in 1644): As It Appears upon the Records of the First Church of New Haven," New Haven Colony Historical Society, *Papers,* V (1894), 133–148; *NHCR,* I, 268–270; Handlin, "Dissent in a Small Community," *New England Quarterly,* LVIII (1985), 193–220; and Isabel M. Calder, *The New Haven Colony* (1934; rpt., New Haven, 1970), 93. On the case against Brewster, see above, this chapter, and Lyle Koehler, *A Search for Power: The "Weaker Sex" in Seventeenth-Century New England* (Urbana, Ill., 1980), 242.

79. Complaint dated June 17, 1730, Rex v. Thomas Walstone et al., NHCC Files, dr. 11; Petition of Susanna Walstone (Oct. 18, 1732), Conn. Archives, Crimes and

Similarly, widow Rebecca English claimed that she did not know that the two men who came to her door one night demanding to see her boarder, Mary Veal, "ware offerseers or had any power to atach the body" of Veal. The widow had become outraged when the men laid "viollant hands" on Veal, "pulling hur acros the sill of the dore," stripping her "coats" off. "Upon . . . surpriseing such disorder in my house . . . and thinking myself in duty bound to ceep good orders in my house as governes theirof I maid resistanc by laying hold of the abused party and commanding those that had been guilty of such unsufillity [incivility] to forbair and goe out of my house or be orderly thierin." When prosecuted for this act of resistance, the widow's protestation that any transgression of the laws on her part might be imputed to her "womanish ignorance" was disingenuous, since she had, surely wittingly, called the constable "dog etc." and prevented the abusive man and his deputy from making the arrest.[80] Although the bench did not accept English's plea, fining her twenty shillings, her fashioning of dual arguments resting on both her obligation as a temporary household head and her sex's attenuation from the realm of laws and politics signaled the pressure that eighteenth-century New England women were under to conform to subordinate, domestic, and largely silent roles.

One final gender distinction emerges in the eighteenth-century slander writs in the ways in which slander plaintiffs and their lawyers described the impact of slander—the fall from social acceptance into "Shame, Infamy, and Disgrace."[81] Not unexpectedly, men, whether tarred with bankruptcy or marital infidelity, emphasized the material losses that were engendered by ruptures in social relations: loss of custom, trading partners, and credit sources, all crucial sources of livelihood. Young women stressed their displacement in the marriage market while older women felt most threatened by being cut off from the society and traffic of their neighbors. What is surprising are the extraordinarily dramatic images of social rejection and exclusion that manifest themselves principally in women's declarations. The smaller geographic range of a woman's social world often protected her from rumors that

---

Misdemeanors, 1st Ser., III, 163; Petition of Susanna Walstone to Nov. 1731 New Haven County Court, NHCC Files, dr. 11.

80. Rex v. Rebecca English (Jan. 1728/9), NHCC, III, 283, NHCC Files, dr. 6. Mary Veal had been convicted of adultery in 1715, branded on the forehead, and required from thenceforth to wear a halter. For the case, see Chapter 4, above.

81. John MacKey v. Elnathan Beech (Apr. 1742 adjourned), NHCC Files, dr. 17 (writ).

became slanderous, but ironically the insularity of that world meant that the consequences of ostracism were dire. Whereas a community could not afford to isolate a male household head entirely, the fears expressed on behalf of women in some slander writs suggest that, since women were dependents, under the wing of a male-governed family, society might choose to dispense with all ties to them.

For men, what was put in jeopardy by "the blemish of scandal" was the security of economic and social place already attained by the plaintiff, along with his ambitions for further prosperity. Although occasionally writs pictured a fictional image of catastrophic loss — of such exclusion from the economic community that the slandered man could no longer make a living — most male plaintiffs formulated their fears of the effect of slander in more realistic ways: as sudden reversal, as an interruption in their careers, as a rent in the social fabric that bound their lives, as displacement from the rank that they had earned through age and hard work.[82] Moses Sanford went so far as to claim that the charge of being found "in a Close hug" with a "Negro Wench" threatened "to reduce him to Want and Indigence" and "Poverty." But most men stressed that defamation interrupted their *ascent* "in the world among men." Vital to the good reputation that had permitted farmers and merchants to acquire "a Large and Plentifull Estate" or gain "a reputable Living with great Profit" were such attributes as: "fulfill[ing] . . . Faith, Contracts and promises in All . . . transactions relating to his Trade," paying debts "with Honour and punctuallity without any appearance . . . of Breaking," "not [being] addicted to any Particular Vice," and possessing the "great Trust and Confidence" of "divers subjects."[83] For slandered men, the lawyers drafting their declarations, and the communities that sat in judgment on their reputations, the central issue was whether their earned place in society was being threatened unjustly or whether they had through immoral conduct forfeited it.

82. Merchant Stephen Howell, Jr., and taverner Abel Merriman included the same phrase in their writs, 19 years apart: each claimed that the slander was intended to "deprive him of the Means of sustaining himself and Family" (Howell v. Eliot et al. [Feb. 1747/8], NHSC Files, dr. 16; Abel Merriman v. Yale Bishop [Apr. 1767], NHCC Files, dr. 327).

83. Moses Sanford v. Edward Allen (Nov. 1779), NHCC Files, dr. 65 (writ); Deposition of Jehiel Royce (Feb. 22, 1762), in Samuel Tyler v. Asa Barns (Feb. 1762), NHSC Files, dr. 330; Keeny v. Beecher (1762), NHSC Files, dr. 330 (writ); Howell v. Eliot et al. (1748), NHCC Files, dr. 16 (writ); Scrantom v. Benton (1768), NHCC Files, dr. 45 (writ).

Phrases painting a visceral portrait of the utter contempt and rejection visited upon the slandered plaintiff appeared in women's declarations from the 1740s on. Molly Hoadley worried not only that she had lost "her preferment" in marriage but also that the story would "Render her so odious to all the good Subjects" of the colony "that they should have nothing to do with her." Mary Lewis claimed that her friends had already "forsaken her." Widow Gould asserted that in the wake of the witchcraft charge she not only had been brought into "Abhorrence" but had actually been "vexed, Grieved, and Molested" by members of her community. And most dramatically, young Eunice Heaton reported that, because of the scandalous report circulating about her, she was "hissed at by her Neighbours."[84] Roxanna Frisbie, the young, single schoolteacher, made most manifest the threat of denial of place that could be embodied in slanderous speech against a woman. Frisbie claimed that the malicious accusation against her would not only cause "good" people to think of her as a thief but that they would also refuse to "imploy her and her said Business." "Nor [would they] entertain her, or Suffer her to live in their Houses and Families; or trade or deal, or *have any Thing to do with her.*"[85]

Two writs thirty years apart contain the phrase that most starkly revealed the nature of the rejection anticipated by these maligned women. In 1753 young Eunice Heaton declared in anguish that, because of the slur of fornication upon her, she was "accounted the ofscouring of her Sex." And in 1781, stung by the charge of perjury and theft, Abigail Dayton lamented that, to her "great and Grievous Wrong," henceforth she would be "treated as the Offscouring of the World." "Offscouring" was a word Scripture-suffused New Englanders would know from two books in the Bible, the Lamentations of Jeremiah and the First Epistle of Paul to the Corinthians. Those biblical texts offered up the potent word as a description of frail human beings caught and suffering in the contexts of defamation, shame, and punishment.[86] That the word was

84. Hoadly v. Barker (Nov. 1757), NHCC Files, dr. 24; Jacob and Mary Lewis v. Moses and Mary Blakeslee (Nov. 1780), dr. 66; Gould v. Chittenden (Apr. 1742), dr. 15. The words "forsaken" and "molested," in addition to Gould's "Abhorrence," were all found only in women's writs and not once in men's declarations. These phrases echo the Bible; see Job 27:23, Zeph. 2:15, 2 Cor. 4:9. "Hissed at" was first used by a woman in 1755; it appeared in a man's declaration in 1787: Charles Hall v. Moses Gaylord (Nov. 1787), dr. 79.

85. My emphasis (Roxanna Frisbie v. Samuel Hoadley [Jan. 1781], ibid., dr. 66).

86. Eunice Heaton v. John Cotter (Feb. 1755), NHSC Files, dr. 329 (writ); Israel and Abigail Dayton v. Thaddeus Cook (Mar. 1782), NHCC Files, dr. 72 (writ). The

chosen for women's eighteenth-century slander declarations suggests that religious vocabulary shaped both society's perceptions and individual women's understandings of female shame in ways that no longer held for most men in the society. Indeed, the intense anticipation of shame and the deep anxiety over rejection that reverberated in the writs of female slander plaintiffs suggest a divergence in male and female ethics in the decades after Puritan enthusiasm had waned. It is as if women continued to be judged — even chose to be judged — in religious terms while the society commenced to measure men's characters in a more secular mode.

The distinct rhetorical patterns in men's and women's slander writs, whether accurate reflections of the most extreme effects of slander or merely gender-based, linguistic conventions, implied that, while loss of reputation for a woman could mean forfeiture of all standing in her community and loss of human dignity, slander caused a man to suffer diminution of rank but not all-encompassing, utter rejection. In the realm of slander litigation, then, as well as in the realm of prosecutions for sexual misconduct, the court records reveal a movement in New England culture toward a middle-class ideology that would demand complete moral virtue from women while tolerating gradations of moral probity in the ranks of men. Virtue had not yet become an attribute attached exclusively to the female sex; it was still an essential asset to men with ambitions for high social rank and material success. To men, slanderous ascription with immoral activities brought them into "Detestation" and "Disesteem," "Mistrust and Discredit," "Great Shame and Disgrace," even "great disquiet in . . . the . . . marriage State" — strong stuff indeed![87] But to women, slander, metaphorically at least, could precipitate a fall beyond the pale of community. As far as we know, women who lost their slander suits in eighteenth-century New Haven County were not literally cast out of their social places, but their lives and sensibilities must have been affected by the presence in their culture of

---

term was used derivatively in a man's 1783 suit over a perjury charge: James Baldwin v. John Rice (Nov. 1783), NHCC Files, dr. 68 (writ). See Lam. 3:45. In 1 Cor. 4:13, the apostles describe their sufferings: "Being defamed, we intreat: we are made as the filth of the world, and are the offscouring of all things unto this day."

87. John Royce, Jr. v. Azor Curtis (Jan. 1767), NHCC Files, dr. 44 (writ); John Keating v. John Wilford (Apr. 1765), dr. 44 (writ); John Danielson v. Nathaniel Kimberly (Jan. 1769), dr. 39 (writ); Samuel Clark v. Nathan Bryan (Apr. 1746 adjourned), dr. 15 (writ); Benedict Arnold v. Capt. Elijah Forbes (Apr. 1771), dr. 49 (writ).

the metaphor of the fallen women as beneath contempt — as the off-scouring of humanity.[88]

———————

The shifts in slander litigation that occurred in New England court-rooms, like those of New Haven County between the 1630s and the 1790s, embodied in microcosm transformations wrought in legal culture and society at large. Seventeenth-century New Englanders placed great importance on legal proceedings as crucial mechanisms for defending the reputations of lay inhabitants and magistrates alike against defamation and insults. The efficacy of exposing misspeech in court and eliciting a spoken apology stemmed from at least two contexts. First, the communal goals of the Puritan experiment were deeply compromised by disruptive speech. And, second, given the tiny European populations planted in the New World, apologies could reach the ears of all community members because many were present in court and news quickly saturated the settlements. Starting in the early eighteenth century, not only did judges restrict the range of litigable slander, but the populace began to see courts as less and less effective sites for seeking relief for harmful speech.

One aspect of this development involved broad, philosophical shifts in ideologies governing the regulation of behavior. Elite and propertied householders were moving from a communal ethos — by which one revealed and repented all sin — to an ethic of privacy in which middle-class respectability was preserved by shielding the family name from public exposure.[89] The waning of slander suits also reflected the declining ap-

———————

88. For one wife who sued with her husband, there is suggestive evidence that they left New Haven County soon after the slander case. Mary Lewis, wife of Jacob, was accused of committing fornication with a black man in her youth; the Lewises lost the case in November 1780 when the county court jury ruled the defendants were not guilty of slander. The last notation concerning the Lewises in the town records of Wallingford, where they both were born and married, was the birth of their second son in July 1777. The genealogist Jacobus believes that Jacob Lewis might have moved his household to Wells, Vermont (*FANH*, 1089).

That a higher proportion of women won slander suits than men may signal that justices and jurors were aware of the special vulnerability of women to slander and were prepared to extend an extra measure of protection to women who could not with certainty be proven transgressors as charged.

89. For one justice of the peace's family engaging in a conspiracy of silence over a scandal, see Cornelia Hughes Dayton, "Taking the Trade: Abortion and Gender

propriateness of public apologies where community, as a result of population growth and social stratification, had become diffuse and less clearly defined. However, one segment of the population *did* find slander an effective legal action in the late colonial and early national periods: men involved in commercial transactions and frequent civil litigation used the forum of the courtroom to clear their names of the taint of bankruptcy and cheating.

All of these trends pushed women out of slander litigation, just as the changed face of the slander caseload itself encapsulated the reasons why women were barely visible in the overall civil caseload. Although court business had expanded enormously in volume by the last quarter of the eighteenth century, its nature had narrowed dramatically so that women's important roles as monitors of sexual behavior were no longer a staple of slander litigation or of other court activity. Morality would henceforth be debated and regulated largely outside the county court: in the more intimate, privatized settings of family, neighborhood, and church and in the newer institutional settings of relief agencies and benevolent organizations. Women's emphases in eighteenth-century slander writs on the centrality of neighborly associational bonds to female place and identity remind us not only of cultural norms that increasingly represented women's work and voices as peripheral but also of the reality of women's invisible community roles, in which many women would choose to display ethical and religious values in counterpoint to those manifest in middle-class manhood.[90]

Relations in an Eighteenth-Century New England Village," *WMQ*, XLVIII (1991), 19–49.

90. For extended discussions of women's agency in advancing distinctive values in a variety of late-18th- and early-19th-century settings, see Ulrich, " 'Daughters of Liberty,' " in Hoffman and Albert, eds., *Women in the Age of the American Revolution*, 211–243; Carroll Smith-Rosenberg, "Beauty, the Beast, and the Militant Women: A Case Study in Sex Roles and Social Stress in Jacksonian America," in Smith-Rosenberg, *Disorderly Conduct: Visions of Gender in Victorian America* (New York, 1985), 109–128; Suzanne Lebsock, *The Free Women of Petersburg: Status and Culture in a Southern Town, 1784–1860* (New York, 1984).

Appendix One

Divorce Petitions, Connecticut and New Haven Colonies, 1639–1710

Date, Residence	Parties	Grounds Cited	Outcome
Court of Magistrates, New Haven Colony (2)			
Ca. 1656 Milford	Hannah v. John Uffit	impotence	granted
October 1661 New Haven	Mary v. Wm. Andrews, Jr.	desertion of 8 years & remarriage	granted
General Court, Connecticut Colony (12)			
May 1655 Fairfield	Goody v. Tho. Beckwith	desertion	granted conditionally
August 1657 Saybook	Robert v. Joan Wade	disowning him for 15 years	granted
March 1660/1 ——	Sarah North v. husband	desertion of 6 years	granted at end of 7th year
May 1662 Hartford?	Bridget v. Tho. Baxter	bigamy?	granted
May 1670 Stonington	Hannah v. Tho. Huitt	absence of 8 years	granted
October 1676 New London	Elizabeth v. John Rogers	heretical opinions, abuse	granted
October 1676 ——	Sarah Towle v. husband	desertion of 6 years	granted
October 1677 ——	Mary v. Patrick Murrain	desertion of 6 years	granted
October 1677 ——	Experience v. Wm. Shepherd	desertion	granted

Date, Residence	Parties	Grounds Cited	Outcome
October 1677 ——	Mercy v. John Nicolson	desertion of 5 years	granted
October 1678 ——	Joanna v. Henry Pember	desertion of 3 years	granted
October 1691 Hartford	Richard v. Eliz. Edwards	desertion of 5 years	granted

	Court of Assistants, Connecticut Colony (43)		
June 1665 ——	Anne v. Robert Morris	impotence	granted
May 1667 New London	Rebecca v. Samuel Smith	desertion of 3 years	granted
January 1667/8 Hartford?	Mary v. John Halloway	impotence	temporary separation/ no final resolution
May 1669 ——	Mary v. Charles Barnes	desertion (& adultery?)	granted
May 1672 ——	Sarah v. Zachary Dibble	recent desertion, cruelty, adultery	granted
October 1672 Wethersfield	John v. Abigail Betts	adultery	granted
October 1674 New Haven	Mary v. John Browne	desertion of 7 years, adultery	granted
October 1674 ——	Elizabeth v. Robt. Jarrad	desertion	granted
October 1674 ——	Elizabeth v. Wm. Sedgwick	desertion	granted
May 1675 New London	Elizabeth v. John Rogers	heretical opinions, abuse	referred to General Court (granted there October 1676)

Date, Residence	Parties	Grounds Cited	Outcome
October 1676 Stonington	Lydia v. William Moore	desertion of 6 years (& probable adultery)	granted
October 1680 Stonington	John v. Martha Fish	desertion of 7 years & adultery	granted
October 1680 Newport, R.I.	James v. Alice Wakely	refusal to live with him	denied
October 1680 Wethersfield	Alice v. James Wakely	desertion of 14 years	denied
December 1681 ——	Thomas v. Sarah Long	adultery	granted
May 1682 Wethersfield	Hugh v. Alice Mackey	adultery, cruelty, recent desertion	denied
October 1682 ——	Mehitable v. David Ensign	adultery	granted
May 1683 Branford	Thomas v. Ruth Gutsell	desertion of 3 years	granted
October 1684 ——	Sarah v. John Jones	desertion of 3 years	granted
May 1685 New London	Rebecca v. Wm. Collins	desertion of 8 years	granted
October 1685 Windsor	Frances v. Henry Goring	desertion of 5 years	granted
May 1686 New London	Margaret v. George Hutchinson	desertion of 3 years	granted
[1680s] ——	Mary Orgor v. husband	desertion of 13 years	unknown
May 1687 ——	Thomas v. Martha Olmstead	fraudulent contract (fornication before marriage)	deferred

Date, Residence	Parties	Grounds Cited	Outcome
October 1690 Hartford	Richard v. Eliz. Edwards	adultery, refusing sex	denied
May 1692 New Haven	Mercy v. Ebenezer Hill	adultery	granted
May 1692 Lyme	Susanna v. John Hodge	adultery, desertion	granted
May 1693 Fairfield	Hannah v. Andrew Winton	desertion of 8 years	granted
May 1693 New Haven	Sarah v. John Dorman	impotence	granted
May 1694 Haddam	John v. Lydia Ventrous	fraudulent contract (fornication before marriage)	denied
October 1695 Saybrook	Joseph Ingram v. wife	desertion of 9 years	denied
May 1697 Windsor	Marie v. John Enno	desertion of 5 years	granted
October 1700 Stonington?	Erasmus v. Marie Babbitt	desertion	granted
May 1702 Hartford	Elizabeth v. Wm. Blancher	desertion	granted
October 1702 New Haven	Elizabeth v. Wm. Reynolds	desertion of 3 years	granted
May 1703 Middletown	Abigail v. James Crow	desertion of 3 years	unknown
Nov. 1703 Fairfield	Marie v. James Bennett	desertion of 4 years	granted
October 1704 ———	Sarah v. Jonathan Whitecus	unknown	denied
May 1705 Wethersfield	Marie v. David Sage	desertion of 9 years	granted

Date, Residence	Parties	Grounds Cited	Outcome
October 1705 Middletown?	Frances v. John Hall	desertion of 4 years	unknown
October 1709 Windham	Jonathan v. Judith Jennings	desertion of 6 years, adultery	deferred (he dies)
October 1709 Woodbury	Jonathan v. Hannah Taylor	adultery, desertion	granted

Note: The dates represent when final action on the case was taken; residence is that of petitioner.

Sources: PR, I–V; *NHCR,* II; Conn. Archives, Crimes and Misdemeanors 1st Ser., I, III; Samuel Wyllys Papers (1632–1709), CSL; *Recs. Ct. of Assts.,* Lacy transcript, I, II; Early General Records, LXVI (1663–1665), R.G. 1, CSL.

Appendix Two

Divorce Petitions, Connecticut General Assembly, 1711–1789

Date, Residence (County)	Parties	Grounds Cited	Outcome
October 1739 Ridgefield (Fairfield)	John v. Abigail Wallis	wife's premarital pregnancy by a black man	denied (twice)
May 1741 Preston (New London)	Jane v. John Mackwier	common law husband remarried	?
May 1753 Enfield (Hartford)	Mary v. Job Larkham	cruelty — she left (he admitted guilt; both had attorneys)	granted
January 1774 Branford (New Haven)	Sarah v. Jeremiah Wolcott	cruelty, he wasted her fortune; loveless courtship	granted (plus property division)
October 1774 Branford (New Haven)	Elizabeth v. James Howd	cruelty, neglect, possible adultery, loveless courtship	denied
May 1785 East Windsor (Hartford)	Jared v. Hepsibah Foot	adultery, cruelty	granted
May 1786 Saybrook (New London)	Susanna v. John Widger	desertion, cruelty	granted
May 1786 New Haven (New Haven)	George v. Mercy Dudley	cruelty, neglect	granted
May 1787 Suffield (Hartford)	Thaddeus v. Alice King	cruelty	granted (plus property division)

Date, Residence County	Parties	Grounds Cited	Outcome
May 1788 Bolton (Tolland)	Betty v. Rev. John Bliss	cruelty, lascivious carriage, intemperance	granted (plus property division, custody)
October 1788 New Haven (New Haven)	Dr. John v. Elizabeth Spaulding	neglect, plot to murder husband	granted
January 1789 Wallingford (New Haven)	Lois v. John Dudley	cruelty, adultery, intemperance, deceit in courtship, wasting of her estate	denied
October 1789 Litchfield (Litchfield)	Ursula v. Thomas Philips	cruelty, adultery, intemperance	granted

Note: The dates represent when final action on the case was taken.

Sources: PR and *PRS*; Conn. Archives, Lotteries and Divorces, 1st and 2d Ser., CSL.

Bibliography

MANUSCRIPT SOURCES

American Antiquarian Society, Worcester, Mass.
    Fiske, Nathan. Manuscript Sermons. Fiske Family Papers, 1757–1799.
    Forward, the Reverend Justus, of Belchertown, Mass. Diaries, 1762,
        1766, 1785–1786, 1797.
Connecticut Historical Society, Hartford
    Farmington Justice Court Records, 1741–1750 [Thomas Hart, Justice of
        Peace]. Microfilm.
    Glastonbury Inferior Court Records, 1753–1765. Microfilm.
    Mead, Dr. Amos, of Greenwich. Account Book, 1776–1794.
    Middletown Inferior Court Records, 1762–1784 [Matthew Talcott,
        Justice of Peace].
    Rose, Solomon, of Branford. Account Book, 1711–1791.
    Simsbury Inferior Court Records, 1742–1753. Microfilm.
    Trumbull, Jonathan, Sr. Papers: Memo Book, 1724–1784, including his
        Justice of Peace Record of Cases Tried for 1738.
    Windham Justice Court Records, 1754–1761: "First Record Book of
        Samuel Gray, Esq. of Windham, from June 6, 1754 to April 2,
        1761." Microfilm.
    Windsor Inferior Court Records, 1719–1734 [Matthew Allyn, Justice of
        Peace]. Microfilm.
    Windsor Records of [Inferior] Courts Kept by Roger Wolcott, Justice of
        Peace, 1722–1753. Microfilm.
    Wolcott, Dr. Alexander, of Wallingford. Account Book, 1744–1751.
Connecticut State Library, State Archives, Hartford
    Church, Land, Probate, Town, and Vital Records
        Barbour Collection of Connecticut Vital Records.
        Branford First Congregational Church Records, 1687–1821: vols. I, II.
            Cataloged Manuscripts.
        Cheshire Congregational Church Records, 1742–1923: vol. III.
            Cataloged Manuscripts.
        Church Records Index.
        Land Records: for the towns of Branford, Derby, Durham, Guilford,
            Milford, New Haven, Wallingford, and Waterbury. Microfilm.
        Milford Town Meeting Records. Cataloged Manuscripts.

New Haven First Church of Christ and Ecclesiastical Society Records,
    1639–1937: vols. I, IX. Record Group 70.

Probate Court Record Books and Indexes: for the districts of Guilford
    (1720–1852), New Haven (1647–1852), Wallingford (1776–
    1855), Waterbury (1779–1851), and Woodbury (1719–1850).
    Record Group 4. Microfilm.

Probate Estate Papers: for the districts of Durham-Middletown (1752–
    1900), Guilford (1719–1900), Hartford (1641–1940), New
    Haven (1683–1922), Wallingford (1776–1909), Waterbury
    (1779–1945), and Woodbury (1720–1949). Record Group 4.
    Microfilm.

Probate Estate Papers Index.

Connecticut Archives. Microfilm

Crimes and Misdemeanors, 1st Ser. (1662–1789), 2d Ser. (1671–1820).

Lotteries and Divorces, 1st Ser. (1755–1789), 2d Ser. (1718–1820).

Private Controversies, 2d Ser. (1636–1811).

Court Records, Record Group 1

Early General Records, vols. LVII, LVIII: Court of Assistants Records,
    1687–1711.

Court Records, Record Group 3

Derby Justice Court Records, 1777–1803 [Thomas Clark, Justice of
    Peace].

Fairfield County Court Records, 1702–1788, and Files, 1713–1853.

Fairfield County Superior Court Files, 1712–1799.

Hartford County Court Records, 1706–1717, 1719–1763, 1771–1774,
    and Files, 1713–1855.

Hartford County Superior Court Files, 1711–1849.

Litchfield County Superior Court Files, 1752–1901.

New Haven County Court Papers by Subject: Conservators and
    Guardians, 1720–1855.

New Haven County Court Records, 1666–1855, and Files, 1700–1855.

New Haven County Superior Court Files, 1712–1798.

New Haven County Superior Court Papers by Subject: Divorce, 1712–
    1798.

New London County Court Trials-Dockets, 1729–1815, and Files, 1691–
    1855.

New London County Superior Court Files, 1711–1881.

Superior Court Records, 1714–1798.

Windham County Court Records, 1726–1855, and Files, 1726–1855.

Windham County Superior Court Files, 1726–1908.

Wyllys, Samuel. Papers: Depositions on Cases of Witchcraft, Assault,

Theft, Drunkenness, and Other Crimes, Tried in Connecticut, 1663–1728. Cataloged Manuscripts.

Wyllys, Samuel. Papers Supplement (1930 photstats). Cataloged Manuscripts.

The Henry Huntington Library, San Marino, Calif.

Hopkins, Samuel, Sermons.

Yale University Library Manuscripts and Archives, New Haven

Blackstone, John, Jr. Farm Account Book, 1772–1839. Blackstone Family Papers.

Hillhouse Family Papers.

Sherman Collection.

Whiting, Nathan. Papers.

PRINTED PRIMARY SOURCES

Newspapers

Advocate of Moral Reform (New York), 1835–1847.

Boston Chronicle, 1767–1770.

Boston Evening-Post, 1735–.

Connecticut Courant (Hartford), 1764–.

Connecticut Gazette (New Haven), 1755–1768.

Connecticut Journal (New Haven), 1767–.

Newport Mercury (Rhode Island), 1758–1820.

Pennsylvania Gazette (Philadelphia), 1728–.

Providence Gazette; and Country Journal (Rhode Island), 1762–.

Statutes, Court Records, and Legal Treatises

Acts and Laws, of His Majesties Colony of Connecticut in New-England. New London, 1715.

Acts and Laws, of His Majesties Colony of Connecticut in New-England, bound together with *Acts Passed by the General Assembly from May 1716 to October 1733.* New London, 1733. (This compilation, marked "Theophilus Munson — His Law Book — 1734," and "Jedidiah Elderkin's Book A.D. 1772," is at the Connecticut State Library.)

Acts and Laws of His Majesties Colony of Connecticut in New England — Passed by the General Assembly, May 1716 to May 1749. Rpt., Hartford, 1919.

Blackstone, William. *Commentaries on the Laws of England.* 4 vols. 1765–1769; rpt., Chicago, 1979.

Colonial Laws of Massachusetts, The. Boston, 1889.

Cushing, John D., ed. *The Earliest Laws of the New Haven and Connecticut Colonies, 1639–1673*. Wilmington, Del., 1977.

[Dalton, Michael]. *The Countrey Justice*. . . . London, 1619.

Dexter, Franklin Bowditch, and Zara Jones Powers, eds. *New Haven Town Records*. 3 vols. Ancient Town Records. New Haven, 1917–1962.

Dow, George Francis, ed. *Records and Files of the Quarterly Courts of Essex County, Massachusetts*. 9 vols. Salem, Mass., 1911–1975.

East, Edward Hyde. *A Treatise of the Pleas of the Crown*. 2 vols. Philadelphia, 1806.

Fane, Francis. *Reports on the Laws of Connecticut*. Ed. Charles M. Andrews. [New Haven], 1915.

Farrell, John T., ed. *The Superior Court Diary of William Samuel Johnson, 1772–1773*. . . . Washington, D.C., 1942.

Hale, Sir Matthew. *Historia Placitorum Coronae: The History of the Pleas of the Crown*. 2 vols. London, 1736.

Hawkins, William. *A Treatise of the Pleas of the Crown*. . . . 2d ed. 2 vols. 1724–1726; rpt., New York, 1972.

Hoadly, Charles J., ed. *Records of the Colony and Plantation of New Haven, from 1638 to 1649*. Hartford, 1857.

———. *Records of the Colony or Jurisdiction of New Haven, from May, 1653, to the Union*. Hartford, 1858.

Hoadly, Charles J., et al., comps. *Public Records of the State of Connecticut, [1776–1803]*. 11 vols. Hartford, 1894–1967.

Jacob, Giles. *Every Man His Own Lawyer*. . . . 7th ed. New York, 1768.

———. *The Modern Justice*. . . . 3d ed. London, 1720.

———. *A New Law-Dictionary*. 7th ed. London, 1756.

Kirby, Ephraim. *Reports of Cases Adjudged in the Superior Court of the State of Connecticut, from the Year 1785, to January 1789; with Some Determinations in the Supreme Court of Errors*. Hartford, 1933 [orig. publ. 1789].

Konig, David Thomas, ed. *Plymouth Court Records, 1686–1859*. 16 vols. Wilmington, Del., 1978–1981.

Public Statute Laws of the State of Connecticut, The. Hartford, 1839.

Records of the Particular Court of the Colony of Connecticut, Administration of Sir Edmond Andros, Royal Governor, 1687–1688. Hartford, 1935.

Reeve, Tapping. *The Law of Baron and Femme, of Parent and Child, Guardian and Ward, Master and Servant*. . . . New Haven, 1816.

Revised Statutes of the State of Connecticut, The. Hartford, 1849.

Root, Jesse. *Reports of Cases Adjudged in the Superior Court and in the Supreme Court of Errors*. . . . 2 vols. Hartford, 1798–1802.

Select Trials at the Sessions-House in the Old-Bailey. 4 vols. London, 1742. Rpt. in 2 vols., New York, 1985.

Smith, Joseph H., ed. *Colonial Justice in Western Massachusetts (1639–1702): The Pynchon Court Record.* . . . Cambridge, Mass., 1961.

Swift, Zephaniah. *A System of the Laws of the State of Connecticut.* New York, 1972. Orig. publ. 2 vols., Windham, Conn., 1795–1796.

Trumbull, J. Hammond, and Charles J. Hoadly, eds. *The Public Records of the Colony of Connecticut, 1636–1776.* 15 vols. Hartford, 1850–1890.

Wroth, L. Kinvin, and Hiller B. Zobel. *Legal Papers of John Adams.* 3 vols. Cambridge, Mass., 1965.

Diaries, Sermons, Travel Accounts, and Other Sources

Ames, Nathaniel. *An Astronomical Diary; or, Almanack for . . . 1769.* New London, [1768].

Bradstreet, Simon. "Bradstreet's Journal, 1664–83." *New England Historical and Genealogical Register,* IX (1855), 43–51, 78–79.

Butterfield, L. H., et al., eds. *The Book of Abigail and John: Selected Letters of the Adams Family, 1762–1784.* Cambridge, Mass., 1975.

Castiglioni, Luigi. *Luigi Castiglioni's Viaggio: Travels in the United States of North America, 1785–87.* . . . Ed. and trans. Antonio Pace. Syracuse, N.Y., 1983.

[Clap, Thomas]. "Memoirs of a College President: Womanhood in Early America." Ed. Edwin Stanley Welles. *Journal of American History,* II (1908), 473–478.

Cooper, James Fenimore. *The Pioneers; or, The Sources of the Susquehanna: A Descriptive Tale.* New York, 1823.

Dana, James. *The Intent of Capital Punishment: A Discourse Delivered in the City of New-Haven, October 20, 1790, Being the Day of the Execution of Joseph Mountain, for a Rape.* New Haven, [1790].

[Davenport, John]. John Cotton. *A Discourse about Civil Government in a New Plantation Whose Design Is Religion.* Cambridge, Mass., [1663].

Gouge, William. *Of Domesticall Duties.* London, 1622.

Gurney, Joseph, comp. *The Trial of Frederick Calvert, Esq.: Baron of Baltimore, in the Kingdom of Ireland for a Rape on the Body of Sarah Woodcock; . . . at the Assizes Held at Kingston for the County of Surry on Saturday the 26th of March, 1768.* . . . London, 1768.

Hall, David D., ed. *The Antinomian Controversy, 1636–1638: A Documentary History.* Middletown, Conn., 1968.

———. *Witch-Hunting in Seventeenth-Century New England: A Documentary History, 1638–1692.* Boston, 1991.

Hamilton, Alexander. *Gentleman's Progress: The Itinerarium of Dr. Alexander Hamilton, 1744.* Ed. Carl Bridenbaugh. Pittsburgh, 1992.

Hempstead, Joshua. *Diary of Joshua Hempstead of New London, Connecticut . . . from September, 1711, to November, 1758.* New London County Historical Society, Collections, I. New London, 1901.

Hubbard, William. *A General History of New England from the Discovery to MDCLXXX.* 2d ed. New York, 1968. Orig. publ. Boston, 1848.

Hunter, Robert, Jr. *Quebec to Carolina in 1785–1786: Being the Travel Diary and Observations of Robert Hunter, Jr., a Young Merchant of London.* Ed. Louis B. Wright and Marion Tinling. San Marino, Calif., 1943.

Knight, Sarah Kemble. "The Journal of Madam Knight [1704]." Ed. Sargent Bush, Jr. In William L. Andrews, ed., *Journeys in New Worlds: Early American Women's Narratives,* 67–116. Madison, Wis., 1990.

Langdon, Timothy. *A Sermon, Preached at Danbury, November 8th, A.D. 1798, Being the Day of the Execution of Anthony, a Free Negro. . . .* [Danbury, Conn., 1798].

Life, and Dying Speech of Arthur, a Negro Man Who Was Executed at Worcester, October 20th 1768, for a Rape Committed on the Body of One Deborah Metcalfe, The. Boston, 1768.

Mather, Cotton. *Magnalia Christi Americana, Books I and II.* Ed. Kenneth B. Murdock. Cambridge, Mass., 1977.

Maverick, Samuel. "A Briefe Discription of New England and the Severall Townes Therein, Together with the Present Government Thereof." Massachusetts Historical Society, *Proceedings,* 2d Ser., I (1884–1885).

Minor, Thomas. *The Diary of Thomas Minor, Stonington, Connecticut, 1653 to 1684.* New London, 1899.

Paine, Robert Treat. *The Papers of Robert Treat Paine.* Ed. Stephen T. Riley and Edward W. Hanson. Vol. II. Boston, 1992.

Patten, Matthew. *The Diary of Matthew Patten of Bedford, N.H.* Concord, N.H., 1903.

Schneir, Miriam, ed. *Feminism: The Essential Historical Writings.* New York, 1972.

Sketches of the Life of Joseph Mountain, a Negro, Who Was Executed at New-Haven, on the 20th Day of October, 1790, for a Rape, Committed on the 26th Day of May Last. New Haven, 1790.

Smyth, Newman, ed. "Mrs. Eaton's Trial (in 1644): As It Appears upon the Records of the First Church of New Haven." New Haven Colony Historical Society, *Papers,* V (1894), 133–148.

Trumbull, Benjamin. *An Appeal to the Public, Especially to the Learned, with Respect to the Unlawfulness of Divorces, in All Cases, excepting Those of Incontinency.* New Haven, 1788.

———. *A Complete History of Connecticut, Civil and Ecclesiastical, from the Emigration of Its First Planters. . . .* 2 vols. Hartford, New Haven, 1797–1818.

Vital Records of New Haven, 1649–1850. 2 vols. Vital Records of Connecticut, 1st Ser., Towns, IV, pt. 1. Hartford, 1917–1924.

Vital Records of Norwich, 1659–1848. Hartford, 1913.

Willard, Samuel. *A Compleat Body of Divinity.* . . . Boston, 1726.

Williams, John. *Warnings to the Unclean: In a Discourse . . . Preacht at Springfield . . . August 25th. 1698, at the Execution of Sarah Smith.* Boston, 1699.

Winthrop, John. *The History of New England from 1630 to 1649.* Ed. James Savage. 2 vols. Boston, 1853.

SECONDARY WORKS

Abbott, Susan Woodruff, comp. *Families of Early Milford, Connecticut.* Baltimore, 1979.

Allen, David Grayson. *In English Ways: The Movement of Societies and the Transferal of English Local Law and Custom to Massachusetts Bay in the Seventeenth Century.* Chapel Hill, N.C., 1981.

Allen, Neal W., Jr. "Law and Authority to the Eastward: Maine Courts, Magistrates, and Lawyers, 1690–1730." In Daniel R. Coquillette, ed., *Law in Colonial Massachusetts, 1630–1800* (Colonial Society of Massachusetts, *Publications,* LXII [Boston, 1984]), 290–311.

Amussen, Susan Dwyer. "Féminin / Masculin: Le genre dans l'Angleterre de l'epoque moderne." *Annales: Economies, sociétés, civilisations,* XL (1985), 269–287.

——. *An Ordered Society: Gender and Class in Early Modern England.* New York, 1988.

Andrews, Charles M. *The Colonial Period of American History.* Vol. II. New Haven, 1936.

——. *The Fathers of New England: A Chronicle of the Puritan Commonwealths.* New Haven, 1921.

Applewhite, Harriet B., and Darline G. Levy, eds. *Women and Politics in the Age of the Democratic Revolution.* Ann Arbor, Mich., 1990.

Arnold, Marybeth Hamilton. " 'The Life of a Citizen in the Hands of a Woman': Sexual Assault in New York City, 1790 to 1820." In Kathy Peiss and Christina Simmons, eds., *Passion and Power: Sexuality in History,* 35–56. Philadelphia, 1989.

Atwater, Edward E., ed. *History of the City of New Haven to the Present Time.* New York, 1887.

Auwers, Linda. "The Social Meaning of Female Literacy: Windsor, Connecticut, 1660–1775." *Newberry Library Papers in Family and Community History,* no. 77-4A. Chicago, 1977.

Backhouse, Constance B. "Nineteenth-Century Canadian Rape Law, 1800–

92." In David H. Flaherty, ed., *Essays in the History of Canadian Law,* II, 200–247. Toronto, 1983.

Bacon, Margaret Hope. *Mothers of Feminism: The Story of Quaker Women in America.* San Francisco, 1986.

Barber, John Warner. *Connecticut Historical Collections. . . .* New Haven, 1838.

Barker-Benfield, G. J. *The Culture of Sensibility: Sex and Society in Eighteenth-Century Britain.* Chicago, 1992.

Basch, Norma. "Invisible Women: The Legal Fiction of Marital Unity in Nineteenth-Century America." *Feminist Studies,* V (1979), 346–366.

Beattie, J. M. *Crime and the Courts in England, 1660–1800.* Princeton, N.J., 1986.

———. "The Criminality of Women in Eighteenth-Century England." *Journal of Social History,* VIII (1974–1975), 80–116.

Black's Law Dictionary. 5th ed. St. Paul, Minn., 1979.

Bloch, E. Maurice. *The Paintings of George Caleb Bingham: A Catalogue Raisonné.* Columbia, Mo., 1986.

Bloch, Ruth H. "The Gendered Meanings of Virtue in Revolutionary America." *Signs: Journal of Women in Culture and Society,* XIII (1987–1988), 37–58.

Bowler, Clara Ann. "Carted Whores and White Shrouded Apologies: Slander in the County Courts of Seventeenth-Century Virginia." *Virginia Magazine of History and Biography,* LXXXV (1977), 411–426.

Boydston, Jeanne. *Home and Work: Housework, Wages, and the Ideology of Labor in the Early Republic.* New York, 1990.

Breen, T. H. " 'Baubles of Britain': The American and Consumer Revolutions of the Eighteenth Century." *Past and Present,* no. 119 (May 1988), 73–104.

———. *The Character of the Good Ruler: A Study of Puritan Political Ideas in New England, 1630–1730.* New Haven, 1970.

———. "An Empire of Goods: The Anglicization of Colonial America, 1690–1776." *Journal of British Studies,* XXV (1986), 467–499.

Brown, Lloyd A. *Loyalist Operations at New Haven.* Meriden, Conn., 1938.

Brown, Richard D. *Knowledge Is Power: The Diffusion of Information in Early America, 1700–1865.* New York, 1989.

Buel, Joy Day, and Richard Buel, Jr. *The Way of Duty: A Woman and Her Family in Revolutionary America.* New York, 1984.

Bumsted, J. M. "A Caution to Erring Christians: Ecclesiastical Disorder on Cape Cod, 1717 to 1738." *William and Mary Quarterly,* 3d Ser., XXVIII (1971), 413–438.

Bushman, Richard L. *From Puritan to Yankee: Character and the Social Order in Connecticut, 1690–1765.* New York, 1970.

———. *The Refinement of America: Persons, Houses, Cities.* New York, 1992.

Calder, Isabel MacBeath. *The New Haven Colony.* 1934; rpt., New Haven, 1970.

Carlton, Charles. "The Widow's Tale: Male Myths and Female Reality in Sixteenth and Seventeenth Century England." *Albion,* X (1978), 118–129.

Carr, Lois Green, and Lorena S. Walsh. "The Planter's Wife: The Experience of White Women in Seventeenth-Century Maryland." *William and Mary Quarterly,* 3d Ser., XXXIV (1977), 542–571.

Clark, Anna. *Women's Silence, Men's Violence: Sexual Assault in England, 1770–1845.* New York, 1987.

Clark, Charles E. *The Eastern Frontier: The Settlement of Northern New England, 1610–1763.* New York, 1970.

Clark, Christopher. "The Household Economy, Market Exchange, and the Rise of Capitalism in the Connecticut Valley, 1800–1860." *Journal of Social History,* XIII (1979–1980), 169–189.

———. *The Roots of Rural Capitalism: Western Massachusetts, 1780–1860.* Ithaca, N.Y., 1990.

Cohen, Daniel A. *Pillars of Salt, Monuments of Grace: New England Crime Literature and the Origins of American Popular Culture, 1674–1860.* New York, 1993.

Cohen, Patricia Cline. *A Calculating People: Numeracy in Early America.* Chicago, 1982.

Cohen, Sheldon S. "The Broken Bond: Divorce in Providence County, 1749–1809." *Rhode Island History,* XLIV (1985), 67–79.

———. " 'To Parts of the World Unknown': The Circumstances of Divorce in Connecticut, 1750–1797." *Canadian Review of American Studies,* XI (1980), 275–293.

———. "What Man Hath Put Asunder: Divorce in New Hampshire, 1681–1784." *Historical New Hampshire,* XLI (1986), 118–141.

Cook, Edward M., Jr. *The Fathers of the Towns: Leadership and Community Structure in Eighteenth-Century New England.* Baltimore, 1976.

Cott, Nancy F. *The Bonds of Womanhood: "Woman's Sphere" in New England, 1780–1825.* New Haven, 1977.

———. "Divorce and the Changing Status of Women in Eighteenth-Century Massachusetts." *William and Mary Quarterly,* 3d Ser., XXXIII (1976), 586–614.

———. "Eighteenth-Century Family and Social Life Revealed in the Massachusetts Divorce Records." *Journal of Social History,* X (1976–1977), 20–43.

———. "Passionlessness: An Interpretation of Victorian Sexual Ideology,

1790–1850." *Signs: Journal of Women in Culture and Society,* IV (1978–1979), 219–236.

Daniels, Bruce C. *The Connecticut Town: Growth and Development, 1635–1790.* Middletown, Conn., 1979.

———. "Economic Development in Colonial and Revolutionary Connecticut: An Overview." *William and Mary Quarterly,* 3d Ser., XXXVII (1980), 429–450.

———. "Money-Value Definitions of Economic Classes in Colonial Connecticut, 1700–1776." *Histoire Sociale — Social History,* VII (1974), 346–352.

Davidson, Cathy N. *Revolution and the Word: The Rise of the Novel in America.* New York, 1986.

Davis, Charles Henry Stanley. *History of Wallingford Connecticut, from Its Settlement in 1670 to the Present Time, Including Meriden . . . and Cheshire.* 2 vols. Meriden, Conn., 1870.

Dayton, Cornelia Hughes. "Taking the Trade: Abortion and Gender Relations in an Eighteenth-Century New England Village." *William and Mary Quarterly,* 3d Ser., XLVIII (1991), 19–49.

Demos, John Putnam. *Entertaining Satan: Witchcraft and the Culture of Early New England.* New York, 1982.

———. *A Little Commonwealth: Family Life in Plymouth Colony.* New York, 1970.

———. "Shame and Guilt in Early New England." In Carol Z. Stearns and Peter N. Stearns, eds., *Emotion and Social Change: Toward a New Psychohistory,* 69–85. New York, 1988.

Dewey, Frank L. "Thomas Jefferson's Notes on Divorce." *William and Mary Quarterly,* 3d Ser., XXXIX (1982), 212–223.

Dexter, Franklin Bowditch. "New Haven in 1784." New Haven Colony Historical Society, *Papers,* IV (1888), 117–138.

Ditz, Toby L. *Property and Kinship: Inheritance in Early Connecticut, 1750–1820.* Princeton, N.J., 1986.

Dolan, Frances E. *Dangerous Familiars: Representations of Domestic Crime in England, 1550–1700.* Ithaca, N.Y., 1994.

Dubois, Ellen Carol. *Feminism and Suffrage: The Emergence of an Independent Women's Movement in America, 1848–1869.* Ithaca, N.Y., 1978.

Dunn, Mary Maples. "Saints and Sisters: Congregational and Quaker Women in the Early Colonial Period." *American Quarterly,* XXX (1978), 582–601.

Estrich, Susan. *Real Rape.* Cambridge, Mass., 1987.

Fairbanks, Jonathan L., and Robert F. Trent, eds. *New England Begins: The Seventeenth Century.* 3 vols. Boston, 1982.

Fairchilds, Cissie. "Female Sexual Attitudes and the Rise of Illegitimacy: A

Case Study." *Journal of Interdisciplinary History*, III (1977–1978), 627–667.

Faragher, John Mack. "History From the Inside-out: Writing the History of Women in Rural America." *American Quarterly*, XXXIII (1981), 537–557.

Federal Writers' Project, Works Progress Administration for the State of Connecticut, comps. *History of Milford, Connecticut: 1639–1939.* Bridgeport, Conn., 1939.

Fischer, David Hackett. *Albion's Seed: Four British Folkways in America.* New York, 1989.

Fitzpatrick, Ellen. "Childbirth and an Unwed Mother in Seventeenth-Century New England." *Signs: Journal of Women in Culture and Society*, VIII (1982–1983), 744–749.

Flaherty, David. "Law and the Enforcement of Morals in Early America." *Perspectives in American History*, V (1971), 203–253.

——. *Privacy in Colonial New England.* Charlottesville, Va., 1972.

——, ed. *Essays in the History of Canadian Law.* 2 vols. Toronto, 1981–1983.

Fletcher, Anthony, and John Stevenson, eds. *Order and Disorder in Early Modern England.* Cambridge, 1985.

Fliegelman, Jay. *Prodigals and Pilgrims: The American Revolution against Patriarchal Authority, 1750–1800.* New York, 1982.

Folbre, Nancy F. "Patriarchy in Colonial New England." *Review of Radical Political Economics*, XII (1980), 4–13.

Fowler, William Chauncey. *History of Durham, Connecticut, from the First Grant of Land in 1662 to 1866.* Hartford, 1866.

Friedman, Lawrence M., and Robert V. Percival. *The Roots of Justice: Crime and Punishment in Alameda County, California, 1870–1910.* Chapel Hill, N.C., 1981.

Garvan, Anthony F. N. *Architecture and Town Planning in Colonial Connecticut.* New Haven, 1951.

Gaskins, Richard. "Changes in the Criminal Law in Eighteenth-Century Connecticut." *American Journal of Legal History*, XXV (1981), 309–342.

Gelles, Edith B. "Gossip: An Eighteenth-Century Case." *Journal of Social History*, XXII (1988–1989), 667–683.

Gillis, John R. "From Ritual to Romance: Toward an Alternative History of Love." In Carol Z. Stearns and Peter N. Stearns, eds., *Emotion and Social Change: Toward a New Psychohistory*, 87–121. New York, 1988.

Gilsdorf, Joy B., and Robert R. Gilsdorf, Jr. "Elites and Electorates: Some Plain Truths for Historians of Colonial America." In David D. Hall et al., eds., *Saints and Revolutionaries: Essays on Early American History*, 207–244. New York, 1984.

Glenn, Myra C. *Campaigns against Corporal Punishment: Prisoners, Sailors, Women, and Children in Antebellum America.* Albany, N.Y., 1984.

Gluckman, Max. "Gossip and Scandal." *Current Anthropology,* IV (1963), 307–316.

Godbeer, Richard. " 'The Cry of Sodom': Discourse, Intercourse, and Desire in Colonial New England." *William and Mary Quarterly,* 3d Ser., LII (1995), 259–286.

Gordon, Linda, and Paul O'Keefe. "Incest as a Form of Family Violence: Evidence from Historical Case Records." *Journal of Marriage and the Family,* XLVI (1984), 27–34.

Gough, Deborah Mathias. "A Further Look at Widows in Early Southeastern Pennsylvania." With a response by Lisa Wilson Waciega. *William and Mary Quarterly,* 3d Ser., XLIV (1987), 829–839.

Grant, Charles S. *Democracy in the Connecticut Frontier Town of Kent.* New York, 1972.

Green, Constance McL. *History of Naugatuck, Connecticut.* New Haven, 1948.

Green, Thomas Andrew. *Verdict according to Conscience: Perspectives on the English Criminal Trial Jury, 1200–1800.* Chicago, 1985.

Greenberg, Douglas. *Crime and Law Enforcement in the Colony of New York, 1691–1776.* Ithaca, N.Y., 1976.

Greene, Evarts B., and Virginia D. Harrington. *American Population before the Federal Census of 1790.* New York, 1932.

Greene, Jack P., and J. R. Pole, eds. *Colonial British America: Essays in the New History of the Early Modern Era.* Baltimore, 1984.

Greven, Philip J., Jr. *Four Generations: Population, Land, and Family in Colonial Andover, Massachusetts.* Ithaca, N.Y., 1970.

Grigg, Susan. "Toward a Theory of Remarriage: A Case Study of Newburyport at the Beginning of the Nineteenth Century." *Journal of Interdisciplinary History,* VIII (1977–1978), 183–220.

Griswold, Robert L. "The Evolution of the Doctrine of Mental Cruelty in Victorian American Divorce, 1790–1900." *Journal of Social History,* XX (1986–1987), 127–148.

Groneman, Carol, and Mary Beth Norton, eds. *"To Toil the Livelong Day": America's Women at Work, 1780–1980.* Ithaca, N.Y., 1987.

Gross, Robert A. *The Minutemen and Their World.* New York, 1976.

Grossberg, Michael. *Governing the Hearth: Law and the Family in Nineteenth-Century America.* Chapel Hill, N.C., 1985.

Gundersen, Joan R. "Independence, Citizenship, and the American Revolution." *Signs: Journal of Women in Culture and Society,* XIII (1987–1988), 59–77.

Gundersen, Joan R., and Gwen Victor Gampel. "Married Women's Legal

Status in Eighteenth-Century New York and Virginia." *William and Mary Quarterly,* 3d Ser., XXXIX (1982), 114–134.

Habermas, Jürgen. *The Structural Transformation of the Public Sphere: An Inquiry into a Category of Bourgeois Society.* Trans. Thomas Burger. Cambridge, Mass., 1989.

Hall, David D. *Worlds of Wonder, Days of Judgment: Popular Religious Belief in Early New England.* New York, 1989.

Hall, David D., et al., eds. *Saints and Revolutionaries: Essays on Early American History.* New York, 1984.

Hall, David D., and David Grayson Allen, eds. *Seventeenth-Century New England.* Boston, 1984.

Hall, Max. *Benjamin Franklin and Polly Baker: The History of a Literary Deception.* Chapel Hill, N.C., 1960.

Handlin, Lilian. "Dissent in a Small Community." *New England Quarterly,* LVIII (1985), 193–220.

Harding, Susan. "Women and Words in a Spanish Village." In Rayna Reiter, ed., *Toward an Anthropology of Women,* 283–308. New York, 1975.

Hart, James D. *The Popular Book: A History of America's Literary Taste.* New York, 1950.

Hartog, Hendrik. "The Public Law of a County Court: Judicial Government in Eighteenth Century Massachusetts." *American Journal of Legal History,* XX (1976), 282–329.

Haskell, Thomas L. "Litigation and Social Status in Seventeenth- Century New Haven." *Journal of Legal Studies,* VII (1978), 219–241.

Haskins, George Lee. *Law and Authority in Early Massachusetts: A Study in Tradition and Design.* New York, 1960.

Helmholz, R. H. "Civil Trials and the Limits of Responsible Speech." In Helmholz and Thomas A. Green, eds., *Juries, Libel, and Justice: The Role of English Juries in Seventeenth- and Eighteenth-Century Trials for Libel and Slander.* Los Angeles, 1984.

———. *Marriage Litigation in Medieval England.* Cambridge, 1974.

Hemphill, C. Dallett. "Women in Court: Sex-Role Differentiation in Salem, Massachusetts, 1636–1683." *William and Mary Quarterly,* 3d Ser., XXXIX (1982), 164–175.

Henretta, James A. "Families and Farms: *Mentalité* in Pre-Industrial America." *William and Mary Quarterly,* 3d Ser., XXXV (1978), 3–32.

Herrup, Cynthia B. *The Common Peace: Participation and the Criminal Law in Seventeenth-Century England.* New York, 1987.

Heyrman, Christine Leigh. *Commerce and Culture: The Maritime Communities of Colonial Massachusetts, 1690–1750.* New York, 1984.

Hindus, Michael Stephen. *Prison and Plantation: Crime, Justice, and Authority* in Massachusetts and South Carolina, 1767–1878. Chapel Hill, N.C., 1980.

Hindus, Michael Stephen, and Douglas Lamar Jones. "Quantitative Methods or *Quantum Meruit?* Tactics for Early American Legal History." *Historical Methods,* XIII (1980), 63–74.

Hirsch, Alison Duncan. "The Thrall Divorce Case: A Family Crisis in Eighteenth-Century Connecticut." *Women and History,* no. 4 (1982), 43–75.

Hoff, Joan. *Law, Gender, and Injustice: A Legal History of U.S. Women.* New York, 1991.

Hoff-Wilson, Joan. "Hidden Riches: Legal Records and Women, 1750–1825." In Mary Kelley, ed., *Woman's Being, Woman's Place: Female Identity and Vocation in American History,* 7–25. Boston, 1979.

Hoffer, Peter C., and N. E. H. Hull. *Murdering Mothers: Infanticide in England and New England, 1558–1803.* New York, 1981.

Hoffman, Ronald, and Peter J. Albert, eds. *Women in the Age of the American Revolution.* Charlottesville, Va., 1989.

Horwitz, Morton J. *The Transformation of American Law, 1780–1860.* Cambridge, Mass., 1977.

Howard, George Elliott. *A History of Matrimonial Institutions, Chiefly in England and the United States, with an Introductory Analysis of the Literature and the Theories of Primitive Marriage and the Family.* 3 vols. Chicago, 1904.

Hull, N. E. H. "The Certain Wages of Sin: Sentence and Punishment of Female Felons in Colonial Massachusetts, 1673–1774." In D. Kelly Weisberg, ed., *Women and the Law: The Social Historical Perspective,* I, 7–25. Cambridge, Mass., 1982.

———. *Female Felons: Women and Serious Crime in Colonial Massachusetts.* Urbana, Ill., 1987.

Hunt, Margaret. "Wife Beating, Domesticity, and Women's Independence in Eighteenth-Century London." *Gender and History,* IV (1992), 10–33.

Hurst, James Willard. *Law and the Conditions of Freedom in the Nineteenth-Century United States.* Madison, Wis., 1956.

Innes, Stephen. *Labor in a New Land: Economy and Society in Seventeenth-Century Springfield.* Princeton, N.J., 1983.

———, ed. *Work and Labor in Early America.* Chapel Hill, N.C., 1988.

Isaac, Rhys. *The Transformation of Virginia, 1740–1790.* Chapel Hill, N.C., 1982.

Jacobus, Donald Lines, comp. *Families of Ancient New Haven.* 3 vols. 1922–1932; rpt., Baltimore, 1981.

———, ed. and comp. *History and Genealogy of the Families of Old Fairfield.* 2 vols. 1930–1932; rpt., Baltimore, 1976.

———, comp. *List of Officials, Civil, Military, and Ecclesiastical of Connecticut Colony . . . and of New Haven Colony. . . .* New Haven, 1935.

Jedrey, Christopher M. *The World of John Cleaveland: Family and Community in Eighteenth-Century New England.* New York, 1979.

Jones, Douglas Lamar. "Poverty and Vagabondage: The Process of Survival in Eighteenth-Century Massachusetts." *New England Historical and Genealogical Register,* CXXXIII (1979), 243–254.

———. "The Strolling Poor: Transiency in Eighteenth-Century Massachusetts." *Journal of Social History,* VIII, no. 3 (Spring 1975), 28–54.

Jordan, William Chester. *Women and Credit in Pre-Industrial and Developing Societies.* Philadelphia, 1993.

Jordan, Winthrop D. *White over Black: American Attitudes toward the Negro, 1550–1812.* Chapel Hill, N.C., 1968.

Karlsen, Carol F. *The Devil in the Shape of a Woman: Witchcraft in Colonial New England.* New York, 1987.

Katz, Stanley N. "The Problem of a Colonial Legal History." In Jack P. Greene and J. R. Pole, eds., *Colonial British America: Essays in the New History of the Early Modern Era,* 457–489. Baltimore, 1984.

Katz, Stanley N., and John M. Murrin, eds. *Colonial America: Essays in Politics and Social Development.* 3d ed. New York, 1983.

Kelley, Mary, ed. *Woman's Being, Woman's Place: Female Identity and Vocation in American History.* Boston, 1979.

Kerber, Linda K. " 'History Can Do It No Justice': Women and the Reinterpretation of the American Revolution." In Ronald Hoffman and Peter J. Albert, eds., *Women in the Age of the American Revolution,* 3–42. Charlottesville, Va., 1989.

———. " 'I Have Don . . . much to Carrey on the Warr': Women and the Shaping of Republican Ideology after the American Revolution." In Harriet B. Applewhite and Darline G. Levy, eds., *Women and Politics in the Age of the Democratic Revolution,* 227–257. Ann Arbor, Mich., 1990.

———. "The Paradox of Women's Citizenship in the Early Republic: The Case of *Martin vs. Massachusetts,* 1805." *American Historical Review,* XCVII (1992), 349–378.

———. "The Republican Mother: Women and the Enlightenment—An American Perspective." *American Quarterly,* XXVIII (1976), 187–205.

———. "Separate Spheres, Female Worlds, Woman's Place: The Rhetoric of Women's History." *Journal of American History,* LXXV (1988–1989), 9–39.

——. *Women of the Republic: Intellect and Ideology in Revolutionary America.* Chapel Hill, N.C., 1980.

Kettner, James H. *The Development of American Citizenship, 1608–1870.* Chapel Hill, N.C., 1978.

Keyssar, Alexander. "Widowhood in Eighteenth-Century Massachusetts: A Problem in the History of the Family." *Perspectives in American History,* VIII (1974), 83–119.

King, Andrew J. "The Law of Slander in Early Antebellum America." *American Journal of Legal History,* XXXV (1991), 1–43.

King, Walter J. "Punishment for Bastardy in Early Seventeenth-Century England." *Albion,* X (1978), 130–151.

Koehler, Lyle. "The Case of the American Jezebels: Anne Hutchinson and Female Agitation during the Years of Antinomian Turmoil, 1636–1640." *William and Mary Quarterly,* 3d Ser., XXXI (1974), 55–78.

——. *A Search for Power: The "Weaker Sex" in Seventeenth-Century New England.* Urbana, Ill., 1980.

Konig, David Thomas. *Law and Society in Puritan Massachusetts: Essex County, 1629–1692.* Chapel Hill, N.C., 1979.

Kulikoff, Allan. *The Agrarian Origins of American Capitalism.* Charlottesville, Va., 1992.

——. *Tobacco and Slaves: The Development of Southern Cultures in the Chesapeake, 1680–1800.* Chapel Hill, N.C., 1986.

Lacey, Barbara E. "Gender, Piety, and Secularization in Connecticut Religion, 1720–1775." *Journal of Social History,* XXIV (1990–1991), 799–821.

——. "The World of Hannah Heaton: The Autobiography of an Eighteenth-Century Connecticut Farm Woman." *William and Mary Quarterly,* 3d Ser., XLV (1988), 280–304.

Landes, Joan B. *Women and the Public Sphere in the Age of the French Revolution.* Ithaca, N.Y., 1988.

Langbein, John H. "The Criminal Trial before the Lawyers." *University of Chicago Law Review,* XLV (1978), 263–316.

——. *Prosecuting Crime in the Renaissance: England, Germany, France.* Cambridge, Mass., 1974.

——. "Shaping the Eighteenth-Century Criminal Trial: A View from the Ryder Sources." *University of Chicago Law Review,* L (1983), 1–136.

Laslett, Peter. "The Bastardy Prone Sub-Society." In Laslett et al., eds., *Bastardy and Its Comparative History: Studies in the History of Illegitimacy and Marital Nonconformism in Britain, France, Germany, Sweden, North America, Jamaica, and Japan,* 217–246. Cambridge, Mass., 1980.

Laslett, Peter, and Karla Oosterveen. "Long-Term Trends in Bastardy in England." *Population Studies*, XXVII (1973), 255–286.

Laslett, Peter, et al., eds. *Bastardy and Its Comparative History: Studies in the History of Illegitimacy and Marital Nonconformism in Britain, France, Germany, Sweden, North America, Jamaica, and Japan.* Cambridge, Mass., 1980.

Lebsock, Suzanne. *The Free Women of Petersburg: Status and Culture in a Southern Town, 1784–1860.* New York, 1984.

Lewis, Jan. "The Republican Wife: Virtue and Seduction in the Early Republic." *William and Mary Quarterly,* 3d Ser., XLIV (1987), 689–721.

Lindemann, Barbara S. " 'To Ravish and Carnally Know': Rape in Eighteenth-Century Massachusetts." *Signs: Journal of Women in Culture and Society,* X (1984–1985), 63–82.

Lockridge, Kenneth A. *Literacy in Colonial New England: An Enquiry into the Social Context of Literacy in the Early Modern West.* New York, 1974.

———. *A New England Town, the First Hundred Years: Dedham, Massachusetts, 1636–1736.* New York, 1970.

———. *On the Sources of Patriarchal Rage: The Commonplace Books of William Byrd and Thomas Jefferson and the Gendering of Power in the Eighteenth Century.* New York, 1992.

Lockwood, Rose Ann. "Birth, Illness, and Death in Eighteenth-Century New England." *Journal of Social History,* XII (1978–1979), 111–128.

Main, Jackson Turner. "The Distribution of Property in Colonial Connecticut." In James Kirby Martin, ed., *The Human Dimensions of Nation Making: Essays on Colonial and Revolutionary America,* 54–104. Madison, Wis., 1976.

———. *The Social Structure of Revolutionary America.* Princeton, N.J., 1965.

———. *Society and Economy in Colonial Connecticut.* Princeton, N.J., 1985.

Malmsheimer, Lonna M. "Daughters of Zion: New England Roots of American Feminism." *New England Quarterly,* L (1977), 484–504.

Manchester, A. H. *A Modern Legal History of England and Wales, 1750–1950.* London, 1980.

Mann, Bruce H. "The Formalization of Informal Law: Arbitration before the American Revolution." *New York University Law Review,* LIX (1984), 443–481.

———. *Neighbors and Strangers: Law and Community in Early Connecticut.* Chapel Hill, N.C., 1987.

———. "Rationality, Legal Change, and Community in Connecticut, 1690–1760." *Law and Society Review,* XIV (1980), 187–221.

Marchant, Ronald A. *The Church under the Law: Justice, Administration, and Discipline in the Diocese of York, 1560–1640.* Cambridge, 1969.

Marcus, Gail Sussman. " 'Due Execution of the Generall Rules of Righteousnesse': Criminal Procedure in New Haven Town and Colony, 1638–1658." In David D. Hall et al., eds., *Saints and Revolutionaries: Essays on Early American History,* 99–137. New York, 1984.

Marsella, Paul D. *Crime and Community in Early Massachusetts: Essex County, 1700–1785.* Acton, Mass., 1990.

Martin, James Kirby, ed. *The Human Dimensions of Nation Making: Essays on Colonial and Revolutionary America.* Madison, Wis., 1976.

Masur, Louis P. *Rites of Execution: Capital Punishment and the Transformation of American Culture, 1776–1865.* New York, 1989.

McManus, Edgar J. *Law and Liberty in Early New England: Criminal Justice and Due Process, 1620–1692.* Amherst, Mass., 1993.

Melder, Keith E. *Beginnings of Sisterhood: The American Woman's Rights Movement, 1800–1850.* New York, 1977.

Menefee, Samuel Pyeatt. *Wives for Sale: An Ethnographic Study of British Popular Divorce.* New York, 1981.

Merrill, Michael. "Cash Is Good to Eat: Self-Sufficiency and Exchange in the Rural Economy of the United States." *Radical History Review,* IV (1977), 42–71.

Miller, Perry. *The New England Mind: From Colony to Province.* Boston, 1953.

——. Review of *The New Haven Colony,* by Isabel M. Calder. *New England Quarterly,* VIII (1935), 582–584.

Monaghan, E. Jennifer. "Literacy Instruction and Gender in Colonial New England." *American Quarterly,* XL (1988), 18–41.

Moogk, Peter N. " 'Thieving Buggers' and 'Stupid Sluts': Insults and Popular Culture in New France." *William and Mary Quarterly,* 3d Ser., XXXVI (1979), 524–547.

Morgan, Edmund S. *The Gentle Puritan: A Life of Ezra Stiles, 1727–1795.* New Haven, 1962.

——. *The Puritan Family: Religion and Domestic Relations in Seventeenth-Century New England.* Rev. ed. New York, 1966.

——. "The Puritans and Sex." *New England Quarterly,* XV (1942), 591–607.

——. *Visible Saints: The History of a Puritan Idea.* New York, 1963.

Morris, Richard B. *Studies in the History of American Law: With Special Reference to the Seventeenth and Eighteenth Centuries.* 2d ed. New York, 1974.

Murrin, John M. "The Legal Transformation: The Bench and Bar of Eighteenth-Century Massachusetts." In Stanley N. Katz and Murrin, eds., *Colonial America: Essays in Politics and Social Development*, 540–572. 3d ed. New York, 1983.

———. "Magistrates, Sinners, and a Precarious Liberty: Trial by Jury in Seventeenth-Century New England." In David D. Hall et al., eds., *Saints and Revolutionaries: Essays on Early American History*, 152–206. New York, 1984.

———. Review essay. *History and Theory*, XI (1972), 226–275.

Narrett, David E. *Inheritance and Family Life in Colonial New York City.* Ithaca, N.Y., 1992.

Nelson, William E. *Americanization of the Common Law: The Impact of Legal Change on Massachusetts Society, 1760–1830.* Cambridge, Mass., 1975.

———. *Dispute and Conflict Resolution in Plymouth County, Massachusetts, 1725–1825.* Chapel Hill, N.C., 1981.

———. "Emerging Notions of Modern Criminal Law in the Revolutionary Era: An Historical Perspective." *New York University Law Review*, XLII (1967), 450–482.

New Haven Colony Historical Society. *Papers.* 10 vols. 1865–1951.

Nissenbaum, Stephen, ed. *The Great Awakening at Yale College.* Belmont, Calif., 1972.

Norton, Mary Beth. "Eighteenth-Century American Women in Peace and War: The Case of the Loyalists." *William and Mary Quarterly*, 3d Ser., XXXIII (1976), 386–409.

———. "The Evolution of White Women's Experience in Early America." *American Historical Review*, LXXXIX (1984), 593–619.

———. "Gender and Defamation in Seventeenth-Century Maryland." *William and Mary Quarterly*, 3d Ser., XLIV (1987), 3–39.

———. *Liberty's Daughters: The Revolutionary Experience of American Women, 1750–1800.* Boston, 1980.

Oberholzer, Emil, Jr. *Delinquent Saints: Disciplinary Action in the Early Congregational Churches of Massachusetts.* New York, 1956.

Oosterveen, Karla, and Richard M. Smith. "Bastardy and the Family Reconstitution Studies of Colyton, Aldenham, Alcester, and Hawkshead." In Peter Laslett et al., eds., *Bastardy and Its Comparative History: Studies in the History of Illegitimacy and Marital Nonconformism in Britain, France, Germany, Sweden, North America, Jamaica, and Japan*, 94–140. Cambridge, Mass., 1980

Orcutt, Samuel, and Ambrose Beardsley. *The History of the Old Town of Derby, Connecticut, 1642–1680.* Springfield, Mass., 1880.

Osterweis, Rollin G. *Three Centuries of New Haven, 1638–1938.* New Haven, 1953.

Parkes, Henry Bamford. "Morals and Law Enforcement in Colonial New England." *New England Quarterly,* V (1932), 431–452.

Parkhurst, Charles Dyer. *Early Families of New London and Vicinity.* Vol. XXXI. Hartford, 1938. At CSL.

Pateman, Carole. *The Sexual Contract.* Stanford, Calif., 1988.

Peiss, Kathy, and Christina Simmons, eds. *Passion and Power: Sexuality in History.* Philadelphia, 1989.

Pennington, Donald, and Keith Thomas, eds. *Puritans and Revolutionaries: Essays in Seventeenth-Century History Presented to Christopher Hill.* New York, 1982.

Powell, Chilton Lathan. *English Domestic Relations, 1487–1653.* . . . New York, 1917.

Powers, Edwin. *Crime and Punishment in Early Massachusetts, 1620–1692: A Documentary History.* Boston, 1966.

Pruitt, Bettye Hobbs. "Self-Sufficiency and the Agricultural Economy of Eighteenth-Century Massachusetts." *William and Mary Quarterly,* 3d Ser., XLI (1984), 333–364.

Quaife, G. R. *Wanton Wenches and Wayward Wives: Peasants and Illicit Sex in Early Seventeenth Century England.* New Brunswick, N.J., 1979.

Reiter, Rayna R., ed. *Toward an Anthropology of Women.* New York, 1975.

Ricketson, William F. "To Be Young, Poor, and Alone: The Experience of Widowhood in the Massachusetts Bay Colony, 1675–1676." *New England Quarterly,* LXIV (1991), 113–127.

Rockey, J. L., ed. *History of New Haven County, Connecticut.* 2 vols. New York, 1892.

Roeber, A. G. "Authority, Law, and Custom: The Rituals of Court Day in Tidewater Virginia, 1720–1750." *William and Mary Quarterly,* 3d Ser., XXXVII (1980), 29–52.

Roetger, R. W. "The Transformation of Sexual Morality in 'Puritan' New England: Evidence from New Haven Court Records, 1639–1698." *Canadian Review of American Studies,* XV (1984), 243–257.

Rogers, Kim Lacy. "Relicts of the New World: Condition of Widowhood in Seventeenth-Century New England." In Mary Kelley, ed., *Woman's Being, Woman's Place: Female Identity and Vocation in American History,* 26–52. Boston, 1979.

Rosenberg, Norman L. *Protecting the Best Men: An Interpretive History of the Law of Libel.* Chapel Hill, N.C., 1986.

Rothenberg, Winifred B. "The Emergence of a Capital Market in Rural Massachusetts, 1730–1838." *Journal of Economic History,* XLV (1985), 781–808.

———. "The Market and Massachusetts Farmers, 1750–1855." *Journal of Economic History,* XLI (1981), 283–314.

Rowe, G. S. "Infanticide, Its Judicial Resolution, and Criminal Code Revision in Early Pennsylvania." American Philosophical Society, *Proceedings,* CXXXV (1991), 200–232.

———. "The Role of Courthouses in the Lives of Eighteenth-Century Pennsylvania Women." *Western Pennsylvania Historical Magazine,* LXVIII (1985), 5–23.

———. "Women's Crime and Criminal Administration in Pennsylvania, 1763–1790." *Pennsylvania Magazine of History and Biography,* CIX (1985), 335–368.

St. George, Robert. " 'Heated' Speech and Literacy in Seventeenth-Century New England." In David D. Hall and David Grayson Allen, eds., *Seventeenth-Century New England,* 275–321. Boston, 1984.

———. " 'Set Thine House in Order': The Domestication of the Yeomanry in Seventeenth-Century New England." In Jonathan L. Fairbanks and Robert F. Trent, eds., *New England Begins: The Seventeenth Century,* II, 139–351. Boston, 1982.

———, ed. *Material Life in America, 1600–1860.* Boston, 1988.

Salmon, Marylynn. "The Legal Status of Women in Early America: A Reappraisal." *Law and History Review,* I (1983), 129–151.

———. *Women and the Law of Property in Early America.* Chapel Hill, N.C., 1986.

Sanday, Peggy Reeves. "The Socio-Cultural Context of Rape: A Cross-Cultural Study." *Journal of Social Issues,* XXXVII, no. 4 (1981), 5–27.

Scholten, Catherine M. " 'On the Importance of the Obstetrick Art': Changing Customs of Childbirth in America, 1760 to 1825." *William and Mary Quarterly,* 3d Ser., XXXIV (1977), 426–445.

Seed, Patricia. "American Law, Hispanic Traces: Some Contemporary Entanglements of Community Property." *William and Mary Quarterly,* 3d Ser., LII (1995), 157–162.

Shammas, Carole. "Anglo-American Household Government in Comparative Perspective." *William and Mary Quarterly,* 3d Ser., LII (1995), 104–144.

———. "The Domestic Environment in Early Modern England and America." *Journal of Social History,* XIV (1980–1981), 3–24.

Shammas, Carole, Marylynn Salmon, and Michel Dahlin. *Inheritance in America from Colonial Times to the Present.* New Brunswick, N.J., 1987.

Sharpe, J. A. *Defamation and Sexual Slander in Early Modern England: The Church Courts at York.* York, Eng., [1980].

Shiels, Richard D. "The Feminization of American Congregationalism, 1730–1835." *American Quarterly,* XXXIII (1981), 46–62.

Shumway, Floyd, and Richard Hegel, eds. *New Haven: An Illustrated History.* Woodland Hills, Calif., 1981.

Silverman, Robert A. *Law and Urban Growth: Civil Litigation in the Boston Trial Courts, 1880–1900.* Princeton, N.J., 1981.

Sklar, Kathryn Kish. "Culture versus Economics: A Case of Fornication in Northampton in the 1740's." University of Michigan, *Papers in Women's Studies,* 1978, 35–56.

Smith, Daniel Scott, and Michael S. Hindus. "Premarital Pregnancy in America, 1640–1971: An Overview and Interpretation." *Journal of Interdisciplinary History,* IV (1974–1975), 537–570.

Smith-Rosenberg, Carroll. "Beauty, the Beast, and the Militant Woman: A Case Study in Sex Roles and Social Stress in Jacksonian America." In Smith-Rosenberg, *Disorderly Conduct: Visions of Gender in Victorian America,* 109–128. New York, 1985.

Somerville, James K. "The Salem (Mass.) Woman in the Home, 1660–1770." *Eighteenth-Century Life,* I (1974), 11–14.

Spalletta, Matteo. "Divorce in Colonial New York." *New-York Historical Society Quarterly,* XXXIX (1955), 422–440.

Speth, Linda E. "More than Her 'Thirds': Wives and Widows in Colonial Virginia." *Women and History,* no. 4 (1982), 5–41.

Spruill, Julia Cherry. *Women's Life and Work in the Southern Colonies.* 1938; rpt., New York, 1972.

Stansell, Christine. *City of Women: Sex and Class in New York, 1789–1860.* New York, 1986.

Stark, Bruce. "Freemanship in Lebanon, Connecticut: A Case Study." *Connecticut History,* no. 15 (1975), 27–49.

Stearns, Carol Z., and Peter N. Stearns, eds. *Emotion and Social Change: Toward a New Psychohistory.* New York, 1988.

Steiner, Bernard Christian. *A History of the Plantation of Menunkatuck and of the Original Town of Guilford, Connecticut. . . .* Baltimore, 1897.

Stiles, Henry Reed. *Bundling: Its Origin, Progress, and Decline in America.* [N.p., 1871].

———. *The History and Genealogies of Ancient Windsor, Connecticut.* 2 vols. Hartford, 1891–1892.

Stiles, Henry Reed, and Sherman W. Adams. *The History of Ancient Wethersfield.* 1904; rpt., Somersworth, N.H., 1974–1975.

Stone, Lawrence. *The Family, Sex, and Marriage in England, 1500–1800.* New York, 1977.

———. *Road to Divorce: England, 1530–1987.* New York, 1990.

Stowell, Marion Barber. *Early American Almanacs: The Colonial Weekday Bible.* New York, 1977.

Sweeney, Kevin M. "Furniture and the Domestic Environment in Wethersfield, Connecticut, 1639–1800." In Robert Blair St. George, ed., *Material Life in America, 1600–1860,* 261–290. Boston, 1988.

Thomas, Keith. "The Double Standard." *Journal of the History of Ideas,* XX (1959), 195–216.

———. "The Puritans and Adultery: The Act of 1650 Reconsidered." In Donald Pennington and Keith Thomas, eds., *Puritans and Revolutionaries: Essays in Seventeenth-Century History Presented to Christopher Hill,* 257–282. New York, 1982.

Thompson, Roger. " 'Holy Watchfulness' and Communal Conformism: The Functions of Defamation in Early New England Communities." *New England Quarterly,* LVI (1983), 504–522.

———. *Sex in Middlesex: Popular Mores in a Massachusetts County, 1649–1699.* Amherst, Mass., 1986.

Thompson, Thomas C. "The Life Course and Labor of a Colonial Farmer." *Historical New Hampshire,* XL (1985), 135–155.

Tomaselli, Sylvana, and Roy Porter, eds. *Rape.* London, 1986.

Tracy, Patricia J. *Jonathan Edwards, Pastor: Religion and Society in Eighteenth-Century Northampton.* New York, 1980.

Trowbridge, Thomas Rutherford, Jr. "History of Ancient Maritime Interests of New Haven." New Haven Colony Historical Society, *Papers,* III (1882), 85–112.

Ulrich, Laurel Thatcher. " 'Daughters of Liberty': Religious Women in Revolutionary New England." In Ronald Hoffman and Peter J. Albert, eds., *Women in the Age of the American Revolution,* 211–243. Charlottesville, Va., 1989.

———. " 'A Friendly Neighbor': Social Dimensions of Daily Work in Northern Colonial New England." *Feminist Studies,* VI (1980), 392–405.

———. *Good Wives: Image and Reality in the Lives of Women in Northern New England, 1650–1750.* New York, 1982.

———. "Housewife and Gadder: Themes of Self-sufficiency and Community in Eighteenth-Century New England." In Carol Groneman and Mary Beth Norton, eds., *"To Toil the Livelong Day": America's Women at Work, 1780–1980,* 21–34. Ithaca, N.Y., 1987.

———. "Martha Ballard and Her Girls: Women's Work in Eighteenth-Century Maine." In Stephen Innes, ed., *Work and Labor in Early America,* 70–105. Chapel Hill, N.C., 1988.

———. *A Midwife's Tale: The Life of Martha Ballard, Based on Her Diary, 1785–1812*. New York, 1990.

———. "Psalm-tunes, Periwigs, and Bastards: Ministerial Authority in Early Eighteenth Century Durham." *Historical New Hampshire*, XXXVI (1981), 255–279.

———. "Vertuous Women Found: New England Ministerial Literature, 1668–1735." *American Quarterly*, XXVIII (1976), 20–40.

Ulrich, Laurel Thatcher, and Lois K. Stabler. " 'Girling of It' in Eighteenth-Century New Hampshire." *Dublin Seminar for New England Folklife*, X (1985), 24–36.

Underdown, David. "The Taming of the Scold: The Enforcement of Patriarchal Authority in Early Modern England." In Anthony Fletcher and John Stevenson, eds., *Order and Disorder in Early Modern England*, 116–136. Cambridge, 1985.

Van Dusen, Albert E. *Connecticut*. New York, 1961.

Veall, Donald. *The Popular Movement for Law Reform, 1640–1660*. Oxford, 1970.

Vickers, Daniel. "Competency and Competition: Economic Culture in Early America." *William and Mary Quarterly*, 3d Ser., XLVII (1990), 3–29.

Waciega, Lisa Wilson. "A 'Man of Business': The Widow of Means in Southeastern Pennsylvania, 1750–1850." *William and Mary Quarterly*, 3d Ser., XLIV (1987), 40–64.

Wall, Helena M. *Fierce Communion: Family and Community in Early America*. Cambridge, Mass., 1990.

Walsh, James. "The Great Awakening in the First Congregational Church of Woodbury, Connecticut." *William and Mary Quarterly*, 3d Ser., XXVIII (1971), 543–567.

Warden, G. B. "Law Reform in England and New England, 1620 to 1660." *William and Mary Quarterly*, 3d Ser., XXXV (1978), 668–690.

Washburn, Georgia Cooper, comp., Mabel Thacher Rosemary Washburn, ed. *Witter Genealogy: Descendants of William Witter of Swampscott, Massachusetts, 1639–1659*. New York, 1929.

Waters, John J. "Family, Inheritance, and Migration in Colonial New England: The Evidence from Guilford, Connecticut." *William and Mary Quarterly*, 3d Ser., XXXIX (1982), 64–86.

———. "Patrimony, Succession, and Social Stability: Guilford, Connecticut in the Eighteenth Century." *Perspectives in American History*, X (1976), 129–160.

Weisberg, D. Kelly. " 'Under Greet Temptations Heer': Women and Divorce in Puritan Massachusetts." *Feminist Studies*, II (1975), 183–193.

——, ed. *Women and the Law: The Social Historical Perspective.* 2 vols. Cambridge, Mass., 1982.

Wells, Robert V. *The Population of the British Colonies in America before 1776.* Princeton, N.J., 1975.

——. "The Illusion of Change: Women and the American Revolution." In Alfred E. Young, ed., *The American Revolution: Explorations in the History of American Radicalism,* 388–485. DeKalb, Ill., 1976.

Wilson, Lisa. *Life after Death: Widows in Pennsylvania, 1750–1850.* Philadelphia, 1992.

Wolfram, Sybil. "Divorce in England, 1700–1857." *Oxford Journal of Legal Studies,* V (1985), 155–186.

Woodbridge, Linda. *Women and the English Renaissance: Literature and the Nature of Womankind, 1540–1620.* Urbana, Ill., 1984.

Zainaldin, Jamil S. "The Emergence of a Modern American Family Law: Child Custody, Adoption, and the Courts, 1796–1851." *Northwestern University Law Review,* LXXIII (1979), 1038–1089.

UNPUBLISHED WORKS

Basch, Norma. "An Open Discussion on Women's Legal History, 1730–1830." 14th Annual Meeting of the American Society for Legal History, Newark, N.J., Oct. 19, 1984.

Bissell, Linda Auwers. "Family, Friends, and Neighbors: Social Interaction in Seventeenth-Century Windsor, Connecticut." Ph.D. diss., Brandeis University, 1973.

Brown, Kathleen Mary. "Gender and the Genesis of a Race and Class System in Virginia, 1630–1750." Ph.D. diss., University of Wisconsin, 1990.

Cleary, Patricia A. " 'She Merchants' of Colonial America: Women and Commerce on the Eve of the Revolution." Ph.D. diss., Northwestern University, 1989.

Crane, Elaine Forman. "When More Means Less: Women and Work in Colonial American Seaports." Paper presented at the 6th Berkshire Conference on the History of Women, Northampton, Mass., June 1–3, 1984.

Dayton, Cornelia Hughes. "Narratives of Infanticide: Changing Configurations of Gender, Race, and Class in Eighteenth-Century New England." Paper presented to the Annual Meeting of the Law and Society Association, Phoenix, Ariz., June 16, 1994.

——. "Satire and Sensationalism: The Emergence of Misogyny in Mid-Eighteenth-Century New England Newspapers and Almanacs." Paper presented to the New England Seminar in American History, Worcester, Mass., Nov. 15, 1991.

——. "Women before the Bar: Gender, Law, and Society in Connecticut, 1710–1790." Ph.D. diss., Princeton University, 1986.

Filiaci, Anne Marie. "Raising the Republic: American Women in the Public Sphere, 1750–1800." Ph.D. diss., State University of New York at Buffalo, 1982.

Friedman, Rachelle E. "To My Well-Beloved Wife: Testamentary Patterns and Female Authority in Boston, 1650–1725." Paper presented at the Annual Meeting of the Organization of American Historians, Anaheim, Calif., Apr. 15–18, 1993.

Hunt, Margaret Rose. "English Urban Families in Trade, 1660–1800: The Culture of Early Modern Capitalism." Ph.D. diss., New York University, 1986.

James, Janet Wilson. "Changing Ideas about Women in the United States, 1776–1825." Ph.D. diss., Radcliffe College, 1954.

Kamensky, Jane Neill. "Governing the Tongue: Speech and Society in Early New England." Ph.D. diss., Yale University, 1993.

Lacy, Norbert B., ed. "Records of the Court of Assistants of Connecticut, 1665–1701." 2 vols. Master's thesis, Yale University, 1937.

McNamara, Martha. "Disciplining Justice: Massachusetts Courthouses and the Legal Profession, 1750–1850." Ph.D. diss., Boston University, 1994.

Malmsheimer, Lonna Myers. "New England Funeral Sermons and Changing Attitudes toward Woman, 1672–1792." Ph.D. diss., University of Minnesota, 1973.

Mann, Bruce Hartling. "Parishes, Law, and Community in Connecticut, 1700–1760." Ph.D. diss., Yale University, 1977.

Murrin, John M. "Anglicizing an American Colony: The Transformation of Provincial Massachusetts." Ph.D. diss., Yale University, 1966.

Roetger, Robert West. "Order and Disorder in Early Connecticut: New Haven, 1639–1701." Ph.D. diss., University of New Hampshire, 1982.

St. George, Robert Blair. "A Retreat from the Wilderness: Pattern in the Domestic Environment of Southeastern New England, 1630–1730." Ph.D. diss., University of Pennsylvania, 1982.

Saxton, Martha. "Puritan Women's Moral Authority: Seeds of a Critical Tradition." Paper presented to the Annual Meeting of the Organization of American Historians, Anaheim, Calif., Apr. 15–18, 1993.

Snyder, Terri Lynne. " 'Rich Widows Are the Best Commodity This Country Affords': Gender Relations and the Rehabilitation of Patriarchy in Virginia, 1660–1700." Ph.D. diss., University of Iowa, 1992.

Index